INCLUSIVE *Learning* 365

Edtech Strategies for Every Day of the Year

Christopher Bugaj, Karen Janowski, Mike Marotta, Beth Poss

D1556172

International Society for Technology in Education
PORTLAND, OREGON • ARLINGTON, VIRGINIA

Inclusive Learning 365
Edtech Strategies For Every Day of the Year
Christopher Bugaj, Karen Janowski, Mike Marotta, Beth Poss

Acquisitions Editor: *Valerie Witte*
Managing Editor: *Emily Reed*
Copy Editors: *Courtney Burkholder, Lynda Gansel*
Proofreader: *Laura Gibson*
Indexer: *Wendy Allex*
Book Design and Production: *Kim McGovern*
Cover Design: *Beth DeWilde*

Library of Congress Cataloging-in-Publication Data

Names: Bugaj, Christopher R., author. | Janowski, Karen, author. | Marotta, Mike, author. | Poss, Beth, author.
Title: Inclusive learning 365 : edtech strategies for every day of the year / Christopher Bugaj, Karen Janowski, Mike Marotta, Beth Poss.
Identifiers: LCCN 2020057139 (print) | LCCN 2020057140 (ebook) | ISBN 9781564848857 (paperback) | ISBN 9781564848826 (epub) | ISBN 9781564848833 (mobi) | ISBN 9781564848840 (pdf)
Subjects: LCSH: Special education—Computer-assisted instruction. | Individualized instruction—Computer-assisted instruction. | Inclusive education. | Educational technology.
Classification: LCC LC3969.5 .B85 2021 (print) | LCC LC3969.5 (ebook) | DDC 371.9/046—dc23
LC record available at https://lccn.loc.gov/2020057139
LC ebook record available at https://lccn.loc.gov/2020057140

First Edition

ISBN: 978-1-56484-885-7

Ebook version available.

Printed in the United States of America.

ISTE® is a registered trademark of the International Society for Technology in Education.

ABOUT ISTE

The International Society for Technology in Education (ISTE) is home to a passionate community of global educators who believe in the power of technology to transform teaching and learning, accelerate innovation and solve tough problems in education.

ISTE inspires the creation of solutions and connections that improve opportunities for all learners by delivering: practical guidance, evidence-based professional learning, virtual networks, thought-provoking events and the ISTE Standards. ISTE is also the leading publisher of books focused on technology in education. For more information or to become an ISTE member, visit iste.org. Subscribe to ISTE's YouTube channel and connect with ISTE on Twitter, Facebook and LinkedIn.

Related ISTE Titles

The New Assistive Tech: Make Learning Awesome for All by Christopher Bugaj

Dive Into UDL: Immersive Practices to Develop Expert Learners by Kendra Grant and Luis Perez

To see all books available from ISTE, please visit **iste.org/books**.

ABOUT THE AUTHORS: WHY THESE FOUR

Who are we and how did we come together to write this book? We come from a variety of backgrounds in education. You can read all about us below, but we wanted to tell you the story of how our different experiences influenced the development of this book. While we all spent much of our careers working in the field of educational and assistive technology, we each bring a unique lens. Beth Poss, a thirty-year veteran of the public schools as a speech/language pathologist and educator, most recently spent her time in school administration as an elementary school assistant principal, and before that as a coordinator for her district's early childhood special education programs. Chris Bugaj, who is also a speech/language pathologist, worked for many years as a member of his district's assistive technology team. Karen Janowski comes from the world of occupational therapy and runs her own consulting business, training and supporting schools throughout the greater Boston area. Mike Marotta is an engineer, private consultant, and trainer. The four of us have all known each other for more than ten years, generally meeting up a few times each year at educational conferences. We present together periodically and appreciate each other's work and expertise.

Together we bring experiences across content areas, developmental levels, ages, and grades, and we are all passionate about creating inclusive environments that leverage technology to support learning. When Chris, who has authored two other ISTE books began thinking about his next book, he approached Beth, Karen, and Mike with the idea of designing a book that provided a digestible strategy-a-day to help educators make learning more accessible and engaging. The result is 365 inclusive strategies that span content, ages, and skills.

About Chris

Christopher R. Bugaj, MA CCC-SLP (**chrisbugaj.com**), is a founding member of the assistive technology team for Loudoun County Public Schools, where he currently works as the assistive technology specialist. Chris is the co-author of *The Practical (and Fun) Guide to Assistive Technology in Public Schools* (**bit.ly/chewatamazon**) and author of *The New Assistive Tech: Make Learning Awesome For All* (**bit.ly/thenewat4all**), both published by ISTE, and he has designed and instructed online courses for ISTE on the topics of assistive technology and universal design for learning (UDL). Chris co-hosts the Talking With Tech podcast (**talkingwithtech.org**), which features interviews and conversations about augmentative and alternative communication. He has also hosted the A.T.TIPSCAST (**attipcast.com**), a multi-award winning podcast featuring strategies to design educational experiences. Chris was also the author of "ATEval2Go," an app for iPad that helps professionals in education perform technology assessments for students. Chris coauthored two chapters for *Technology Tools for Students with Autism*, published by Brookes Publishing. Together with his wife, Chris coproduces and coauthors the popular Night Light Stories (**nightlightstories.net**) podcast, which features original stories for children of all ages. Chris serves as the K–12 subcommittee chair for the National Center on Accessible Educational Materials Advisory Council. He also serves on the advisory board for the Center on Inclusive Technology and Education systems (CITES). Chris has presented over five hundred live or digital sessions (**bit.ly/bugajpresentations**) at local, regional, state, national, and international events, including TEDx (**bit.ly/bugajtedx**).

About Karen

Karen Janowski, MS Ed, OTL, is an assistive and inclusive technology consultant, a former adjunct professor at Simmons College in Boston, and has worked as a school-based occupational therapist. She presents both locally and nationally about the importance of using ubiquitous technologies, which remove the obstacles to learning for all learners. She is a passionate advocate for UDL and inclusive technology for learners of all ages. She is an EdCampBoston and EdCampAccess organizer, and the founder and co-moderator of #ATchat on Twitter. She has blogged at "Teaching Every Student" (**teachingeverystudent.blogspot.com**) since 2005. Karen is the president and owner of EdTech Solutions, Inc., in Reading, Massachusetts, which provides professional development, coaching, consultations, and assessments in the areas of assistive technology and assistive technology for communication throughout the greater Boston area.

About Mike

Mike Marotta is an assistive technology professional certified by the Rehabilitation Engineering and Assistive Technology Society of North America, as well as the ISTE Inclusive Learning Network 2017 Outstanding Educator. He has been providing direct services to individuals with all disabilities for thirty years and runs his own technology consulting firm, Inclusive Technology Solutions, LLC. As an evaluator, Mike works collaboratively with teams in all environments (school, workplace, and community) to effectively match each individual's needs to technology supports. Mike is a nationally and internationally recognized presenter and was previously a trainer for California State University at Northridge (CSUN), where he provided practical and in-depth training to professionals interested in specializing in assistive technology. In addition, Mike is an adjunct professor at Ramapo College of New Jersey, where he teaches courses for graduate-level educators in assistive technology and UDL. Mike is the director of the Richard West Assistive Technology Advocacy Center at Disability Rights New Jersey, the statewide Assistive Technology Act program for New Jersey. Mike serves on the advisory boards for both CAST Accessible Educational Materials and CITES.

About Beth

Beth Poss has worked as a speech/language pathologist, technology consultant, curriculum writer, and school administrator. She is currently the Director of Educational Programs for LessonPix, an online tool used to create educational resources, and she has a private educational consulting practice. She is also a member of the editorial board of the *Assistive Technology Outcome Benefits Journal*. Having spent more than thirty years working for Montgomery County Public Schools in Maryland, Beth is passionate about designing educational environments that support all students in accessing a rigorous curriculum and meeting educational outcomes. In her ongoing work with school districts, universities, and national- and state-level educational organizations, she focuses on technology as an essential component in designing equitable and inclusive learning environments for learners of all ages. Find her on Twitter at **twitter.com/possbeth**.

WHY THIS BOOK: AN ORIGIN STORY

A Word from Chris

In 2003 I was working as an assistive technology trainer with a dynamic team of innovative and driven individuals when one of my colleagues approached me with an idea. He knew I was interested in making videos as a mechanism for training others. He had a word of the day calendar on his desk and thought I could make an educational video of the day. Back then, before the existence of YouTube, making engaging, high quality video took hours of planning, shooting, and editing. It just wasn't feasible at the time. What was possible was the idea of a Word of the Day calendar that replaced the word with a tool, resource, or strategy. In late April of that school year, I pitched the idea to our team. Everyone agreed, and we went to work creating PowerPoint slides which eventually became our very first calendar, which we called the AT-A-Day calendar (where AT = assistive technology). We were able to put it together in roughly two weeks with the help of students in design classes who did the cutting and gluing to bring the digital version into print media. When it was distributed to teachers, specifically special education teachers, it was an instant hit. Everyone stated how much they loved using it as a resource for short yet meaningful bursts of information which not only raised their awareness of different philosophies, practices, and technologies but also proved to change their implementation practices. In the ensuing years, the project grew, collaborating with more people, gathering content from different departments, and expanding the usefulness of the product with QR codes to additional resources. We shared the idea with colleagues at different conferences, where we gave out limited samples of what came to be called the Strategy-A-Day calendar. Different organizations replicated the idea, making their own versions. Some of the calendars are still in production to this day!

I was saddened when the decision was made to halt the production of the calendars a few years ago. Working with my creative and inspiring colleagues on this project included some of the most rewarding experiences in my professional life. I look back fondly at the trials and tribulations we overcame to bring a meaningful change agent to thousands of educators everywhere! To all my colleagues with whom I worked so closely with to make those calendars a reality, I am eternally grateful for your time, dedication, passion, and commitment. Thank you all for modeling what it means to be awesome.

Despite the end of the Strategy-A-Day calendar, the idea of presenting educators with small, bite-sized chunks of information each day persisted. This book is the evolution of that idea.

A Word from Karen

After working in medical settings as an occupational therapist, I made the transition to school-based occupational therapy in the late 80s. Like Beth, I remember those Apple IIe green screens and almost immediately saw the potential. It started with working with a third-grade student. The intent of the program we explored together was to improve his understanding of CVC words. A lightbulb went off. Instead, I was using it to encourage him to pause, visually scan and finally, select the item, to help decrease his impulsivity, in this case, with purposeful computer navigation. We thought outside the box to envision using the software beyond the intent. Technology could be used in innovative ways to build skills, support strengths and bypass learning challenges. I was hooked.

It soon became apparent to me, unfortunately, that schools assign adult supports before they consider the use of assistive technology. It became my mission and passion to promote the use of assistive and inclusive technology to meet the needs of all learners for success and independence. And when I heard the objection, "Well, the student doesn't want to be seen as different," my response was, "Don't let them be seen as different. Make the tools and resources available to all!" With my background as an OT, it's in my DNA to promote independence with life skills and the life skills for learners include the ability to complete academic tasks and thrive in the school setting. I honestly can't think in any other way. Effective inclusion promotes independence and competence and no one is seen as different. Variety and choice are valued and offered and learners can finally thrive.

When Chris reached out to me to consider joining him in this book endeavor, I jumped at the chance to spread the gospel of success and independence through inclusive technology to meet the needs of all learners. It is the practical application of readily available, intuitive technologies that can make a difference in the lives of learners. We need to break the cycle of dependence with engaging, innovative, inclusive practices that instill a love for life-long learning. My participation in this book collaboration is based on that premise and I am thrilled to contribute to the growing and necessary field of inclusive education.

A Word from Mike

Looking back thirty years to the start of my career, I would never have thought I would be working in the field of technology for individuals with disabilities. As an engineer, I was always interested in how things worked (specifically, taking things apart and hopefully putting them back together!) The field of assistive technology looks very different today than it did when I started as a "wheelchair fix-it guy." Fast forward to today and computers are everywhere. We carry them around in our pocket. We access digital files in the cloud. Many of our technology tools are "everyday" tools, designed for consumers and customized to meet the unique needs of each individual. This is an exciting time to focus on building inclusive systems that value individuals and their unique needs and abilities.

Working on this book while holding down a fulltime job, teaching as an adjunct professor and various consulting gigs has been an adventure, but I wouldn't have had it any other way. Chris, Beth, Karen, and I have collaborated on presentations and smaller projects in the past. At the end of each of those collaborations, I would reflect on how these were "my people." We share similar philosophies on the intersection of education and technology that provides opportunities for each individual to achieve success.

A Word from Beth

In my more than thirty years as an educator, I've had the opportunity to see technology arrive, evolve, and irrevocably change the lives of learners, educators, families, and indeed, society. I remember when I first used a computer program as an educational tool, in graduate school (way back in 1986!) with a learner that I was working to engage in reading aloud. It was a game that involved a quest and had multiple layers with directions for success at each level. As he played the game, I had him read each component of the quest aloud. He was excited and began to make progress in reading fluently. I then began working with learners with physically complex bodies who needed technology to be able to communicate and access education. This was in the infancy of the world of assistive technology, long before iPads, and just as electronic devices and early computer systems (remember the Apple IIE? I do!) were able to be programmed to talk using synthesized speech. This soon became my passion, as I saw individuals being given a voice and a means to access education. As my career progressed, technology boomed, and my journey as an educator evolved. From being classroom based, to consulting, to being the individual with an eye on special education and Universal Design for Learning in writing curriculum for the district, to finally being in a supervisory role as an assistant principal of an elementary school, I continued to see how technology had the power to change education. What I came to realize, however, was that technology without sound pedagogy is just technology for technology's sake. That was why I was so excited when Chris reached out to me about being a part of this book. Chris, Mike, Karen, and I all agreed that putting the strategy ahead of the technology in this book was the way to communicate to you, our readers, that it is what you and your learners do with technology that makes the difference. Technology is simply a tool for learning—it is not learning on its own. It is with this viewpoint that I hope that you find that this book has a place in your educational toolbox.

ACKNOWLEDGMENTS

From Chris

I'd like to thank long-time friends and colleagues Beth, Karen, and Mike for answering the call to create this book. They could have run for the hills knowing how long and arduous the task would be. Instead, they embraced it with passion and dedication. We spent countless hours drafting, discussing, deliberating, and deciding what should and should not appear within these pages. Spending that time with them has been the greatest reward of this experience and has further opened my mind to the possibilities of what the future can be when we work collaboratively with a shared vision. Beth, Karen, and Mike, thank you all for your awesomeness.

Writing this book while having a fulltime job and family, and during a pandemic was no easy feat. It was necessary to work into the evening, on weekends, and even during holidays to get this book out to all of you as expeditiously as possible. Every hour spent working on this book was one less hour spent with the family. Without their understanding, support, and sacrifice, this book would not have been possible. To Melissa, Tucker, and Margaret, thank you for your understanding, patience, and encouragement. With your support, anything is possible! Love is a pretty strong word and it still isn't enough to express how I feel. You're the "most awesomest" family there ever was.

Finally, I want to acknowledge you, the reader, for picking up this book. We can all work to make more money but time is a limited commodity. I thank you for the vote of confidence you are giving us by spending your valuable time with the strategies of this book. Learners are relying on you to craft a better future and I hope this book makes that burden a little easier. As educational experience designers and inclusive design facilitators, I believe this book will act as a catalyst which propels you forward on your mission of leading others in the implementation of inclusive practices. Learning is awesome and so are you.

From Karen

I need to thank my family for all they have endured to prepare me for this time. My husband, John, has been a tremendous support and my biggest cheerleader and I can't thank him enough. My three children, Alexa, Amanda, and Chris—now all awesome adults—taught me a great deal during their own academic journeys and we have many discussions about educational philosophy. I apply those lessons in my daily professional practice with a passion to ensure all learners feel valued, respected, successful, and independent.

Most importantly, I need to thank all the learners with whom I've worked over the years. You have taught me to listen and have inspired me to always consider your perspectives and needs first. I dedicate this book to you and thank you immensely.

From Mike

I want to first thank my coauthors for this opportunity. While I may not miss the late nights of working on this manuscript, I will miss our two-hour-long Zoom calls, where we discussed this book, and anything else going on in our worlds. These three have become more than colleagues—they have become friends and I am proud to be part of this endeavor with them.

I wanted to save my most important thank you for last. To say I am thankful for the support of my family would be a huge understatement. I dedicate this book to them. My wife, Diane, provided constant support throughout this project while I carried my laptop around the house saying, "I just gotta do one more thing for the book!" Thank you for always being there to provide an encouraging word when it all felt like too much and I had piles of deadlines staring me in the face. Having you by my side makes me feel like I can take on any project and succeed. Love you, honey! For my kids, Matt and Haley, thanks for always listening to my stories about the book and how awesome it was going to be—even if you may not have understood what I was talking about! Watching you go after your goals and start your "adult lives" was an inspiration to me to conquer this project. You guys are the best, love you both.

From Beth

I would like to say a special thank you to my family; to my husband, Stephen, who has put up with my countless weekend hours working on this book and every other passion project I have taken on, and to my daughters, Madeline and Morgan, who taught me so much about using technology in education, including that just because you are young doesn't mean that you prefer to read digital text. I also want to thank every educator and learner who helped shape my views on how technology can change our world, including how the people behind the tool are always more important than the tool. And a special thank you to you, our readers, for being motivated to make your educational space an inclusive one. I hope that this book supports you in this critical work.

DEDICATION

To every learner of every ability, everywhere, who was told you couldn't and then you did: Thank you for letting us learn from you. This book is for you.

CONTENTS

Foreword xii

Introduction: Before You Begin xiv

Read First! Do Not Skip This Part! xiv

Adopting an Inclusive Mindset xiv

How To Use This Book xix

Strategies By Purpose

CROSS-CONTENT STRATEGIES 1

READING STRATEGIES 98

WRITING STRATEGIES 157

STEAM STRATEGIES 202

RESEARCH AND STUDYING STRATEGIES 240

EXECUTIVE FUNCTIONING STRATEGIES 275

SOCIAL EMOTIONAL STRATEGIES 309

PROFESSIONAL LEARNING STRATEGIES 341

THE UN-STRATEGY 366

Afterword 368

References 369

Indexes 372

Index of Strategies 372

Index of Tools 372

Book Index 378

FOREWORD

I began my career in public education teaching global studies to high school students labeled severely emotionally disturbed. In those days, technology in classrooms meant wheeling the television and DVD player from room to room when you wanted to show a documentary (assuming you had signed up for the TV cart a few days prior), or using an overhead projector to highlight a key passage in the text. Teaching students with special needs taught me about the power of individualizing education, a key element of successful instruction that applies to all student populations. Now that teachers and students have the world at their fingertips and more technology than they know what to do with, using that tech strategically to address each student's individual needs is not only possible, it's necessary. Educators need guidance and support as they apply new strategies to their work, and *Inclusive Learning 365* provides exactly that.

When I was a young system leader, I was given the responsibility to oversee the new district information technology office, after we had built the technology infrastructure for the system. This was during the late 90s, and we needed routers, wiring, and servers to support the nascent world of technology that was booming in schools. The marketplace and policymakers were promising that with more computers, the classroom would be transformed, students would flourish, and the boring old teacher who droned on in front of the class would be replaced by engaging lessons delivered through a screen. Getting technology into schools was seen as both a moral and political imperative. But once our infrastructure was built, the IT director left, and the superintendent had a different problem on his hands that he asked me to tackle. Now that we had the technology, how were teachers expected to use it? I worked closely with the curriculum and instruction department to figure out how to infuse technology into regular daily instruction, without making it an "extra" thing that teachers were expected to do. This experience stayed with me as I became a superintendent, where I greatly increased access to and use of various technologies. The key, however, was to always ground a new technology in the needs of students and the leadership and vision of educators. Simply having the technology isn't enough; knowing which tools to use and when is the key, and that's where too many schools fall down.

In the last twenty years we've continued to see increases in the use of technology amidst the calls for both greater personalization of instruction and the need to address long-standing inequities in our schools. And we know that technology alone won't do any of that, despite claims by many technologists and companies. It is but one tool that we have, just like the selection of texts that accurately depict historical events, or the design of math problems that help students understand both concepts and operations. We've also seen increased stratification, as some educators—especially those who teach students with special needs—have become evangelists and highly capable users of technology, while others have been allowed to continue to use the overhead projector and DVD player. *Inclusive Learning 365* is such a valuable resource for practitioners and could not have come at a better time. Educators must learn from and with other educators who have done the work. The authors, having successfully used technology to address the needs of their students, are exactly the kind of guides that we need now more than ever.

As I write this, we are still learning the lessons of 2020 and the COVID-19 crisis. One thing that is abundantly clear is that some educators are more facile than others in the use of technology. Unlike pre-COVID times, however, using technology is no longer a choice. Moreover, now that more educators have been forced to use technology, it's expected that their comfort will increase, and they'll continue to improve their practice. That's a silver lining amidst the darkness of the 2020–2021 school year. Guidance by and for practitioners is more important than ever, and the strategy-a-day structure of this book is exactly what educators need. Even more important, we know that too many students will be re-entering school needing significant support and remediation to accelerate their progress. The skills, knowledge, and tactics of special educators are more valuable today than ever before, as educators will have to differentiate their lessons, regularly assess progress, and constantly adjust instruction. Educators can't be expected to know how to do all of that, and schools will have to be organized to promote educator learning. *Inclusive Learning 365* is a powerful starting point for every educator who wants to learn how to address the challenges of today and embrace the opportunities of tomorrow.

— Dr. Joshua P. Starr
CEO of PDK International and former Superintendent of Montgomery County
Public Schools in Maryland

Introduction: Before You Begin

We understand the curiosity monster living inside you wants to break free from its shackles to explore the content on the ensuing pages. It is understandable that you'd want to flip to the other sections of this book to find practical applications to help the learners you serve. When the water is this warm, who wouldn't want to dive right in?

READ FIRST! DO NOT SKIP THIS PART!

Resist the urge to skip this introduction. It is foundational to the journey on which you're about to set sail. The rationale described here not only offers guidance to help you navigate the structure of the book, but also presents the fundamental reasoning for how the content within can help (re)shape every educational experience you design and deliver. This introduction is essential to understanding how the strategies within this book can truly transform educational practices for everyone!

Figure i. The authors strongly urge you to read this introduction before you jump into the strategies.

ADOPTING AN INCLUSIVE MINDSET

Inclusion may have different meanings and interpretations depending on the experiences of each person. Therefore, we thought it might be a good idea to explain what inclusion means to us, the authors, to help develop a common understanding and shared vision with you, the one experiencing the strategies within this learning experience.

The first step in designing authentically inclusive educational experiences is believing that it can be done. Adopting an *inclusive mindset* is a necessary prerequisite before one can design educational experiences that will meet all learners' needs. Educators working to design such experiences do so by embracing and respecting the fact that everyone is unique with different abilities, backgrounds, and preferences. Innovation and progress are accelerated when heterogeneous individuals work together to solve problems. An inclusive mindset means that these variances are celebrated as a source of strength not just for each individual, but for the class, the community, and society as a whole.

The principle element in inclusive design is flexibility. Providing options promotes learner agency and intrinsically motivates individuals to actively engage in their own learning. Individually, the strategies outlined in the book can help you immediately provide more options to learners. Our greater hope is that by experiencing, practicing, and implementing these strategies you will further your own professional (and personal) goal of adopting and spreading an inclusive mindset. Using these strategies will help you, your colleagues, and your entire local education agency create a culture where every learner, regardless of ability, cultural background, or demographic group, is valued, respected, and honored equally.

Building a culture of inclusivity in your practice, school, and/or agency will have lasting results. Learners brought up in inclusive environments will shape the culture for future generations. Each decision we make now as educators will act as an example of how to build an inclusive culture into the future. As educators, we hold great power over shaping the future of society. This book is meant to help you shape that future into one of acceptance where everyone is included.

Authentic Inclusion

Some local educational agencies actively work to increase inclusive practices. Goals are established, strategies are employed, data is collected, and reflection transpires, all in an attempt to increase inclusion. The metrics some use to measure inclusive practices are based on how much time learners with disabilities spend engaging in educational experiences with non-disabled learners. That sounds pretty good, right? Not only does it seem noble, but it shows an attempt to adhere to legal requirements, which vary depending on which part of the world you're in.

Yet being in the same space, virtually or physically, does not mean every learner is authentically included. Take, for example, a learner who has an individualized education program (IEP) that states that they will be fully included by receiving academic support services in a general education environment with non-disabled peers. Again, this sounds fantastic, right? However, when the learner is actually in the general education environment, the educators have decided that sometimes the learner needs to be segregated to an assigned section of the room where they will work with a related services provider, teaching assistant, or special educator separately. Is this inclusion? If we are tracking metrics based on what is written in the IEP, it would seem that this learner is included one hundred percent of the time, which will really help make the local educational agency's achievement of goals look great! However, in truth, despite being in the same room as others, the learner is not really included in the same way the other learners are. If the table the learner was sitting at were three feet further away on the other side of a classroom wall, perhaps in an adjacent room, the service delivery would be called a special education setting. What difference does three feet make? Whether someone is placed at a table in a separate part of the room, or placed at a table in another room, true inclusion is not happening.

Should a wall be the determining factor between what is inclusive and what isn't? We invite you to think of inclusion as something deeper than the space where someone learns and who else might be in that space. True inclusion happens when we design educational experiences with everyone in mind. A truly inclusive experience is designed in such a way that any learner, regardless of ability, can participate in it and learn from it. An experience that is authentically inclusive means that anyone, even people the educator hasn't met yet, can come into it and leave having made progress toward achieving educational goals.

Our Philosophy is Learner-Centered

Imagine a group of people who want to learn the skill of fishing. Some people might have years of experience, growing up with family members who taught them something about how to bait hooks, cast into open waters, and scout out the best holes to catch the biggest fish. Others may have only ever seen fishing on television or on the internet, having never touched a fishing pole in their lives. It is very likely that every individual in that room is starting at different places with their fishing knowledge and ability. If you were going to teach fishing to the people in this room, would it make sense to teach them all the same way, starting them off learning the same skills, and doing the same thing? We think not. Instead, it might be better to design an experience where the learners assess their own abilities and then engage in different opportunities to grow their skills based on the results of that assessment. Learners who are novices might participate in an entirely different set of experiences than those who already have mastered some aspects of fishing. Beyond experience level, other variances include how much time it might take individuals to learn to fish. For some, it might come quickly and easily. For others, it might take hours of sustained effort. Depending on other circumstances, some people might be able to dedicate several hours a day to learning how to fish. Others might only be able to commit a few hours a week to the endeavor. Each learner will also have different physical, cognitive, and social-emotional abilities which might impact how long it might take to learn the skill. So, how do we design a learning experience that meets the needs of each learner? How do we teach each individual learner to fish?

The End of Flipped Learning

Flipped learning is defined by the Flipped Learning Network as "a pedagogical approach in which direct instruction moves from the group learning space to the individual learning space, and the resulting group space is transformed into a dynamic, interactive learning environment where the educator guides learners as they apply concepts and engage creatively in the subject matter." (2014) Ultimately it is a learner-centered means of asynchronously presenting content via technology outside the traditional classroom and using structured time in class to provide learners with personalized instruction to address the topic of the asynchronous experience in greater depth, clarify concepts, and address specific learner needs.

The term "flipped" implies that this approach is the opposite of the typical approach. We're ready to stop calling this approach "flipped" and start using it as the premier way to design educational experiences. Instead of calling it flipped, we're going to start calling it "The way we all should do it now." Congratulations, pioneers and champions of flipped learning, we've done it! Instruction is now flipped! Boom! It's the new, inclusive way of designing educational experiences—one that meets everyone's needs—and we are not going back.

Function First

If you are reading this book, chances are you like technology. As the authors of this book, we do too. We get excited when a new tool becomes available, and as early adopters of many technology resources we are always eager to try something different. However, we made a deliberate decision to structure this book around strategies and the function that technology provides to learners and educators, and then supply tools as a means of implementing that strategy and accessing that function. Tools may change, be incompatible when hardware changes, and much to our frustration, even go away at times. By focusing on strategies and the function of technology, we are better able to align our use of technology with pedagogy, which is, of course, what sound instructional practices are based on. If you love tools, don't worry—you will learn all about technology tools when you read this book, but we want to be sure that you understand the *why* and not just the *how* of using an educational tool. We hope that as you browse the strategies that fill these pages, you have many "aha" moments, discovering new reasons to use familiar tools, and discovering new tools that help you implement strategies with which you may already be familiar. Just remember, it's about the function and the learning that is occurring; the tool just helps you get there.

Design Over Accommodations

For our purposes, the term *accommodation* means that educators make changes to the educational experience to fit the needs of someone who otherwise couldn't participate in the same way as their peers. This term implies that there is one main or "correct" way of participating. Accommodations are changes made to the experience for those who can't participate in that main way. This idea also means that everyone engaging in that educational experience is meant to do so in the same or similar fashion, with exceptions made for those who can't. Examples of traditional educational experiences include: Everyone must complete a worksheet, produce the same or similar product (such as an essay or multimedia slideshow), or take a test. Traditional accommodations might be made based on individual needs to help those individuals engage in these educational experiences in an equitable fashion. Perhaps a worksheet would be made available digitally and the student would be allowed to type instead of handwrite. Another student might be invited to produce five slides for a multimedia slideshow instead of the ten required of others. Yet another student might be allowed to have test questions read aloud to them.

Accommodations propagate the notion that there is one main way of engaging in an experience. We invite you to consider the idea that educational experiences might be personalized and designed with variability and flexibility in mind so that there is not one main way of doing things. We invite you to use the strategies in this book to design experiences with multiple options from which learners can choose but we emphasize: the strategies in this book are not meant to be accommodations. They are meant to help you design educational experiences so inclusively that there is minimal or even no need for accommodations, because every learner would have one or more achievable options available. To put it simply, if you design educational experiences for everyone, then you don't need to provide accommodations to anyone.

An Introduction to Universal Design for Learning

Learners often know how they learn best, but unfortunately, educators are not always listening. The principles of Universal Design for Learning (UDL) are sprinkled throughout this book, and we encourage you to find ways to bring these ideas into the learning environment. Our goal as educators is to build an inclusive learning environment where every learner can thrive. The UDL guiding principles can be our roadmap to inclusive learning success. Designed around three main principles, the UDL Guidelines focus on creating a learning environment that provides:

- Multiple means of engagement,
- Multiple means of representation, and
- Multiple means of action and expression.

CAST (**cast.org**) has led this charge with the development and implementation of the UDL Guidelines. Flexibility is at the core of inclusive learning and the UDL Guidelines provide strategies for meeting the unique learning needs of each individual. In fact, CAST provides educators a free, interactive ebook (Meyer, Rose, and Gordon, 2014) that helps outline a path to inclusive learning that not only provides strategies related to inclusive goals, methods, materials, and assessments, but also "walks the walk" by providing information in audio formats, hyperlinked text leading to supporting resources, video clips of demonstrations, and more. Visit **udltheorypractice.cast.org** to sign up for a free account to access the digital book.

The Cost of Tools

Nothing in life is free. Your grandmother said it to your mother, your mother said it to you, and if you have kids you probably said it to them. It's true. Especially in the world of edtech. There are many "free" tools out there, but at what cost? Alphabet, the parent company of Google, didn't become one of the most profitable companies in the world in 2020 rankings (Statista, 2021) by giving you a free search tool. The data collected is worth millions, if not billions, to the company. It is often the same with other companies working in the field of edtech. They may offer a free tool, but beware of what you are really signing up for. Have you ever looked at the user agreement before installing a tool? OK, stop laughing. We already know the answer. You probably haven't, because you just want to get that tool installed so you can start using it. But what rights have you just given away? What is the company doing with your data?

In the world of edtech, what starts as free doesn't always remain that way. Once upon a time to get software installed on a computer people would purchase compact disks (wait, what is that?) for a one-time price. Now, most tools are web-based and have moved to a subscription model. Many of these tools have adopted some version of a "freemium" model, where a portion of the tool does not cost money to use but other features require a paid subscription. In this way, users can try a tool to see if it would meet their needs. It may be possible to use the features of the free version for learners to be successful. Depending on their needs, yearly purchases might be needed. The basic question is "Is this tool meeting the learners' needs?"

There are other concerns about free tools. First, they may go away. Those of us with years of experience can name at least one favorite free tool that disappeared. This is one reason why this book places the emphasis on strategies and functions of tools rather than on the tools themselves. Strategies have longer legs and persist over time, even when tools don't. Second, free tools may suddenly become "freemium" tools that require a fee to fully use all the features. One example is Padlet, which used to be free with unlimited pads, but now comes only with three pads for free. While for some, three pads might be all that is needed; for others, more active pads might be necessary and, therefore, worth the fee.

Another reality of free tools is that there may be ads that may make the tool more complicated to use or possibly inappropriate in an educational setting. The paid version of the tool might eliminate the ads.

When possible, we have tried to identify multiple tools that can support the same strategy. The more options available, the more likely it is that we can effectively meet the unique needs of each learner without breaking the budget.

A Word About Privacy and Security

COPPA (Children's Online Privacy Protection Act) and FERPA (Family Educational Rights and Privacy Act) are two US laws meant to protect the privacy and security of students. In our quest to provide readers with an outstanding resource for inclusive strategies, one area we chose not to specifically address was individual tool and resource privacy compliance. Companies may update policies, and it is not possible to ensure the most recent compliance information in this book. We encourage you to check with your own local educational agency for their specific policies about adopting tools including those listed as samples in this book. If a tool is currently not allowed in your district, remember that the function and strategy are what is paramount. You can always look for a different tool that offers a similar function. If you can't find something already available, you may advocate for the adoption of a tool that does provide the function, if that tool is determined to be compliant. Many of the resources highlighted in this book include legal statements about their privacy policies. The reader is encouraged to review those statements when considering implementation.

For additional information about student privacy, the US Department of Education has created a comprehensive website, "Protecting Student Privacy, A Service of the Privacy Technical Assistance Center and the Student Privacy Policy Office," which may be accessed at studentprivacy.ed.gov.

StudentPrivacyCompass (**studentprivacycompass.org**), formally known as FERPA/Sherpa, is a comprehensive web resource that has a wealth of information about student data privacy issues. Resources are provided for all stakeholder groups: educators, students, families, local and state education agencies, lawyers, educational technology companies, higher education institutions, and policymakers.

HOW TO USE THIS BOOK

Passionate educators set personal goals and work to intentionally meet those goals every day. One of your goals might be centered around increasing inclusive practices. We believe you'll find that inclusive practices not only benefit learners with disabilities, or those in other underrepresented groups, but everyone else as well.

Learning Something New Everyday

One powerful strategy to help you achieve your goals is to learn one new thing every day. That is one major theme of this book: learn one new nugget of information every day that you can apply to the educational experiences you design. Educators model learning for learners. With that in mind, we encourage you to share your learning with the learners you support. Share these strategies with individuals or groups, invite feedback, and work together to demonstrate that learning is an ongoing process that happens persistently little by little, not all at once. Today is the best day to learn!

Strategies Are Grouped By Purpose

The book is organized according to the primary purpose of the strategy. Tags with corresponding icons represent both the primary purpose of the strategy as well as any other related area. Many strategies fit in more than one category. The icons in the margins represent all of the tags listed on the page.

Two Indexes

Beyond the Table of Contents, Indexes are included at the end of the book. Depending on the need at the time, readers might want to search for strategies for different purposes. The Indexes are meant to help you quickly find what you need based on why you need it. Strategies are organized both by page number (which corresponds with the strategy number) and alphabetically by the name of every tool that appears in the book.

Multiple Strategies in One Tool

Some tools provide a single function or purpose. Others provide a multitude of functions, allowing you to use the tool to implement a wide variety of strategies. A tool that provides comprehensive features that can be used for a variety of purposes may have certain advantages. For instance, learners might find having just one tool to locate and use is easier than learning multiple tools. A single tool with multiple functions often provides a consistent look and feel for the user, with similarly designed elements, such as color schemes and icon choices. This consistency can help a learner recognize, navigate, and use the tool. One tool with many functions might also be easier for administrators and informational technology personnel to manage. Multiple tools means multiple checks of security, privacy, and technical aspects to ensure compatibility. One tool that consolidates functions minimizes the efforts of those meant to support its implementation, leading to increased efficiency, improved productivity, and decreased frustration for learners and the educators who support them. Examples of robust contemporary tools that provide multiple functions include Read&Write for Google Chrome, Google Keep, OneNote, PearDeck, ActivelyLearn, Book Creator, and Geogebra. Beyond these examples, the Sample Tools Index may be used to understand how some tools have multiple functions. The same tool might be listed as an option to use with multiple strategies. This indicates that the tool could be used in multiple ways, for a variety of purposes, and by a diverse set of learners.

Figure ii. Use this QR Code to visit inclusive365.com

Compendium Website and Hashtag

Due to the number of web-based resources listed in this book we thought it prudent to create a compendium website that lists all of the hyperlinks found in the book. Beyond the hyperlinks, the website is meant to serve as a portal to engage in conversations around the experiences that can be designed using the strategies and tools in this book. You may also engage on the social media platform of your choice by using the hashtag #Inclusive365. The website can be found at **inclusive365.com**

Be Part of the Community That Shares

As educators who are often siloed in a learning environment, we look for communities with whom to interact and engage. In reading this book you will become part of an inclusive education community. Other educators are reading this book and working to implement these inclusive strategies. This shared experience provides us all with a unique opportunity to compare notes, experiences, trials, and triumphs. What worked for you? What tips and tricks did you learn that could help someone else apply the strategy? The book is meant to be a catalyst for conversation; the companion website is designed to be a shared community space to foster these exchanges. Visit the website at **inclusive365.com** and click the Share Your Story link on the navigation toolbar. There you will find a web form to share your story. You're invited to share artifacts in any format you choose including text, audio, video, or anything else that works for you. These inclusive stories will be added into the corresponding inclusive strategy page on the Inclusive365 website. The more stories shared by educators, the larger our shared inclusive education community becomes. Let's work collaboratively to raise awareness of inclusive strategies where everyone succeeds!

Strategy Section Descriptions

Each of the 365 strategies is organized in the same way, with the following sections.

Title. The title of each strategy starts with a verb (or adjective + verb) to help illustrate the idea that action needs to be taken.

Description. This section describes the strategy in detail including why it is beneficial to learners.

Inclusive Uses. This section describes how the strategy supports the diverse needs of learners all of which have varied abilities and skills.

Sample Tools. This section suggests some tools that might help educators and learners implement the strategy. The tools listed in this section are not meant to be exhaustive but rather a set of possibilities. Other tools may exist that would do the job in similar or even better ways.

Extension Opportunities. This section describes additional ways educators and learners might use the strategy and/or tools to design educational experiences in ways beyond those provided in the initial description.

Related Resources. This section lists content that further supports or explains the strategy and/or sample tool(s) described on the page.

Figures. Each strategy features at least one captioned figure meant to provide a visual representation of the strategy and/or sample tools described on the page.

ISTE Standards for Students and Educators. This section aligns the strategy with the ISTE Standards for Students and Educators, indicating the standard number and indicator. The complete standards can be found online at **iste.org/standards**.

QR Code. The QR code on each page connects to a corresponding website (**inclusive365.com**) that lists all of the URLs on the page. Readers are encouraged to scan the QR code to navigate to active links.

Defining Common Terms

Words matter. The authors specifically chose a selection of terms to use consistently. A description and explanation of each follow.

Learner

We intentionally used the word *learner* instead of *student* in this book. The term *student* tends to create a short-term connotation indicating enrollment in or around one class, topic, or time frame. The term *learner* follows us throughout the expanse of our life as we intentionally work to further knowledge, abilities, and skills. Learners are self-driven and motivated to explore, solve, and create not by societal expectations but out of an internal curiosity and passion for the content. Learners set personal educational goals for the areas in which they want to grow, develop a plan of action, establish timelines for how to meet these goals, and measure their own progress toward mastery. Learners are responsible for their own learning. For an engaged learner, the constructs of school may be helpful, but are not necessary. Learners want to learn, not to achieve a grade, impress a teacher, or even get a job. Instead, learners seek the next evolution of themselves, working to achieve their greatest potential through the acquisition and mastery of new knowledge, skills, and abilities. Passionate learners dive deep into educational experiences not because someone tells them they have to, but because they want to.

Educator

We use the word *educator* rather than the word *teacher*. Teachers are one specific profession that can support a learner on their journey. The broader term of *educator* is meant to illustrate that learners have a wide array of professionals who can help them achieve their goals. Administrators, specialists, therapists, consultants, facilitators, and parents are just some of those who can help a learner achieve success. As we explore the boundaries of inclusive education, *everyone* can play a role.

How do we, as educators, support learners on their quest? By facilitating the learning process, not dictating it. Educators design educational experiences and provide authentic opportunities for learners to achieve their educational goals. Educators ask reflective questions, probe for insights to generate higher-order thinking, provide supportive and meaningful feedback, and encourage learners by celebrating progress and achievements and viewing mistakes as an opportunity to learn.

Experiences

We intentionally use the term *experience* rather than *assignment, activity,* or *lesson.* Although people can assign themselves a task, most don't think of it that way. Assignments and lessons are often given by someone else, removing agency. Experiences are more likely to foster internal motivation. The term *experience* also connotes choice. Learners can choose whether they'd like to participate in an experience. Activities have the potential to be purposeless. Walking around in circles when bored is an activity. Bouncing a ball aimlessly is an activity. Sitting and staring at the wall could be considered an activity. Instead, experiences are intentional and purposeful. Learners engage in experiences for a reason. The experience of bouncing a ball could be purposeful: to increase hand-eye coordination, for example.

Learning Spaces

We intentionally used the term *learning spaces* rather than *classroom* (unless we absolutely mean classroom). Learning isn't confined to the classroom, nor should it be. Learning can happen at home, in the hallways, in the library, in the cafeteria, in the back of the car, on the bus, on a bed, under a bed, at a desk, in a pillow fort, in the backyard, on the playground, behind a screen, and more. Learning does not happen in one place. Learning can happen everywhere!

Learning Environments

We intentionally use the term *learning environment* rather than *school.* A building called a school is but one place learning can happen. Learning strategies can happen anywhere. A sense of community can be fostered around a school, but may be fostered in other learning environments as well, including online communities, clubs, and teams, which can all take place outside of school. The majority of the strategies in this book can be used outside of school, in different environments such as homes, daycare centers, after-school programs, and anywhere else the learner travels.

Learning Groups

We intentionally use the term *group* rather than the terms *class* or *grade level* (unless we absolutely mean class or grade level). Classes and grade levels are societal constructs for grouping learners. These groupings have largely been based on age, following the idea that learners of a similar age have similar skills and abilities. When you consider that age is just one of many variables that factor into one's knowledge, skills, and abilities, learners can and should work together in groups with others who are of different ages. There are some institutions that have abandoned the idea of grade levels altogether to adopt a more communal and connectivist approach, where learners of different ages work together to achieve skills and broaden their knowledge. A group can be made up of a much more eclectic and diverse set of individuals. The term *group* is more inclusive of various numbers of learners as well. Whether the size of the group is three or three hundred, the idea is that learners can collaborate and cooperate to support each other's learning.

Invite (and Synonyms)

We intentionally used terms like *invite, entice, offer, encourage, support, guide, facilitate,* and *suggest* rather than the terms *have, assign,* and *allow.* Educators made the choice to work in the profession. In many cases, learners go to schools not by choice but because of laws, societal expectations, or familial economic needs (i.e., parents need to go to work). Learners are often not given a choice of where they'd like to spend their time. Adopting the learner-first approach means individual learners choose the experiences in which they'd like to participate. Learners are the drivers of their own experiences, and the role of the educator is to support those efforts. In a learner-first environment, learners are not forced to participate in an experience designed by educators. Instead, educators work to design experiences that are so engaging and empowering, the learner chooses to participate in them. The strategies in this book are meant to help educators design learning spaces, environments, and experiences that are so enticing, learners participate in them not because they have to, but because they want to.

Scaffolds

In the construction industry, scaffolds are temporary supports used when building structures, and are adapted depending on the situation. Without scaffolds, it is impossible to safely construct buildings, bridges, and other structures. In the same way, scaffolds in education are tiered supports that are temporary and customized depending on the needs of the learner. Scaffolds are individualized for multilingual learners, learners with varied abilities, or learners who need additional supports for a particular content area.

The Future is Inclusive

As we compiled the strategies shared in this book, we had long discussions about the power of inclusive strategies—not just for you, the educator, as you create engaging, meaningful, inclusive learning experiences; it's also an opportunity to model an inclusive mindset for all learners. If learners are exposed to inclusive strategies during educational experiences (like those listed in this book), they develop an understanding that these types of supports can be utilized by anyone, not just by a peer with a disability. Modeling and expecting inclusivity helps ensure that future generations create a world for everyone.

Evaluating Apps for Educational Effectiveness Using a Quality Assurance Rubric

There are thousands of apps available for people to use to promote learning. The National Educational Technology Plan, the American Academy of Pediatrics, and the National Association for the Education of Young Children, as well as ISTE advocate for the use of high quality technology in education. A series of considerations based on recommendations compiled from these organizations provides a means to evaluate educational effectiveness. Responses can be charted on a rubric with a rating scale from 1 to 5. These considerations include the following. The technology:

- Is open-ended to support problem solving and creativity, as opposed to simply providing drill and practice.

- Includes rich, engaging experiences that invite a high degree of interactivity and control by the user.

- Provides opportunities for or encourages movement.

- Enhances and encourages interactions with adults or peers for collaborative reflection, rather than only solitary exploration.

- Is free of stereotypes and promotes cultural and linguistic diversity as a strength.

- Is accessible to a wide range of learners, including those with physical or sensory-related disabilities.

- Meets a stated learning need that encourages development of literacy, language, STEAM, or artistic expression or supports learning that addresses educational standards.

INCLUSIVE USES

When sound pedagogy, cultural competency, and accessibility are used to select a tool, it is far more likely to support inclusive practices and meet the needs of every learner.

SAMPLE TOOL

Google Docs can be used to create rubrics (**docs.google.com**). Create your own or use this rubric which uses the considerations listed above: **bit.ly/inclusive365-1a**.

EXTENSION OPPORTUNITIES

Invite learners to evaluate a resource, modifying the language based on age and abilities of the learner. Invite learners to create a collaborative review portal on the website of your local education agency, where authentic evaluations of resources can be kept to be reviewed by other learners and educators. A common practice could be to search the portal prior to conducting one's own app review.

RELATED RESOURCES

Better Edtech Buying for Educators (**bit.ly/inclusive365-1b**)

Educational Apps Checklist Poster (**smore.com/72qsc**)

Figure 1. Summary of Educational Apps Checklist.

ISTE STANDARDS FOR STUDENTS
1a, 1b, 1c, 3a, 3b, 4b, 7b, 7c

ISTE STANDARDS FOR EDUCATORS
5a, 5b, 5c, 6b

Inspiring Agency With Twenty Percent Time

When individuals are invited to choose the topics they are studying, and educators act as facilitators rather than directors of learning, learners are more likely to actively participate. Focusing on a learner's personal interests and passions makes learning empowering and increases investment in learning. One step educators can take to move toward a completely learner-centered environment is to allocate a minimum of one hour a week to a learner passion project. Made popular by companies like Google, Twenty Percent Time promotes the idea that an individual should be able to freely engage in a topic of interest. The individual chooses what they want to investigate or create and spends approximately twenty percent of their time on it. While a final project can be a culminating event, examining the learning throughout is critical in helping both learners and educators see how the project is beneficial to meeting outcomes. Learners can share their progress along the way by blogging, microblogging, podcasting, or other means. Educators, peers, and others can provide feedback, input, and guidance.

INCLUSIVE USES

Learners become motivated when their learning preferences and passions are honored and respected. Providing the opportunity to engage in self-selected tasks empowers learners while increasing ownership and agency. Providing options for how to share the learning allows learners additional autonomy.

SAMPLE TOOLS

Facebook, Twitter, and Instagram provide microblogging options for learners to write or post media to chronicle the progress of their projects. Edublogs, from WordPress, allows learners to set up more formal blogs that can be dedicated to their projects (**edublogs.org**).

EXTENSION OPPORTUNITIES

Use a digital form to survey learners about their interests and passions. The learner and educator can then set personalized goals to monitor outcomes and the steps taken to achieve them as described in Strategy 13, Centering the Learner Using Preference and Interest Surveys.

Invite learners to imagine what would happen if the strategy were inverted, and instead was called Eighty Percent Time. Ask what they think the learning experience would be like if eighty percent of their time were engaged in projects driven by their own passions.

RELATED RESOURCES

A. J. Juliani provides a free self-paced, online course on how to implement Twenty Percent Time for educators (**ajjuliani.com/20-time-guide**).

The "20% Time Project" provides information and directions for educators to set up Twenty Percent Time and for learners to present on their projects (**20timeineducation.com**).

Ten Reasons to Try Genius Hour (**ajjuliani.com/try-genius-hour**)

Figure 2. Learners share Twenty Percent Time projects.

ISTE STANDARDS FOR STUDENTS
1a, 1c, 4b, 6a

ISTE STANDARDS FOR EDUCATORS
1a, 1b, 1c, 4d, 7b, 7c

Reviewing Learning Materials for Accessibility Prior to Implementation

Educators often choose which learning materials learners access. Adopting a consistent review process prior to implementation helps ensure materials meet the needs of any learner. Educators can ask questions about accessibility, such as:

- If the resource has digital text, can it be read aloud by a text-to-speech application?

- Can the resource be magnified or enlarged?

- Can the colors be changed to provide varied contrast?

- Is there a corresponding text representation when audio plays (i.e., captions)?

- Is there a corresponding optional audio track that can be played, describing the action in video (i.e., video descriptions)?

- Do images have corresponding text describing the image and, if so, can this text be presented in audio format (i.e., ALT tags)?

- Does the user interface have multiple input options to allow for access by someone who uses a switch?

- Is the resource portable, moveable, adjustable, or mountable to allow for access by someone in a wheelchair?

INCLUSIVE USES

When items are implemented without considering accessibility, educators may end up spending a significant amount of time and energy adapting materials to meet individual needs. Considering the accessibility of potential learning material helps to limit additional work.

SAMPLE TOOL

The following Google Doc can be used as a template for reviewing the accessibility of tools being considered: **bit.ly/inclusive365-3a**. The AEM Pilot tool provides guidance on the inclusive educational design of materials, including self assessment, goal setting, and progress monitoring (**aem-pilot.cast.org**).

EXTENSION OPPORTUNITY

Invite learners to participate in or contribute to the review of potential learning materials. Provide learners with a rubric with accessibility considerations, and ask them to provide input prior to implementation. This feedback could be used to help inform the actual decision-making process, while providing the added benefit of teaching future generations about the importance of considering accessibility.

RELATED RESOURCES

Choose Accessible Learning Materials Initiative at Virginia Tech (**assist.vt.edu/calm.html**)

Designing for Accessibility with POUR (**bit.ly/inclusive365-3b**)

AEM Pilot introduction (**bit.ly/inclusive365-3c**)

Quality Indicators for the Provision of AEM in K12 (**bit.ly/inclusive365-3d**)

Figure 3. This meme could be turned into a poster to help people remember to choose accessible learning materials.

ISTE STANDARDS FOR STUDENTS
1b, 1d, 3b, 4b, 4c

ISTE STANDARDS FOR EDUCATORS
2a, 2b, 2c, 3b, 3c, 4a, 4b, 4d, 5a, 5c, 6b

STRATEGY 4

Designing Instruction Using Information from Digital Pre-Assessment Tools

Gathering objective data from well-designed, inclusive, digital pre-assessment tools provides valuable information for future instruction. Carol Ann Tomlinson stated, "Assessment is today's means of modifying tomorrow's instruction" (2017). Pre-assessment guides instruction, so that educators know what learners already know about a subject or topic. Educators can then tailor instruction to meet each learner's needs. Pre-assessment also activates prior knowledge, creating connections to previous learning. Digital pre-assessment can also be automated, examined more quickly, and is generally more accessible than traditional pencil and paper assessment tools.

INCLUSIVE USES

Digital pre-assessment tools may bypass barriers of traditional paper and pencil methods for learners who have fine motor impairments, those working to improve verbal expression, and those who have yet to master decoding abilities. Learners can utilize screen readers to support decoding for pre-assessments on any topic that is not assessing the specific skill of decoding. Multimedia and interactive elements can be built into digital pre-assessments; these additions can increase engagement and accessibility as well.

SAMPLE TOOLS

Google Forms provides multimedia options and easy data analysis (**google.com/forms**).

Quizizz has engaging multimedia options for creating assessments (**quizizz.com**).

EXTENSION OPPORTUNITIES

As part of the pre-assessment data collection, ask your learners what they would like to learn about the topic. What problems would they hope to solve through learning the information?

Invite learners to reflect on their growth by comparing what they learned to the pre-assessment results.

RELATED RESOURCES

Does Pre-Assessment Work? (**bit.ly/inclusive365-4a**)

"Assessment is Today's Means of Modifying Tomorrow's Instruction" (**bit.ly/inclusive365-4b**)

Tomlinson, C. (1999) *The differentiated classroom: Responding to the needs of all learners.* Alexandria, VA: ASCD.

Figure 4. A pre-assessment created in Quizizz.

ISTE STANDARDS FOR STUDENTS
1a, 1c

ISTE STANDARDS FOR EDUCATORS
6a, 6b, 6c, 7b, 7c

Adopting a Platform-Agnostic Mindset

Many educators find that the technology decisions made by others often limit what they can access. For example, maybe your local educational agency predominantly uses Google Suite or Microsoft Office. Whichever platform the district administration mandates, there are still opportunities to use features from other platforms. Many tools are now web-based, allowing access from any internet-capable device. This allows learners the flexibility to choose the technology that works best based on individual needs.

INCLUSIVE USES

Ensuring that learners have access to what they need is essential in every learning environment. Agencies might adopt a multi-tiered system of supports, where tier one supports are available to every learner, tier two supports are available to groups of learners, and tier three supports are selected and implemented based on individual needs. Further, "Bring Your Own Technology" initiatives allow learners to use their own devices, inviting choice and agency. In these structures, learners have an opportunity to select the technology that works best for them.

SAMPLE TOOLS

With the advent of Office 365, the Microsoft Productivity Suite is available on multiple platforms (**bit.ly/inclusive365-5a**).

Immersive Reader is a feature embedded into most Microsoft and partner tools, providing an array of customizable support for evolving readers. An unofficial version of Immersive Reader exists as an extension in the Chrome browser (**bit.ly/inclusive365-5b**).

EXTENSION OPPORTUNITY

In an effort to adopt a more agnostic mindset, focused on the use of tools regardless of the platform, invite learners to advocate to IT staff for the technology learners find useful.

RELATED RESOURCE

Introducing Office 365 New Features (**bit.ly/inclusive365-5c**)

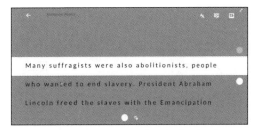

Figure 5a. Activate Immersive Reader for the Chrome extension by selecting website text, then right clicking the access menu.

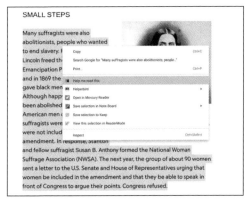

Figure 5b. Adapted website text with the background color, font style, and line spacing modified—plus a line focus tool has been activated.

ISTE STANDARDS FOR STUDENTS
1a, 1d, 3c, 5c, 6a.

ISTE STANDARDS FOR EDUCATORS
2b, 3b, 5a, 5c, 6a, 6b

Celebrating Diversity in Educational Materials

Learners are diverse. Traditionally, instructional materials have not reflected this reality. Learners need to see themselves represented in a non-stereotypical manner in the teaching and learning resources used in their learning spaces, including images in slide decks and educator-created instructional materials. Beyond simply seeing themselves, learners also need to see accurate images of the diversity in the world around them. Ensure that learners of all backgrounds are represented equitably.

INCLUSIVE USES

When considering diverse images, be sure to include individuals with disabilities. Learners of all abilities need to see individuals with disabilities represented in their educational resources.

SAMPLE TOOLS

Pics4Learning is designed with learners in mind. It is a curated image library of copyright-friendly photos and illustrations that are safe and free for educational purposes (**pics4learning.com**).

Pixabay is a web library that provides learners with an amazing collection of pictures, videos, and music. Almost two million images are available for use at this website (**pixabay.com**).

Unsplash includes more tha one million images that can be freely used in learner projects (**unsplash.com**).

Flickr provides access to thousands of images licensed under Creative Commons. Individuals can set up accounts to share their images as well (**flickr.com/creativecommons**).

EXTENSION OPPORTUNITIES

Invite learners to create a bank of images and photographs that highlight diversity and then use them across their learning community.

Invite learners to be photographers. Be sure to secure family permission to use and share photos that feature learners or their families.

RELATED RESOURCE

Culturally Responsive Teaching: Celebrating

Figure 6. Flickr picture of learners taken by Victoria Choi, USAG Humphreys Public Affairs, licensed under Attribution 2.0 Generic (CC BY 2.0).

Diversity in Our Schools (**bit.ly/inclusive365-6**)

ISTE STANDARDS FOR STUDENTS
2c

ISTE STANDARDS FOR EDUCATORS
3b, 4d

Matching Learner Needs to the Features of Technology

With the multitude of apps, web tools, and resources out there, one can become overwhelmed by the sheer number of options. It would be impossible to know every detail of every tool available. When considering what technology to put in place to help an individual learner or groups of learners, focus on examining their needs first, and then go hunting for technology with the features that would best support those needs. Referring to a resource list designed to match features to names of tools can become a helpful way to identify what specific resource should be put in place. Many resource lists currently exist and are updated regularly to support educators.

INCLUSIVE USES

Effectively matching learners' needs to appropriate tools promotes the intentional use of technology to promote inclusive learning. You can serve learners more effectively by offering a list of thoughtfully considered options selected because they will likely meet specific needs, rather than having unlimited, unfettered access to every tool under the sun.

SAMPLE TOOLS

The Periodic Table of iPad Apps for Primary Students is designed to resemble the Periodic Table of Elements to provide app suggestions under different categories (creativity, teaching, demonstration, collaboration, literacy, numeracy, etc) (**bit.ly/inclusive365-7a**).

The Shake Up Learning Chrome Extension Database is a web-based directory focused exclusively on Chrome Extensions. With more than 150 extensions listed, educators can search this directory by category, grade level or subject area (**shakeuplearning.com/chrome-database**).

EXTENSION OPPORTUNITY

Invite learners to reflect on the ways they believe technology could support their learning experience, and create a list in the first column of a table. For some it might be helpful to provide a starter sentence such as, "I wish my technology could …" to guide their thinking. Some learner responses might be, "Read words aloud to me," "Help me keep on track," or "Become better at typing." Once the list is complete, challenge learners to use resource lists and databases to find at least three different options with features that might meet all those needs. Invite the learners to evaluate the effectiveness of these tools to find the right fit.

RELATED RESOURCE

CALL Scotland Downloadable Posters and Leaflets (**bit.ly/inclusive365-7b**)

Figure 7. The CALL Scotland Chromebook apps and extensions wheel.

ISTE STANDARDS FOR STUDENTS

1a, 1b, 1c, 1d, 3a, 4b

ISTE STANDARDS FOR EDUCATORS

1b, 1c, 2a, 2c, 3a, 3b, 4a, 5c, 7b

STRATEGY 7

STRATEGY 8

Providing Learning Spaces With Multiple Sources of Natural Light

Spaces designed to maximize natural light help increase work performance while promoting improved ratings of worker happiness and satisfaction. Whenever possible, design and structure learning spaces to maximize natural light. Simple strategies include keeping windows clear of clutter, placing work areas near the windows, and filling learning environments with multiple sources of soft light using lamps and bulbs that artificially produce "natural" light.

INCLUSIVE USES

Some learners who are working to regulate sensory stimulation may have an added level of distraction caused by the pulsing and/or buzzing produced by fluorescent lighting. These distractions might be so subtle that they are not necessarily readily perceived by others. Having multiple sources of natural light provides options for different areas where learners can choose to work without the distractions presented by fluorescent lights.

SAMPLE TOOL

Floorplanner allows users to design a 3D representation of the learning space they'd like to build, including multiple sources of natural light (**floorplanner.com**).

EXTENSION OPPORTUNITY

Invite learners to design their learning space by drafting, drawing, or digitally rendering designs of the room, common areas, and other learning spaces to include multiple sources of natural light.

RELATED RESOURCES

Flexible Seating and Student-Centered Classroom Redesign (**bit.ly/inclusive365-8a**)

A.T.TIPSCAST Episode #61: Room (Re-) Arranging (**bit.ly/attipscast61**)

The Benefits of Natural Light in Office Spaces: Lighting Design for Increased Employee Satisfaction (**bit.ly/inclusive365-8b**)

Figure 8. A learning space with soft lighting.

ISTE STANDARDS FOR STUDENTS
1a, 1b, 1c, 1d, 4b, 4c

ISTE STANDARDS FOR EDUCATORS
2b, 3a, 4a, 4b, 4c, 4d, 5a, 5b, 5c, 6a, 6b

Providing Work Surfaces at Multiple Heights

People choose to work in locations that best suit individual preferences. Work locations vary based on the parameters and cognitive demands of the task, and each person's physical needs at the time. Sometimes it is prudent to stand to get work done. At other times, a person might choose to sit or even lie down to complete work. Provide work surfaces that are adjustable and available at varying heights to facilitate task completion. While there are a variety of commercially-available adjustable tables and flexible seating pieces on the market, educators can make low-cost adaptations. For example, use bed risers to make a desk comfortable for standing, or place pillows next to a low table to allow learners to sit on the floor to work.

INCLUSIVE USES

Adjustable work surfaces acknowledge the reality that one size does not fit all. Learners of varying heights, sizes, and abilities can choose the work surface that's right for them to complete their work most comfortably and effectively. Learners in wheelchairs or positioning equipment benefit from having adjustable work surfaces to suit the height needed for their equipment. When educators create a learning environment with work surfaces at differing heights, the environment becomes accessible for all.

SAMPLE TOOL

Floorplanner is a website that can be used to design a 3D representation of the learning space you'd like to build, including work surfaces at varying or adjustable heights (**floorplanner.com**).

EXTENSION OPPORTUNITY

Invite learners to design the learning space by drafting, drawing, or digitally rendering designs of the room, common areas, and other learning spaces to include work surfaces of multiple heights.

RELATED RESOURCES

Reimagining Classrooms: Teachers as Learners and Students as Leaders, Kayla Delzer, TEDxFargo (**bit.ly/inclusive365-9a**)

Walker, J. D., Brooks, D. C., & Baepler, P. (2011). "Pedagogy and space: empirical research in new learning environments." *EDUCAUSE Quarterly, 34*(4) (**bit.ly/inclusive365-9b**)

Figure 9a. A learning space with a variety of work surfaces at multiple heights.

Figure 9b. Tables with heights that can be adjusted using a foot pedal.

ISTE STANDARDS FOR STUDENTS
1a, 1b, 1c, 1d, 4b, 4c

ISTE STANDARDS FOR EDUCATORS
2b, 3a, 4a, 4b, 4c, 4d, 5a, 5b, 5c, 6a, 6b

STRATEGY 10

Creating Learning Spaces Using Flexible and Adjustable Work Locations

Learning spaces can be designed in such a way that educators and learners can transform the arrangement of the furniture, including work locations, based on the instructional needs of the experience. Furniture can be moved to support independent study, small group work, or whole group instruction. Learners can be invited to choose work locations based on the learning task.

INCLUSIVE USES

Individuals practicing strategies to regulate attention might be empowered to maintain focus during learning experiences when they are given the choice of where they'd like to work.

SAMPLE TOOLS

Gynzy provides a library of icons and other graphics, including representations of a variety of furniture, that can be dragged onto a virtual whiteboard to design learning spaces (**bit.ly/inclusive365-10a**).

Design Your Classroom allows learners to design a space with technology, furniture, and wall items (**bit.ly/inclusive365-10b**).

EXTENSION OPPORTUNITIES

Invite learners to design the learning space to include multiple work locations for independent, small group, or whole group learning experiences.

Invite learners to choose different locations in the room and evaluate the impact the locations have on their attention, focus, and task completion.

RELATED RESOURCES

Campfires, Caves, and Watering Holes (**bit.ly/inclusive365-10c**)

A.T.TIPSCAST Episode #61: Room (Re-) Arranging (**bit.ly/inclusive365-10d**)

Figure 10. A room with flexible seating.

ISTE STANDARDS FOR STUDENTS
1a, 1b, 1c, 1d, 4b, 4c

ISTE STANDARDS FOR EDUCATORS
2b, 3a, 4a, 4b, 4c, 4d, 5a, 5b, 5c, 6a, 6b

Using Virtual Backgrounds for Distance Learning

Various platforms allow users to set up virtual backgrounds, including uploading a custom image. Educators can use virtual backgrounds to complement and enhance a learning experience. Studying the rainforest? Find a rainforest image to help spark discussion or reinforce concepts. Reading Edgar Allen Poe? Find something dark and moody to set the tone. Select images that support the learning, rather than distracting from it.

INCLUSIVE USES

Learners who use augmentative communication devices may benefit from having their communication device in view on the screen behind their educator or speech/language pathologist, who can then use the background to model language.

A virtual background can also serve as an equity resource for learners who may not wish to show their own home setting in the background of their screen. A virtual background can provide privacy for families, learners, and educators.

SAMPLE TOOLS

Virtual Background in Zoom allows you to select any image as the background for your environment. Once the Zoom software is updated, the Virtual Background appears even if the learner does not have a green screen behind them (**zoom.us**).

Visual Effects for Google Meet is a Chrome extension that provides background support directly in Google Meet. Learners can apply effects to their personal background including blur and pixelate, and they can even connect a custom background picture (**bit.ly/inclusive365-11a**).

Unsplash has thousands of copyright-free images, including a variety of high resolution wallpaper images that work well as virtual backgrounds (**unsplash.com/t/wallpapers**).

EXTENSION OPPORTUNITY

Invite learners to help select the virtual background for the day using a poll or other method of voting as part of a morning routine.

RELATED RESOURCES

Virtual Background—Zoom Help Center (**bit.ly/inclusive365-11b**)

Visual Effects for Google Meet Chrome Extension (**bit.ly/inclusive365-11c**)

PBS offers virtual background resources for educators (**bit.ly/inclusive365-11d**).

Figure 11. Rainforest image from Unsplash along with a screenshot of a student's augmentative communication device used as a virtual background.

ISTE STANDARDS FOR STUDENTS
2d

ISTE STANDARDS FOR EDUCATORS
5b, 5c

Providing Learning Spaces with Flexible and Kinesthetic Seating Surfaces

Active movement helps the brain learn. Rather than using movement as a break during long stints of sitting or stationary work, design the environment and learning experiences with seating options that provide movement. Sitting on a hard surface during stationary tasks could be considered the break in an environment predominantly built with movement in mind.

Provide learners with opportunities to choose seating based on preferences necessary to complete the learning task at hand. Seating options could include both soft and hard surfaces upon which to sit and work. Options could include surfaces that provide for vestibular and kinesthetic movement, such as bouncy balls, swivel chairs, and durable cushions.

INCLUSIVE USES

Learners who are practicing to regulate attention may find they can maintain focus longer with fewer distractions while their body is involved in spontaneous motor movements.

SAMPLE TOOL

Gynzy provides a library of icons and other graphics, including representations of a variety of furniture, that can be dragged onto a virtual whiteboard to design learning spaces (**bit.ly/inclusive365-12a**).

EXTENSION OPPORTUNITIES

Invite learners to design the learning space by researching, selecting, budgeting for, proposing, and ordering soft and hard seating options.

Invite learners to adapt current furniture options using commonly found materials. For instance, tennis balls could be cut and placed on two opposing corners of chair legs. When seated in this chair, learners can wobble back and forth.

Learners participating in family and consumer science experiences could make secure cushions for furniture.

RELATED RESOURCES

The Kinesthetic Classroom: Teaching and Learning through Movement, Michael Kuczala, TEDxAshburn (**bit.ly/inclusive365-12b**)

Brain Rules Exercise by John Medina (**bit.ly/inclusive365-12c**)

Figure 12. Learning spaces with seating surfaces that promote kinesthetic movement. These include bean bag chairs, bouncy chairs, and wobbly stools.

ISTE STANDARDS FOR STUDENTS
1a, 1b, 1c, 1d, 4b, 4c

ISTE STANDARDS FOR EDUCATORS
2b, 3a, 4a, 4b, 4c, 4d, 5a, 5b, 5c, 6a, 6b

Centering the Learner Using Preference and Interest Surveys

As the principle benefactor of every educational experience, learners should be in the driver's seat. A digital form can be used to survey learner preferences to help guide the design process of an educational experience. The results of the form automatically populate a spreadsheet which can be copied for each learner. The learner and educator can then use the results of the survey to establish learning goals and outline steps to help achieve them.

INCLUSIVE USES

Learners become motivated when their learning preferences and passions are honored and respected. The simple act of inviting learners to share preferences and then spending time reflecting on the responses can help build trust and positive relationships, especially with those who have been marginalized or who have adopted a mindset of doubt around their ability to learn.

SAMPLE TOOLS

Google Forms allows users to collect data and sort the data displayed in a Google Sheet (**docs.google.com/forms**).

Microsoft Forms allows users to collect data and sort the data displayed in an Excel spreadsheet (**forms.office.com**).

The following is an example of an interest inventory in Google Forms: **bit.ly/inclusive365-13a**.

EXTENSION OPPORTUNITIES

Invite each learner or small groups of learners to lead an online learning experience based on a passion or preference.

Invite learners to complete the preference or interest survey multiple times throughout the year. Interests and preferences may evolve as time progresses.

RELATED RESOURCES

Developing a Student Centered Classroom (**bit.ly/inclusive365-13b**)

How to Create a Student Interest Survey with Microsoft Forms (**bit.ly/inclusive365-13c**)

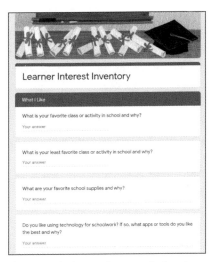

Figure 13. An interest inventory in Google Forms.

ISTE STANDARDS FOR STUDENTS

1a, 1c, 4b, 6a

ISTE STANDARDS FOR EDUCATORS

1a, 1b, 1c, 4d, 7b, 7c

STRATEGY 14

Building a Sensory Path

A sensory path is a series of colorful stickers or other objects placed on the ground in a hallway or room which help learners understand how to integrate and regulate different sensory inputs. Like an obstacle course, learners complete a series of tasks or actions to traverse the path. Along the way, learners develop motor, vestibular (balance), spatial, and other cognitive skills. Different stickers might include letters, numbers, words, colors, shapes, and decorative objects centered around a theme. Although there are commercial packs available, customized stickers can be made as well.

INCLUSIVE USES

Learners can be invited to traverse the sensory path as they travel down the hallway, whenever they decide they need to move, as part of an academic experience, or anytime they find it necessary. Providing opportunities for movement is a culturally responsive and inclusive means of addressing a learner's need to be active and move to be ready to engage with learning tasks.

SAMPLE TOOL

Fit and Fun Playscapes provides commercially available items to help build a sensory path (**fitandfunplayscapes.com**).

EXTENSION OPPORTUNITIES

Invite learners to design sensory paths for their peers, challenging them to attempt to structure it with different modalities in mind.

Invite learners to reconfigure an existing sensory path.

Invite learners to test and provide feedback about the experience they had traversing a path created by a peer.

RELATED RESOURCES

Movement and Sensory Pathway: How to Create Your Own (**bit.ly/inclusive365-14a**)

DIY Sensory Path and Motor Path (**bit.ly/inclusive365-14b**)

Figure 14. Sensory paths.

ISTE STANDARDS FOR STUDENTS
1b, 5c

ISTE STANDARDS FOR EDUCATORS
4d, 5b

Experiencing Stories of People with Disabilities Through Art

An effective way to learn about diversity and the perspectives of other people is to experience the artistic expression created by people of different cultures and communities. Invite learners to expand their world view by experiencing artistic content, including stories, paintings, sculptures, photographs, music, and more, created by people with disabilities.

INCLUSIVE USES

Learners need role models. Learners with disabilities can benefit from the experiences and perspectives of those who have come before. Hearing stories of strategies effectively used by others can help learners adopt and employ that strategy for themselves. Experiencing art created by people with disabilities offers learners different modalities to develop a shared perspective.

SAMPLE TOOL

Disability Arts Online is a web-based resource that shares blog posts and magazine articles related to art created by people with disabilities (**disabilityarts.online**).

EXTENSION OPPORTUNITIES

Invite learners to create their own works of art to share online for others to experience and enjoy. Ideas include drawings, paintings, music, or writing that helps someone else learn more about a particular disability.

After participating in an experience where learners have learned about making respectful, meaningful comments, invite learners to take turns moderating comments before posting publicly.

RELATED RESOURCE

Disability Art
(**britannica.com/art/disability-art**)

Figure 15. Comments from the Google Art and Culture YouTube Channel of Vincent Van Gogh's work, Starry Night.

ISTE STANDARDS FOR STUDENTS
2a, 2b, 3d, 6b, 6c, 6d, 7a, 7b

ISTE STANDARDS FOR EDUCATORS
3a, 3b, 3c, 6d, 7a

STRATEGY 15

STRATEGY 16

Collaborative Problem Solving Using Virtual Escape Rooms

Virtual escape rooms provide an opportunity for learners to engage in collaborative problem solving in an interactive, game-based environment. Learners work to complete a series of challenges to move through the virtual room to escape. Each challenge provides the learners with a key to unlock the next challenge, until they have completed all the tasks. Learners engage in critical thinking, risk taking, and problem solving while exploring the content.

INCLUSIVE USES

Presenting a learning task in a game-based context increases engagement. Working together with peers can help build relationships for learners who are working to improve social skills. When designing an escape room experience, ensure that the problems can be solved by using more than one modality or sense. It may be impossible For some learners to solve a particular problem if the solution requires use of a particular sense, such as sight or hearing only.

SAMPLE TOOLS

OneNote can be used to create an interactive notebook that takes learners through a series of challenges to escape the virtual room. OneNote provides educators with templates to create escape rooms at both the elementary and secondary level. If OneNote is used to design and present the escape room, learners can use the built in accessibility features, including text-to-speech with Immersive Reader (**onenote.com**).

Breakout EDU has options for both in-person and virtual escape room experiences (**breakoutedu.com**).

Google Forms can be used to create a virtual escape room where each clue must be solved

before the learner may progress to the next item (**docs.google.com/forms**).

EXTENSION OPPORTUNITIES

Invite educators to use a virtual escape room as part of a professional learning experience. Escape rooms can provide a means of engaging in collaboration and collegiality when participating virtually. And they're fun!

Did you spot the clue hidden within this page? There are certain hints and clues peppered throughout this page that, once deciphered, unlock super secret bonus content. There is no such thing as cheating in this experience. Phone a friend! Do an internet search! Bribe an author! Do whatever it takes because this is bonus content you won't want to miss.

RELATED RESOURCES

OneNote Break Out Templates (**bit.ly/inclusive365-16a**)

30 Digital Escape Rooms Plus Tips for Creating Your Own (**bit.ly/inclusive365-16b**)

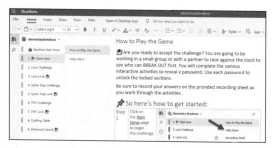

Figure 16. An introduction to a virtual escape room experience using OneNote.

ISTE STANDARDS FOR STUDENTS
5b, 7b, 7c

ISTE STANDARDS FOR EDUCATORS
4c, 5a, 5b, 5c

Manipulating Documents into Manageable Components

How do we provide a platform for learners to interact with PDFs? As educators share documents with learners, there may be instances where these documents need to be manipulated for easier access. Large documents may need to be broken up into more manageable chunks, or multiple smaller documents may need to be combined into one larger document. Learners need the ability to manipulate these files independently. Online file management and creation can be a powerful solution for utilization of digital files.

INCLUSIVE USES

File management is critical for building an inclusive learning environment. Not every learner can access the documents shared with them by educators. Learners can be shown how to independently combine or break apart files for annotation or easier navigation.

SAMPLE TOOLS

SodaPDF is a web tool that allows manipulation of PDFs to ensure usability. Features include creating, converting, optical character recognition, merging PDFs, and separating PDFs. PDFs can exist on your local device, or PDFs can be made directly from URLs (**sodapdf.com**).

Adobe Acrobat also allows learners or educators to be able to split a PDF into multiple documents (**acrobat.adobe.com**).

EXTENSION OPPORTUNITY

Visit this web tool and collaborate with learners to modify a PDF file. Take a large PDF file (e.g., a study guide) and edit the file to split the large file into smaller, more manageable files to increase access to learners.

RELATED RESOURCES

Chunking Reading Materials
(**bit.ly/inclusive365-17a**)

How to Split PDF Pages
(**bit.ly/inclusive365-17b**)

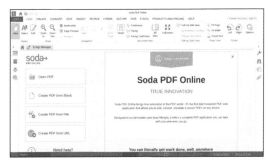

Figure 17. SodaPDFOnline.

STE STANDARDS FOR STUDENTS
1a, 1d, 3a, 3c, 6a

ISTE STANDARDS FOR EDUCATORS
3b, 4b, 5a, 6a

Backchanneling for Learner Discussions

All learners have something to contribute, but not everyone prefers to speak during discussions. Furthermore, some learning spaces, environments, or experiences aren't conducive to synchronous verbal exchanges. A backchannel discussion is a digital space where learners can add thoughts, questions, and other contributions to what is being discussed verbally. Backchannel tools provide a location for this discussion, and learners can choose which modality works best for them to contribute. Some of the most powerful moments of learning can come from these "behind the scenes" sharing opportunities. Backchannel discussions promote choice, respect different forms of communication, reduce stress, and provide evidence of learning.

INCLUSIVE USES

Learners who have oral language challenges or who are multilingual learners can take the time needed to compose their messages. Learners who are hesitant to share can take time to compose their thoughts or contribute with resources they have had time to research. Learners who tend to dominate a conversation can add to the backchannel discussion as often as they want without preventing others from participating. Learners who are not comfortable turning on their microphone during distance learning can still be active participants. A backchannel tool allows all of these learners the opportunity to actively participate.

SAMPLE TOOLS

YoTeach! is a chat tool to use as a backchannel discussion board (**yoteachapp.com**).

Padlet provides educators the opportunity to moderate posts and has a profanity filter which prevents messages containing expletives (**padlet.com**).

Backchannel Chat was made specifically for educators to use for backchannel discussions. It provides moderation and does not require a participant email address. Learners can use their educational Google accounts to access it (**backchannelchat.com**).

EXTENSION OPPORTUNITIES

Bring a backchannel discussion into the "front channel" and review the information together to validate the sharing.

Invite learners to use a backchannel asynchronously to participate whenever and wherever. In this way, the backchannel fosters a sense of community around the topic about which a group is learning.

RELATED RESOURCES

New Features of Yo Teach!
(**bit.ly/inclusive365-18a**)

The Backchannel: Giving Every Student a Voice in the Blended Mobile Classroom (**bit.ly/inclusive365-18b**)

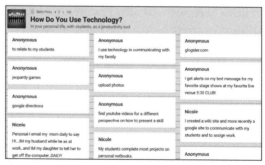

Figure 18. Padlet used as a forum for backchannel discussion on how educators are using technology in their lives.

ISTE STANDARDS FOR STUDENTS
1b, 2a, 2b, 3d, 6c

ISTE STANDARDS FOR EDUCATORS
2a, 3a, 3d, 4c, 5b, 6d

Using Private Chats in Distance Learning Platforms to Meet Individual Needs

Most distance learning platforms include a public chat box for commentary, discussion, or questions. Some learners may find it difficult to ask a public question due to embarrassment or anxiety. Using the private chat option allows educators to reach out to a specific learner, or for a learner to ask a question directed only to the educator for individualized support.

INCLUSIVE USES

Educators can prompt individual learners to use a specific strategy or accommodation without breaching confidentiality. Paraeducators who are co-hosts in a remote learning session can also use this tool to meet individual needs, even when the educator leading instruction is not able to monitor the chat.

SAMPLE TOOLS

Zoom, Google Meet, Microsoft Teams, and Adobe Connect all allow private chats between the host (the educator) and individual learners.

- **zoom.us**
- **meet.google.com**
- **bit.ly/inclusive365-19a**
- **adobe.com/products/adobeconnect.html**

EXTENSION OPPORTUNITY

Educators can keep a bank of commonly needed private chat messages in a Word or Google Doc available to touch base with a learner. Some common messages might include, "How's the reading going?," "I can see how hard you are working!," "What do you think might help you with this?," "Your face looks puzzled. Did I not explain this well?," and "You look a little bored. Is this too easy for you?"

RELATED RESOURCE

The Human Element in Online Learning (**bit.ly/inclusive365-19b**)

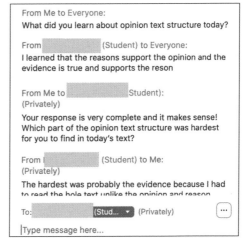

From Me to Everyone:
What did you learn about opinion text structure today?

From ▇▇▇▇▇ (Student) to Everyone:
I learned that the reasons support the opinion and the evidence is true and supports the reson

From Me to ▇▇▇▇ Student):
(Privately)
Your response is very complete and it makes sense! Which part of the opinion text structure was hardest for you to find in today's text?

From ▇▇▇▇ (Student) to Me:
(Privately)
The hardest was probably the evidence because I had to read the hole text unlike the opinion and reason

To: ▇▇▇ (Stud... ▾) (Privately)   (...)

Type message here...

Figure 19. A private Zoom chat between a learner and an educator.

ISTE STANDARDS FOR STUDENTS
1b, 1c

ISTE STANDARDS FOR EDUCATORS
4b, 4c

Promoting Participation Using Audio/Video Recordings

Every learner has something to contribute. However, some learners are reluctant to participate for a variety of reasons. They may need additional time to process questions and comments. They may be shy, or introverted, or fear providing an incorrect response. Audio recordings offer alternatives to the traditional method of asking questions and calling on those who raise their hands. This option can be empowering for learners who remain uncomfortable speaking out. Audio and video recordings promote a culture in which every voice matters.

INCLUSIVE USES

Some learners may use communication devices and need additional time to formulate a response. Offering audio recording tools gives learners time to process their thoughts, and also provides the option for a learner to re-record until satisfied with their recording. This has the potential to be beneficial for all learners, not just those working on improving communication skills.

SAMPLE TOOLS

Flipgrid is a free audio and video recording tool that gives every learner a voice. It allows learners to respond to questions and leave comments to build collaborative knowledge (**flipgrid.com**).

VoiceThread also provides learners the ability to use text, images, video, and audio responses (**voicethread.com**).

EXTENSION OPPORTUNITIES

Encourage learners to respond to videos made by peers to build a collaborative community.

Educators can collaborate using short audio and video recordings. Educators could comment on a collaborative project, reflect on a strategy, share their thoughts to help plan an upcoming event, or provide input on any other topic.

RELATED RESOURCE

Flipgrid Resources (**bit.ly/inclusive365-20**)

Figure 20. Learner responses in Flipgrid.

ISTE STANDARDS FOR STUDENTS

6a, 6c, 7b

ISTE STANDARDS FOR EDUCATORS

3a, 3b, 5a, 4c, 6a, 6b, 6d

Facilitating Discussions Using Think, Pair, Share

Think, Pair, Share is a collaborative learning strategy that encourages independent thinking and the exchange of ideas. Educators can use this strategy in face-to-face settings by asking learners to consider an answer to a question or their ideas on a topic and then turning to a partner to share their ideas and discuss whether they each agree, disagree, or should consider alternatives. In an online environment, learners instead are paired or grouped in the digital learning platform to exchange direct text or audio messages synchronously or asynchronously.

INCLUSIVE USES

Introverted learners, learners working to improve short or long memory, those who have difficulty processing information in a large group setting, those who have trouble focusing for long periods of time, as well as multilingual learners can get lost in a whole group discussion or a lecture-only format. Small groups are critical for keeping these learners engaged and giving every learner a voice. Think, Pair, Share provides an opportunity for learners to interact with peers in a low stress, no judgement environment using multiple modalities that don't require in-the-moment reading or writing proficiency.

SAMPLE TOOLS

Voxer provides real time push-to-talk capabilities on phones or via a web browser. Voxer provides the opportunity to send text or voice messages with a "walkie-talkie" feature (**voxer.com**).

Edmodo is a learning management system that allows educators to create learner groups for collaboration and discussion (**new.edmodo.com**).

EXTENSION OPPORTUNITIES

Invite learners to expand their discussions in a variation called Think, Pair, Share, Square. Think, Pair, Share, Square brings two pairs together to continue the discussion, adding more ideas and perspectives. Each pair explains their thoughts to each other and considers how the new information may change or solidify their thinking.

RELATED RESOURCES

Edmodo Teacher Guide (**bit.ly/inclusive365-21a**)

Think, Pair, Share (**readingrockets.org/strategies/think-pair-share**)

Seven Think-Pair-Share Variations (**bit.ly/inclusive365-21b**)

Figure 21. Learners engage in Think, Pair, Share via Voxer.

ISTE STANDARDS FOR STUDENTS
7b

ISTE STANDARDS FOR EDUCATORS
4c, 5a

STRATEGY 22

Polling for Learner Engagement and Checks for Understanding

Polls can help educators check the understanding of a particular concept in a small or large group of learners all at once. Using mobile devices, computers, or even low tech means such as QR codes on cards, learners can provide input to a poll to demonstrate what they know, which can help an educator find out which learners might be struggling with a concept or skill. Provide polls synchronously to serve as a check-in with learners while delivering new information, or asynchronously while learners are working independently. Educators can then make adjustments and provide targeted supports to specific learners. Consider also how to collect opinions and spark discussions with polls. Additionally, educators can collect feedback on the pace of a group, interest in a topic, or the appeal of a learning experience, to gain insight into learner preferences.

INCLUSIVE USES

Polls can give an educator feedback privately, without drawing attention to individual learners. Polls also keep learners from being influenced by the answers that their peers may be providing, so that an educator can get a true idea of what a learner is thinking.

SAMPLE TOOLS

Poll Everywhere is a live response tool for group use in in-person or virtual settings (**polleverywhere.com**).

Plickers is a low-tech method of polling in which educators print out cards with QR codes on them that send learners to answer poll questions online (**get.plickers.com**).

Polling is a feature in Zoom Meetings (**zoom.us**).

Google Forms can be used to create a poll (docs.google.com/forms). Take a poll about your favorite inclusive learning strategy here: (**bit.ly/inclusive365-22a**).

EXTENSION OPPORTUNITY

Invite learners to create their own poll questions based on a project they are creating. Space polling questions throughout the experience.

RELATED RESOURCE

Polling the Classroom: Four Free Polling Tools to Keep Students Engaged (**bit.ly/inclusive365-22b**).

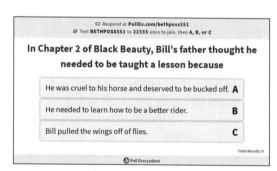

Figure 22. Check for Understanding created in Poll Everywhere.

ISTE STANDARDS FOR STUDENTS
1c

ISTE STANDARDS FOR EDUCATORS
4a, 5a, 5b

Facilitating Asynchronous Discussions with Audio

Learners may be reluctant, or struggle, to write thoughts cohesively. Inviting learners to record their voices as an option for participation promotes the sharing of ideas. The use of audio also enables learners to hear the voices of peers, gleaning insights from tone, rate, and emphasis, which might minimize the potential of misinterpreting written text. Hearing the voices of peers may help learners make connections during distance learning as well as provide an opportunity to experience perspectives from different backgrounds and cultures to broaden the scope of understanding.

INCLUSIVE USES

Learners not yet confident in their writing abilities may find that using audio provides a more equitable opportunity to participate.

Individuals working on improving articulation or working on increasing particular language skills, including those learning how to become proficient in multiple languages, may find recording their voices to participate in authentic discussions a useful and motivating way to practice. Learners can record, listen, reflect, and re-record repeatedly until they are satisfied.

SAMPLE TOOLS

Synth is an audio conversation tool accessible on most web enabled devices. Unique features include the ability to set up and record audio for one-time access. Once the audio has been completed, the educator can download the file to share (**gosynth.com**).

Voxer is an audio conversation tool accessible on most web-enabled devices. Groups can be created that have a specific focus, and then learners can join the conversation (**voxer.com**).

Read&Write for Google Chrome allows users to record audio which is embedded as comments in a Google Doc (**bit.ly/inclusive365-23a**).

EXTENSION OPPORTUNITIES

Pose an audio prompt to engage learners in a conversation about a current event. Race and equity, the implications of scientific discoveries, technological advances, and financial trends are just some of the topics that could be discussed. Facilitate the discussion with feedback throughout to ensure all voices have an opportunity to be heard.

Create an audiobook club. As the group reads a novel, ask questions, and invite learners to discuss their thoughts regarding characters, plot, author's message, and more.

Invite colleagues to participate in asynchronous audio discussions on topics related to educational practices, including technology, useful strategies, book studies (perhaps around the strategies in this book!), and the latest research.

RELATED RESOURCES

Easy Podcasting for Teachers and Students Using Synth (**bit.ly/inclusive365-23b**)

Seven Ways to Use Synth with K12 Students (**bit.ly/inclusive365-23c**)

Voxer Versatility: New Ways to Communicate (**bit.ly/inclusive365-23d**)

Figure 23. A Synth audio discussion.

ISTE STANDARDS FOR STUDENTS
1b, 1c, 2a, 6d, 7a, 7b

ISTE STANDARDS FOR EDUCATORS
5a, 5b, 5c, 6a, 7a

STRATEGY 23

Creating Small Group Opportunities During Distance Learning

Educators often need to think in new, creative ways when providing distance learning opportunities. How does an educator provide small-group collaborative learning or small-group support? Breakout rooms provide an opportunity for educators to group learners either randomly or by design into small groups, which the educator can join to monitor and facilitate the discussion. Learners now have the opportunity to participate more easily than in a larger, whole group meeting. Educators can use learning strategies, including Think, Pair, Share as described in Strategy 21, in the breakout rooms. Depending on the distance learning platform, educators can pre-set the discussions to end after a specific time, provide a warning message to the small groups, and have learners automatically rejoin the larger group when the time is up.

INCLUSIVE USES

Introverted learners, learners with memory issues, or those who take more time to process information in a large group setting—as well as multilingual learners—can often get lost in a whole-group discussion or a lecture-only format. Small groups are critical for keeping these learners engaged and giving every learner a voice.

SAMPLE TOOLS

Zoom Breakout Room meetings can be divided in up to fifty different groups. The meeting host can split the participants automatically or manually (**zoom.us**).

Google Meet also allows for breakout rooms (**meet.google.com**).

EXTENSION OPPORTUNITY

Create opportunities for learners to connect with peers in other groups, other schools, or even other countries through breakout rooms in digital meetings. Learners can engage with others outside their four walls to gain new perspectives.

RELATED RESOURCES

How to Use Breakout Rooms in Zoom (**bit.ly/inclusive365-24a**)

Using Breakout Rooms in Google Meet (**bit.ly/inclusive365-24b**)

How to Use Breakout Rooms in Zoom for Teaching and Learning (**bit.ly/inclusive365-24c**)

Figure 24. Learners and an educator in a Zoom breakout room for small group instruction.

ISTE STANDARDS FOR STUDENTS

1a, 1b, 2b, 6a, 7b

ISTE STANDARDS FOR EDUCATORS

2b, 3a, 4c, 6a

Creating Scavenger Hunts with QR Codes Leading to Video Content

The first principle in the Universal Design for Learning framework suggests educators should provide multiple means of engagement, focusing on recruiting interest and sustaining effort and persistence in a variety of ways. The sense of discovery experienced when finding clues, unraveling a mystery, or solving a puzzle intrinsically motivates many learners. Scavenger hunts designed using QR codes that link to video prompts promote engagement and sustained attention. When designing a scavenger hunt, the QR codes can be integrated into the physical space in which the hunt is occurring or can be built into digital resources if the hunt is designed to be digital in nature.

INCLUSIVE USES

Video content with captions and corresponding text or video descriptions removes the need to read text independently. Although sighted individuals might benefit from captions, they may be particularly important to learners with hearing impairments. Text transcripts of the audio content along with descriptions of the action in a video make it accessible to learners who are blind or who use screen readers.

QR codes for a physical scavenger hunt should be placed at heights and in locations accessible to all learners, including those who are shorter or in wheelchairs.

SAMPLE TOOL

Flipgrid from Microsoft allows users to create short videos with automatic QR code generation (**info.flipgrid.com**).

EXTENSION OPPORTUNITY

Invite learners to explore how to create their own QR codes and design their own virtual or physical scavenger hunts. For example, learners could be invited to create a "welcome to our community" scavenger hunt for those who are new to the learning environment.

RELATED RESOURCE

Flipgrid Shorts with QR Code/AR blog post (**blog.flipgrid.com/ar**)

Figure 25. Flipgrid shorts showing a QR code generator.

ISTE STANDARDS FOR STUDENTS
4a, 4b, 7a

ISTE STANDARDS FOR EDUCATORS
3b, 3d, 5a, 5c, 6a, 6b, 6c

Discovering Hidden Artifacts Using Geocaching and Augmented Reality

Humans have an innate drive to uncover that which is hidden. This thirst for discovery can be a powerful way to engage learners. Seeking clues that lead to an artifact hidden by others hooks learners' imaginations, sending them on a journey promoting critical thinking, problem solving, collaboration, and creativity. Educators can create indoor or outdoor augmented reality (AR) hunts using geocaches. Geocaching, a location-based treasure hunt, can be used either on its own or in context with a story or mystery to solve. Geocaches can be physical objects hidden in different geographic locations or virtual artifacts discovered through a mobile device. Learners decipher clues, coordinates, distances, and waypoints to navigate to locations containing a virtual or physical question or clue. Learners document their discoveries through text, audio, photos, and video, and then share, providing feedback on their progress.

INCLUSIVE USES

Learners who are practicing problem-solving or visual spatial skills may find seeking and locating physical and virtual geocaches a fun and exciting way to hone these abilities.

SAMPLE TOOL

Waypoint EDU is an iOS app designed for small scale geocaching in a limited area, such as a room or outdoor space up to the size of a football field (**waypointedu.com**).

EXTENSION OPPORTUNITIES

Invite learners to maintain a journal with multimedia entries cataloging their experiences as they progress through their discoveries.

Create an immersive experience where learners are engaged in a mystery: stumbling across a map to a treasure, an ancient journal, or a mysterious letter from some secret adventurer. The clues, once discovered, prompt further exploration of content to decipher the puzzle and find the ultimate hidden treasure!

Invite learners to create their own scavenger hunt to demonstrate knowledge of a topic.

RELATED RESOURCES

GeocachingEdu
(**newsroom.geocaching.com/geocachingedu**)

GPS and Geocaching in Education
(**bit.ly/inclusive365-26a**)

Night Light Stories: Terrapene Ornata, Parts 1, 2, and 3 (**bit.ly/inclusive365-26b**) (**bit.ly/inclusive365-26c**) (**bit.ly/inclusive365-26d**)

Figure 26. A Waypoint EDU map and AR image after completing part of a treasure hunt for inventions.

ISTE STANDARDS FOR STUDENTS
1c, 3c

ISTE STANDARDS FOR EDUCATORS
2c, 3b, 4b, 5a, 5b

Promoting Movement During Distance Learning

Learners can participate in movement-based experiences to overcome inactivity. Create an experience that involves finding geometric patterns in different places in the building, learning space, or home setting. Educators can provide tips on how to help learners set up standing desks or use seats that allow movement. Education today needs to promote the notion that good design is not sedentary but rather kinesthetic. The educator shouldn't be saying, "Move because you've been sitting so long!" but rather, "Sit because you've been moving so much!"

INCLUSIVE USES

Learners with physical disabilities or impairments may be at greater risk of prolonged times of inactivity during distance learning. Providing models that have physical or cognitive challenges helps these learners see themselves as athletes.

SAMPLE TOOLS

Special Olympics Virtual Movement is a user-generated website filled with scheduled movement experiences using online meeting platforms or videos (**virtualsomd.com**).

A movement choice board can be created using LessonPix (**bit.ly/inclusive365-27a**).

Go Noodle organizes resources via curriculum categories (**app.gonoodle.com/categories**).

EXTENSION OPPORTUNITY

Invite learners to design and record their own movement-based learning activities, share them with peers, and even lead the experiences.

RELATED RESOURCES

To Boost Learning, Just Add Movement (**cultofpedagogy.com/movement**)

Movement and Learning in Elementary School (**bit.ly/inclusive365-27b**)

Movement and Learning (**bit.ly/inclusive365-27c**)

Figure 27. Example of a LessonPix movement choice board.

ISTE STANDARDS FOR STUDENTS
1a, 5c

ISTE STANDARDS FOR EDUCATORS
5a, 6a

Selecting Public Domain and Copyright-Free Media

Respecting intellectual property must be considered during content creation. Learners and educators must understand copyright in terms of using images and music ethically and legally in their work. Learners should know about websites and searches that yield images and music that are in the public domain, under certain Creative Commons licenses, or otherwise copyright-free. Online databases of images, videos, and sounds that are royalty- and copyright-free provide a valuable resource for learners and educators alike.

INCLUSIVE USES

Finding the perfect image, audio, or video clip can be a distraction from the creative process. Learners who are working to maintain focus may find searching through a small set of reliable royalty-free and copyright-free resources more manageable than having every item on the internet at their disposal—reducing the cognitive, language, and time demands of having to use advanced search tools to find these same types of images.

SAMPLE TOOLS

Pixabay has millions of free stock photos, illustrations, music, and video files (**pixabay.com**).

Unsplash has images shared by the community (**unsplash.com**).

Public Domain Images has thousands of public-domain images available (**publicdomainpictures.net**).

Granger Academic offers historical images to educators and learners (**grangeracademic.com/index.asp**).

Pics4Learning is a curated image library of copyright-friendly photos and illustrations (**pics4learning.com**).

Bensound is a web collection that includes royalty-free audio files (**bensound.com**).

EXTENSION OPPORTUNITIES

Invite learners to investigate the various ways to copyright digital work using lessons like this one from CommonsSense Media: **bit.ly/inclusive365-28a**. This can help demonstrate respect for intellectual property.

Ask learners, "Would you be okay with allowing someone to take your work and use it in their own remix?" Many websites have a mechanism for learners to upload their own digital materials (photos, videos, etc.) for other users.

RELATED RESOURCES

Research Guides: Finding Public Domain and Creative Commons Media (**bit.ly/inclusive365-28b**)

Wanna Work Together? (**bit.ly/inclusive365-28c**)

Find Free and Fair Use Images (**bit.ly/inclusive365-28d**)

Why Teach Copyright? (**bit.ly/inclusive365-28e**)

Copyright and Fair Use: Stanford University Libraries (**fairuse.stanford.edu**)

Figure 28. A search on the Creative Commons website.

ISTE STANDARDS FOR STUDENTS
1c, 2c, 3c, 6a, 6b

ISTE STANDARDS FOR EDUCATORS
2b, 3b, 3c, 4c, 5

Protecting Privacy With Cartoon Avatars

Learners are increasingly leaving a digital footprint as they move through their academic years. Working together, educators and families should help learners understand which information they should keep private and which may be shared. One way to maintain privacy when resources include a profile image (or avatar) is to have learners generate cartoon avatars. This allows learners to personalize their profile image while avoiding using an actual photograph of themselves.

INCLUSIVE USES

When learners in a community all use a cartoon as a profile image, they eventually become familiar with each other's avatars. Cartoon avatars protect underage learners from having their actual likenesses appear on websites and apps.

SAMPLE TOOLS

Pixton EDU allows learners to create avatars. Creating avatars is one of the many comic style resources that can be created in Pixton EDU (**edu.pixton.com/educators**).

Storyboard That allows educators to enroll learners through Google Classroom rosters. Avatars can be created as characters to be used in comics and other resources that can be customized from pre-made examples (**storyboardthat.com**).

EXTENSION OPPORTUNITIES

Create a group picture with educators and learners from the avatars that learners have created. Post it on a website, blog, or within a distance learning platform.

Invite or challenge learners to get creative with their avatars. Learners can be whatever they'd like to be! The only limit is one's imagination!

RELATED RESOURCE

Video Introduction to Pixton EDU (**bit.ly/inclusive365-29**)

Figure 29. Avatar and learning space layout created in Pixton EDU.

ISTE STANDARDS FOR STUDENTS
2a, 2d

ISTE STANDARDS FOR EDUCATORS
3d, 6b

STRATEGY 30

Using Creative Commons to Support Digital Citizenship and Ethical Content Creation

Creative Commons licensed resources allow learners and educators to use images, audio, and video legally and ethically in their own presentations, social media, blog posts, or other shared creations. Explicitly teaching learners the importance of attribution and legal use of images, audio, and video in their own work as content remixers and creators is a critical digital citizenship skill. Learners should understand how to find media for use under the various Creative Commons licenses.

INCLUSIVE USES

Learners working on building skills related to reading and writing may find it useful to create products meant for an authentic audience. Learning how to label content so that audiences know if they can or cannot use it benefits both the content producer and those consuming it.

SAMPLE TOOLS

The Creative Commons website has a search engine for Creative Commons images by license (**search.creativecommons.org**).

CreativeCommons.org also has resources for audio that can be used by content creators (**bit.ly/inclusive365-30a**). YouTube and Vimeo both have Creative Commons options for content that is original and uploaded to these video portals.

With the CC Search Browser Extension installed users can find images from more than a dozen hosts of Creative Commons licensed works. The extension not only provides images for download; it also provides all of the attribution information needed for the images (**bit.ly/inclusive365-30b**).

EXTENSION OPPORTUNITIES

Creators may choose to retain copyright of their creations however, learners and educators can also be invited to consider branding their own unique resources, including photos, digital art and music under a range of Creative Commons licensing options. They could upload these creations to websites such as **CreativeCommons.org**.

Learners and educators can create accessible books with easy-to-access Creative Commons licensed images using the TarHeel Reader website. Educators should explain clearly that the images available in the TarHeel Reader authoring program are all Creative Commons licensed and are available to use because the creators of those images have given explicit permission to others to do so.

RELATED RESOURCE

The Harvard Law School Library has an excellent article detailing the difference between Public Domain and the different types of Creative Commons Licenses (**bit.ly/inclusive365-30c**).

 CC Search Browser Extension
Offered by: creativecommons.extension

Figure 30. The Creative Commons search browser extension.

ISTE STANDARDS FOR STUDENTS
2c, 6b

ISTE STANDARDS FOR EDUCATORS
3b, 3c

Designing Safe Video Playlists

Video is a powerful instructional tool for engaged learning. However, unfiltered videos can lead users down a rabbit hole filled with ads, distractions, and inappropriate content or comments. Fortunately, there are tools that allow educators to provide a safe space for video exploration, taking advantage of the power of video for learning.

INCLUSIVE USES

Learners who benefit from structure and a distraction-free environment may find safe video playlists especially helpful.

SAMPLE TOOLS

SafeShare.TV is an online video playlist creation space (**safeshare.tv**).

Class YouTube Channel free template for Google Slides or PowerPoint provides the option to create video playlists in a controlled space while keeping the YouTube aesthetics (**bit.ly/inclusive365-31a**).

Save curated videos to a tool such as Wakelet to create safe video playlists (**wakelet.com**).

EXTENSION OPPORTUNITY

Invite learners to create videos and upload them to a collaborative Wakelet or Google Slide presentation.

RELATED RESOURCE

Creating Video Playlists with Wakelet (**bi.ly/inclusive365-31b**)

Figure 31. An example of a safe video playlist about habitats created in SafeShare.TV.

ISTE STANDARDS FOR STUDENTS

3c, 4a, 4b, 6a, 6b

ISTE STANDARDS FOR EDUCATORS

3a, 4c, 5a, 5b, 5c, 6a, 6b

STRATEGY 31

Accessing Digital Books Using Switches

While digital books can open up a world of literacy for learners, the inability to turn digital pages is a barrier for some. A switch is an external device, often a button, that allows users to activate a command with a single movement to enable a function within the software. Switches connect to the device, enabling learners to perform certain functions upon activation. Switch-accessible digital books allow learners to access pages by activating one or more switches. Turning a page or accessing any given page through the table of contents can be made fully accessible to all readers.

INCLUSIVE USES

A paper book may pose a barrier for learners who are unable to physically turn a page. Digital books may provide the same roadblock. Switch-accessible digital books allow switch clicks to turn pages. Certain digital reading tools can recognize switch clicks as a mouse click or the Enter key. These functions enable all learners to interact with the digital page.

SAMPLE TOOLS

TarHeel Reader is a website devoted to the creation and display of digital books. Learners and educators can make their own digital books, with text, pictures, and embedded audio, directly on the internet. These books are made switch accessible (**tarheelreader.org**).

Switch Control is part of the built in accessibility of iOS, enabling an individual to control functions by connecting a single switch to the device. Educators can use this functionality to provide access to digital learning material. A Switch Recipe is a programmed series of defined functions activated by a single switch click. This can automate a very complicated series of screen activations into a single click.

EXTENSION OPPORTUNITY

Invite learners to explore the Switch Control feature in an iOS device to make the entire screen a switch. Go into the device Settings and select Accessibility to find Switch Control features. The device can be set to scan and the user can tap the screen as the highlight moves to the area you wish to activate. Use this function as a display for a full group reading experience. As the group reads aloud, ask one of the learners to tap the screen to move to the next page.

RELATED RESOURCES

TarHeel Reader Switch Access (**bit.ly/inclusive365-32a**)

How to Set Up "Turn Pages" in iOS Switch Control (**bit.ly/inclusive365-32b**)

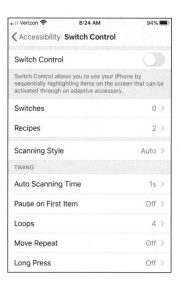

Figure 32. iOS Switch Control.

ISTE STANDARDS FOR STUDENTS
1b, 1d, 6a

ISTE STANDARDS FOR EDUCATORS
5a

Accessing a Screen with a Do-It-Yourself Stylus

A stylus can help individuals more precisely navigate a screen. Although commercial styluses are available, learners may tend to use a stylus with greater frequency and regularity when they have created it themselves. Further, when designing and making a stylus, it can be customized and personalized to meet the needs of the individual learner. Variations such as size, shape, thickness, color, and handle can lead to unique and useful designs.

INCLUSIVE USES

Learners who have difficulty accessing a touchscreen with their finger may find the use of a customized stylus helpful.

SAMPLE TOOL

A pen, aluminum foil, a cotton swab, and a small amount of water can be used to create a functioning stylus.

EXTENSION OPPORTUNITIES

Invite learners to view a video on how to create their own stylus, adding features such as hardened clay around the outside formed to the learner's unique grip.

Invite learners to create a tutorial demonstrating how they created their stylus and what purpose their customizations serve.

RELATED RESOURCES

Make a Two-Minute Stylus
(**bit.ly/inclusive365-33a**)

How to Make a Stylus Using Any Pen/Pencil
(**bit.ly/inclusive365-33b**)

DIY iPad Brush
(**instructables.com/DIY-iPad-brush**)

Figure 33. Homemade styluses made by sixth graders.

ISTE STANDARDS FOR STUDENTS
1b, 1d, 3d, 4a, 4c, 4d, 6a, 7a, 7b, 7d

ISTE STANDARDS FOR EDUCATORS
3a, 4c, 5a, 6a, 6b, 6c, 6d

Increasing Efficiency with Keyboard Shortcuts

Keyboard shortcuts are found on all operating systems and popular applications. Knowing keyboard shortcuts makes learners and educators more efficient across content areas and tasks. In addition to universal basics such as copy, paste, and print, there are other essential keystroke combinations that are useful for learners and educators.

INCLUSIVE USES

Keyboard shortcuts are essential for learners who have challenges using a mouse or who use speech-to-text to navigate on their device. Keyboard shortcuts can also provide an opportunity to increase input speed and efficiency by keeping hands on the keyboard and automating computing tasks.

SAMPLE TOOLS

For a list of some of our most used keyboard shortcuts, check out: **bit.ly/inclusive365-34a**.

EXTENSION OPPORTUNITY

Invite learners to create custom keyboard shortcuts in their most-used applications to increase efficiency.

RELATED RESOURCES

Keyboard Shortcuts in Microsoft Office (**bit.ly/inclusive365-34b**)

Chromebook Keyboard Shortcuts (**bit.ly/inclusive365-34c**)

47 Keyboard Shortcuts That Work in All Browsers (**bit.ly/inclusive365-34d**)

Customize Keyboard Shortcuts (**bit.ly/inclusive365-34e**)

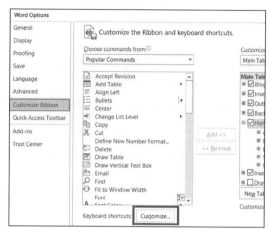

Figure 34. How to customize keyboard shortcuts in Microsoft Word.

ISTE STANDARDS FOR STUDENTS
1a, 1b, 1d

ISTE STANDARDS FOR EDUCATORS
2b, 5a, 6a

Ensuring Accessibility of Slide Decks by Using Consistent Text Order and Pre-Made Templates

Slide decks are often used by educators to support lectures. Learners create them to demonstrate understanding of content. Not all slides decks are created equally—with equity and inclusivity in mind. Text in slide decks typically works with technologies that read the text aloud. However, if the text on the screen is not placed in an ordered, consistent manner, the user of the screen reader technology may have trouble following the flow of the text. Erratic or random ordering of the text causes the screen reading technology to jump around rather than progressing linearly through the content. Predefined slide layouts in popular presentation tools including Microsoft PowerPoint and Google Slides are specially coded to work effectively with screen reader tools. By following some simple rules and using predefined slide templates, rather than manually adding text boxes, anyone can put the content in your slides in the intended reading order so that screen readers read it correctly for users with a vision or reading disability.

INCLUSIVE USES

Considering the order that text is added to a slide deck supports learners with visual impairments and those with who use text-to-speech tools. Learners who are building executive functioning skills might also find that using templates that have built-in accessibility for screen readers encourages placing text in a consistent order, and helps these learners consider the most efficient way to build a slide or slide deck of their own. Using a predefined template also creates a more uniform and professional-looking presentation.

SAMPLE TOOLS

Microsoft PowerPoint, Google Slides, and Keynote all support screen readers, allow for the input of alternative text for images, and have built-in captioning and other accessibility features (**google.com/slides**, **apple.com/keynote**, **office.com/launch/powerpoint**).

EXTENSION OPPORTUNITY

Invite learners to build their own slide decks with accessibility in mind.

RELATED RESOURCES

Make your document or presentation more accessible (**bit.ly/inclusive365-35a**).

Microsoft Accessibility Checker (**bit.ly/inclusive365-35b**)

Creating Accessible Documents in Apple Products (**bit.ly/inclusive365-35c**)

Figure 35. A master slide in Google Docs. Following the layout of the master slide assists screen reader technology in being able to easily read text on slides in the order that is intended.

ISTE STANDARDS FOR STUDENTS
1d

ISTE STANDARDS FOREDUCATORS
5a

STRATEGY 36

Describing the Salient Features of an Image with Captions and Alt Text

It has been said that a picture is worth a thousand words. Which words of those thousand are the most important? Placing a caption under and alternative text (alt text) behind an image helps those looking at the picture and listening to the text know what aspects of the image might be most important. Describing what is in an image forces the person creating the educational content to identify the most important or relevant aspects of an image and then describe them succinctly via text.

INCLUSIVE USES

Learners who use audio supports, such as those with visual impairments, may find the text describing images necessary in understanding what is in the image and why it is important. If an image is simply decorative and does not convey information, using alt text that tells screen reader software to ignore the image also helps the learner focus on the information that is important.

SAMPLE TOOL

Alt text is a feature of most word processing, multimedia presentation, and website creation tools.

EXTENSION OPPORTUNITIES

Invite learners who are creating materials for public consumption to practice adding alt text to images, both to think through why the imagery is important and to ensure accessibility for anyone who might be consuming the content. Alt text and captions can be added to any images in guidance documents and performance feedback rubrics to increase accessibility.

When reviewing educational materials, invite learners to check for alt text. If a particular resource has not provided this accessibility feature, learners could use it as an opportunity for an authentic writing experience to ask the resource provider to include alt text.

RELATED RESOURCES

What is alt text? (**bit.ly/inclusive365-36a**)

What is alt text and why is it important for SEO? (**bit.ly/inclusive365-36b**)

Figure 36. An alt text window in Google Docs.

ISTE STANDARDS FOR STUDENTS
6a, 6b, 6c, 6d, 7a, 7b

ISTE STANDARDS FOR EDUCATORS
2b, 3c, 4d, 5a, 5b, 5c, 6d

Improving Navigation with Links to Text Fragments

Educators frequently provide digital resources to learners. These resources are often in the form of a hyperlink that takes the learner to a website with text. If the link simply takes the learner to the website in general, it is often up to the learner to follow directions to find the specific content on a site. Navigating to the exact section of relevant content can be challenging and even frustrating. When the educator shares a link to a fragment of text rather than a general link, the learner's attention is taken to the exact spot in the text that the educator intended for the learner to review.

INCLUSIVE USES

Learners with print-related disabilities, such as dyslexia or vision impairments, may find navigating websites with large amounts of text challenging. Links to text fragments help learners more quickly be taken to the relevant portion of the text without wasting time hunting through irrelevant text.

Learners with attention issues may find that links to text fragments increase their focus and reduce their distractions.

SAMPLE TOOL

Link to Text Fragments is an extension for the Google Chrome browser that allows a user to create a hyperlink to a specific block of text on a website (**bit.ly/inclusive365-37a**).

EXTENSION OPPORTUNITIES

Invite learners to create and share their own hyperlinks to fragments of text when sharing information with others.

Invite learners to create a library of words they are learning by creating a hyperlink to that specific target word.

Invite learners to demonstrate their knowledge by creating hyperlinks to text to provide evidence that they understand a particular concept. Educators could follow the hyperlink to verify the learner understands the concept. For instance, a learner might share a link to a word or portion of a sentence to demonstrate the understanding of prepositional phrases.

RELATED RESOURCE

Targeting Text Fragments
(**bit.ly/inclusive365-37b**)

Figure 37. Selecting text in a document to create a link to that selected text.

ISTE STANDARDS FOR STUDENTS

3c, 6d, 7c

ISTE STANDARDS FOR EDUCATORS

3c, 5a, 5c

Differentiating Materials Based on Personalized Needs

Educators guiding individuals to chart their own paths in becoming expert learners must differentiate materials based on personalized learner needs. Rarely, if ever, does one singular piece of material meet the varied and diverse needs of every individual. Contemporary learning management systems typically offer a function that allows educators to differentiate material distribution to provide customized experiences for each learner. Examples of variations might include the quantity of materials, visual presentation of the material, inclusion or exclusion of audio or video supports, presentation of text at various reading levels, and more.

INCLUSIVE USES

Discreet differentiation acknowledges learner variability; all learners benefit. Learners who are working on gaining agency and ownership over their own learning particularly benefit from materials selected and allocated to meet their personalized needs.

SAMPLE TOOLS

Seesaw provides a function that allows educators to individually select learners when distributing materials (**seesaw.com**).

Google Classroom offers a function that allows educators to individually select learners when distributing materials (**classroom.google.com**).

EXTENSION OPPORTUNITY

The idea that each learner is unique extends to families and parents as well. Consider providing customized resources when distributing materials for parents and caregivers. This sort of customized care will save parents time and energy in trying to whittle through a sea

of materials that may or may not pertain to the learner they are working to support. Like with learners, personal conversations with families about the types, amounts, and formats that work best for them can foster improved communication.

RELATED RESOURCE

How do I assign activities in Seesaw? (**bit.ly/inclusive365-38**)

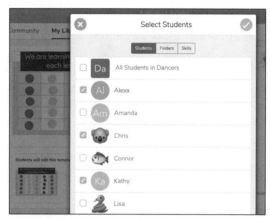

Figure 38. Selected learners receive specific content in Seesaw.

ISTE STANDARDS FOR STUDENTS
1a, 1c

ISTE STANDARDS FOR EDUCATORS
5a, 5b, 5c, 6a, 6b, 7a

Selecting Mistake-Tolerant Instructional Tools

Promoting a culture where failure and risk-taking are opportunities for growth is important for learners and educators. Part of developing this type of culture means carefully selecting instructional tools that allow learners to make and then fix mistakes, while embracing the idea that being comfortable making mistakes promotes learner confidence and independence. Low-tech whiteboards are an example of a tool that allows learners to make marks and then easily erase those marks if necessary. Learners can write, reflect, erase, and try again. Educators should ask, "Does this tool offer the learner the ability to make and correct mistakes" when selecting resources to provide as options. Markers, pens, and crayons might be examples which are less tolerant of mistakes than pencils, dry-erase markers, chalk, or digital annotation tools.

INCLUSIVE USES

All learners benefit from instructional tools that allow them to correct errors, review their work, or begin again, especially those who have adopted a mindset that they must produce perfect work on the first try. Providing mistake-tolerant tools is an example of universal design to reach all learners.

SAMPLE TOOLS

Seesaw is a learning platform that provides a means to create, reflect, share, and collaborate as well as delete and edit work (**seesaw.com**).

Book Creator is a multimedia book creation tool that allows user to make corrections to fix mistakes, even after a work is published (**bookcreator.com**).

Flipgrid is a collaborative video response tool which allows users to pull down and re-post content (**flipgrid.com**).

EXTENSION OPPORTUNITY

Invite learners to track when they fail and start over, and praise their willingness to share their failures and the completed outcomes with peers. Seeing multiple attempts helps illustrate to peers how risk-taking and mistake-making are part of learning, and that the process is as valuable as the product. This can be especially important when initially establishing relationships in a new learning environment.

RELATED RESOURCES

Why Taking Risks in the Classroom Pays off for Students—and Teachers (**bit.ly/inclusive365-39a**)

Why Students Who Embrace Short-Term Failure Have a Better Shot at Long-Term Success (**bit.ly/inclusive365-39b**)

Figure 39. A middle-school-aged girl uses a dry erase marker on a whiteboard to illustrate how she accidentally made a spelling mistake, erased it, and made a correction.

ISTE STANDARDS FOR STUDENTS
1a, 4b, 6a, 6b, 6d

ISTE STANDARDS FOR EDUCATORS
5a, 5b 5c, 6a, 6b, 7a, 7b

STRATEGY 40

Controlling A Tablet With A Mouse

In a world of smartphones, tablets, and touch screen computers there is still a need for external navigation devices. Having multiple input and navigation methods available means more options for users to access and control devices. While it has been easy enough to connect an external mouse to a computer or Chromebook, the world of tablets has remained a primarily touch-access medium. Some tablets with Bluetooth capabilities make it possible for users to control the device with a mouse, joystick, trackpad, trackball, or other external inputs.

INCLUSIVE USES

Some individuals may find the use of a mouse preferable or even necessary to control a tablet. Learners with fine or gross motor impairments may find that a mouse provides a more suitable way to interact and control a device. Alternative devices beyond a standard mouse can be connected to provide customized access to individuals who need more support for pointer control.

SAMPLE TOOL

iPadOS Pointing Devices are located in Accessibility settings under Touch. Pointing Devices functionality enables a Bluetooth pointing device to connect to an iPad. Once connected, the pointing device activates a Touch icon that appears on the screen and follows the movement of the pointing device. Learners can customize the response to movement to increase or decrease speed and accuracy. For this feature to work, the iPad must be running iPad OS 13.4 or above. This feature is available only on these iPad models: iPad Pro (all models), iPad Air 2 or later; iPad Fifth Generation or later; and iPad Mini 4 or later.

EXTENSION OPPORTUNITIES

Encourage learners to explore an app used for drawing after connecting an alternative access device to an iPad. Invite learners to reflect on the experience and ask, "Was the creation easier to do with a pointing device?"

Like using an external keyboard with an iPad, some educators may feel more comfortable controlling touch screen devices with a mouse or trackball.

RELATED RESOURCE

Use a Bluetooth Mouse or Trackpad on Your iPad (**bit.ly/inclusive365-40**)

Figure 40. Accessibility settings in iPadOS, where you can choose devices and connect Bluetooth pointing devices.

ISTE STANDARDS FOR STUDENTS
1a, 1d, 5d, 6a

ISTE STANDARDS FOR EDUCATORS
1a, 2b, 2c, 5a, 6d

Scanning Text to Make it Accessible

When planning educational experiences, educators must ensure accessibility of materials. We all have our favorite instructional material, but is it accessible? How can educators make that material accessible without a fancy scanner or app? Many copy machines have scanning functionality built right into the device; some copy machines even include an Optical Character Recognition (OCR) feature which converts the text from that document into editable, accessible text. When a copy machine is unavailable, try a scanning app instead. A copy store will also have a high speed scanner that may be able to scan a book quickly. However, to scan the book they may have to cut the binding off so it can fit on the scanner. If this happens, simply three-hole punch the pages and insert into a 3 ring binder. Many book publishers will provide PDFs of their books to serve learners with disabilities— all you have to do is inquire.

INCLUSIVE USES

For learners who are evolving readers, text-to-speech audio support for reading tasks may be crucial for comprehension. To utilize the inclusive tools that can provide that level of support, text needs to be digitized and available in the electronic format. OCR provides the ability to convert text so it is accessible for these inclusive tools.

SAMPLE TOOLS

Many copy machines include a scanning feature that allows you to scan a page and send the electronic version directly to an email address as a digital file. Some may even have an OCR feature that will convert print text to editable, acccessible digital text.

ScannerBin allows you to use a pre-made cardboard stand to make a smartphone a scanning station. This pre-made stand comes with magnets to hold the sides together along with an option for a light (**scannerbin.com**).

EXTENSION OPPORTUNITY

Invite learners to create their own mobile device scanning station from either a cardboard box or wire basket. Position the book under the mobile device so the image fills the screen. Make sure the light source is not blocked from above and is instead coming from the sides to illuminate the page.

RELATED RESOURCES

DIY BookScanner (**diybookscanner.org**)

Is it legal to digitize a book? (**bit.ly/inclusive365-41**)

Figure 41. ScanBox (no longer commercially available) consists of a cardboard box that can used as a scanning solution.

ISTE STANDARDS FOR STUDENTS
1c, 2b, 3c, 6b

ISTE STANDARDS FOR EDUCATORS
2b, 5a, 5b, 6a

Presenting with Auto Captions

Making curriculum materials accessible to all learners is not just a best practice; it is mandatory under special education IDEA law. Captioning of spoken words is one way of making a lecture or discussion more accessible for learners with hearing impairments or other learning needs. When presenting to learners, auto captioning can be enabled on some presentation tools, which automatically converts speech into text. Educators demonstrate that they value all learners and are building truly inclusive learning environments by using captioning.

INCLUSIVE USES

Automatically generated captions not only support those with hearing impairments but can be a literacy support for learners who are learning to read, multilingual learners, or as a general support to anyone who may benefit from a multimodal learning experience. Auto captions can also be displayed in a different language from what is being spoken, providing increased accessibility for multilingual learners.

SAMPLE TOOLS

Google Slides allows a presentation mode that displays automatically generated captions (**google.com/slides**).

Microsoft Powerpoint in Office 365 has an auto caption mode (**microsoft.com/en-us/microsoft-365/powerpoint**).

EXTENSION OPPORTUNITIES

Use a screen recording tool to record the audio and presentation when giving a presentation using auto captions. This creates a fully accessible recorded learning module to share with anyone.

By modeling the use of auto captions, learners will come to understand the value of providing materials with accessibility in mind. As learners move forward in an ever evolving world of technology, we hope that they build accessibility supports into their content, not as an afterthought but as a component of the construction of that content.

RELATED RESOURCES

Present with Real-Time Automatic Captions or Subtitles in Powerpoint (**bit.ly/inclusive365-42a**)

Present Slides with Captions (**bit.ly/inclusive365-42b**)

Figure 42. An example of captioning during a presentation.

ISTE STANDARDS FOR STUDENTS
6a, 6d

ISTE STANDARDS FOR EDUCATORS
5a, 6a

Making Learning Materials Switch-Accessible

Electronic, battery operated toys and other items with moving parts, lights, and sounds can be used to teach cognitive and language concepts, particularly for young learners or those with emergent language and learning skills. Items such as a talking toy animal or a motorized vehicle can even be used as an engaging way to convey story elements including character and plot. Battery operated items often require fine motor abilities to turn on or activate. Mechanical adaptations using battery interrupters and switches provide an alternative way to activate the object with an external on/off switch that can be activated with a push, tap, breath, or any other motor movement. Making these mechanical adaptations can be a meaningful and authentic STEM experience for any learner.

INCLUSIVE USES

Any learner who maintains consistent volitional control of at least one muscle movement can learn to access a switch-adapted item. Individuals without disabilities can also use switch adaptations to activate the same item.

SAMPLE TOOL

Battery interrupters can be made or purchased to fit individual needs. Battery interrupters interrupt the flow of electrical current coming from the battery. When a switch connected to the interrupter is activated, the electrical circuit is completed and the device then functions (**bit.ly/inclusive365-43a**).

EXTENSION OPPORTUNITIES

Present learners who are participating in makerspaces with the authentic task of helping to switch-adapt items.

Invite learners exploring circuits in physics or other STEAM-related experiences to switch-adapt items.

RELATED RESOURCES

AT Makers (**atmakers.org**)

Talking with Tech Podcast Episode 63: Interviews from ATIA & FETC: Christine Baudin of "AAC for the SLP," Michael Dicpinigaitis, and Mike Marotta (**bit.ly/inclusive365-43b**)

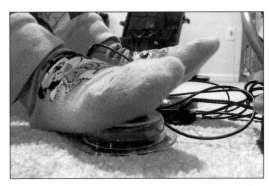

Figure 43. A young learner activating two switches with each foot.

ISTE STANDARDS FOR STUDENTS

1b, 1d, 3d, 4a, 4b, 4c, 4d, 5c, 5d, 6a, 6b, 6c, 6d, 7a, 7b, 7c, 7d

ISTE STANDARDS FOR EDUCATORS

2b, 3a, 4c, 4d, 6c

Navigating Video Conference Tools Using Keyboard Commands

Effective use of video conferencing requires understanding, practicing, and using some specific skills that have become essential for participating in contemporary society. These skills include, but are not limited to, muting microphones, toggling video on and off, and blurring backgrounds. Knowing what to do when the dog suddenly starts barking at something outside or when another family member bursts into the space can help improve the experience for everyone participating in the conference. Learned and practiced keyboard commands can be used to mute or unmute, activate or deactivate the camera, or do any number of other functions to help maintain the professional nature of the video call.

INCLUSIVE USES

Proper virtual learning etiquette is an important set of skills for learners to develop as part of their ongoing quest to be good digital citizens. Practicing the use of keyboard shortcuts can help learners develop methods that save them time, energy, and frustration. Keyboard shortcuts also support individuals with physical or visual impairments to control the computer without the need to navigate using a mouse, trackpad, or touchscreen.

SAMPLE TOOLS

Zoom (**zoom.us**)

- Alt+V: Toggle video on/off
- Alt+A: Mute / unmute microphone
- Alt+H: Show the chat

Google Meet (**meet.google.com**)

- CTRL+E (CMD+E): Toggle video on/off
- CTRL+D (CMD+D): Mute / unmute microphone

EXTENSION OPPORTUNITIES

Invite learners to set up a test video call in the format of an interview show. A moderator (a peer or an educator) will interview each learner. Set guidelines prior to the start of the interview. Each speaker only appears on video, with a live microphone, when called upon by the moderator. The moderator can ask questions and randomly call on learners to answer the questions. This provides a situation where the learner needs to quickly turn on and off both video and microphone.

Invite learners to create and display a keyboard shortcut reminder card near a learning space, like a desk or table. For some learners, the card could be a sticky note placed near the trackpad of a computer.

RELATED RESOURCES

Google Meet Keyboard Shortcuts (**bit.ly/inclusive365-44a**)

Zoom Keyboard Shortcuts (**bit.ly/inclusive365-44b**)

Figure 44. A Google Meet shortcut.

ISTE STANDARDS FOR STUDENTS
2b, 6a, 7b

ISTE STANDARDS FOR EDUCATORS
3a, 3c, 4c

Maintaining Closed Captioning with Multiple Open Tabs

When offering presentations to learners or other educators, it is essential to ensure text captions are available throughout the presentation. Google Slides and Microsoft PowerPoint for Office 365 both provide captioning for the presentation while in slide show mode. If there are embedded links in the presentation or the presenter needs to open another tab, closed captioning is no longer available, as it only appears in the original presentation. Fortunately, there is a really cool hack that keeps the captioning available even when you leave the presentation; open two different browser windows and within them two slide decks. In one window, put the slide deck in Present mode, enable captions and then exit full screen. In the other window, go to Present and exit full screen, then resize the presentation to be layered on top of the caption slides, ensuring that the captions will show below or above the presentation deck.

INCLUSIVE USES

Captioning may be critical for individuals with hearing loss. It can also be useful for multilingual learners to assist in the comprehension of spoken English when accompanied by text. Captions can also help most everyone else learn content, keep focus, or catch something they missed auditorily.

SAMPLE TOOLS

Google Slides and Microsoft PowerPoint for Office 365 both offer captioning when in present or slide show mode (**microsoft.com/ en-us/microsoft-365/powerpoint** and **docs.google.com/presentation**).

EXTENSION OPPORTUNITIES

Invite learners to monitor their speaking skills by having captions turned on. When they see their speech transcribed it can help them decrease use of "umm" and "like" and be more aware of the word choice and grammatical complexity that they are using as they speak.

Encourage educators to consider using captions in a language other than English that may be representative of a large number of learners.

RELATED RESOURCES

A Rising Tide: How Closed Captions Can Benefit All Students (**bit.ly/inclusive365-45a**)

How to Maintain Closed Captioning with Open Tabs (**bit.ly/inclusive365-45b**)

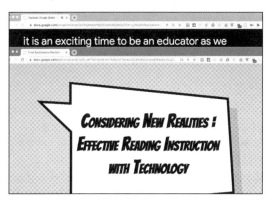

Figure 45. Two windows open showing closed captioning in the rear window.

ISTE STANDARDS FOR STUDENTS
1b

ISTE STANDARDS FOR EDUCATORS
3a, 5a

Reviewing Learning Materials for Accessibility Prior to Purchase

Educators influence the purchasing decisions made by learning agencies developing curriculum. Educators should ask questions of vendors related to accessibility prior to purchase. Adopting a consistent process of accessibility review prior to the purchase or acquisition of the learning material helps educate developers about the importance of accessibility and ensure developers design future products with accessibility in mind.

INCLUSIVE USES

When items are purchased without considering accessibility, special educators may end up spending a significant amount of time and energy adapting materials to meet individual needs. Proactively inquiring about the accessibility features of potential curriculum material helps ensure that all learners' needs are met. Time, energy, and money is not wasted creating accessibility after purchase.

SAMPLE TOOLS

AEM Pilot is a free web based tool which provides guidance to educators as they create teams to focus on inclusive educational design and accessible educational materials, and as they work to develop and maintain an effective team through self assessment, goal setting, and progress monitoring (**aem-pilot.cast.org**).

An accessibility review checklist (**bit.ly/inclusive365-46a**)

EXTENSION OPPORTUNITY

Invite learners to participate in or contribute to the review of potential learning materials. Learners could be provided a rubric which contains accessibility considerations and asked to provide input prior to acquisition. This feedback could be used to help inform the actual decision making process while providing the added benefit of teaching future generations about the importance of considering accessibility.

RELATED RESOURCES

Purchase Accessible Learning Materials (PALM) Initiative in Maine (**maine-aim.org/palm-initiative**)

POUR from CAST (**bit.ly/inclusive365-46b**)

A.T.TIPSCAST Episode #133: Purchasing Accessible Learning Materials, Story 3 (**bit.ly/attipscast133**)

Google Doc Template of Sample Questions (**bit.ly/inclusive365-46c**)

Introduction to AEM Pilot (**bit.ly/inclusive365-46d**)

Quality Indicators for the Provision of AEM in K1 (**bit.ly/inclusive365-46e**)

Figure 46. A cartoon highlighting the need to ask vendors about accessibility.

ISTE STANDARDS FOR STUDENTS
1b, 1d, 3b, 4b, 4c

ISTE STANDARDS FOR EDUCATORS
2a, 2b, 2c, 3b, 3c, 4a, 4b, 4d, 5a, 5c, 6b

Removing or Replacing Backgrounds of Images to Improve Understanding

Busy images can be distracting. Objects in the background may detract from the main idea or subject of an image. Removing or replacing the background in an image can help learners focus on and understand that pertinent information that is being conveyed in the picture.

INCLUSIVE USES

Learners who are distracted by background information may find themselves focusing on the wrong part of an image. Replacing or removing the background helps limit distractions.

Learners with visual impairments may find it difficult to see items in a picture when the picture is obscured with a busy background. Replacing the background with a lighter or darker solid color emphasizes the information presented in the foreground by providing visual contrast between colors. Learners can then better discriminate between what is in the foreground and focus on the most important information in the image.

SAMPLE TOOLS

Microsoft Powerpoint allows the user to remove the background of individual images (**bit.ly/inclusive365-47a**).

Remove is a free website that allows users to remove and replace the backgrounds of images (**remove.bg**).

Photo Scissors is a free website that allows users to remove and replace the backgrounds of images (**photoscissors.com**).

EXTENSION OPPORTUNITIES

Invite learners to create fun images of people or avatars where the backgrounds have been removed and place them in visual scenes to tell stories. Add images to the foreground of a picture, embed in multimedia slide decks, or add to comic strip style panels as an engaging way to share a digital story.

Replace backgrounds with different environmental scenes to depict that a person in the foreground is actually in a remote location, such as in space, a rainforest, a desert, the Arctic or Antarctic, or anywhere.

RELATED RESOURCE

Classroom Adaptations for Students with Low Vision (**bit.ly/inclusive365-47b**)

Figure 47. An image of a man standing in front of a golf course in Arizona, followed by a cutout of the same image of the man with the background removed, followed by a final image of the man on a boardwalk on a beach with the ocean in the background.

ISTE STANDARDS FOR STUDENTS

6a, 6b, 6c, 6d

ISTE STANDARDS FOR EDUCATORS

3a, 3b, 5c, 6b, 6d

Controlling a Mobile Device with Voice Commands

It is now commonplace for people to control their environment by voice. People interact with household voice assistants (such as Amazon Alexa or Google Home) daily. Smartphones and tablet functions can be controlled by voice as well. Learners can control many, if not all, of the functions of specific mobile devices, including the features of apps, with voice commands and screen navigation. For example, a user could say, "Open Mail" to access email or, "Volume up" to make whatever is playing louder. Using voice as an option to control a device provides an opportunity for learners who have difficulty with motor skills.

INCLUSIVE USES

Voice control may be the only way some learners or educators with physical impairments can autonomously access a mobile device. The ability to control device functions via voice could be the difference between independence and dependence.

SAMPLE TOOL

Voice control is a feature added to devices running iOS 13 and iPad OS 13. Voice control allows the user to speak commands aloud to the device and have the device perform functions. If a user isn't sure what the proper voice command might be, that individual can just try saying something. The device will provide hints to lead the user to the correct command. There is also a grid overlay, with numbers in each block, that allows a user to speak numbers aloud to navigate the screen. The grid gets smaller and smaller until the user hones in on the desired function (**bit.ly/inclusive365-48a**).

EXTENSION OPPORTUNITIES

Invite learners to access their mobile devices via voice to determine if they could access all the necessary features to complete a task.

Invite learners who use augmentative or alternative communication devices to control other devices with a synthetic voice to complete learning tasks.

RELATED RESOURCES

How to Navigate with Voice Control on Your iPhone (**bit.ly/inclusive365-48b**)

Talking with Tech Podcast Episode #112: Jane Odom: Takeaways from the Future of Educational Technology Conference (**bit.ly/inclusive365-48c**)

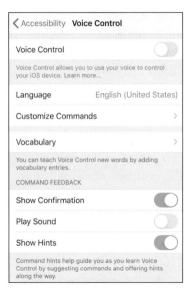

Figure 48. A voice control grid in iOS.

ISTE STANDARDS FOR STUDENTS
1d, 5d, 6c

ISTE STANDARDS FOR EDUCATORS
2b, 5a, 6a

Listening to Ambient Background Noise or Music to Increase Productivity

Ambient noises or music can help learners focus on the task in which they are engaged. Different sounds might be preferred (or disliked) based on individual choices. While classical music might help one person focus, another might find it distracting. Some learners might enjoy a particular set of natural sounds while others prefer a tune with a funky beat. Additionally, learners might find that preferences change based on the nature of the task. Select something with an upbeat tempo for a kinesthetic learning task or something slower with a calming feeling when working on a more sedate task.

INCLUSIVE USES

Learners who are distracted by noises made by peers might find it beneficial or necessary to listen to ambient noises or music. Some learners prefer white noise to block out distractions while others prefer music or nature sounds. The sensory input provided by ambient noise allows some learners to better focus on educational tasks.

SAMPLE TOOLS

YouTube allows users to search for various background noise tracks which can be played in an open browser tab (**bit.ly/inclusive365-49a**).

Noisli is a website and Google Chrome extension that provides users with a wide array of background noises and sounds (**noisli.com**).

TableTop Audio is a website with ambient sounds designed for tabletop gaming experiences. It can also be useful for background sound while working on learning tasks (**tabletopaudio.com**).

EXTENSION OPPORTUNITY

Invite learners to reflect on the effectiveness of the sounds they selected according to the task they are completing. If keeping events in a calendar or to do list, the learner can cite the ambient sounds they used per task and rank each sound's effectiveness on a scale from 1 to 5. This reflection can help learners internalize whether the sounds are truly helping them achieve their goals, or if they are finding that sounds they selected are proving to be an unwelcome distraction.

RELATED RESOURCE

How Background Noise Affects Productivity (**bit.ly/inclusive365-49b**)

Figure 49. Nature Sounds, Forest Sounds on YouTube by JohnnieLawson.

ISTE STANDARDS FOR STUDENTS
1a, 1b, 1c

ISTE STANDARDS FOR EDUCATORS
2b, 5a, 5b, 5c

Regulating Background Volume in Learning Spaces with Visual Feedback

If background noise becomes too loud in a learning environment, it can be distracting to some learners. Noise levels can rise slowly and subtly without everyone in the environment being aware of the increase. Although some learners might not notice, for others this rise in noise level can impact their sensory system, making it difficult for them to continue learning. Providing a way for learners to visually see the rise in volume can help individuals and the group as a whole become aware and make adjustments to the volume in the environment.

INCLUSIVE USES

Learners need to develop skills to regulate their own actions within an environment to demonstrate respect for the others learning alongside them, including by learning to regulate their own voice volume. An auditory or visual cue may provide the means to independently monitor and adjust volume within a learning space. Those who are learning skills to regulate their behaviors, respect the needs and emotions of others, and use appropriate voice volume levels may find audio and visual cues for background volume useful.

SAMPLE TOOL

Bouncy Balls is a free website that provides a visual cue representing levels of environmental noise. Using the microphone to detect room noise, a visual display of bouncing balls, emojis, bubbles, or eyeballs indicates the noise level. The visualization changes as the noise increases, and users are alerted with either a "shhh" or a beep when certain thresholds are exceeded (**bouncyballs.org**).

EXTENSION OPPORTUNITIES

When learners are working in groups, invite one learner to activate the background noise monitor. The feedback received from the tool should assist with managing speaking levels and reduce the possibility of people speaking over each other.

Invite groups of learners to establish acceptable thresholds so they have collectively collaborated on what they consider too noisy. Learners may have more agency and motivation to change behaviors when they are included in this decision.

RELATED RESOURCE

Digital Visual Feedback Modulators (**bit.ly/inclusive365-50**)

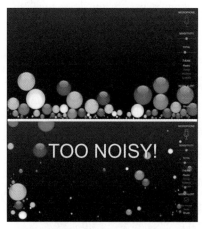

Figure 50. Bouncy Balls in a quieter room, and Bouncy Balls in a room that is too noisy.

ISTE STANDARDS FOR STUDENTS

1c

ISTE STANDARDS FOR EDUCATORS

5a, 6a

Decorating Learning Spaces Purposefully

While many educators love eye-catching decor, keeping decorations functional should take priority. Many learners can be easily overstimulated by over-decorated learning spaces. Researchers found that increased visual stimulation correlated with decreased cognitive performance (Fisher, Godwin, and Seltman, 2014; Rodrigues and Pandierada, 2018). Leave wall and bulletin board space for learner work. When learners see their work displayed and their peers as their audience, educators promote ownership and greater participation in the learning process. When choosing learner work to display, educators should be conscientious of how a learner might feel to see their work made public, and make an effort to showcase work that a learner is pleased with. It is also critical to display work in different formats, including digital products that can be showcased via QR codes.

INCLUSIVE USES

Learners working to regulate sensory information may find an abundance of visual materials distracting or disturbing.

EXTENSION OPPORTUNITIES

Learning spaces can be both in-person and virtual. Consider creating a virtual background for distance learning or a digital scene for your online links that is purposeful and intentional.

Invite learners to reflect on what materials they would like to see posted in the learning spaces. Learners can be invited to provide input before material is placed where others might see it.

RELATED RESOURCES

Heavily Decorated Classrooms Disrupt Attention and Learning in Young Children (**bit.ly/inclusive365-51a**)

Do's and Don'ts on Designing for Accessibility (**bit.ly/inclusive365-51b**)

Night Light Stories Podcast Episode #12: A Place for Everyone (**bit.ly/inclusive365-51c**)

Figure 51. This learning space from @thegirldoodles, with its monochromatic theme, is attractive, projects a positive message, and has plenty of blank space.

ISTE STANDARDS FOR STUDENTS
1b, 6d

ISTE STANDARDS FOR EDUCATORS
5a, 5c

STRATEGY 51

STRATEGY 52

Inspiring Artists with Artificial Intelligence

As important as technology can be in supporting learners academically, it is just as important to support their creativity and ability to experience the world of art. Artificial intelligence provides options for aspiring artists to engage with tools and techniques used by art masters. When learners are given novel resources with which to create they can consider the influences of the artists who came before them and how works of art in museums around the world tie into their own lived experiences.

INCLUSIVE USES

Google Arts and Culture is an online art museum that includes multiple languages, and many of the works and exhibits have descriptive captions for the visually impaired. Augmented reality allows learners, who might not otherwise be able to interact with art from galleries and museums all over the world, the ability to see it up close and in 3D. Digital art tools allow learners with limited motor skills or those who do not feel confident with their own art ability to explore tools and resources they might otherwise be unable to experience.

SAMPLE TOOLS

Google Arts and Culture is available as an app for iOS and Android and also as a website (**artsandculture.google.com/partner**). It uses artificial intelligence to provide the following features:

- **Art Transfer:** Take a photo and transform it with classic artworks
- **Art Selfie:** Discover portraits that look like you
- **Color Palette:** Find art by using the colors of your photo

Tate for Kids provides inspiration from the Tate Museum in London for aspiring artists, with a range of fun and funky art tools, games, and more (**tate.org.uk/kids**).

EXTENSION OPPORTUNITIES

Invite learners to find a portrait that looks like them using the Art Selfie feature on Google Arts and Culture. They could then explore more about that artist and the style of art in which the portrait was done, and use digital or physical art tools to create their own self-portrait.

Invite learners to create their own shared digital art gallery by creating a website of artwork.

RELATED RESOURCES

Google Arts and Culture YouTube Channel (**bit.ly/inclusive365-52a**)

The Museum Art and Culture Consortium: At Home Activities (**bit.ly/inclusive365-52b**)

Inspired by Irises
Vincent van Gogh
The J. Paul Getty Museum | Google Arts & Culture

Figure 52. A photo transformed with Google Arts and Culture's Art Transfer.

ISTE STANDARDS FOR STUDENTS
3a, 6b, 6c

ISTE STANDARDS FOR EDUCATORS
5a, 5b, 5c, 6

Creating Works of Art with Animated Video

Artistic expression is a powerful way to connect the learner to a learning experience. Video animation is a growing field, and video animation tools are easily available through a variety of websites and apps, allowing even young learners the opportunity to bring drawings to life as animated videos. Animation tools provide a platform for learners to demonstrate what they know while promoting creative expression. Creating custom animations about curriculum content and learning topics supports engagement with learning, and the creation of visual arts has been demonstrated to build neural connections in the brain (Sousa, 2006).

INCLUSIVE USES

Using digital creation tools can make art accessible to all learners. Animation cells can be created right in the browser, using the trackpad without a need to manipulate hand-held drawing tools.

SAMPLE TOOLS

ABCya Animate is a simple web-based tool that enables learners to create their own unique custom animations. Animate individual frames to create a video masterpiece. Save and share the final projects to create a digital portfolio (**abcya.com/games/animate**).

Animaker is a Chrome browser extension that provides a digital canvas to create a video animation project (**bit.ly/inclusive365-53a**).

Toontastic 3D is an app that provides creators with an opportunity to build custom 3D animated video clips (**toontastic.withgoogle.com**).

EXTENSION OPPORTUNITY

Using a browser-based video animation tool, encourage learners to develop a digital story to highlight an important concept from a lesson. Each video animation should have at least four panels that highlight a key component. Animations can be shared to a main repository of digital artifacts. Want to save this as a video clip? Try using a tool like Screencastify to record the screen and save the clip to Google Drive. Now it can be embedded in slide presentations or even on a website.

RELATED RESOURCES

Use of Animation in Learning (**bit.ly/inclusive365-53b**)

"How the Arts Develop the Young Brain" by David A. Sousa (**bit.ly/inclusive365-53c**)

Figure 53. Learner artwork created with ABCya Animate.

ISTE STANDARDS FOR STUDENTS
1c, 2b, 5c, 6a, 6b, 6d

ISTE STANDARDS FOR EDUCATORS
5a, 6d

Providing Opportunities for Self-paced Review with Video Learning

Screen recordings and video presentations of information have many different purposes as an instructional tool and are of particular value when posted online for later review by learners. Making the videos available online allows learners multiple opportunities to experience the instruction. They can pause the video and watch a segment as many times as necessary to understand a challenging concept. The repetition and review that this allows is a truly empowering instructional method.

INCLUSIVE USES

When instructional videos are available for viewing, learners can review the recordings as many times as needed. It is possible to pause, reflect, rewind, and review at their leisure. Learners who need additional processing time can pause or even slow down the video speed, while learners who need a simple refresh of just one part of a lesson can fast forward to the specific section they need to review.

SAMPLE TOOLS

Screencastify is an easy-to-use screen recording Chrome extension. The free version allows up to five minutes of recording (**screencastify.com/education**).

Loom is a chrome extension and desktop or iOS app that allows users to create video recordings of the screen, voice, and face (**bit.ly/inclusive365-54a**).

Every version of iOS from 11 to the current version has screen recording built into the device. Screen recording is located in the control panel. Make sure you do a force press (apply more pressure) on the record button to activate the microphone. Otherwise, you won't be able to narrate the action, and the

video will have only system sounds for audio. When finished, the video saves automatically to the camera roll. Simply share it out to your publishing platform for learner access.

Document camera software with recording capabilities allows educators to employ a lower-tech method to record instruction.

EXTENSION OPPORTUNITY

Invite learners to volunteer to record their own instructional screencasts and videos. When learners teach the concept, research demonstrates they better understand and remember it.

RELATED RESOURCE

Best Screencasting Tools for Classrooms (**bit.ly/inclusive365-54b**)

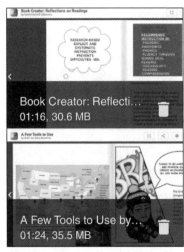

Figure 54. Screencast recordings created in Screencastify for self-paced viewing by learners.

ISTE STANDARDS FOR STUDENTS
1a, 6a, 6c, 6d

ISTE STANDARDS FOR EDUCATORS
5a, 5b, 5c

Improving Visualizations Using Interactive Image Hot Spots

How can a learner take in new information about a topic if they lack basic background information about that topic? Let's look at Wikipedia for a second. (Wait! Hear us out!) One of the most powerful aspects of any entry in Wikipedia is the hyperlinked resources on each page. If a learner is reading about ancient Greece but isn't familiar with Plato, no problem. The name *Plato* is hyperlinked to an entire entry about his life and contributions. These hyperlinks allow each learner to interact with the information at their own level. The same strategy can be used with pictures embedded with hot spots that create additional learning opportunities. Online digital images can contain either subtle or overt hot spots, so that when a cursor moves over a particular region, additional content pops up. This content might be text or a thumbnail view of audio, video, another image, or a website. Learners can use this interactive image to help them understand or remember content.

INCLUSIVE USES

Learners might prefer particular modalities for how they experience content. An interactive image allows for a person to use their visual processing abilities to recall information. Visualizing a piece of content often helps someone remember it. When that content is interactive, learners understand and then recall more specific details about it.

SAMPLE TOOL

ThingLink allows learners and educators to create images with rich, engaging content embedded into the picture to support learning. Embed audio, video, text, and pictures directly into a background picture. These materials can be accessed via hot spots placed directly on the background picture. Thinglink can be embedded in a website, shared on social media, or visited via the link (**thinglink.com**).

EXTENSION OPPORTUNITIES

Invite learners to create their own images to express what they've learned. Using hot spots, they can add their own content to an image to make it interactive.

Use an image of a text representation of a word. Use the interactive hot spots to link to different media that helps explain that particular vocabulary word.

RELATED RESOURCES

ThingLink Tutorial (**bit.ly/inclusive365-55a**)

ThingLink Tutorial Image (**bit.ly/inclusive365-55b**)

Figure 55. A Thinglink image with embedded information.

ISTE STANDARDS FOR STUDENTS
6b, 6c, 6d

ISTE STANDARDS FOR EDUCATORS
5a, 5c, 6b, 6d

STRATEGY 56

Turning Web Content into Audio to Listen Any Time

We've all encountered the challenge of having too much to read and not enough time. For some individuals, listening to audio (reading with your ears) can save time, promote efficiency, and enhance learning. Individuals can convert any digital content or articles into podcast-style audio files for listening at any time.

INCLUSIVE USES

For learners who have yet to master the ability to decode text and read fluently, and for those who need to experience content repeatedly, listening to content can promote success and independence.

SAMPLE TOOLS

Podcastle AI is a Chrome extension that turns any digital text into a digital audio file with high-quality male or female voices, for listening when it works best (**podcastle.ai**).

AudioMaker, one of the features in the premium version of the Read&Write Chrome extension, turns any digital content into audio (**bit.ly/inclusive365-56a**).

EXTENSION OPPORTUNITY

Invite learners to create a personal audio library of online articles of interest for later review.

RELATED RESOURCES

Podcastle AI video (**bit.ly/inclusive365-56b**)

Audio Maker Tutorial (**bit.ly/inclusive365-56c**)

Figure 56. A podcast created from a website.

ISTE STANDARDS FOR STUDENTS
1a, 1b, 3c, 7b

ISTE STANDARDS FOR EDUCATORS
2a, 5b, 5c

Creating Visually Engaging Slide Decks

Slide templates that come standard with Microsoft PowerPoint and Google Slides quickly become overused and boring, and they do not always convey the tone or message intended. Not all educators have the graphic design talent to develop their own slide deck templates, particularly when keeping slide accessibility in mind. A variety of websites provide slide deck design templates that are free to use and set just the right tone to create visually appealing presentations and materials.

INCLUSIVE USES

Learners who have difficulty refocusing attention back to a presenter may find a slide deck with an engaging template helps draw them back in when focus has shifted. Some learners with low vision or other visual impairments might find that templates with black backgrounds and white text might be easier to see. Even learners who don't have visual impairments might find templates with high contrast elements appealing.

SAMPLE TOOLS

SlidesMania has bright, colorful slide decks for Google Slides and PowerPoint that are designed with educators and learners in mind. Their slide decks include layouts for interactive treasure hunts, file cabinets for links for distance learning, game boards, and much more (**slidesmania.com**).

Slides Carnival provides decks that can be searched by color and theme, and include a variety of seasonal decks with a new deck added every month (**slidescarnival.com**).

PowerPoint templates from Microsoft offer a variety of templates for different purposes, including ones specifically designed for education (**bit.ly/inclusive365-57a**).

EXTENSION OPPORTUNITIES

Invite learners to evaluate the effectiveness of a given template. Do they find the design engaging? Distracting? Too busy? Easy to use?

When creating their own slide decks, invite learners to consider their potential audience when choosing a template.

RELATED RESOURCE

10 Tips for Better Slide Decks (**bit.ly/inclusive365-57b**)

Figure 57. A slide deck template from SlidesMania.

ISTE STANDARDS FOR STUDENTS
6a, 6b, 6c, 6d

ISTE STANDARDS FOR EDUCATORS
5c

Designing Educational Experiences Using Empathy Mapping

A traditional lesson design process invites educators to place the content at the center. In this model, the educators begin by thinking about the best way to teach the content. Starting with the content, however, can lead to a design that is not personalized for each learner. One technique for designing personalized educational experiences is to put the learner at the core of the process. A visualization strategy called "empathy mapping" invites educators to plot a series of answers to a consistent set of questions, which helps shape the design by considering the learner first. Variations exist, but empathy maps generally ask questions such as: Who is the learner? What does that individual want or need to learn? What does that person see in the learning environment around them? What has that person expressed about the learning task? What actions has the person taken to achieve the goal?

INCLUSIVE USES

Educators who either individually or collaboratively use empathy mapping to design learning experiences can meet the unique needs of each learner, including those with diverse neurological needs, physical abilities, and cultural backgrounds.

SAMPLE TOOLS

Google Forms allows users to answer a series of reflective questions when developing an empathy map (**bit.ly/aboutgoogleforms**).

Visual Paradigms Online Diagrams is a free website featuring online diagrams including an empathy map maker (**bit.ly/vpodempathymap**).

Padlet is an interactive, web-based, virtual corkboard that allows users to add information to templates arranged in different columns (**padlet.com**).

EXTENSION OPPORTUNITIES

Invite learners to complete an empathy map to learn social-emotional goals or to help think about the needs of those who will be experiencing products they are designing.

Use an empathy map to frame discussions about an individual learner's needs. The empathy map provides a way to organize the conversation while documenting and visualizing the results, which may lead to more streamlined and productive outcomes.

Invite educators to use an empathy map to reflect on previous educational experiences. What changes might they make to the design of future educational experiences after completing the empathy map?

RELATED RESOURCES

Using an Empathy Map for Education (**bit.ly/inclusive365-58a**)

Empathy Maps for Teachers (**bit.ly/inclusive365-58b**)

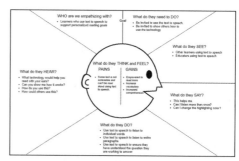

Figure 58. A completed empathy map created using a template from Visual Paradigms Online Diagrams.

ISTE STANDARDS FOR STUDENTS

1b, 1c, 2a, 2b, 2c, 3a, 3d, 4d, 5c, 6c, 6d, 7a, 7b, 7c

ISTE STANDARDS FOR EDUCATORS

2b, 3a, 3c, 4a, 4d, 5a

Creating Interactive, Multimedia Virtual Tours

Make learning come alive by creating virtual tours using digital maps and globes when studying literature, history, or geography. A virtual tour allows learners to experience the location, including distance, topography, architecture, and landmasses. In digital maps and globes, street view allows learners to immerse themselves in the location they are studying. Virtual tours offer a unique learning experience that broadens a learner's understanding of a location, culture, or period of time. Learners can tour Tanzania's Gombe National Park with Jane Goodall or take a trip to Crater Lake National Park with Charlie the Park Ranger.

INCLUSIVE USES

Virtual field trips transport learners into environments they may not be able to travel to in real life. Virtual tours provide a 360-degree visual representation to bring to life what learners are studying. Virtual tours allow learners to overcome physical, financial, and time barriers that impede travel to the actual locations.

Learners working to improve visual-spatial skills and those with physical disabilities who may not otherwise be able to traverse certain areas may especially find virtual tours beneficial.

SAMPLE TOOLS

Google Tour Builder and Google Earth Web allow learners and educators to build maps and stories within Google Maps (**tourbuilder. withgoogle.com**, **bit.ly/inclusive365-59a**).

Virtual Tours of National Parks allows learners to virtually visit national parks and map out their tour (**bit.ly/inclusive365-59b**).

EXTENSION OPPORTUNITY

Using Google's Tour Builder, invite learners to create their own tours of places meaningful to them. Encourage them to add meaningful descriptive text and invite their peers to take the tour.

RELATED RESOURCE

Storytelling with Maps Using Tour Builder (**bit.ly/inclusive365-59c**)

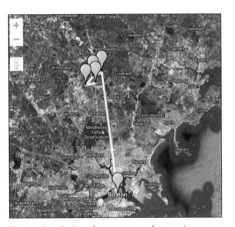

Figure 59. A virtual tour mapped out using Google Earth.

ISTE STANDARDS FOR STUDENTS

6a, 6b, 6c, 6d, 7a, 7b

ISTE STANDARDS FOR EDUCATORS

2b, 3b, 5a, 5b, 5c, 6a, 6b

STRATEGY 60

Using Open Educational Resources to Create Content

Open Educational Resources (OER) are public digital repositories of open source resources used by educators around the world. Creative Commons defines OER as "teaching, learning, and research materials that are either (a) in the public domain or (b) licensed in a manner that provides everyone with free and perpetual permission to engage in the 5R activities— retaining, remixing, revising, reusing and redistributing the resources." OER, coined by the United Nations Educational, Scientific, and Cultural Organization at the 2002 Forum on the Impact of Open Courseware for Higher Education in Developing Countries, with the intent to make high-quality education materials available to all learners at no cost, and to engage learners and educators to provide better learning opportunities.

INCLUSIVE USES

OER democratizes instructional materials so that cost is no longer a factor in the availability of high-quality, well-designed materials. Depending on the repository used, material is available by grade or difficulty level with multi-sensory support and resources.

SAMPLE TOOLS

OER Commons is a web repository that acts as a clearinghouse for open educational resources. Users post their information to this website; you can search for materials to download. Search functions for subject, education level, and standard help you narrow down your search. Once you have identified materials, simply download them to start using. There is even a function to download materials directly into Google Classroom (**oercommons.org**).

Ck12.org is a web-based repository of open educational resources. Educators can create groups and provide materials. Explore available materials by resource type, standards, and subjects (**ck12.org**).

EXTENSION OPPORTUNITIES

Invite learners to remix, revise, and redistribute the open-source materials and design their own learning around topics of interest.

Educators can use filters to find resources by education standard, subject area, and material type, including videos and simulations. Educators can control the design and create engaging, customized, remixed curriculum based on the needs of learners.

RELATED RESOURCE

OER: Open Educational Resources (**bit.ly/inclusive365-60**)

Figure 60. An OER Commons lesson plan and linked resources.

ISTE STANDARDS FOR STUDENTS
3b, 3c, 4a, 5a, 5b, 6a, 7a, 7b, 7d

ISTE STANDARDS FOR EDUCATORS
5a, 5b, 5c, 6a, 6b, 7a, 7b

Customizing Web Links to Access Internet Materials

Learners and educators create an abundance of digital materials, but sharing those materials can become frustrating if the weblink is difficult to remember or to type. A solution is shortened links. Using a tool to create small, customized web links can make it easier to find and interact with materials. Throughout this book there are links shortened in a consistent way to make them more accessible and memorable.

INCLUSIVE USES

Long URL links consisting of numbers, letters, and symbols are difficult for anyone to recreate, type, and navigate. Link customizers provide learners with a descriptive way to connect the material to the learning task. For learners, incorporating short, descriptive links can provide a platform to share their information with educators. Learners and educators who have difficulty typing and those with short-term memory difficulties may find customized hyperlinks easier to access.

SAMPLE TOOLS

Bit.ly is a free link customizing website that enables users to create short, memorable links to access content. Educators can create free accounts to track links. Bit.ly allows users to see how many people clicked a link and keep a running list of all shortened links in one centralized location (**app.bitly.com**).

TinyURL is a free link shortening tool that allows customization of links (**tinyurl.com**).

EXTENSION OPPORTUNITIES

Review the digital materials used in a learning experience. Think about some descriptive links that could make it easier to navigate to these materials. If an experience has several websites to visit, consider a consistent naming convention such as bit.ly/<educatorname1>, bit.ly/<educatorname2>, and so on.

Invite learners to create digital artifacts to share. Encourage them to make customized shortened links for easy access.

RELATED RESOURCES

How to Shorten and Customize Links with Bit.ly (**bit.ly/inclusive365-61a**)

Best Link Shorteners Reviewed: Bit.ly vs. TinyURL vs. BL.INK (**bit.ly/inclusive365-61b**)

Figure 61. Using a link shortener like bit.ly can make your long, difficult links easy to remember.

ISTE STANDARDS FOR STUDENTS

1b, 6d, 7a

ISTE STANDARDS FOR EDUCATORS

2c, 3b, 4c, 5a

STRATEGY 61

Creating Books with Embedded Audio in Slide Decks

Digital books with embedded audio provide a way to engage learners beyond print-based media. While there are commercial websites that sell ebooks with audio, educators and learners can create their own customized ebooks with audio to support learning. One way to create custom books with audio is by using Google Slides. Slide presentations are basically digital books already, with each slide representing a page, and educators can incorporate options for learner engagement by adding audio.

INCLUSIVE USES

For some learners, materials that use print exclusively create a barrier to learning. This barrier can be reduced, or even eliminated, by adding audio support. Learners can embed pictures on slides and then narrate the picture to provide an alternative to the written word. Incorporating accessible text, pictures, and embedded audio help learners who are working on building their decoding, reading comprehension, and writing skills.

SAMPLE TOOLS

Google Slides now includes an option in the Insert menu to insert audio. The audio appears on the slide as a Play button. As the cursor hovers over the button, an audio control slider appears that allows you to play or pause the audio (**docs.google.com/presentation**).

Cloud Audio Recorder is a free web-based audio recording tool that integrates with Google Drive. It has buttons to record and save audio directly in Google Drive. The audio can then be added to a slide (**bit.ly/inclusive365-62a**).

You can also embed audio in Microsoft PowerPoint presentations.

EXTENSION OPPORTUNITIES

Educators can take an existing slide presentation and embed audio clips throughout the slides to highlight key points, information, and takeaways.

Invite learners to gather pictures related to a topic about which they are learning, and then record narration into audio files that can be inserted into slides with the images.

RELATED RESOURCES

Insert Audio into Google Slides (**bit.ly/inclusive365-62b**)

Add or Delete Audio in Your PowerPoint Presentation (**bit.ly/inclusive365-62c**)

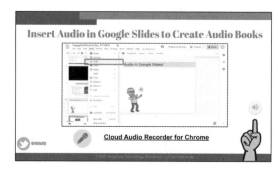

Figure 62. Inserting audio into Google Slides.

ISTE STANDARDS FOR STUDENTS
1c, 3c, 6a, 6b, 6d

ISTE STANDARDS FOR EDUCATORS
5a, 5b

Teaching Social Studies Concepts Using a Digital Sandbox

Have you ever built a castle out of sand? How about a sculpture or a moat? The shape, structure, and size of each creation is determined by its creator. Digital sandbox tools allow users to create objects in a virtual world without limitations. Educators and learners can use digital sandbox tools to produce virtual manipulatives to demonstrate and illustrate content and concepts. Sandbox tools often provide blocks or other units to create the environment. These blocks can be used as virtual items to construct artifacts, reconstruct events from history, or build virtual environments.

INCLUSIVE USES

Engage learners who are not motivated by traditional learning tasks using digital sandbox tools.

SAMPLE TOOLS

Minecraft Education Edition allows users to create in a digital sandbox (**education.minecraft.net**).

Roblox invites users to create digital objects and experiences for others (**roblox.com**).

Eco Education invites players to maintain a simulated ecosystem through virtual creations (**play.eco/education**).

EXTENSION OPPORTUNITIES

Invite learners to demonstrate their knowledge of historical events through the use of digital sandbox tools.

Invite learners to incorporate text tools, such as signs, to label and describe items created in the virtual environment.

RELATED RESOURCES

Jamestown in Minecraft (**bit.ly/inclusive365-62a**)

Minecraft History and Culture Subject Kits (**bit.ly/inclusive365-62b**)

Using Minecraft for Educational Purposes (**bit.ly/inclusive365-62c**)

Figure 63. Recreation of the USS Arizona made in Minecraft.

ISTE STANDARDS FOR STUDENTS
1b, 4a, 4b, 4c 4d, 6a, 6b, 6c, 6d

ISTE STANDARDS FOR EDUCATORS
4c, 5a, 5c, 6b, 6c, 6d, 7a

Reframing History to Include Herstory

US history textbooks focus predominantly on the role of men. A recent exhaustive study demonstrated that only 17% of stories in US textbooks are about women (Maurer et al., 2017). It's time to reframe history and include the many diverse, powerful women who have been overlooked.

INCLUSIVE USES

The novel experience of using augmented reality may engage those who are reluctant to learn about the past by reading textbooks, listening to podcasts, or watching videos. Augmented reality provides yet another modality by which learners can become engaged in learning. The opportunity to learn about powerful women from US history may empower and inspire a new generation of learners.

SAMPLE TOOLS

Lessons in Herstory is a unique, augmented reality app that allows the user to hold the device camera over a picture in a specific textbook to read about an overlooked historical woman. You can also scroll through the historical women who are included in the app and bypass the augmented reality experience (**lessonsinherstory.com**).

The Ducksters website includes a section devoted to biographies of women leaders in history as well as present-day (**bit.ly/inclusive365-64a**).

If you use EpicBooks, bookmark the curated collection of books about women in history (**bit.ly/inclusive365-64b**).

A curated collection of books about women is available from the A Mighty Girl website (**bit.ly/inclusive365-64c**).

Smithsonian American "Because of Her Story" Women's History Initiative provides virtual exhibits and resources on women in history (**womenshistory.si.edu**).

EXTENSION OPPORTUNITIES

Invite learners to track how many historical women they were familiar with and how many were new to them.

Encourage learners to create another resource, such as a book in Book Creator or videos in Flipgrid, to share what they learned with peers.

Invite learners to dress up and pretend to be a famous woman from history. The learner can tell others about the life of the famous woman speaking from a first-person perspective.

RELATED RESOURCE

"Where Are the Women?" A report on the status of women in the United State Social Studies Standards (**womenshistory.org/social-studies-standards**)

Figure 64. An image of Sojourner Truth from the Smithsonian's "Because of Her Story" virtual exhibit.

ISTE STANDARDS FOR STUDENTS
3a, 3c

ISTE STANDARDS FOR EDUCATORS
3b, 5a, 5b, 5c, 6a

Adjusting the Size of On-Screen Information for Vision Health or Accommodation

We all spend more time on devices than ever before. Because of this, considering the size of text and objects on a screen is important. Smaller items cause eye strain and fatigue. There are multiple ways to present information in a larger size. Operating systems offer display and resolution settings that can be adjusted to meet user preferences. Zoom has features that allow users to rapidly scale items on the screen. Magnifiers can help make on-screen items larger and protect against eye strain.

INCLUSIVE USES

Although adjusting the size of on-screen information may be useful for any sighted educator or learner to decrease eye strain, it may be absolutely necessary for individuals with vision impairments.

SAMPLE TOOLS

The Chrome built-in magnifier includes two built-in settings for magnifying screen information. There is a docked magnifier that places an enlarged screen area along the top of the screen. This magnified section follows the cursor placement on the main screen. The full screen magnifier enlarges the entire screen and provides enlarged screen elements as the cursor moves across the screen (**bit.ly/inclusive365-65a**).

The iOS built-in magnifier can be used in conjunction with the device camera to provide enlarged information. It is found under Settings > Accessibility (**bit.ly/inclusive365-65b**).

Windows provides a variety of settings and features for customizing the display (**bit.ly/inclusive365-65c**).

EXTENSION OPPORTUNITIES

Invite learners to explore the magnification settings on their devices to determine if they are useful.

Invite learners to create a product or presentation that teaches others about the settings and options on various devices that can magnify the screen. Learners could deliver the product or presentation to others who might benefit from this information, including relatives or people in the community.

RELATED RESOURCES

How to Use Screen Magnification on Your Chromebook (**bit.ly/inclusive365-65d**)

How to Use Hover Text to Display Larger Text on Your Mac (**bit.ly/inclusive365-65e**)

How to Zoom in on Your iPhone or iPad Screen with Window Zoom (**bit.ly/inclusive365-65f**)

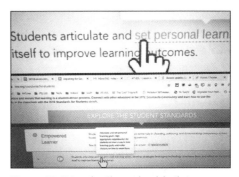

Figure 65. Using the Chromebook built-in docked magnifier, enlarged text is displayed in a box on the top of the screen.

ISTE STANDARDS FOR STUDENTS
1d, 3c

ISTE STANDARDS FOR EDUCATORS
1a, 2b, 4b, 5a, 7a

STRATEGY 65

Customizing Cursors to Increase Engagement

The traditional mouse cursor is a small white arrow that converts to the icon of a hand when it hovers over something selectable on the screen. Some learners may have difficulty visually tracking a cursor on the screen when watching a video or participating in a synchronous distance learning session. Losing the cursor location can make it more difficult to follow along, causing frustration and disengagement. Educators or learners can customize their cursor by changing it into an object other than the white pointer/hand combination. Learners can choose an object, color, and size based on their personal preferences.

INCLUSIVE USES

Although any learner might benefit from a larger, more engaging cursor, those with visual impairments or attention difficulties may find the personalized cursor particularly helpful in keeping the cursor in their visual field.

SAMPLE TOOL

Custom Cursor is an extension for the Chrome browser that allows users to change their icon into a wide array of objects, including popular culture icons. Users can also upload their own pictures (**custom-cursor.com**).

EXTENSION OPPORTUNITY

Invite learners to create their own customized cursors by selecting from a predetermined set of options. Learners can customize their own cursors to use on their own devices.

Upload pictures of positive role models the learner might find reinforcing or motivating to use as a cursor icon.

RELATED RESOURCE

Creating Custom Cursors to Maximize Engagement (**bit.ly/inclusive365-66**)

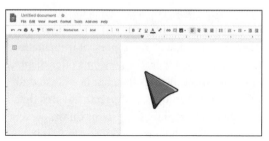

Figure 66. Customized cursor: a large blue arrow.

ISTE STANDARDS FOR STUDENTS
1d

ISTE STANDARDS FOR EDUCATORS
5c, 6a, 6b

Demonstrating Knowledge Using Screen Recordings

Learners can use screen recordings to demonstrate what they know. Learners can record their screen to demonstrate their thinking in any content area. Reviewing the screen recording provides educators the opportunity to ensure the learner understands the concept. Educators can also identify instances where the learner has made an error to then provide targeted assistance. Screen recordings provide evidence of learning and can be placed in a digital portfolio of work. Multiple screen recordings can be compared to illustrate growth.

INCLUSIVE USES

Learners can take their time when creating a screen recording and edit the video before providing it to an educator for feedback. Individuals who experience anxiety around assessments may find making a screen recording less stressful and more authentic.

SAMPLE TOOLS

Screencastify is a Chrome extension which allows users to produce videos. No internet connection is needed to record. An internet connection is only needed to upload the video file. Record using a full browser window or a specific application. Turn on the microphone to narrate the video. You can record and share up to five minutes of video content with the free version (**screencastify.com**).

WeVideo is an online video editor with screen recording capabilities (**wevideo.com**).

Screen recording is a feature of iOS devices (**bit.ly/inclusive365-67a**).

EXTENSION OPPORTUNITY

Learners can flaunt their personalities in video content, sharing favorite pop culture references, quotes, memes, or animations, which can make the experience more engaging for the audience watching the video. An engaging video is an opportunity to build relationships with educators, peers, and members of the community.

Invite learners to make screen recordings of error messages that occur when operating a device. The video can be shared with support personnel who can use it to troubleshoot the issue.

RELATED RESOURCE

7 Classroom Screen Recording Activities (**bit.ly/inclusive365-67b**)

Figure 67. Using Screencastify to narrate a Google Slides presentation for added engagement.

ISTE STANDARDS FOR STUDENTS

1b, 2c, 3c, 6a, 6b, 6d

ISTE STANDARDS FOR EDUCATORS

2b, 3b, 4a, 5a, 5c, 7a

Collaborating with Shared Slide Decks

Collaborative online slide decks provide a means for learners to work together regardless of location. Learners can use a slide deck to divide up the learning tasks. The degree of structure provided in the slide deck template could be driven by the complexity of the task, the skill level of the learners, and the familiarity of the learners with the tool they are using. Learners collaborate to decide which specific slides they will complete. Learners can work in whole or small groups and track who has contributed to each slide using the slide history function. Learners can provide feedback to each other using comments and work together to produce a cohesive product.

INCLUSIVE USES

Because adaptive technologies, such as screen readers, word prediction tools, and speech-to-text are essentially invisible within the final product, and each learner can use the tools they prefer or require, collaborative projects using slides have built-in accessibility that is not always found in face-to-face collaboration.

Learners can choose specific components of the learning task, or choose specific slides designed to help that learner practice particular skills.

SAMPLE TOOLS

PowerPoint in Office 365 and Google Slides both allow learners to work collaboratively within the same slide deck (**bit.ly/inclusive365-68a** and **google.com/slides**).

EXTENSION OPPORTUNITY

Invite learners to take different roles within their collaboration, such as graphic designer, fact checker, font stylist, and hyperlink checker. Ensure that learners rotate through these jobs in future projects so that they understand the importance of all of these details in a slide deck.

RELATED RESOURCES

Collaborative Learning (**bit.ly/inclusive365-68b**)

Not Just Group Work—Productive Group Work (**bit.ly/inclusive365-68c**)

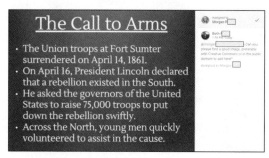

Figure 68. Learners collaborate to build a Google Slides deck for an assignment.

ISTE STANDARDS FOR STUDENTS
7b, 7c, 7d

ISTE STANDARDS FOR EDUCATORS
3a, 3b, 5a, 5c, 6a, 6c, 6d

Creating Artifacts Using Three Dimensions and Virtual Reality

There are times when adding visual depth to an image better expresses proportions, adds greater meaning, or provides a more immersive experience than two dimensions alone. Learners can create drawings, paintings, and other objects to express themselves in 3D, which is then viewed using virtual reality (VR) headsets. Learners can demonstrate their knowledge by sketching out people, places, diagrams, equations, words, environments, and more. You can then view their work using a VR headset, where it will appear in 3D.

INCLUSIVE USES

Some learners may find items presented in VR highly engaging, including those with learning challenges. Viewing letters, words, word families, math facts, shapes, money, and numbers in 3D may be more memorable and engaging than the same information shown in 2D. Learners who have demonstrated a preference for expressing themselves via drawing, painting, or expressions other than writing may find creating images for VR empowering.

SAMPLE TOOLS

Google Cardboard turns most mobile devices into an inexpensive VR viewer (**arvr.google.com/cardboard**).

Panoform is a free website with downloadable and printable templates that allow users to transform 2D pictures into 3D experiences (**panoform.com**).

EXTENSION OPPORTUNITIES

Invite learners to create their own drawings or other artwork and organize it in photo albums to access and refer back to.

Invite learners to create a library of shared creations for use by others.

RELATED RESOURCE

Through a Child's Eyes (**bit.ly/inclusive365-69**)

Figure 69. The word empowering drawn on the Panoform template, with each syllable separated by differing background colors. When viewed through a VR viewer, each syllable of the word is in a different area of space.

ISTE STANDARDS FOR STUDENTS
1c, 4a, 6b, 6c, 6d, 7a

ISTE STANDARDS FOR EDUCATORS
5c, 6d

STRATEGY 69

STRATEGY 70

Improving Expression with Picture Prediction

Drawing is a skill that takes practice. Expressing themselves through drawing can be an empowering way for learners to share what they know and make an impact on the world. Whether due to the effort or the perceived lack of ability, some learners may find drawing challenging or even frustrating. Picture prediction technology analyzes a simple drawing and provides images that might be a representation of the image the learner was attempting to draw. The learner selects the image close to their vision, and it is embedded in the canvas, replacing the original drawing.

INCLUSIVE USES

Learners with fine motor difficulties may find picture prediction useful, enjoyable, and empowering, giving them an opportunity to illustrate their work.

SAMPLE TOOL

AutoDraw by Google is a website that allows a user to begin drawing an image and select from an array of images to represent their rough drawing (**autodraw.com**).

EXTENSION OPPORTUNITIES

Invite learners to keep a portfolio of creations by downloading them and then adding them to a shared file location. Comparing early artifacts to later ones can demonstrate growth.

Invite learners to draw for a purpose. Adding a drawing to enhance a project, illustrate a point, or convey a message to make an impact on the world can be inherently motivating.

RELATED RESOURCE

Quick, Draw! (**quickdraw.withgoogle.com**)

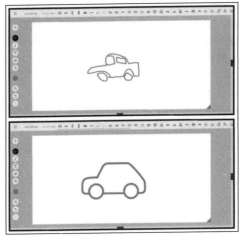

Figure 70. A hand-drawn car converted to a computer-generated image using Google AutoDraw.

ISTE STANDARDS FOR STUDENTS
6b, 6c, 6d

ISTE STANDARDS FOR EDUCATORS
6d

Creating Interactive Venn Diagrams

Venn diagrams are graphical representations using overlapping circles to compare and contrast two or more objects, ideas, or concepts. Venn diagrams help learners visualize similarities and differences and classify information. Online, interactive Venn diagrams help learners easily create an artifact with items that can be manipulated or moved from one area to another to see the relationships between concepts.

INCLUSIVE USES

Interactive digital tools offer a flexible, mistake-tolerant option that can decrease frustration when a learner needs to reposition or delete something when editing work. Digital Venn diagrams provide ever-increasing space to add text, images, and weblinks.

SAMPLE TOOLS

ReadWriteThink provides an interactive Venn diagram for iPads or Android devices (**bit.ly/inclusive365-71a**).

Inspiration Maps, an iOS app, provides multiple versions of Venn diagram templates for different content areas, as well as the ability to generate a novel Venn diagram from scratch. Inspiration Maps provides text-to-speech, as well as the ability to record audio in a diagram (**bit.ly/inclusive365-71b**).

EXTENSION OPPORTUNITIES

Invite learners to use Venn diagrams to analyze multiple points of view during discussions about characters in books they are reading, historical events, or gender and racial issues.

Invite learners to use Venn diagrams to analyze the similarities and differences between different words while studying vocabulary terms.

RELATED RESOURCE

Additional Ideas for How to Use Venn Diagrams for Instruction (**bit.ly/ readwritethinkvenn**)

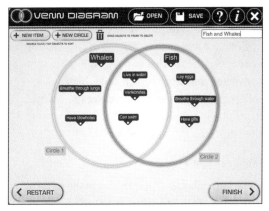

Figure 71. A Venn diagram created in ReadWriteThink.

ISTE STANDARDS FOR STUDENTS

1a, 5a, 5b, 6b, 6c

ISTE STANDARDS FOR EDUCATORS

5a, 5b, 5c, 6a, 6b

STRATEGY 72

Converting Files to Different Formats for Use in Projects

We have all been there. Inspiration strikes, and you are creating an amazing digital artifact that is going to blow your learners away with how inventive, funny, clever, or awesome it is. But wait—your file is the wrong format! It won't work the way it is. The software you need to use beeps an error message, saying it can't read this type of file. All progress stops, and inspiration slowly drains away as you desperately attempt to find a way to import your digital file into the project. Educators aren't alone in this dilemma. Learners run into this issue, too. A file converter can help keep enthusiasm alive and well. Upload the file you have, set the controls to tell it what type of file you want it to be, and then convert. Problem solved.

INCLUSIVE USES

Creating a digital artifact often takes multiple steps. The wrong file type can stop all the creating and build frustration instead. This might be enough to cause the learner to abandon the experience altogether. Providing a simple way to avoid this issue enables learners to continue their work with less frustration. Overcoming an obstacle is useful for learners working to understand and complete the steps of a process, demonstrate resiliency, and demonstrate troubleshooting ability.

SAMPLE TOOL

Free Online File Converter allows a learner to upload any type of file for conversion. Accepted formats include: archive, vector, document, image, audio, video, ebook, font, and presentation. Basically, any file type can be converted to something else (**freefileconvert.com**).

EXTENSION OPPORTUNITY

Encourage learners to gain a better understanding of file formats and the file requirements for their digital creation tools. Explore the files they use and discuss ways to create a catalog of different formats of the same file for use in different projects. Building a reference table of common file formats helps learners understand and remember these formats.

RELATED RESOURCE

The Ultimate Guide to File Formats (**bit.ly/inclusive365-72**)

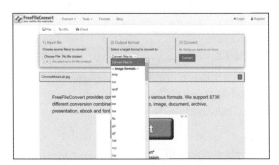

Figure 72. A file being converted to another file format using Free Online File Converter.

ISTE STANDARDS FOR STUDENTS
1d, 3c, 4a, 5d, 6a

ISTE STANDARDS FOR EDUCATORS
4b, 5a, 5b

Collaborating to Create a Video Masterpiece

Today's learners often shoot video as a matter of habit and can even use videos as artifacts to demonstrate learning. Shooting a video happens with relative ease now that most devices are equipped with cameras. However, editing video is an entirely different process. Creating a compelling, edited video clip—with transitions, title cards, and credits—takes some practice. Professional video editing tools can be very expensive, but there are powerful free video editing tools that can be accessed within your web browser. Take advantage of the skills of various learners by providing an opportunity for them to collaborate on a video project, regardless of their location. The shared workspace can be accessed and edited by all group members simultaneously.

INCLUSIVE USES

While most of the features of video editing tools focus on the visual aspects of a product, we must also consider accessibility features in video creation. Captions are critical to ensure accessibility. Providing "open captions" in your video clip means that the captions are visible at all times, which ensures that all viewers can appreciate and access your video clip.

SAMPLE TOOL

WeVideo is a web-based video editing tool that provides a feature-rich video editing experience directly in the browser window. Upload video clips and add transitions and text. Make sure to include those captions for accessibility (**wevideo.com**).

EXTENSION OPPORTUNITY

Discuss the various aspects of a finished video clip and assign roles to each learner: director, credits, editor, etc. Each learner can add their unique style to the finished clip while learning the importance of each role in the video creation and editing process.

RELATED RESOURCES

How to Use WeVideo with Students in the Classroom (**bit.ly/inclusive365-73a**)

WeVideo Technology Resources for Teachers (**bit.ly/inclusive365-73b**)

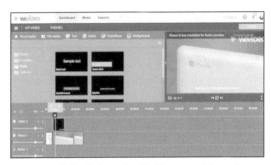

Figure 73. Video being edited in WeVideo with captions.

ISTE STANDARDS FOR STUDENTS
1d, 3c, 6a, 6b, 6d

ISTE STANDARDS FOR EDUCATORS
2b, 3b, 4b, 5a

Podcasting to Share Learner Voices

Podcasting has become a popular medium for individuals to share information and opinions on topics they are passionate about. Anyone can podcast, including learners. The opportunity for learners to share their knowledge and ideas to an authentic audience via audio creates engagement often exceeding the enthusiasm shown for written projects. Free podcasting platforms provide the structure necessary to bring a podcast to an audience. Recording audio can happen on any number of devices. The podcast platform then automates the other aspects of producing and delivering content to the masses. Using a podcast platform is also an opportunity to teach technology skills in a practical and meaningful manner.

INCLUSIVE USES

While a written script may still be needed to produce a coherent and effective podcast, for evolving writers, producing audio as the final product may reduce the barriers that spelling and mechanics may present. Some learners find their best creative expression when they share their thoughts aloud.

SAMPLE TOOL

Anchor is a free podcasting platform that has all the features necessary to take an idea and broadcast it to an audience. The simple, easy-to-use interface assists with recording audio clips directly on the site, uploading other audio files, and adding sound effects. Anchor even provides a feature that allows multiple speakers to connect into the audio file, in real time, to be part of an episode (**anchor.fm**).

EXTENSION OPPORTUNITY

Invite learners to produce a group podcast. Each learner can have a role to play and can collaborate on different aspects of a podcast

such as the name, the frequency of episodes, the audio components that will make up each episode, and where it will be available. Other roles include writing scripts and being the "on air" talent. Not every learner will want to be the voice of the podcast. There are plenty of jobs to go around.

RELATED RESOURCES

How to Start a Podcast: A Complete Step by Step Tutorial (**podcastinsights.com/start-a-podcast**)

The Easiest Way to Make a Podcast (**anchor.fm/switch**)

Teaching Podcasting: A Curriculum Guide for Educators (**bit.ly/inclusive365-74**)

Figure 74. The Talking With Tech podcast.

ISTE STANDARDS FOR STUDENTS
6a, 6b, 6d, 7a, 7b, 7c

ISTE STANDARDS FOR EDUCATORS
3a, 3b, 3c, 4a, 4b, 4c, 5a, 5b, 7a, 7b

Creating Sophisticated Audio Recordings for Projects

Incorporating voice and sound effects into presentations can enhance a learner's project. There are many audio recording tools available for expression; however, several of these tools are simply a record button that saves the recording to a digital file. Using a full-featured audio editing tool allows learners to fully express themselves and create an audio experience that has added depth, sophistication, and complexity. Using a resource that allows for the combination of spoken audio, sound effects, and more unleashes the creativity in learners.

INCLUSIVE USES

Demonstrating understanding via audio may enable an evolving writer to demonstrate mastery of a subject. Creating a layered audio experience can showcase creativity and depth of knowledge.

SAMPLE TOOLS

Audacity is a fully functional, robust, open source audio editing tool freely available for download on both Windows and Mac computers. Upload audio files, layer multiple tracks into one file, add effects, export files in current formats, and much more (**audacityteam.org**).

Twisted Wave is a browser-based audio editing tool. Perfect for use on Chromebooks, the free version has a five-minute project limit and only exports in mono audio. This resource may be ideal for shorter learner projects (**twistedwave.com/online**).

EXTENSION OPPORTUNITIES

Invite learners to listen to podcasts that interest them to see how the various uses of audio enhance the quality of the product.

Invite learners to create a series of audio projects around a central theme and to put them out as a limited-run podcast.

Invite learners to write and record audio dramas where the learners perform to demonstrate knowledge, share information, or simply entertain an audience.

Consider creating your own podcast sharing your experiences as a professional.

RELATED RESOURCE

A.T.TIPSCAST Episode #21: Audacity for Reading Fluency has wonderful examples of how to incorporate fun audio effects, as well as information on how to use Audacity (**bit.ly/inclusive365-75**)

Figure 75. Recording on Audacity.

ISTE STANDARDS FOR STUDENTS
1c, 2a, 3c, 4b, 5c, 6b, 6d

ISTE STANDARDS FOR EDUCATORS
2c, 3b, 4a, 6d

Demonstrating Knowledge Using Infographics

Infographics provide visual representations of information, data, or knowledge. If done well, the result is accurate information presented concisely, understandably, and in an appealing way. Infographics can make information more comprehensible by tapping into an individual's ability to see patterns and trends. Infographics enable learners to showcase their knowledge with visual representations, which may include both text and images, designed to maximize their expression.

INCLUSIVE USES

Learners challenged by traditional writing tasks may be liberated by the opportunity to express themselves with a pictorial representation of their mastery of a subject. Learners working on improving math and science skills may find demonstrating their knowledge through an infographic a meaningful form of expression.

SAMPLE TOOLS

Google Drawings is an application in the Google Suite that can be used by learners to create an infographic. While there are many different ways to create infographics, including websites and apps specifically designed for this purpose, learners may prefer to use a tool to which they already have access! Google Drawings provides a blank canvas for learners to express themselves (**docs.google.com/drawings**).

Piktochart is a web tool that has templates, icons, and other graphics that invite users to create an infographic on any topic (**piktochart.com**).

EXTENSION OPPORTUNITY

Pair the creation of an infographic with literature. Invite learners to demonstrate their understanding of the character traits of the main character of a story and the journey they completed. Learners can pair text with pictures to highlight connections.

RELATED RESOURCE

The Google Drawings Manifesto for Teachers from Ditch That Textbook (**bit.ly/inclusive365-76**)

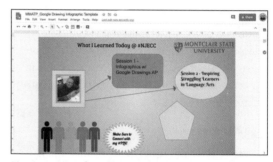

Figure 76. An infographic created using Google Drawings.

ISTE STANDARDS FOR STUDENTS
1b, 1c, 5a, 6c

ISTE STANDARDS FOR EDUCATORS
5a, 5b, 5c

Pairing Audio and Video to Facilitate Expression

When a product is created in only one medium, it limits the number of people who can access that material effectively. If the product is exclusively text, that limits those who rely on visual imagery for support. If the item is exclusively video, those who prefer reading text may find that material less engaging. Although audio might provide an advantage of being able to listen while participating in other hands-on tasks, those who prefer video or text may find audio alone difficult to comprehend. Providing materials in multiple modalities ensures learners can choose which modality they prefer. Text-to-speech can turn text into an audio experience. Captions add text to a video or audio experience. Audio files can be transformed into accessible video clips, and text can be transcribed simultaneously. Producing video clips with captioning opens up learner work to a whole new audience and provides options to increase engagement.

INCLUSIVE USES

Learners with hearing impairments may need audio to be transcribed into text, presented with captions, or transformed into video with captions. Learners improving auditory comprehension skills may find the visuals presented in a video more helpful than files containing exclusively audio information. Learners improving their reading skills may find seeing text while listening helpful when practicing decoding and reading comprehension skills.

SAMPLE TOOL

Headliner is a free web tool that takes audio clips and infuses them into a video package. Videos can be captioned and transcribed for accessibility. A waveform can be placed over still pictures to simulate action during a video clip and provide a visual clue that audio is playing. Audio files up to two hours long can be uploaded, edited, clipped, and modified to create a gallery of video projects (**headliner.app**).

EXTENSION OPPORTUNITIES

Encourage a learner to record an audio file answering reflective questions on a topic of study. Once the audio file is created, invite the learner to convert this audio file into an engaging video clip that can be formatted and shared on Instagram, YouTube, or any video platform. Remind the learner to provide captions and a transcription.

RELATED RESOURCE

How to Create a Headliner Video
(**bit.ly/inclusive365-77**)

Figure 77. Import audio into the Headliner web app to create engaging visuals with transcripts.

ISTE STANDARDS FOR STUDENTS
1c, 2a, 2c, 6a, 6b, 6c, 6d

ISTE STANDARDS FOR EDUCATORS
5a, 6a

Making Movies with Green Screens

Green screen technology allows learners to drop into any digital scene. Video editing software recognizes a color (typically green) and replaces instances of that color with a background image or video file. This is a creative way to engage learners in a topic by allowing them a realistic or imaginative backdrop or setting for a video. Whether it is outer space or a Revolutionary War battle, using an interactive virtual background enhances the learning experience. The ability to create an immersive experience forms powerful connections to the educational materials. Learners flex their creative muscle and demonstrate their skills using a virtual environment to demonstrate mastery of content through video.

INCLUSIVE USES

Using green screen technology, learners can experience a situation and connect that back to the learning. Learners working to convey ideas via writing might find that video creation using a virtual environment provides a fun, multimodal experience which incorporates both visuals and sounds.

SAMPLE TOOLS

Green Screen by Do Ink, an iOS app, provides a video editing solution enabling learners to create video clips that can be inserted into any virtual background (**doink.com**).

Chromavid is a free app (available for both iOS and Android) that lets learners drop themselves into the action. Add a picture or video clip into the background, stand in front of a green screen, hit record, and create! Files can be downloaded and shared on other platforms (**chromavid.com**).

EXTENSION OPPORTUNITIES

Invite learners to insert themselves into a scenario to share facts. Develop a news team and each learner can report from the scene of their story. Incorporating background images and video, learners can draft a news story to share the key elements of the story. These stories can then be stitched together to create the newscast.

Invite learners to wear green clothing in videos, and then use green screen tools to provide animations of that clothing. A green shirt, for instance, can be replaced with a picture or video, to make it look like the person in the video is wearing something extraordinary.

RELATED RESOURCES

Lesson Plans for Green Screen by Do Ink (**bit.ly/inclusive365-78a**)

Using Green Screens for Adapted PE (**bit.ly/inclusive365-78b**)

Figure 78. Insert yourself in the action with a green screen using the Chromavid app.

ISTE STANDARDS FOR STUDENTS
1b, 3c, 4b, 6b

ISTE STANDARDS FOR EDUCATORS
4b, 5a, 5b, 6a, 6d

Controlling Moveable Elements in Slide Decks

Just like with a felt board, magnetic letters, or a traditional tabletop board game, learners can move elements, add text, and even play interactive games over distance learning platforms when combined with remote cursor control, or via a shared collaborative slide deck. Presentation mode may not allow remote cursor control, but edit mode often does. Either method allows learners, along with the educator, to actively participate in the learning. Moveable on-screen elements can be used as digital manipulatives for math, interactive storytelling resources, or game pieces. Integrating game controls such as spinners, dice, and drawing from a hat further engages learners.

INCLUSIVE USES

An interactive slide deck is ideal for a learner to demonstrate understanding of a concept, even if they do not yet have the literacy skills to use chat tools or the language skills to participate in a discussion.

SAMPLE TOOLS

Google Slides and PowerPoint allows educators and learners to create their own custom slide decks that when utilized in edit mode rather than present mode allow elements to be moved and manipulated (**google.com/slides** and **office.com/launch/powerpoint**).

LessonPix allows educators to download any custom content into PowerPoint or Google Slides and utilize moveable images, digital dice, and digital spinners (**lessonpix.com**).

EXTENSION OPPORTUNITY

Invite learners to create their own interactive slide decks to demonstrate their understanding of a concept. Learners can share their slide decks remotely with a peer or a younger learner and invite them to engage in synchronous, collaborative learning experiences.

RELATED RESOURCES

Remote Learning Using Google Slides and LessonPix (**bit.ly/inclusive365-79a**)

Ten simple tips for PowerPoint with LessonPix (**bit.ly/inclusive365-79b**)

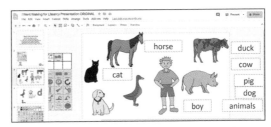

Figure 79. Google Slides with moveable elements from LessonPix.

ISTE STANDARDS FOR STUDENTS

1b, 3c, 5c, 6a

ISTE STANDARDS FOR EDUCATORS

5a, 5b, 5c

Practicing Speaking Publicly Using a Teleprompter

Public speaking. Just saying those two words to some people causes anxiety. One strategy to help lessen that stress is to remember the old adage, "Practice makes perfect." Providing learners with opportunities to practice public speaking and refine their presentation skills bolsters confidence. As with most skills, the more opportunities to practice, the easier it becomes. Using a teleprompter can instill a sense of comfort with public speaking by encouraging learners to keep their eyes on the crowd. Learners can repeatedly practice reading until they feel comfortable with the flow, pace, and wording.

Some technologies utilize speech recognition technology to automatically scroll the text at the same rate at which a person is speaking. When a person speaks slower, the text slows down. When a person speeds up, the text scrolls faster. The learner automatically controls the pace.

INCLUSIVE USES

Learners working to regulate anxiety and stress may find the use of a teleprompter useful when presenting to others. The comfort of having the words scroll while reading can lessen anxiety.

Learners who are emergent readers working on decoding and reading fluency may find practicing the same text repeatedly and at their own pace helps them gain proficiency.

SAMPLE TOOL

Speakflow is a free website that provides a scrolling teleprompter feature for pacing presentations. Copy and paste any text into the website and adjust the text size and colors according to learner preferences (**speakflow.com**).

EXTENSION OPPORTUNITY

Invite learners to search for famous speeches and practice reading them publicly. Learners might consider listening to a recorded version of how the speech was originally presented by the person who first gave the speech. Using the original as a guide, learners can record themselves giving the speeches using the camera connected to the device. Learners can play back the video, edit, re-record, and critique their delivery to reflect on areas where they'd like to improve.

RELATED RESOURCE

Teleprompter: How to Use One
(**bit.ly/inclusive365-80**)

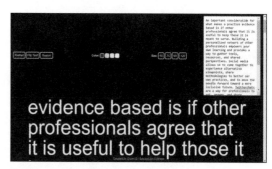

Figure 80. Speakflow in action.

ISTE STANDARDS FOR STUDENTS
1c, 2a, 5b, 6a, 6c, 6d

ISTE STANDARDS FOR EDUCATORS
5a, 5b, 5c, 6a

Setting Learning Goals by Using Radar Chart Ability Infographics

While all learners have different talents and abilities, nurturing a growth mindset includes supporting all learners in believing that with concerted effort they can make progress in any skill area. Learners can take assessments to determine their level of mastery of a particular skill. Learners can use these assessment results to determine strengths and areas where they want to improve. The quantitative results can be plotted on a radar chart to provide a visual representation of each ability on a graph that looks like a spiderweb, with each ability plotted separately. The learner can then use the score to set a measurable goal and take action steps to achieve this goal.

INCLUSIVE USES

Although most learners benefit from setting goals, providing the information in a visual way may be particularly helpful for learners who need support. Analyzing a radar chart of personal abilities can help an individual foster a mindset that given time, effort, tools, and strategies, one can improve the targeted ability.

SAMPLE TOOLS

Google Forms is a web-based tool that provides a means for users to answer a series of questions that can be used to provide scores to create a radar chart (**google.com/forms/about**).

Visual Paradigms is a free website featuring online diagrams, including a radar chart maker (**bit.ly/inclusive365-81a**).

EXTENSION OPPORTUNITIES

Invite learners to complete the ability survey quarterly and plot the results on the same chart to see growth over time.

Invite adult learners to complete ability surveys prior to and after a professional development experience to visualize growth over time.

RELATED RESOURCES

The Radar Chart and its Caveat (**bit.ly/inclusive365-81b**)

Radar Chart CS 465: Information Visualization (**bit.ly/inclusive365-81c**)

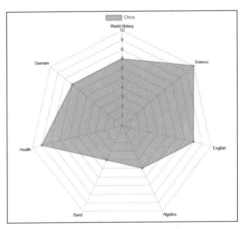

Figure 81. A radar chart illustrating abilities as an infographic.

ISTE STANDARDS FOR STUDENTS
1a, 5b

ISTE STANDARDS FOR EDUCATORS
1a, 6a, 7c

Welcoming New Learners through Video Introductions

Transitioning into a new learning environment can be a difficult experience for some learners, whether they have moved from one building within a district to another or are new residents to the area. A welcoming video available online for all learners to review prior to entering the building for the first time can alleviate anxiety, reduce stress, and cultivate a culture of acceptance. The video can include welcoming comments from adults such as the principal, office staff, nurse, custodian, lunch staff, as well as comments from current learners. The videos should include a visual name tag for each featured individual to help viewers start to put names to faces. The video should also be captioned.

INCLUSIVE USES

Creating videos as part of transitioning from one program within the district to another can be a helpful strategy for easing the transition for learners. Videos can be watched repeatedly for anyone who needs it to help foster connections and build community awareness. Anyone can view the video as many times as necessary to learn names and grow their familiarity with those in the new learning environment.

SAMPLE TOOLS

Clips is a mobile video recording application that automatically adds closed captioning (**apple.com/clips**).

Flipgrid can be used to create a welcome grid. Having the tool available on any device enables learners to create welcome videos that highlight their personality in any location. Flipgrid also has the ability to have captions in the video for inclusive support (**info.flipgrid.com**).

EXTENSION OPPORTUNITY

In small, collaborative groups, invite learners to storyboard the welcoming video and then film, edit, and share. The group can decide which one should be uploaded to a shared website.

RELATED RESOURCE

How and Why Students Should Make Storyboards (**bit.ly/inclusive365-82**)

Figure 82. Welcome back video shown to a school community.

ISTE STANDARDS FOR STUDENTS
4a, 4b, 6a, 6b, 6d

ISTE STANDARDS FOR EDUCATORS
1a, 3a, 3c, 4a, 5a, 5c

Preparing for Transitions Using Virtual Reality

Learners transition from environment to environment. Whether moving from room to room, level to level, or leaving a building to go home or to work, transitions occur with regularity. Virtual reality (VR) allows learners to experience the new environment while remaining physically in the current one.

INCLUSIVE USES

Preparing for transitions by going to the new location for a visit can help orient learners to the new environment. However, a one-time event can be a limiting experience for an individual who might require more time to process, reflect, and become acclimated to the new environment. Field trips using VR can allow a learner to experience the new environment repeatedly, examining details of the environment to provide a more secure sense of well-being, and to craft questions prior to the event.

SAMPLE TOOLS

Google Tour Creator is a free website that allows users to stitch together images to create a 360° view of that environment (**bit.ly/inclusive365-83a**).

Poly from Google is a library of shared virtual tours and 3D objects (**poly.google.com**).

EXTENSION OPPORTUNITIES

Invite learners to create their own virtual tours of environments and habitats. Learners can create tours of different locations, public places, and work sites to provide an interactive simulation that will help fellow learners prepare for that experience.

Invite learners to create a searchable repository of virtual field trips of local areas that can be accessed in a shared location.

RELATED RESOURCES

25+ Amazing Educational Virtual Field Trips (**weareteachers.com/best-virtual-field-trips**)

Virtual Field Trips (**bit.ly/inclusive365-83b**)

University of North Carolina, Asheville, Virtual Tour, September 2018 (**bit.ly/inclusive365-83c**)

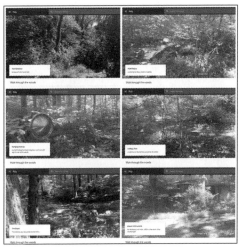

Figure 83. A collage of images from a virtual field trip made by a group of high school-aged learners using Poly by Google.

ISTE STANDARDS FOR STUDENTS

1b, 5c

ISTE STANDARDS FOR EDUCATORS

2b, 2c, 3a, 4c, 4d, 5a, 5b, 5c, 6a, 6b

Ensuring Assessment Accuracy by Providing Familiar Supports

Assessments provide data reflecting progress toward skills acquisition. Assessments should be designed and delivered to give an accurate reflection of learners' abilities. You should ensure that learners have access to the support tools with which they are familiar, and are not locked out of familiar tools during assessments, standardized or otherwise. Customizations and personalizations play a role in successfuly using a tool. A learner's inability to access customizations, including audio, speech recognition, captions, or word prediction tools may skew results, negatively impacting assessment accuracy. Instead, create and implement assessments that work with tools used by the learner.

INCLUSIVE USES

Aside from learners who are hearing impaired, any learner might choose to listen to text in assessments (other than reading assessments) to help ensure accuracy and that they are comprehending questions appropriately. Learners who are working on improving reading comprehension skills might find audio support particularly necessary.

Learners can listen to the audio of the text as often as necessary to ensure they understand the question without feeling embarrassed asking another person to re-read a question.

SAMPLE TOOLS

Google Forms works with various extensions providing text-to-speech, offering a locked mode restricting what external tools can be used, (e.g., looking up answers in a different browser tab). Consider not using this feature, but instead generating assessments with questions probing deeper understanding. If the answer can be found using an internet search, consider drafting a different question (**google.com/forms**).

EXTENSION OPPORTUNITIES

Invite learners to evaluate which assessment tool works best for them, considering all features: visual presentation, audio support features, and other unique supports of the tool.

Invite learners to advocate for the tool they are accustomed to during instruction to be used for assessments. Some platforms lock learners out of the supports they are proficient with, requiring the use of built-in supports.

RELATED RESOURCES

The National Educational Technology Plan, Section 4: Assessment (**tech.ed.gov/netp/assessment**)

Enable Accessibility in Locked Mode in Quizzes in Google Forms with Read&Write and EquatIO (**bit.ly/inclusive365-84a**)

Ditch That Textbook Podcast Episode #078: Concerns about "locked mode" in Google Forms Quizzes (**bit.ly/inclusive365-84b**)

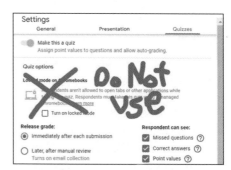

Figure 84. Instead of turning on locked mode for quizzes in Google Forms, consider drafting questions so learners can use information they find to synthesize meaningful responses.

ISTE STANDARDS FOR STUDENTS
1a, 1c, 1d, 5b

ISTE STANDARDS FOR EDUCATORS
3b, 5a, 5b, 5c, 6a, 6b

Creating Multimedia Formative Assessments

Formative assessment provides feedback to educators and guides instruction. Formative assessments should be designed to measure the acquisition of specific skills, and determine what supports or interventions a learner may need. A question when designing a formative assessment is, "Does the design of this assessment truly assess the target skills?" Assessments that are timed or require text decoding might mask a learner's mastery of content. Online formative assessment tools that can be customized with multiple modalities, including images, videos, and sounds, can ensure an accurate measurement of a learner's true competencies.

INCLUSIVE USES

Learners with emerging decoding skills may find that self-paced and engaging formative assessments that provide text-to-speech functions provide accurate results while simultaneously decreasing stress and anxiety. Formative assessments that are self-paced respect the notion that processing speeds vary among learners.

The opportunity to respond using a variety of modalities honors the idea that learners can express what they know in more than one way. Learners who are working on writing skills, including spelling, grammar, and letter formation, may more effectively demonstrate what they know when offered the opportunity to respond using text, audio recording, speech-to-text, or video.

SAMPLE TOOLS

Quizizz allows educators to create their own formative assessments or to use one created by others. It includes image supports, videos, and text-to-speech for both the questions and responses, without time restrictions (**quizizz.com**).

Google Forms can be used to create formative assessments. The assessor can also generate a spreadsheet with responses. Multimedia can be added to questions and responses. Results can be easily shared with others (**google.com/forms**).

EXTENSION OPPORTUNITIES

Invite learners to create a formative assessment for others. This will help ensure they are aware of the purpose of assessments as well as help prove content mastery.

Invite learners to evaluate the quality of formative assessment, providing feedback about the design. What would they change or add to make it more meaningful to support their own learning? Did the formative assessment give them confidence in their learning?

RELATED RESOURCES

Quizizz Tutorial for Teachers (**bit.ly/inclusive365-85a**)

Creating Assessments Using Google Forms (**bit.ly/inclusive365-85b**)

15 Form-ative Assessments with Google Forms (**bit.ly/inclusive365-85c**)

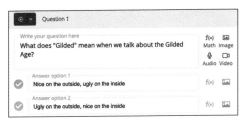

Figure 85. Multimedia options are available for questions in a Quizizz assessment.

ISTE STANDARDS FOR STUDENTS

1a, 1c, 6b, 6c, 6d

ISTE STANDARDS FOR EDUCATORS

6a, 6b, 6c, 6d, 7a, 7b, 7c

Checking for Understanding with Memes

We have all seen them on social media. Memes (pronounced "meemz") are pictures with text overlaid. These simple images not only produce a laugh, but are a powerful tool to use as a check for understanding. Using a meme, learners boil down all the information they gather into one picture and a few lines of text that represent that concept. Concisely summarizing a concept in a meme helps learners show they truly understand the essential point surrounding it.

INCLUSIVE USES

Learners working on summarizing information may find using memes a fun way to demonstrate their knowledge. Those who prefer to use methods other than paper and pencil may find typing on images engaging.

SAMPLE TOOL

IMGFlip Meme Generator is a free website that provides a library of pictures to choose from, or users can upload their own images. Select an image, and then simply overlay text. Then click generate to download or post to social media (**imgflip.com/memegenerator**).

EXTENSION OPPORTUNITIES

After completing a reading passage, invite learners to create a meme to check their understanding of the passage. For a longer article or chapter, learners could split up different sections of the article and create a collaborative slide deck that summarizes the key points.

Invite learners to analyze memes that perpetuate stereotypes and to make decisions about using meme images that may not be appropriate for use in an academic setting. Memes provide a valuable opportunity for a digital citizenship discussion as well as an opportunity to provide a check for understanding.

RELATED RESOURCES

5 Ways to Use Memes with Students (**bit.ly/inclusive365-86a**)

Using Humor to Improve Student Learning (**bit.ly/inclusive365-86b**)

Figure 86. A learner-generated book review via meme made with IMGFlip Meme Generator.

ISTE STANDARDS FOR STUDENTS
1c, 6b, 6c, 6d

ISTE STANDARDS FOR EDUCATORS
3b, 3c, 7a, 7b

Generating Assessments Using Arcade Games

Who doesn't love classic arcade games? Whether it's Asteroids, Pac Man, or even Pong, arcade games get the competitive juices flowing. Educators can harness that excitement for arcade games by embedding assessments into the game. Questions and answers can be programmed into game activities for greater learner engagement.

INCLUSIVE USES

Learners may find they sustain attention longer and perform better when an assessment is made into a game. Developing a custom arcade-style game with questions and answers directly linked to topics of learning provides a platform for learners to demonstrate their understanding.

SAMPLE TOOL

Arcade Game Generator is a website that invites users to create arcade games with embedded educational content. For example, learners can answer questions while shooting aliens and progressing to more difficult levels (**classtools.net/arcade**).

EXTENSION OPPORTUNITIES

Invite learners to design their own arcade game quizzes based on the information from a learning experience. Learners could create their own game and the entire group could engage in a game tournament. Points could be awarded for high score and best game, both in terms of design and development of questions.

Educators can build professional learning experiences using arcade games to share with colleagues.

RELATED RESOURCE

Adapting Arcade Games for Learning (**bit.ly/inclusive365-87**)

Figure 87. Some of the available options from Arcade Game Generator.

ISTE STANDARDS FOR STUDENTS
1c, 5a, 5c, 6c

ISTE STANDARDS FOR EDUCATORS
5b, 5c

STRATEGY 88

Creating Self-Grading Assessments with Certificates

Web-based formative and summative assessments can be used to gauge a learner's progress toward mastery of a subject. Learners can use any web-enabled device to access and complete the assessment. Web-based assessments can provide feedback to the learner with each question and/or at the end. Further, web-based assessments can auto-generate certificates that the learner can use to provide evidence of progress or mastery. Learners can place the digital certificates in an ongoing portfolio to demonstrate growth.

INCLUSIVE USES

For web-based assessments that are measuring skills other than decoding, learners can use text-to-speech tools to have text read aloud with highlighting for reading support, to experience questions and answers using multiple modalities, which can help to ensure a greater level of accuracy. To facilitate writing answers, learners can use dictation tools to speak answers, or can use a virtual keyboard to provide word prediction for vocabulary support. Auto-generation of certificates can provide immediate reinforcement to learners who might otherwise feel anxiety while waiting for results.

SAMPLE TOOLS

Google Forms, part of the G Suite for Education, includes a feature to instantly transform a form into a quiz. Visit Settings, select Quizzes to create a quiz from the form, and select grading options (**docs.google.com/forms**).

Certify'em is a Google Forms add-on with certificate generating features directly in Google Forms. Once active on a form, educators can assign points to each question and

denote acceptable levels of performance. Individuals can use one of the premade certificates or create their own unique certificate in Google Slides (**bit.ly/inclusive365-88a**).

EXTENSION OPPORTUNITY

Encourage learners to create their own Google Forms quiz to accompany a learning experience. In addition to generating the types and number of questions, promote creativity by including the opportunity to make a unique completion certificate.

RELATED RESOURCE

Create and Grade Quizzes with Google Forms (**bit.ly/inclusive365-88b**)

Figure 88. The setup for a Google Forms quiz.

ISTE STANDARDS FOR STUDENTS
1a, 1c, 4a, 5b, 5d

ISTE STANDARDS FOR EDUCATORS
7a, 7b, 7c

Creating a Web-Based Digital Resume

Developing a resume to highlight skills and expertise is a necessity for learners as they prepare to transition to life beyond high school. In today's digital world, a digital web presence complete with artifacts illustrating experience demonstrates accomplishments that can be customized to highlight unique skill sets. A web-based resume also demonstrates a level of proficiency and comfort with digital skills to prospective employers. There is a saying, "Tell your story before somebody else does." This has never been more true and more accomplishable through the creation of an online digital resume. Managing a digital presence is a critical skill for today's learners. With more of their lives available digitally and online, individuals need to learn to take control of the narrative and focus on the areas they wish to highlight.

INCLUSIVE USES

Learners working on developing skills related to acquiring employment and preparing to transition from a learning environment to a working environment may find spending time on building their digital resume gives them the competitive edge they need to become gainfully employed.

SAMPLE TOOL

Google Sites is a free, fully functional website builder that is part of the Google Suite. The edit mode provides tools to structure the website—including the ability to add pages and add a variety of multimedia content to each page—and provides options for publishing the website. Learners can map their Google Site to a different domain (for example, YOURNAME.com) or they can simply publish it at sites (**sites.google.com**).

EXTENSION OPPORTUNITIES

Invite learners to set a monthly or bi-monthly date to review their digital resume to update and add information. The resume should dynamically grow right along with the skills of the learner.

Invite learners to review and critique the resumes of learning partners or others in their learning groups.

Invite educators to reflect: As an educational professional, do you have an online digital resume?

RELATED RESOURCES

How to Write a Resume: The Complete Guide (**bit.ly/inclusive365-89a**)

How to Create Your First Google Site (**bit.ly/inclusive365-89b**)

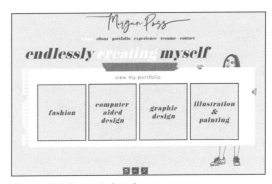

Figure 89. A learner's digital resume.

ISTE STANDARDS FOR STUDENTS
2a, 2d, 3c, 6d, 7a

ISTE STANDARDS FOR EDUCATORS
1b, 2c, 3d, 6d

STRATEGY 90

Creating Online Portfolios

Portfolios are collections of learner's work that document progress. Online portfolios provide a repository showcasing multimedia artifacts that could also include educator, peer, and parent comments. When learners review their growth and are encouraged to intentionally reflect on their learning, they develop metacognitive skills and a mindset that with time and effort they can learn almost anything.

Traditional summative tests can reflect one's abilities at any given moment in time. Factors such as fatigue, hunger, and stress can influence test performance. Test design can also influence performance, including how the text and images are displayed, unconscious bias in how test questions may be worded, and the length of questions. Online portfolios provide a way to demonstrate acquired summative skills and knowledge over time rather than at one moment in time.

INCLUSIVE USE

Online portfolios are inherently inclusive as they offer multimedia features to engage and match the abilities of all learners. Learners can record their voice, take videos or photos, explain their thinking using the video recording tool, draw, and add text. Learners who have expressed disappointment in their perceived lack of progress may find reflecting on past artifacts useful in realizing how they've grown.

SAMPLE TOOLS

Seesaw is a learner-centered digital portfolio tool (**app.seesaw.me**).

Google Drive is a place where learners can house and share all the artifacts they've created (**google.com/drive**).

EXTENSION OPPORTUNITIES

Invite learners to consistently ask themselves the question, "Should this go in my portfolio?" when they've completed a learning task. When first creating an online portfolio, learners could work to draft a list of other questions they might ask themselves when considering what should or should not go into the portfolio. Sample follow up questions they might consider include, "Is this work something I'd want others to see?", "What skills does this demonstrate I have learned?", and "Do I think what I produced is awesome?"

Encourage learners to reflect on their growth and progress by reviewing the artifacts they have placed in their portfolios at various points during their educational journey.

Encourage agency-wide adoption of online portfolios that expand beyond a single year of use.

RELATED RESOURCE

How to Make Digital Portfolios (**bit.ly/inclusive365-90**)

Figure 90. A collection of learner artifacts created and housed in Seesaw.

ISTE STANDARDS FOR STUDENTS

1a, 1c, 4a, 6a, 6b, 6c, 6d

ISTE STANDARDS FOR EDUCATORS

5a, 6a, 6d

Creating Collaborative, Learner-Centered Rubrics Using Forms

Rubrics provide a structure that learners can use to evaluate to what extent their work meets the learning objectives. When rubrics are carefully aligned with learning outcomes, they communicate what mastery would look like for learners. They are a critical means of providing objective feedback. Invite learners to collaborate on the creation of a rubric based on what they understand about a mastery objective and the task. When learners participate in the design and determine their own criteria for meeting learning goals, they are more invested in their own success. Using digital forms to disseminate a rubric to learners and record observations provides a uniform way to consolidate data and share feedback. Many digital forms tools allow collected data to be transferred to a spreadsheet. Using a corresponding spreadsheet, learners can then see feedback from multiple assessors.

INCLUSIVE USES

Clear expectations and targets help individuals pinpoint learning objectives. Rubrics provide a visual way to organize and communicate these expectations and targets. Although all learners likely benefit from having agreed-upon and defined expectations and targets, some might require them to make sense of what might otherwise seem like arbitrary feedback. Individuals learning to regulate emotions and build social skills might find the objectivity of a rubric useful in realizing the feedback being provided is meant as formative guidance.

SAMPLE TOOLS

Google Forms allows educators to transfer all data collected to a Google Sheet for easy grading. It also allows educators to provide learners with feedback via Google Drive or Google Classroom (**google.com/forms**).

Microsoft Forms allows educators to transfer all data to Excel for easy grading. It also allows educators to provide learners with feedback via a PDF, Google Classroom, or MS Teams (**forms.office.com**).

EXTENSION OPPORTUNITY

Invite learners to evaluate the effectiveness of their own created rubrics.

RELATED RESOURCES

What Are Rubrics and Why Are They Important? (**bit.ly/inclusive365-91a**)

How and Why to Move Toward Student-Designed Rubrics (**bit.ly/inclusive365-91b**)

The Trouble with Rubrics (**bit.ly/inclusive365-91c**)

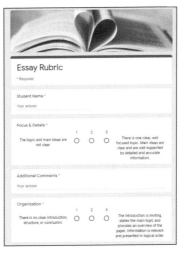

Figure 91. A grading rubric in Google Forms.

ISTE STANDARDS FOR STUDENTS
1c

ISTE STANDARDS FOR EDUCATORS
6a,7a, 7b, 7c

Using Forms for Feedback

Providing learner feedback is one of the top ten influences on learner achievement, according to education researcher John Hattie (2011). When feedback is provided as part of the formative assessment process, learners can act on the feedback to make changes, and educators can see how their instruction needs to change to support the learner. Using a digital form to collect and share feedback allows for educators and learners both to engage in a feedback loop that is meaningful and quick, and can be customized to meet the specific needs of a specific learner. A feedback form can be particularly effective for tasks in which there is not a written product that allows for digital comments, such as an oral presentation, a video recording, or a physical piece of artwork. A digital feedback form can be used multiple times to provide feedback to the same learner. The feedback informs the learner of what they are doing well and what they need to improve. With automatic data generated by forms, the learner and educator can track the effect of the feedback over time.

INCLUSIVE USES

Using forms allows educators to send personalized feedback to learners in a digital format that can be used with any accessibility tools that the learner typically uses, including text-to-speech. Educators can also include symbols, icons, audio, or even video in their feedback.

SAMPLE TOOL

Google Forms and Microsoft 365 Forms both allow educators to create custom forms that can be disseminated to learners (**docs.google.com/forms** and **forms.office.com**).

EXTENSION OPPORTUNITIES

Utilize themed feedback forms, such as a Glow and Grow, for peer to peer feedback (**bit.ly/inlusive365-92a**).

Invite learners to use forms to provide feedback to educators on the impact of a lesson or other learning experiences.

RELATED RESOURCE

John Hattie in Sutton, Hornsey, & Douglas (2011), "Feedback: The communication of praise, criticism, and advice" (**bit.ly/inlusive365-92b**)

Figure 92. A Glow and Grow form created in Google Forms.

ISTE STANDARDS FOR STUDENTS
1a, 1b, 1c

ISTE STANDARDS FOR EDUCATORS
6a, 7b

Providing Audio Feedback to Promote Achievement

Providing effective feedback is critical to the learning process. Effective feedback is among the most powerful influences on how people learn (Hattie, 2012). Meaningful feedback enhances learning and achievement. Educators often provide learners with handwritten or typed comments as feedback. An additional modality is to provide audio commentary, in which the learner hears the educator's voice, which can provide more authentic feedback—such as intonation, which contributes meaning.

INCLUSIVE USES

Learners may receive more meaningful feedback from audio comments than written comments. With audio comments, the learner hears the authentic voice of the person reviewing their work, including tone of voice. It may be easier for educators to scaffold and provide specific support with audio comments. Some learners may prefer audio feedback as a motivational or engaging tool. Learners who are working on decoding text may struggle with written feedback; audio comments can be replayed as often as needed.

SAMPLE TOOLS

The Voice Note feature of the premium version of the Read&Write for Chrome extension is always free for educators (**bit.ly/inclusive365-93a**).

OneNote Class Notebooks, part of Office 365, allows for embedded audio recording for learner feedback (**onenote.com/classnotebook**).

Kaizena is an add-on for Google Docs and Google Slides. It allows for the recording of audio (**bit.ly/inclusive365-93b**).

EXTENSION OPPORTUNITY

Invite learners to use audio to ask questions to educators, provide feedback to peers, or leave themselves a reminder.

RELATED RESOURCES

5 Research-Based Tips for Providing Students with Meaningful Feedback (**bit.ly/inclusive365-93c**)

Hattie, John (2012). *Visible Learning for Teachers: Maximizing impact on learning.* Taylor & Francis.

Making Time for Voice Recordings (**bit.ly/inclusive365-93d**)

Provide Written, Audio, or Video Feedback in OneNote (**bit.ly/inclusive365-93e**)

Figure 93. The Voice Note tool in TextHelp's Read&Write for Google.

ISTE STANDARDS FOR STUDENTS
1a, 1b, 1c

ISTE STANDARDS FOR EDUCATORS
5a, 5b, 6a, 7a, 7b

STRATEGY 94

Reflecting on Learning Using 3-2-1

The 3-2-1 strategy helps promote reflection during and at the conclusion of a learning experience by providing a structure for learners to summarize, organize, and brainstorm how they are going to apply and integrate what they are learning. Although variations exist, one application of the strategy invites participants to reflect and document three new things they discovered or learned during the event or experience, followed by two things they found interesting or intriguing. Then, the participants are invited to document one follow-up or clarifying question or action step they plan to take related to the learning. Learners and educators alike can use this structured reflection strategy throughout and at the end of a learning experience to organize thoughts and takeaways.

INCLUSIVE USES

Learners working to maintain structure for how they organize thoughts may find that completing a template using this format helps them make sense of the content, internalize what they are learning, and actualize next steps.

SAMPLE TOOLS

Sample 3-2-1 Reflection Template
(**bit.ly/inclusive365-94a**)

Sample 3-2-1 Reflection Template
(**bit.ly/inclusive365-94b**)

EXTENSION OPPORTUNITIES

Invite learners and/or educators to complete a 3-2-1 template collaboratively as part of a small group discussion on a given topic.

Invite learners and/or educators to develop their own 3-2-1 template to provide to participants to reflect on a learning experience they've designed.

Create a shared 3-2-1 template using a survey or polling tool, such as Google Forms, to collect and analyze group responses, providing formative information to help shape and design future learning experiences.

RELATED RESOURCE

The Teacher Toolkit: 3-2-1
(**bit.ly/inclusive365-94c**)

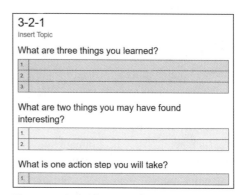

Figure 94. A sample 3-2-1 reflection template made in Google Docs.

ISTE STANDARDS FOR STUDENTS

1a, 1b, 1c

ISTE STANDARDS FOR EDUCATORS

2a, 4a, 5c, 6a, 7a, 7b, 7c

Preparing for Transitions with Reflections

Learners undergo a variety of transitions during their academic years. Allow learners to reflect on their current experience before transitioning to the next learning environment. Learners can then compare and reflect on the similarities and differences from when they entered and when they are about to exit to a new opportunity. Learners could analyze what changes have occurred and how those changes demonstrate growth. Learners can use a variety of multimedia tools to help tap into their creativity, originality, and personalities.

INCLUSIVE USES

Multimedia resources promote universal design for learning and allow learners choices for content creation. They can use photos, videos, text, audio, and music to create a more engaging and entertaining product to record their reflections.

SAMPLE TOOLS

Animoto is a free video creation tool (**animoto.com**).

BookCreator is a full-featured book creation tool. Created books can be published on the web (**bookcreator.com**).

EXTENSION OPPORTUNITIES

Invite learners to share their artifacts with one another to discuss their similarities and differences and compare their growth over time.

Invite learners to use cartoon avatars, stickers, or emojis to represent people, animals, objects, or places if actual pictures are not available, or if avatars, stickers, and emojis are preferred by the individual.

RELATED RESOURCES

Animoto Tutorial (**bit.ly/inclusive365-95a**)

Book Creator Tutorial (**bit.ly/inclusive365-95b**)

Figure 95. The title page from a reflections book created using Book Creator.

ISTE STANDARDS FOR STUDENTS
6a, 6b, 6d

ISTE STANDARDS FOR EDUCATORS
3b, 5a, 5b, 5c, 6a

STRATEGY 96

Helping Families Access Learning Resources with QR Codes

QR (Quick Response) codes provide a quick and simple way to access to files, websites, and pretty much anything else that can be stored digitally online. Educators and learners can use QR codes to share access to these digital resources with anyone who has a smartphone or tablet and internet connection. When used in distance learning, educators and learners can use a QR code to provide family member access to a file or website without having to know the URL, as long as they have access to a device on which to scan the QR code. This is especially helpful when an educator is sharing links and resources within a slide deck with an audience who may not easily be able to type in a URL. Participants point their device camera at the QR code, and the file or website opens up on their device.

INCLUSIVE USES

QR codes decrease the cognitive and fine motor demand of learners and families, who can simply scan the code with their smartphone or tablet camera to access a resource. QR codes also simplify and increase equitable access to digital resources: just print one or more QR codes on paper materials such as postcards or newsletters mailed to a family. With QR codes, they do not need to login to an email or learning management system to access the digital materials.

SAMPLE TOOL

QR Code Monkey makes it easy to create QR codes that can then be downloaded and pasted into a document. QR Code Monkey also allows for custom colors and logos to be added to any QR code (**qrcode-monkey.com**).

EXTENSION OPPORTUNITIES

Invite learners to share their work with others using a custom-designed QR code.

Provide participants in a professional learning experience with QR codes (like we have in this book) for easy access to slide decks, resources, or digital handouts.

RELATED RESOURCE

8 Ways I Make Learning Fun by Using QR Codes in the Classroom (**bit.ly/inclusive365-96**)

Figure 96. An example of a custom QR Code.

ISTE STANDARDS FOR STUDENTS
1b, 1c, 7a

ISTE STANDARDS FOR EDUCATORS
2b, 4d

Building a Brand with Logo Generation

The world competes for attention in a dizzying array of media. Logos help to capture that attention and provide a way for people to instantly recognize and relate to a brand. Learners working to create meaningful products meant to solve authentic problems may find branding an initiative with a logo helps the potential audience immediately recognize it. For example, if a group of learners were working on producing products like videos, posters, T-shirts, and brochures to "Save The Bees," they might find that creating a logo and placing it on the products unifies the initiative for people experiencing the products out in the community. Logos can be placed strategically on products to illustrate key points in text, on pertinent slides in a multimedia presentation, or as the centerpiece of podcast art.

Additionally, logos can be personal, used to highlight an individual's brand. The logo can be used to call attention to the body of work a learner has produced as that learner continues to add to a portfolio.

INCLUSIVE USES

Learners that are working on improving their writing may find that creating a logo can be used to reflect and enhance what they are trying to express. Creating a logo related to any project, including anything with written text, forces a learner to identify the key aspects they are trying to communicate.

SAMPLE TOOLS

Hipster Logo Generator is a free website that lets users design and download a basic black and white logo with shapes and text (**hipsterlogogenerator.com**).

Free Logo Design is a logo generator with many samples that can be customized (**freelogodesign.org**).

Assembly from Pixite Apps is a free logo generator for iOS (**pixiteapps.com/assembly**).

EXTENSION OPPORTUNITY

As a professional educator working to share ideas, thoughts, strategies, knowledge, and passions, do you have a logo to match your brand?

RELATED RESOURCE

How to Design a Logo: The Ultimate Guide (**bit.ly/inclusive365-97**)

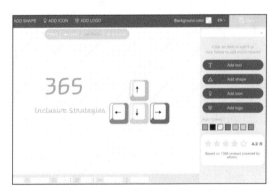

Figure 97. A logo generated using Free Logo Design.

ISTE STANDARDS FOR STUDENTS
2a, 2c, 4c. 6b, 6d

ISTE STANDARDS FOR EDUCATORS
3a, 3b, 4b, 5a, 6b

STRATEGY 98

Assessing a Learner's Reading Mindset

Self-selected reading based on topics of interest is a highly impactful way to promote joyful reading and reading comprehension. Using an inventory helps educators identify how learners feel about reading and what topics are of interest. The information obtained by completing the inventory guides reading instruction and support. Also, educators can use the inventory to assess changes over time.

INCLUSIVE USES

An online digital inventory includes text-to-speech for learners who need or prefer it. Learners respond by using emojis (feelings or thumbs up/down), which minimizes the amount of independent reading needed to provide accurate results.

SAMPLE TOOL

Reading Mindset Snapshot is a survey-style inventory that assesses learner attitudes about reading, and areas of interest (**bit.ly/inclusive365-98a**).

EXTENSION OPPORTUNITIES

Invite learners to create their own list of interests they uncovered while participating in the Reading Mindset Snapshot. Creating a personal list might help reframe how they see themselves as learners and readers.

Encourage learners to complete the Reading Mindset Snapshot periodically to reflect on changes.

RELATED RESOURCES

How To: The Reading Mindset
(**bit.ly/inclusive365-98b**)

Finding Their Story: Access Matters
(**bit.ly/inclusive365-98c**)

Figure 98. Gauging a learner's reading mindset with emojis.

ISTE STANDARDS FOR STUDENTS
1a, 3c, 5b

ISTE STANDARDS FOR EDUCATORS
1a, 5a, 6a, 6b

Teaching the Forty-Four Phonemes in the English Language Using Video

Teaching phonemic awareness is one of the five basic components of reading remediation, along with phonics, vocabulary, fluency, and reading comprehension. Phonemic awareness focuses on the sounds within words. It is considered one of the first steps in the development of reading skills. It is an auditory skill, and intact phonemic awareness is a strong predictor of early success with reading. Videos with music and movement help learners by repeatedly hearing the sounds paired with the orthographic representation. Learners can also pause and repeatedly practice the sounds that are challenging for them to produce.

INCLUSIVE USES

Learning new skills with music enhances memory and retention. Using videos that include song and hand signs provides a multisensory method to learn phonemic awareness.

SAMPLE TOOLS

The "44 Phonemes" video teaches how to pronounce each individual phoneme correctly (**bit.ly/inclusive365-99a**).

"Interactive Phonics Song with Hand Motions" is a video that teaches letter sounds combined with hand motions to get learners moving. (**bit.ly/inclusive365-99b**).

EXTENSION OPPORTUNITY

Invite learners to create their own songs that include vowel sounds and challenging consonants.

RELATED RESOURCE

Phonemic Awareness: Concepts and Research (**bit.ly/inclusive365-99c**)

Figure 99. Examples of videos demonstrating phonemic awareness.

ISTE STANDARDS FOR STUDENTS

1c

ISTE STANDARDS FOR EDUCATORS

5a, 6b

STRATEGY 100

Simulating Dyslexia Experiences

Educators may better understand and appreciate what actions and steps they can take to support the learning of individuals with dyslexia when they explore simulations. Educators can intentionally work to create learning environments and experiences that help support these learners. Difficulties accessing text independently can be defeating, demoralizing, and frustrating for people with dyslexia. The opportunity to simulate the experience of dyslexia, however brief, raises awareness, sensitivity, and understanding for how best to craft educational experiences, as well as how to offer guidance and feedback.

Despite commonalities, it is important to recognize that characteristics of dyslexia vary from person to person. Simulations can raise general awareness, but there should be an understanding that the experience is not meant to be an exact replication of any one person's abilities.

INCLUSIVE USES

Learners with dyslexia or similar learning challenges that impact reading and writing abilities benefit from educators, peers, and family members having had the opportunity to simulate dyslexic experiences.

After experiencing through simulations the challenges learners with dyslexia face, educators who work in inclusive settings can prepare to support those learners more effectively in an inclusive environment.

SAMPLE TOOLS

Understood.org offers web-based simulation experiences (**bit.ly/inclusive365-100a**).

Experience what it may be like for someone with dyslexia with this quick Dyslexia Simulator (**bit.ly/inclusive365-100b**).

EXTENSION OPPORTUNITY

Encourage educators, peers, and parents to reflect on the simulation experiences, record responses, and discuss them in small groups.

RELATED RESOURCES

What Is It Like to Be Dyslexic? University Project–Dyslexia Simulation (**bit.ly/inclusive365-100c**)

Dyslexia for a Day–Writing Simulation (**bit.ly/inclusive365-100d**)

Figure 100. Learning about dyslexia using the Dyslexia Simulator from Understood.org.

ISTE STANDARDS FOR STUDENTS
3d, 6c

ISTE STANDARDS FOR EDUCATORS
2b, 3a, 5a, 5c

Designing Learning Spaces with Diversity in Mind

When designing learning spaces, it is essential to consider diversity in the artifacts represented in the environment. Consider the books, posters, objects, and other imagery in your learning space. Do they reflect different cultures, backgrounds, and experiences? Create a learning environment that allows learners to broaden their own understanding of cultures that are different from their own. Learners who are typically underrepresented in learning spaces will instead see themselves represented.

INCLUSIVE USES

Creating learning spaces that represent all learners speaks to the value of each individual. Learners want to see their cultural experiences reflected in their environment.

Filling bookshelves with books that represent diverse voices promotes awareness and empathy, qualities that are important life skills. Additionally, learners want to read about characters and historical figures that represent their own cultural experiences.

SAMPLE TOOLS

A Mighty Girl is a book curation website of more than four thousand "girl-empowering" titles. The Prejudice and Discrimination category includes more than sixteen hundred titles (**bit.ly/inclusive365-101a**).

Social Justice Books is a collection of multicultural and social justice books for elementary, young adult, and high school readers. (**socialjusticebooks.org**).

One World Posters offers beautiful posters representing a variety of cultures and diverse sayings (**bit.ly/inclusive365-101b**).

Lee and Low is the largest multicultural children's book publisher in the US (**leeandlow.com**).

EXTENSION OPPORTUNITY

Invite learners to record book reviews of books in the learning space that reflect cultures other than their own, using the FlipGrid Shorts tool. Place a QR code linking to the audio response at the front or back of the book.

RELATED RESOURCES

Guide for Selecting Anti-Bias Children's Books (**bit.ly/inclusive365-101c**)

Reading Diversity: A Tool for Selecting Diverse Texts (**bit.ly/inclusive365-101d**)

How to Create a Culturally-Responsive Bitmoji Classroom (**bit.ly/inclusive365-101e**)

Three Ways to Use Flipgrid Shorts (**bit.ly/inclusive365-101f**)

Figure 101. A bitmoji learning space designed with diversity in mind.

ISTE STANDARDS FOR STUDENTS
1b

ISTE STANDARDS FOR EDUCATORS
2b, 5b, 6a

Using Readable Fonts

Fun fonts on both digital and print learning materials as well as in decorations are very popular; you can find examples on Instagram and loads of educator-created fonts for sale on Teachers Pay Teachers. However, educators need to consider readability when creating materials and room decorations. Sans serif fonts are generally more readable than serif fonts (Rello and Baeza-Yates, 2013). Consider using fonts that are most easily read, such as Arial or Calibri. Further, these fonts can provide a model for proper letter formation, especially for young learners who may be looking to use the fonts around the room as a cue for their own handwriting.

INCLUSIVE USES

Those learning to read benefit from seeing highly readable fonts in the text in their environment. Learners practicing handwriting skills would benefit from materials that support consistent letter formation.

SAMPLE TOOLS

Teachers Pay Teachers has many fonts for sale and for free. Try searching for "easy to read fonts," "sans serif fonts," "dyslexia fonts," or "primary fonts" when looking for a font for resources (**teacherspayteachers.com**).

Extensis Fonts is a Chrome extension that provides access to the entire Google Font collection of more than nine hundred fonts in G Suite for Education. Sort by "handwriting," "sans serif fonts," or "serif fonts" (**bit.ly/inclusive365-102a**).

EXTENSION OPPORTUNITIES

Learning spaces can be both in-person and virtual. Consider both font and color choices and how they will appear on screen, as well as in print.

Invite learners to share the fonts they like best in their learning materials.

When learners are creating materials with text for authentic audiences, encourage them to use less stylized fonts.

RELATED RESOURCES

"Good Fonts for Dyslexia" by Rello and Baeza-Yates, 2013 (**bit.ly/inclusive365-102b**)

Formatting Font for Readability (**bit.ly/inclusive365-102c**)

TTP Jot is a sans serif font from Teachers Pay Teachers

Century Gothic is a commonly found sans serif font

Gill Sans Nova is also a sans serif font, but the lower case a maybe more difficult for readers

Figure 102. Examples of sans serif fonts.

ISTE STANDARDS FOR STUDENTS
6a, 6c, 6d

ISTE STANDARDS FOR EDUCATORS
5c

Stoking a Love of Reading with Ebooks and Audiobooks

Digital books and audiobooks provide two powerful options to engage learners in reading. Empowering learners to choose their own books also encourages a love of reading, and removing the barriers to accessing these materials promotes independence. Providing options helps learners read because they *want* to, not because they *have* to. Experiencing digital books and audiobooks does not have to be an expensive undertaking. There are free resources available to promote the love of reading.

INCLUSIVE USES

Learners may not be quick to pick up a book for pleasure reading, because they haven't been given opportunities to read for pleasure. Learners who have yet to master decoding or comprehension skills may prefer to read books using the supports built into digital tools.

SAMPLE TOOLS

Overdrive.com and the Libby app are available through most public libraries. Learners may already have access to this library and not even know it. Books include current popular selections as well as beloved favorites from all genres (**overdrive.com**).

Project Gutenberg is a web-based library with more than sixty thousand free ebooks available to read on the web or to download to your device. These are books that are in the public domain, which means they can be used without concerns of violating copyright laws. (**Gutenberg.org**).

LibriVox has over fourteen thousand audiobooks. Think of this as the audiobook version of Project Gutenberg, with classics that are in the public domain. Books can be listened to directly on the website, or MP3 files can be downloaded for offline listening (**Librivox.org**).

EXTENSION OPPORTUNITIES

Encourage learners to customize the settings and preferences for playback of audiobooks or visual representation of ebooks. Having choices in how they experience books can make the reading experience more personal and meaningful for learners.

Invite learners to volunteer to read an audiobook for Librivox. Learners could work on a solo or collaborative project to help bring to life a story for an authentic audience.

RELATED RESOURCES

Research Review on the Benefits of Audiobooks on Literacy (**bit.ly/inclusive365-103a**)

A.T.TIPSCAST Episode #87: Listening Station Strategies (**bit.ly/inclusive365-103b**)

Figure 103. OverDrive and the Libby App.

ISTE STANDARDS FOR STUDENTS

1c, 3c, 6a

ISTE STANDARDS FOR EDUCATORS

5a

STRATEGY 104

Creating DIY Audiobook Libraries

Great learning spaces are filled with shelves of books for eager readers to use during Drop Everything and Read (DEAR) time, and beyond. For readers whose decoding and comprehension skills are still developing, their independent reading skills may fall short of their auditory comprehension abilities. To instill a love for reading, the obstacles to success need to be removed. Print-based books prevalent in traditional learning spaces can be converted into read-aloud experiences. With a robust library of audiobook options, learners can have a choice to either read or listen to be transported to faraway imaginary lands through book adventures. The audio recording could be linked to each page of the print-based version of the book by the addition of a corresponding QR code on every page.

INCLUSIVE USES

Creating a read-aloud version of print books in the learning space library allows all learners to choose the access method that works for them, no matter their underlying reading skills. When creating QR codes for the book, a tactile cue such as Braille sticky dots can be added so that learners with visual impairments know where to place the QR code reader.

SAMPLE TOOL

Flipgrid Shorts has a QR code generator that can be used to record audio for each page of a book while instantly creating a corresponding QR code. Individuals who have already developed the skill of reading fluently can be asked to volunteer to create the audio recordings. The generated QR codes can be printed on label paper and affixed to the page. Learners can use a tablet camera to listen to human narration as they study the illustrations (**bit.ly/inclusive365-104a**).

EXTENSION OPPORTUNITY

As learners finish reading a book, invite them to record a book review and attach it to the front or back of the book using the same method employed to convert the book into audio format.

RELATED RESOURCES

Three Ways to Use Flipgrid Shorts (**bit.ly/inclusive365-104b**)

Is Listening to an Audiobook Cheating? (**bit.ly/inclusive365-104c**)

Do Audiobooks Get in the Way of Learning to Read? (**bit.ly/inclusive365-104d**)

Figure 104. A page of a book with the QR code affixed to provide alternative information. The QR code actually works—try it for yourself.

ISTE STANDARDS FOR STUDENTS
1b, 6a

ISTE STANDARDS FOR EDUCATORS
5a, 5b, 5c

Creating Customized Libraries of Audiobooks and Accessible eBooks

Learning spaces should be filled with a variety of books for readers of all abilities. Beginning readers are often guided to books identified as more appropriate for them based on their independent reading levels, which are often below their independent comprehension skills. Text that is not engaging may lead to a lack of enthusiasm for reading and the loss of exposure to imaginary lands, new information, and vocabulary. Educators can create a personalized library with each beginning reader, combining areas of interest with read-aloud supports to help instill excitement during independent reading. When learners are involved in book selections, they feel empowered and more motivated to persist with reading, which in turn helps improve reading comprehension, promotes continued vocabulary growth, and fosters a love of literature.

INCLUSIVE USES

Evolving readers who have ready access to a variety of read-aloud books of interest build stamina and vocabulary, which will be reflected in the quality of their writing. When a customized library is available, they can easily transition from one great book to another, all of which are personalized and aligned with their interests.

Learners experiencing anxiety about reading may find that listening to audio versions of texts promotes emotional well-being by removing the stress of decoding while trying to comprehend.

SAMPLE TOOLS

Google Docs, Sheets, or Keep can be used to create customized online libraries with hyperlinks to audiobooks or accessible ebooks.

Padlet can be used to collect links to audiobooks or accessible ebooks (**padlet.com**).

Epic Books includes a feature that allows educators to create a personalized reading list for each learner (**getepic.com**).

Kidlit and Storyline Online each provide audiobooks that can be added to a library (**bit.ly/inclusive365-105a, storylineonline.net**).

EXTENSION OPPORTUNITIES

Invite learners to create a rating system that corresponds to the texts they are experiencing. Once they've experienced a text, learners can leave feedback in the form of text or audio comments.

Invite learners to share their personalized libraries with one another (like playlists) to spread their love of the content they are reading.

RELATED RESOURCE

NCTE Statement on Independent Reading (**bit.ly/inclusive365-105b**)

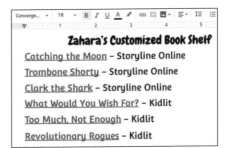

Figure 105. An audio library customized for a learner in Google Docs with embedded links.

ISTE STANDARDS FOR STUDENTS

1a, 1c, 3a

ISTE STANDARDS FOR EDUCATORS

5a, 5b, 6a, 6b

Selecting Appropriate Voice Options for Text-to-Speech

Access to audio and written text together enhances decoding skills beyond reading the text without audio support. However, some text-to-speech can sound unappealing using default settings. Some learners might find the voice to be too robotic or using a pitch that is either too high or too low. Setting the voice option can be a critical step to ensure effective learner support. Most text-to-speech tools provide a level of voice customization. Settings can include using different voices, customized pitch levels, and more to allow a user to find the right combination of preferred settings.

INCLUSIVE USES

Learners working to improve decoding and reading fluency skills may find text-to-speech beneficial. Using the text-to-speech feature of digital text enables learners to interact with written materials, regardless of reading ability. Learners can select specific words to have them spoken aloud or choose to have the entire page read aloud. Additional features include the ability to choose a voice, adjust the reading speed, and select the highlight color.

SAMPLE TOOLS

Users can customize voice options using the built-in accessibility feature of iOS devices by going to Settings > Accessibility > Spoken Content > Voices (**bit.ly/inclusive365-106a**).

Change the voices used on Chromebook by going to Settings > Advanced > Accessibility > Manage accessibility features > Text-to-Speech (**bit.ly/inclusive365-106b**).

EXTENSION OPPORTUNITIES

Invite learners to instruct a fellow learner or a family member on how to locate and activate a text-to-speech function.

Depending on how the digital text is created and coded, text-to-speech might be incapable of reading it. For example, a locked PDF or text rendered in an image may not be as easy to use with text-to-speech. Invite other educators to ensure the materials they are selecting have text that can be read aloud.

Invite learners to try different combinations of settings to select a preferred voice. Learners may find they enjoy several different combinations used at different times for different purposes. Invite learners to document their preferences for later reference, should anything happen to the device and a replacement is necessary.

RELATED RESOURCES

Text-to-Speech Technology: What It Is and How It Works (**bit.ly/inclusive365-106c**)

Does Use of Text-to-Speech and Related Read-Aloud Tools Improve Reading Comprehension for Students with Reading Disabilities? A Meta-Analysis (**bit.ly/inclusive365-106d**)

Figure 106. Voice options built into the iOS operating system.

ISTE STANDARDS FOR STUDENTS
1d, 3c

ISTE STANDARDS FOR EDUCATORS
1a, 2b, 4b, 5a, 7a

Adjusting the Playback Speed When Using Text-to-Speech

Some learners need or prefer to experience literature and other printed content by reading with their ears rather than or in addition to reading with their eyes. Both methods allow a learner to gain information from text and both are still forms of reading. Text-to-speech is a useful function built into the accessibility features of many contemporary technologies which allows a user to listen to text displayed (and sometimes hidden, such as with Alt Text on images) on the screen. The combination of audio and text enhances decoding skills. Learners may find the default settings of the playback speed are either too fast or too slow to meet their individual needs or preferences. Learners might consider adjusting the play-back speed to one that allows them to process the information at a rate at which they feel comfortable.

INCLUSIVE USES

Turning on the text-to-speech/speak selection feature of digital devices enables learners to interact with written materials, regardless of reading ability/preference. Adjusting and reflecting on the playback speed builds both operational competency and agency.

SAMPLE TOOL

IOS devices include text-to-speech features which allow for the adjustment of the playback speed of text-to-speech (**bit.ly/inclusive365-107a**).

EXTENSION OPPORTUNITIES

Invite learners to instruct a peer or a family member on how to locate and adjust the play-back speed of text-to-speech on a device they use.

Invite learners to listen to any text read aloud at the absolute fastest speed and then again at the absolute slowest speed and reflect on what they've heard. Many learners find it fun to hear the text read aloud quickly and then slowly. Then, once they've had a chance to experiment and play with the different speeds, invite them to select a speed that would work for them.

RELATED RESOURCES

Text-To-Speech Technology: What It Is And How It Works (**bit.ly/inclusive365-107b**)

Does Use of Text-to-Speech and Related Read-Aloud Tools Improve Reading Comprehension for Students with Reading Disabilities? A Meta-Analysis (**bit.ly/inclusive365-107c**)

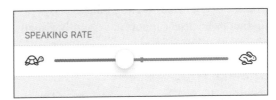

Figure 107. Voice speed setting in iOS showing the sliding button for adjusting the rate of speed.

ISTE STANDARDS FOR STUDENTS

1d, 3c

ISTE STANDARDS FOR EDUCATORS

1a, 2b, 4b, 5a, 7a

STRATEGY 108

Choosing High-Contrast Colors When Using Dual Highlighting in Text-to-Speech

Text-to-speech is a useful function built into the accessibility features of many contemporary technologies. It allows the learner to listen to text displayed (and sometimes hidden) on the screen. One of the features of many of these tools is the ability to highlight spoken text in dual colors. Typically, this means setting one color for the current sentence or paragraph and a different color for the word being spoken aloud. Access to audio and written text together enhances decoding skills beyond reading written materials without audio support. The use of two-color highlights can improve the visual distinction of the current word being read aloud to the learner.

INCLUSIVE USES

The use of dual-color highlighting assists learners who need support to smoothly visually track across lines of text.

SAMPLE TOOL

Read&Write for Chrome is a browser extension that provides customized dual-color high-lighting support for reading materials (**bit.ly/inclusive365-108a**).

EXTENSION OPPORTUNITY

Invite learners to explore the color options available in the text-to-speech tool of choice and customize the visual display to best support their reading.

RELATED RESOURCES

Text-to-Speech Technology: What It Is And How It Works (**bit.ly/inclusive365-108b**)

Does Use of Text-to-Speech and Related Read-Aloud Tools Improve Reading Comprehension for Students with Reading Disabilities? A Meta-Analysis (**bit.ly/inclusive365-108c**)

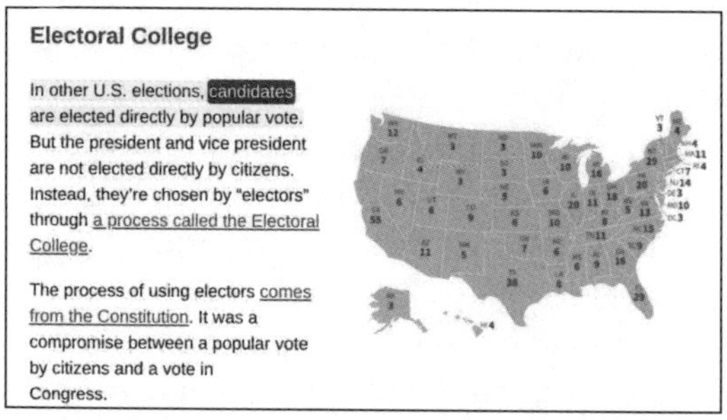

Electoral College

In other U.S. elections, candidates are elected directly by popular vote. But the president and vice president are not elected directly by citizens. Instead, they're chosen by "electors" through a process called the Electoral College.

The process of using electors comes from the Constitution. It was a compromise between a popular vote by citizens and a vote in Congress.

Figure 108. Dual-color highlight support for reading material shows sentences in yellow and the spoken word in blue.

ISTE STANDARDS FOR LEARNERS
1d, 3c

ISTE STANDARDS FOR EDUCATORS
1a, 2b, 4b, 5a, 7a

Online Decoding Instruction Using Shared Letter Tiles

Magnetic letter tiles are a common instructional tool for systematic phonics instruction. Manipulating and sequencing the letter tiles in response to instruction provides a kinesthetic means to enhance learning. A digital option provides an additional way to create a synchronous tile experience where both learners and educators work from the same online tool simultaneously. Both learner and educator can move the tiles to form words and sentences.

INCLUSIVE USES

Learners who have difficulties controlling fine motor movements may find manipulating digital tiles more accessible, using either touch technology, mouse control, or customized cursor control options. Adapting color choices and the size of tiles may be useful for learners who have organic visual impairments, visual processing impairments, or fine motor difficulties.

SAMPLE TOOLS

Jamboard from Google is an interactive, online whiteboard. When shared with editing capabilities, it can be used for synchronous or asynchronous learning experiences (**edu.google.com/products/jamboard**).

Microsoft Whiteboard is an interactive, online whiteboard that learners and educators can use to provide both synchronous and asynchronous learning experiences (**bit.ly/inclusive365-109a**).

EXTENSION OPPORTUNITY

Encourage learners to create their own letter and word boards with images of the alphabet retrieved from Google Search, or to create their own alphabet images and share with peers.

RELATED RESOURCES

Research-Based Methods of Phonics Instruction, Grades K–3 (**bit.ly/inclusive365-109b**)

Enhancing Structured Literacy Instruction with Educational Technology (**bit.ly/inclusive365-109c**)

Figure 109. Letter tiles created in Jamboard.

ISTE STANDARDS FOR STUDENTS

1c, 6a

ISTE STANDARDS FOR EDUCATORS

5a, 5b, 5c, 6a, 6b

Learning Letters and Words Using Augmented Reality

Learners can explore letters and words using augmented reality (AR). AR applications can engage learners in a variety of ways, including by showing a letter and providing a 3D illustration or video of a representation of a word or object starting with that letter; or by giving the opportunity to catch letters with their device to spell a word.

INCLUSIVE USES

Engage and maintain the engagement of learners who are developing skills to regulate attention by using AR.

Some learners might find exploring letters using AR to be an effective mode for remembering letter sounds and usage.

SAMPLE TOOLS

AR Flashcards is an iOS and Android AR application that allows a user to hover over flashcards of letters. Each letter presents a 3D object (**arflashcards.com**).

Catchy Words is an iOS application that prompts learners to find letters floating in a space and put them together to form a word (**bit.ly/inclusive365-110a**).

EXTENSION OPPORTUNITY

Using an AR application, letters could be hidden around different learning spaces. Learners then use the AR application to find the letters, which then display the corresponding objects.

RELATED RESOURCE

Learning Words Using Augmented Reality (**bit.ly/inclusive365-110b**)

Figure 110. Hovering a mobile device over the screen provides added AR animals to support letter recognition.

ISTE STANDARDS FOR STUDENTS

1a, 1b, 1c, 1d, 4b, 4c

ISTE STANDARDS FOR EDUCATORS

2b, 5a, 5c, 6b

Coding to Develop Early Literacy Skills

Computer science skills are almost as critical for learners as reading, writing, and mathematics skills. Coding is a universal language that crosses geographic boundaries. Most coding programs use words that match sight word lists or align with early decoding skills. Young learners can build programs that develop letter recognition, phonemic awareness skills, sight word recognition, and other early literacy skills. These programs can then be shared with other learners to build vocabulary or practice reading.

INCLUSIVE USES

With easily accessible online coding programs and apps, educators can challenge learners with the task of using code to create an interactive program meant to teach other learners relevant content that correlates to early reading programs. Just as they presume anyone can learn to read, educators can start with the presumption that anyone can learn to code. Using coding software, learners can be empowered to work together in collaborative groups to develop code to address an authentic problem, such as reinforcing the spelling of a word, teaching the proper use of punctuation, or illustrating the aspects of a story element.

SAMPLE TOOLS

Scratch is a free coding platform made available by the Massachusetts Institute of Technology which uses interlocking blocks to create code. Scratch also provides a virtual space for finding and sharing programs (**scratch.com**).

ScratchJr is a free coding tool that provides learners between the ages of five and seven the ability to create their own interactive programs. Users snap together graphical programming blocks to make items in the program perform various functions such as singing and running (**scratchjr.org**).

EXTENSION OPPORTUNITY

Invite learners to create a program to teach the meaning of words that appear frequently on the devices of learners who use augmentative or alternative communication. The vocabulary used on these devices is often very similar to early sight word lists. Developing a program to practice the meaning of a word not only helps the learner using the communication device but also helps the programmer better remember the spelling and proper use of the word.

RELATED RESOURCES

Get with the Programming (**bit.ly/inclusive365-111a**)

GO! (**bit.ly/inclusive365-111b**)

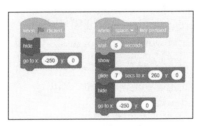

Figure 111a. An example of block coding used to create the word GO!

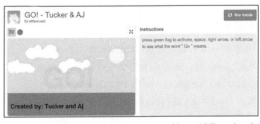

Figure 111b. This program was created by middle-school-aged learners to teach the word Go to younger learners.

ISTE STANDARDS FOR STUDENTS
4a, 4b, 4c, 5c, 5d, 7a, 7b, 7c, 7d

ISTE STANDARDS FOR EDUCATORS
3a, 4c, 5a, 5b, 5c, 6b, 6c, 6d

Making Digital Words into Phonics Experiences

"Making Words" is a strategy (Cunningham and Hall, 2008) designed to teach emergent readers to look for and use common spelling patterns to decode and spell words. Often used with letter cards, white boards, magnetic letters, or letter tiles, it is also easy to replicate this strategy with digital tools, including magnetic letter apps, virtual whiteboards, and digital sticky notes.

Most often the experience begins with a set of individual letters that, when combined, form a single word, such as a learner's name, a word that has a specific word family or rhyme, or a word from a curriculum unit. According to Erickson and Koppenhaver (2020), the three components of a Making Words lesson are:

1. Students use the letters provided to build as many different words as possible, starting with two-letter words and progressing to the final word using all the letters.

2. Students sort the words built to identify spelling patterns.

3. Students transfer learning by using the words they have made to spell new words with similar patterns.

INCLUSIVE USES

Text-to-speech can provide support to emerging readers, depending on the digital tool used. Learners with motor impairments may find digital tools easier to manipulate than physical cards or pencil and paper tasks. Other learners may simply find the digital version more engaging.

SAMPLE TOOLS

Jamboard (iOS, Android, and a part of Google Suite) and MS Whiteboard (on the web and on iOS) are both digital whiteboard tools that allow for collaboration. Learners can interact with letters by moving digital sticky notes, or can draw their own letters using the pen (**edu.google.com/products/jamboard**).

Talking Magnetic Alphabet is an iOS app that looks and functions much like a traditional magnetic letter set; however, it also provides text-to-speech for individual letters, the sounds of letter combinations, and the sounds of complete words as they are made (**bit.ly/inclusive365-112**).

EXTENSION OPPORTUNITY

Invite learners to use additional letters and make more words with the same rhyme or word ending that they made with the initial set of letters.

RELATED RESOURCE

Comprehensive Literacy Instruction for All: Teaching Students with Significant Disabilities to Read and Write, Erickson, K. and Koppenhaver, D. 2020.

Figure 112. A "Making Words" experience using the Magnetic Board iOS app.

ISTE STANDARDS FOR STUDENTS
1b, 4a, 5c, 6a

ISTE STANDARDS FOR EDUCATORS
2b, 4b, 5a, 6a, 7a

Teaching Reading with 3D Printed Letters and Words

Many learning environments and public libraries have 3D printers. 3D representations of sight words can be printed to help learners learn to read and spell. Individual letters can be printed to help learners put together novel words and explore how they are spelled. Individual words can be printed to help learners more immediately recognize sight words. Whole printed 3D words in different colors and with different textures to represent different parts of speech help provide correlations and differentiations between words and how they are used.

INCLUSIVE USES

Although any learner might benefit from using tactile letters, learners with visual impairments might particularly find 3D printed letters useful in learning the alphabet, letter formation, and spelling. Learners who are managing the integration of different sensory stimuli benefit from a multimodal approach to learning letters by combining auditory, visual, tactile, and kinesthetic information to help them master both the skill of sensory regulation while simultaneously learning the letters of the alphabet.

3D words and symbols are often used as a methodology to provide augmentative/alternative communication for learners with multiple sensory impairments who do not primarily use verbal speech. Learners who are both blind and deaf might indeed find that the presentation of 3D printed words in a consistent location can help them learn how and when the words are used. Providing the 3D printed words with corresponding symbols to all learners can help provide any learner with a memorable way to learn sight words.

SAMPLE TOOLS

Thingiverse allows users to find and share files for objects that can be 3D printed (**bit.ly/inclusive365-113a**).

Tinkercad allows users to create 3D objects (**tinkercad.com**).

EXTENSION OPPORTUNITIES

Learners can practice fine motor skills by painting the 3D letters.

Consider attaching magnets to the back of the 3D printed letters and placing them on a cookie sheet to provide a mobile yet stable work surface that can be angled to help improve accessibility.

Invite learners to create 3D letters or words for peers with complex sensory needs. Authentic opportunities to solve problems by making tangible objects that assist real people provide higher levels of engagement.

RELATED RESOURCE

Letters & Numbers (**bit.ly/inclusive365-113**)

Figure 113. 3D printed letters to used to create a sight word.

ISTE STANDARDS FOR STUDENTS

1a, 1b, 1c

ISTE STANDARDS FOR EDUCATORS

5a, 6b, 6d, 7a

Digital Finger Tracking for Beginning Readers

When reading, learners use their vision to smoothly track across the page, from word to word and line to line. Efficient eye tracking is necessary for effective reading so that learners maintain their place, not skipping words or lines. Beginning readers often use their finger and point to each word to focus their eyes on the words they are working to decode. Digital technologies allow the emerging reader to finger read text while benefiting from the additional scaffolded supports available with the technology.

INCLUSIVE USES

For emerging readers, smoothly scanning across lines of text in a left to right manner can be challenging. Providing finger tracking technologies for reading combined with text-to-speech tools supports the development of reading skills. Tools that include finger reading features bypass eye-tracking and visual convergence issues that interfere with independent reading.

SAMPLE TOOL

MDA Avaz Reader for Dyslexia is an iOS app that develops reading skills with any print book. Take pictures of the book pages and use the finger reading and text-to-speech features to promote independence (**dyslexiareader.com**).

EXTENSION OPPORTUNITY

Encourage learners to convert paper books into a digital library within the app so that the books are available for all learners in the learning space.

RELATED RESOURCES

Avaz Reader Helps Children with Dyslexia Read at Their Own Pace (**bit.ly/inclusive365-114a**)

Finger Tracking for At-Risk Readers (**bit.ly/inclusive365-114b**).

Figure 114. The pencil icon shown when finger reading across each line in a book.

ISTE STANDARDS FOR STUDENTS
1a, 1b, 1d, 6a

ISTE STANDARDS FOR EDUCATORS
2b, 5a, 5b, 5c, 6a, 6b

Teaching Sight Words Using Augmentative and Alternative Communication

Learners over the age of three who do not use verbal speech as their primary form of expression should be provided with an alternative or augmentative form of communication (AAC). Most forms of AAC use high frequency words (known as core words). Words are typically paired with symbols and arranged strategically with colors matching the part of speech (ex. words with yellow backgrounds are pronouns). There is a significant overlap when comparing lists of these high frequency words and early sight words. For this reason, AAC can support the learning of sight words for learners who don't necessarily require AAC for expression.

INCLUSIVE USES

Those learning to use AAC for expression benefit when others consistently model usage of words on the AAC throughout the day. This strategy is called aided language stimulation, partner augmented input, or aided language input. The more opportunities learners have to experience the AAC system, the more familiar each becomes with where the words are, how they are used, and how they are spelled.

SAMPLE TOOLS

Nuvoice is software for Windows which allows for the emulation of a variety of AAC systems (**bit.ly/inclusive365-115a**).

Chat Editor is software for Windows which allows for the emulation of a variety of AAC systems (**bit.ly/inclusive365-115b**).

EXTENSION OPPORTUNITIES

Create a poster from the home page of an AAC system and display it as a sight word resource for everyone.

Use emulation software to display a working version of the AAC on an interactive whiteboard. Invite learners to take turns formulating sentences using the AAC in whole or small group experiences to increase familiarity with both the AAC system and the sight words.

Invite learners to put posters, stickers, or other versions of the AAC around the playground or other recreational areas (See Strategy 129).

RELATED RESOURCE

Twin Powers Unite! Teaching AAC Core & Dolch Sight Words (**bit.ly/inclusive365-115c**)

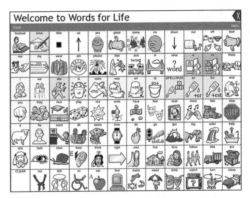

Figure 115. The home screen of the "Language Acquisition through Motor Planning: Words For Life" application for iOS devices.

ISTE STANDARDS FOR STUDENTS
1b, 1c, 1d, 6a, 6c, 7a, 7d

ISTE STANDARDS FOR EDUCATORS
2b, 3a, 4a, 5a, 5b, 5c, 6d

Recording Audio to Improve Reading Fluency

The more fluently one can read correlates to how well one can decode and comprehend in general. One strategy to improve reading fluency is for a learner to record himself reading a passage aloud. Educators and learners can analyze the audio recording to provide a number of quantitative measurements to gauge strengths and areas for improvement. Measurements can include the number of words read fluently, number of errors, and length of time to read the passage. Measurements can be charted to demonstrate improvement, which can build confidence that progress is occurring.

INCLUSIVE USES

Those learning to read may find recording audio passages and then analyzing and visualizing results useful for improving reading fluency.

SAMPLE TOOLS

Audacity is free, open source software that provides a visualization of the audio being recorded and demonstrates duration (**audacityteam.org**).

Fluency Tutor for Chrome is an extension that invites learners to record the passages they read. The audio recording is then analyzed and metrics are provided to educators, who can use that information to design personalized experiences to target errors (**bit.ly/inclusive365-116a**).

EXTENSION OPPORTUNITIES

Invite learners to compare two audio recordings recorded months apart. Recognition of improvement can be difficult to perceive when those improvements happen incrementally. Listening to an audio recording from the past and contrasting that reading with one made in the present can help build confidence in learners who feel like they are not improving, or who perceive themselves as not good at reading.

Invite parents or other caregivers of learners to listen to and compare audio recordings of past and current recordings to demonstrate evidence of progress.

RELATED RESOURCES

Digital Audio Recording to Improve Reading Fluency (**bit.ly/inclusive365-116b**)

A.T.TIPSCAST Episode #21: Audacity for Reading Fluency (**bit.ly/inclusive365-116c**)

Figure 116. A learner reading a book aloud while recording his voice.

ISTE STANDARDS FOR STUDENTS
1a, 1c

ISTE STANDARDS FOR EDUCATORS
2b, 4d, 5a, 5b, 5c, 6a, 7a

Increasing Reading Fluency with Automatic Scrolling

Typically, words are presented in a static way, where the reader scrolls, swipes, or otherwise navigates through the text. The reader's eyes are constantly shifting from left to right and then moving down to the next row of text. One way to practice reading fluency is to have the text auto-scroll. This changes the way the text is presented to the eyes of the reader. The eyes do not need to continuously shift downward to gather the next line of text. Instead, the text moves up to meet the user's gaze. The auto-scroll can be set at a specific rate using a teleprompting tool. The learner can repeatedly nudge up the speed to challenge themselves to read at an increased rate.

INCLUSIVE USES

Learners who are working on increasing their ability to read fluently may find autoscrolling helpful. Emergent readers working on decoding and reading fluency may find repeatedly practicing the same text at their own pace helps them gain proficiency.

SAMPLE TOOL

Speakflow is a free website that provides an auto-scrolling teleprompter feature. Users can paste any text into the website and adjust the text size and colors to match learner preferences (**speakflow.com**).

EXTENSION OPPORTUNITY

Invite learners to record each practice session to reflect on the number and types of mistakes made. Learners can chart both the rate and the number of mistakes to visualize progress. Comparing the audio and video footage of first attempts at reading a passage to later attempts can be both enlightening and a confidence builder.

RELATED RESOURCE

Teleprompter: How to Use One
(**bit.ly/inclusive365-117**)

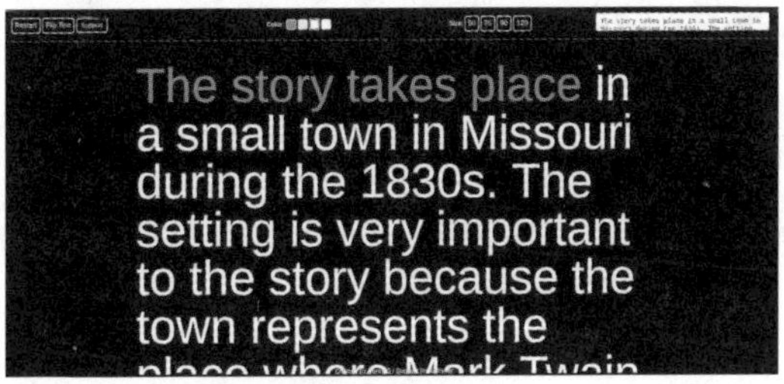

The story takes place in a small town in Missouri during the 1830s. The setting is very important to the story because the town represents the place where Mark Twain

Figure 117. Speakflow in action.

ISTE STANDARDS FOR STUDENTS

1c, 2a, 5b, 6a, 6c, 6d

ISTE STANDARDS FOR EDUCATORS

5a, 5b, 5c, 6a

Improving Reading Fluency with Sequential Single Word Display

When reading, there is typically a great deal of eye movement from left to right, repeated multiple times across lines of text. By streaming individual words in a body of text through a display window, eye movement is negligible, and readers can focus on single words displayed one at a time to increase reading fluency. The reading speed can be adjusted as the learner becomes more fluent.

INCLUSIVE USES

Learners working on improving reading skills may find visual tracking easier when presented with individual words in isolation at an appropriate rate of speed.

SAMPLE TOOL

Spritz, available as an iOS or Android app, or a bookmarklet, allows the user to input preferred content from any website and have it read back at a rate up to 1100 words per minute. Spritz technology highlights one letter in red within the midpoint of each word to maintain eye focus on that part of the screen and eliminate eye movement. The rate of reading speed is fully adjustable (**spritz.com**).

EXTENSION OPPORTUNITY

Encourage learners to track their words per minute over time and evaluate any changes in reading comprehension or reading enjoyment.

RELATED RESOURCES

Are You Ready to Change the Way You Read? (**bit.ly/inclusive365-118a**)

Speed Reading Apps: Can You Really Read a Novel in Your Lunch Hour? (**bit.ly/inclusive365-118b**)

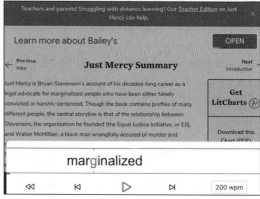

Figure 118. Spritz text showing a single-word focus and red-letter highlight.

ISTE STANDARDS FOR STUDENTS
1c, 1d, 6a

ISTE STANDARDS FOR EDUCATORS
5a, 5b, 5c, 6a

Using Text-to-Speech Silently to Improve Reading Fluency

Text-to-speech is a useful function of many operating systems, apps, and browser extensions. It allows the learner to listen to text displayed on the screen. Most text-to-speech tools provide dual highlighting (as described in Strategy 108), which colors the text being read aloud. One way a learner can practice reading fluency is to mute the sound and use the highlighting feature to provide a visual prompt as she independently reads through the passage. As the learner grows more fluent, the playback speed (as described in Strategy 103) can be adjusted to gradually increase the pace. This speed adjustment can also act as a quantifiable measure of progress by noting the settings at which the speed of the text-to-speech are placed.

INCLUSIVE USES

Learners can customize the pace of the highlighting to best meet their current independent reading speed by adjusting the text-to-speech tool reading speed. Learners working to improve reading fluency may find it useful to mute the audio and read aloud at the pace of the highlighted text.

SAMPLE TOOLS

Read&Write for Chrome is a browser extension that provides text-to-speech for Google Docs or online articles (**texthelp.com/en-us/products/read-write**).

Snap and Read Universal is a browser extension that provides text-to-speech support for web-based reading content (**snapandread.com**).

EXTENSION OPPORTUNITIES

Invite learners to adjust the reading speed of text-to-speech tools for read-along activities. Encourage them to explore different types of reading materials to see if the speed needs to be adjusted to support their reading ability.

Invite learners to record the settings they are using in text-to-speech and reflect on their improvements over time. When would they feel ready to increase reading speed?

RELATED RESOURCES

Text-to-Speech Technology: What It Is And How It Works (**bit.ly/inclusive365-119a**)

Does Use of Text-to-Speech and Related Read-Aloud Tools Improve Reading Comprehension for Students with Reading Disabilities? A Meta-Analysis (**bit.ly/inclusive365-119b**)

Figure 119. Adjust the speed of the text-to-speech function in Read&Write for Chrome to support reading fluency.

ISTE STANDARDS FOR LEARNERS
1d, 3c

ISTE STANDARDS FOR EDUCATORS
1a, 2b, 4b, 5a, 7a

STRATEGY 120

Building Background Knowledge By Reading an Article a Day

Background knowledge is essential to making connections and comprehending text. Deeper learning occurs when the learner is familiar with a topic and able to activate prior knowledge. When new information is introduced, learners attempt to make connections to what they already know to make sense of new ideas and experiences. This is particularly important for multilingual learners, who utilize background knowledge to unpack unfamiliar vocabulary and language structures. Learners can challenge themselves to read at least one article a day as a part of their language arts, science, or social studies instruction. Articles from digital subscription services geared toward school-aged learners provide easy access to flexible digital text. Reading articles that describe various perspectives, situations, circumstances, and cultures can be foundational to encouraging learners to become respectful global collaborators.

INCLUSIVE USES

Learners who are working to improve their reading or language comprehension skills may find reading one short article a day an appealing and manageable strategy to build background knowledge, expand vocabulary, and deepen connections to content.

SAMPLE TOOLS

ReadWorks was specifically designed as a ten-minute instructional tool to build background knowledge, stamina, and vocabulary (**bit.ly/inclusive365-120a**).

Newsela is a subscription service with curated, leveled, text articles on news and current events concerning the arts, government, the environment, and other topics (**newsela.com**).

EXTENSION OPPORTUNITIES

Invite learners to select from an array of articles based on their interests. Once they've read an article, invite learners to reflect on it or discuss it with peers who also chose the same article. This exercise could be done after reading individual articles or, if the articles are part of a theme, discussed once everyone has had a chance to read all of the articles.

Encourage learners to experience the content using text-to-speech, comment using text or audio annotations, and share insights and takeaways using audio or video recording tools.

RELATED RESOURCES

Building Background Knowledge (**bit.ly/inclusive365-120b**)

Introduction to ReadWorks Article-a-Day feature (**bit.ly/inclusive365-120c**)

Figure 120. An example of Article-A-Day options.

ISTE STANDARDS FOR STUDENTS
3b, 3c, 7d

ISTE STANDARDS FOR EDUCATORS
1a, 5a, 5b, 6a, 6b, 7a

Strengthening Comprehension Skills with Digital Dictionaries

Using a dictionary to look up the meaning of an unfamiliar vocabulary word is a long-standing but not particularly convenient reading comprehension strategy. Stopping the act of reading to grab a dictionary, look up the word. and then go back to the text is tedious and can lead to distraction and disrupted focus. Digital text has the advantage of providing instant access to a dictionary with a simple right-click of the mouse or a tap and hold on-screen. Depending on the situation, digital dictionaries may be available online, within an app, or a device may have a dictionary downloaded to it. Learners can find the meaning of a word and not lose their place in the text.

INCLUSIVE USES

Learners are more likely to stop to look up a word when all they have to do is click on it, rather than having to page through a print dictionary. Additionally, depending on the device, text-to-speech may also be available so that a learner can hear the pronunciation of the new word and hear the definition read aloud.

SAMPLE TOOLS

iOS has multiple built-in dictionaries, including the New Oxford American Dictionary, that are available in most applications and browsers.

Google Dictionary is a Chrome extension that allows learners to select a word and get a pop-up dictionary definition using Google's own dictionary tool (**bit.ly/inclusive365-121a**).

EXTENSION OPPORTUNITY

Invite learners to keep a list of new vocabulary with definitions in a spreadsheet, creating a searchable, easily-alphabetized personal dictionary.

RELATED RESOURCE

From Paper to Electronic Dictionaries, Evolving Dictionary Skills (**bit.ly/inclusive365-121b**)

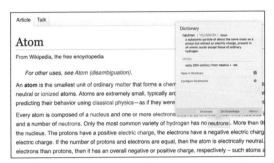

Figure 121. Viewing a word's definition using a digital dictionary.

ISTE STANDARDS FOR STUDENTS

1a, 3a

ISTE STANDARDS FOR EDUCATORS

5a, 5b, 6a

Summarizing Text to Support Comprehension

The sheer length of a text passage can be a barrier to comprehension. Long bodies of text can be intimidating and overwhelming for anyone, but especially so for individuals with learning challenges that impact decoding and comprehension. Automatic text summarizers allow a user to reduce the number of words in a given passage while attempting to maintain the integrity of the meaning. Teaching learners to use automatic text summarizers increases their independence when tackling rigorous and complex texts.

INCLUSIVE USES

Place text into a word summarizer to provide a shortened version of lengthy text-based content. Compare and contrast the results to ensure that the meaning remains intact. Present the shortened version as an option for learning the content. Invite learners to use a text summarizer as a pre-reading strategy to build understanding and then re-read the passage in the original format as part of a close reading experience.

SAMPLE TOOL

Textcompactor is a web-based tool that allows for text summaries. Drag the slider, or enter a number, to set the percentage of text to be kept in the summarization. Paste the summarized text into any shared document or file (**textcompactor.com**).

EXTENSION OPPORTUNITIES

Invite learners to use text summarizers on different types of passages and then compare or contrast the results. Learners can discuss the effects of a summarization tool when used with poetry versus a fact-based article.

Invite learners to perform their own summarization of a piece of text and compare their results with that of the automatic text summarizer. The process of summarizing text helps improve comprehension (Jones, 2007). The automatic text summarizer helps learners consider the accuracy of their human-generated summary.

RELATED RESOURCE

Automatic Summarising: The State of the Art (**bit.ly/inclusive365-122**)

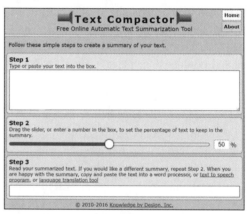

Figure 122. Text Compactor.

ISTE STANDARDS FOR STUDENTS
1a, 1d

ISTE STANDARDS FOR EDUCATORS
3b, 5a, 5b, 6a

Integrating Scaffolded Supports to Improve Reading Comprehension

Effective readers use active strategies to better comprehend text and sustain engagement when reading. These cognitive strategies include predicting, inferring, connecting, clarifying, visualizing, and analyzing the text. Some learners need explicit instruction to incorporate and implement these skills when reading complex text. Embedding supports throughout the text, including questions, notes, videos, and comments, provides scaffolded supports to build background knowledge, improve reading comprehension, and engage with the text.

INCLUSIVE USES

Provide customized scaffolded support to individual learners at the level that enhances their understanding and promotes success, which acknowledges learner variability. Learners who require or prefer text-to-speech support to assist in building decoding and reading fluency skills can use scaffolded supports while reading. All learners can benefit from the ability to add white space and change the font and font size to facilitate independent reading.

SAMPLE TOOL

Actively Learn is an online curriculum platform that allows educators to import their own text or use the thousands of fiction and non-fiction texts included in the platform. It is possible to embed questions, notes, videos, definitions, and comments to instill higher-order thinking and promote understanding (**activelylearn.com**).

EXTENSION OPPORTUNITY

Invite learners to engage in the collaborative interactive reading opportunities afforded through Actively Learn. Encourage learners to customize the visual presentation of text and background in all reading materials.

RELATED RESOURCE

The Limitations of Paper: How "Actively Learn" Enables New Teaching Opportunities for Literacy (**bit.ly/inclusive365-123**)

Figure 123. An assignments page from Actively Learn.

ISTE STANDARDS FOR STUDENTS

1a, 1b, 1c, 2c

ISTE STANDARDS FOR EDUCATORS

3b, 5a, 5b, 5c, 6a, 6b

Comprehending Vocabulary Using Animated GIFs

Repetitive moving pictures—animated GIFs—can support comprehension of vocabulary by providing a short visualization of the word in an engaging manner. The animations help learners visualize definitions in ways that a static image might not and can help with word recall and usage.

INCLUSIVE USES

Learners who have emerging vocabulary skills may find using GIFs to animate the word supports their ability to visualize, recall, and use the word in other contexts.

SAMPLE TOOLS

Giphy is a database of GIFs with hyperlinks that can be shared, embedded, or otherwise incorporated into websites, files, and other resources (**giphy.com**).

Giphy also provides people with a web-based resource that allows learners or educators to create their own GIFs (**giphy.com/create/gifmaker**).

EZ GIF Makers is a web-based tool for making GIFs (**ezgif.com/maker**).

EXTENSION OPPORTUNITIES

Develop a personalized library of GIFs to match the individual needs of each learner. The links can be housed in a multimedia slide deck with one word and GIF per slide.

Learners might find creating GIFs to teach others the meaning of a vocabulary word intriguing. The creation of a GIF can help learners better recall the word they are attempting to remember.

RELATED RESOURCES

Using GIFs to Make Learning Vocabulary Fun (**bit.ly/inclusive365-124a**)

Teach Verbs with Animated GIFs and Quizlet (**bit.ly/inclusive365-124b**)

Figure 124. Pictures illustrating the word tubing. Use the QR code on this page to watch the pictures come to life as an animated GIF.

ISTE STANDARDS FOR STUDENTS
1c, 3a, 3c, 6a, 6b, 6c, 6d, 7a

ISTE STANDARDS FOR EDUCATORS
3b, 5c, 6d

Improving Listening and Reading Comprehension Using Audio Versions of Literature

Literature provided in an audio format invites users to experience stories in a way that does not require the decoding of text. Research suggests listening to audio narratives also improves reading comprehension (Whittingham et al., 2013).

INCLUSIVE USES

Literature provided in audio formats allow learners who prefer or require audio support to experience and learn the concepts and themes embedded in the narrative without being dependent on decoding abilities.

When available, the text version of the literature can be provided in conjunction with the audio to provide a multi-model experience.

SAMPLE TOOLS

Librivox is an open-source library of audio versions of narratives in the public domain including multiple classic texts (**librivox.org**).

Cast of Wonders is a fantasy-themed podcast featuring short audio stories for young adults (**castofwonders.org**).

EXTENSION OPPORTUNITIES

Listening to narratives can provide learners with the opportunity to do other activities at the same time. Reading with one's ears provides a hands-free, eyes-free experience where learners can draw, write, or move around to sustain attention.

Families could be invited to listen to audio narratives together while in the car or sharing public transportation.

Local libraries often have audiobooks available for checkout. Invite learners to investigate available titles.

RELATED RESOURCES

Use of Audiobooks in a School Library and Positive Effects of Struggling Readers' Participation in a Library-Sponsored Audiobook Club (**bit.ly/inclusive365-125a**)

A.T.TIPSCAST Episode #127: Audio Stories for Secondary Students (**bit.ly/inclusive365-125b**)

Do Audiobooks Get in the Way of Learning to Read? (**bit.ly/inclusive365-125c**)

How Audiobooks Can Help Kids Who Struggle with Reading (**bit.ly/inclusive365-125d**)

Figure 125. A high-school aged learner listening to an audio story from Cast of Wonders on his smartphone.

ISTE STANDARDS FOR STUDENTS
1c, 3a, 3c, 7a

ISTE STANDARDS FOR EDUCATORS
3a, 3b, 4b, 4c, 6a, 6b

Self-Selecting Reading Materials

Learner self-selection of text can aid engagement, a key element for building the skills necessary for sustained reading. In addition to fostering intrinsic motivation, inviting learners to make choices promotes agency, confidence, and joyful learning. Providing opportunities to experience texts at a range of levels, including multi-leveled texts, invites autonomy with the option to try a challenging level or to simply enjoy an easier text.

INCLUSIVE USES

Learners who are evolving readers can choose texts they want to read, rather than having to limit themselves to texts that an educator has determined appropriate. Providing the same texts to learners at varied levels further empowers learners as they can engage in conversation about the same text with peers who may be reading at a different level. Learners can also use text-to-speech to listen to the text at the highest level to experience robust language and vocabulary.

SAMPLE TOOLS

Newsela and TweenTribune provide articles at multiple Lexile levels (**newsela.com, tweentribune.com**).

Readtopia has graphic novel texts adapted from classic books, such as *Anne of Green Gables* and *The Gold Bug*, with multiple versions of the same text at different reading levels (**learning-tools.donjohnston.com/product/readtopia**).

Common Lit has texts at different reading levels that are organized around a common topic or theme (**commonlit.org**).

EXTENSION OPPORTUNITIES

Invite learners to engage in literature circles or discussion groups around a text that is available at multiple reading levels or around a topic with a variety of leveled texts available.

For texts that allow comments, such as Newsela and TweenTribune, invite learners to read comments and leave their own.

If a learner has expressed difficulty reading a text because the reading level is too high, consider inviting that learner to search for an audio version or to use text-to-speech to listen.

RELATED RESOURCE

The Importance and Use of Student Self-Selected Literature to Reading Engagement in an Elementary Reading Curriculum (**bit.ly/ inclusive365-126**)

Figure 126a. Multiple Lexile levels for articles in TweenTribune.

Figure 126b. Multiple versions of the classic novel *Frankenstein* at different reading levels, from Readtopia.

ISTE STANDARDS FOR STUDENTS
1a, 1b, 7b

ISTE STANDARDS FOR EDUCATORS
2b, 5a

Diversifying Reading Materials

Learners want and deserve to see themselves and the greater diversity in the world around them represented in books and other learning materials. Research highlights the significant underrepresentation of many communities, including poor quality and quantity of existing literature about them (*School Library Journal*, 2019). Educators must ensure that underrepresented populations see themselves in their reading. Additionally, all learners should see diversity in what they read: to expand their world view, reduce bias, and discourage stereotyping. Resources should include texts that feature and celebrate the lives of diverse characters, cultures, and experiences—not ones that feature a token or stereotyped character.

INCLUSIVE USES

Ensuring that available physical and digital texts showcase diversity and are written by diverse authors is important in all learning spaces. As an educator, try to go beyond featuring books based on the celebration of the culture of the month; instead, include many books that feature individuals that represent different cultures, languages, abilities, genders, and sexual orientations.

SAMPLE TOOLS

Unite for Literacy provides digital fiction and non-fiction picture books in multiple languages that feature people from diverse cultures (**uniteforliteracy.com**).

Epic Books features thousands of books for preschool- through middle-school-aged learners. Many texts are available that feature diverse characters, including both literary and informational texts. Epic includes a collection of books about African American fictional and real characters written by African American authors (**bit.ly/inclusive365-127a**, **getepic.com**).

EXTENSION OPPORTUNITIES

Invite learners to create book reviews about books that they've read that showcase diversity. View both **instagram.com/weneeddiversebooks** and **instagram.com/hereweeread** for ideas.

Take this quiz from Lee and Low Books to examine how diverse the texts in your learning space are (**bit.ly/inclusive365-127b**).

RELATED RESOURCES

An Updated Look at Diversity in Children's Books (**bit.ly/inclusive365-127c**)

Publishing Statistics on Children's/YA Books about People of Color and First/Native Nations and by People of Color and First/Native Nations (**bit.ly/inclusive365-127d**)

The Open Book Blog (**blog.leeandlow.com**)

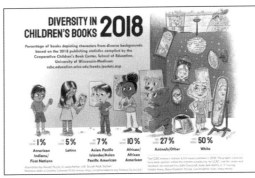

Figure 127. Infographic "Diversity in Children's Books" 2018.

ISTE STANDARDS FOR EDUCATORS
4d

ISTE STANDARDS FOR STUDENTS
7a

STRATEGY 128

Understanding Complex Literature Using Humorous Study Guides

Too often, learners groan, "Why are you making me read this?" instead of exclaiming, "I can't wait to read this! This looks like so much fun!" Joy and humor activate dopamine, a neurotransmitter that is released when we are experiencing something enjoyable. When we experience joy, information travels more easily to the frontal lobe, where it is analyzed and retained. Digital study guides infused with humor, jokes, and ludicrous videos can create a shared, enjoyable, and engaging experience conducive to learning and retention.

INCLUSIVE USES

Learners who find themselves distracted or disengaged by materials which they perceive to be boring may find a fun, joyful, comedic video laced with humor enticing.

SAMPLE TOOL

Shmoop infuses teen-friendly language and humor throughout its numerous study guides that cover commonly-used texts (**shmoop.com/study-guides/literature**).

EXTENSION OPPORTUNITY

Invite learners to work in small groups to create their own videos of a favorite scene from a book, or to compose humorous chapter summaries, in a manner similar to Shmoop, to solidify their understanding of the books they are reading.

RELATED RESOURCE

Laughter and Learning: Humor Boosts Retention (**bit.ly/inclusive365-128a**)

Figure 128. A still from a humorous video created about George Orwell's *1984* provided by Shmoop.

ISTE STANDARDS FOR STUDENTS
1a, 1b, 3a, 3b

ISTE STANDARDS FOR EDUCATORS
5a, 5b, 6a, 6b

Symbolizing Playground Equipment to Promote Language and Literacy

Playgrounds provide a fun environment for gross motor play, kinesthetic learning, exercise, and socialization. They can also be infused with supports to help individuals learn language and reading skills. Symbols with matching orthography can be placed around the playground. These symbols can match contemporary augmentative or alternative communication systems (AAC) to support those learning to use these systems as well. As learners play on the equipment they can point to symbols to make comments and requests, ask and answer questions, and communicate their thoughts.

INCLUSIVE USES

Individuals using AAC to learn language benefit from experiencing others using the same system. Those learning multiple languages might also find the symbols helpful for communicating and learning the language. Any sighted learner can benefit from these symbols and words, as they are another opportunity to read sight words.

SAMPLE TOOLS

The free PASS software from Prentke Romich Company can be used to create customized picture symbols (**bit.ly/inclusive365-129a**).

LessonPix can be used to create customized symbol supports and includes symbols (**LessonPix.com**).

EXTENSION OPPORTUNITIES

Print on card stock the home screen of one or more AAC systems used by those in the learning environment. Place the boards you've created in a clear plastic sleeve and seal the open end with clear tape, or laminate them.

Give them to a team of learners and ask them to place them strategically on the playground equipment where they think they will get the most use. Secure the boards in place using tape or external fasteners such as removable rings.

Invite a team of learners to do monthly maintenance on the symbol supports, Looking for supports that are worn or old and working to replace them.

Work with a printing company to create durable signs containing words with symbols from an AAC system that can be placed around the playground equipment.

Why stop at the playground? Place symbols around other shared learning environments, and other spaces including the cafeteria, gymnasium, and foyers.

RELATED RESOURCE

Playground Core Communication Boards from PRC-Saltillo (**bit.ly/inclusive365-129b**)

Figure 129. Front and back of a sign near the playground equipment at Cedar Lane Elementary School in Ashburn, Virginia.

ISTE STANDARDS FOR STUDENTS
1b, 1c, 3d, 6a, 6c, 7a, 7b, 7c, 7d

ISTE STANDARDS FOR EDUCATORS
2a, 2b, 2c, 3a, 4b, 4d, 5a, 5b, 5c, 6d

Shared Reading to Support Communication

STRATEGY 130

Shared reading is an evidence-based instructional strategy that emphasizes communication and interactions between adults and learners as they read a book together. Adding the additional strategy of Comment, Ask, and Respond (C.A.R.) provides an opportunity for the learner to make comments and respond to a text. When using the C.A.R. strategy, an educator reads aloud and pauses, provides a comment as a model, and then pauses for learners to respond with their own comments. If learners do not respond with a comment after the expectant pause, the educator would then explicitly ask for participation, with a question such as "What do you think?" Then, based on any response from the learner, the educator would reiterate and expand on the learner's comment. The goal of the strategy is communication and interaction, not correct answers.

INCLUSIVE USES

Although all early learners benefit from shared reading to build and expand emergent literacy skills, those learning language using augmentative and alternative communication (AAC) benefit when communication partners demonstrate the use of AAC while engaged in shared reading. Learners with physical impairments can interact with digital books through the use of switches to turn the page. Books with accessible text can support readers with features including text and background color options, and text-to-speech functionality.

SAMPLE TOOL

Tarheel Shared Reader is a repository of custom books from the University of North Carolina's Center For Literacy and Disabilities Studies. Tarheel Shared Reader is fully switch accessible and has a variety of supports to assist those with visual impairments (**shared.tarheelreader.org**).

EXTENSION OPPORTUNITIES

Invite learners to write their own books using the TarHeel Reader platform, and then employ shared reading strategies. Learners who have internet access at home can invite family members to participate in a shared reading experience using a book they have authored. Books can also be printed and sent home.

Invite older learners to demonstrate their knowledge of sophisticated topics by creating an accessible book for younger learners. Then, once this authentic project is completed, invite the older learners to participate in a shared reading experience with younger learners.

RELATED RESOURCES

Literacy Instruction for Students with Significant Disabilities (**literacyforallinstruction.ca/shared-reading**)

How Do I Create Opportunities to Promote the Use of AAC? (**bit.ly/inclusive365-130a**)

Shared Reading: Follow the Car (**bit.ly/inclusive365-130b**)

Figure 130. Book page in Tarheel Shared Reader with symbols available at the bottom for learners to use to communicate about the book.

ISTE STANDARDS FOR STUDENTS
1a, 1c, 1d, 2a, 2b, 2c, 6b

ISTE STANDARDS FOR EDUCATORS
2b, 3b, 5a, 5b, 6a

Converting Analog Text to Read Alouds on the Fly

The ability to comprehend an audio version of a text can, at times, greatly surpass one's ability to decode that same text. Without the use of audio supports, learners are limited to reading content at their own decoding and fluency levels, rather than their level of independent comprehension.

There are times when a learner may find they've come across a text that is inaccessible. In these situations, learners could be taught to convert the resource themselves using technology that can scan text, convert the text to digital, and read the converted text aloud.

INCLUSIVE USES

Converting inaccessible text into something digital that can be read aloud is an important skill for learners to practice when preparing to leave an educational agency. Any learner preparing to transition out of the K–12 learning environment will benefit from this life skill to promote independence.

SAMPLE TOOLS

Microsoft Lens is an iOS application that uses the device camera to take pictures of text. Office Lens uses optical character recognition (OCR) to convert the printed text to digital text. Individuals can then use the Immersive Reader tool to listen to the content using text-to-speech features. It is possible to change the font size, background color, and reading rate (**bit.ly/inclusive365-131a**).

Seeing AI is a scanning app from Microsoft that captures printed text and converts it, via OCR, to digital text. Once converted, learners can use Immersive Reader to customize the visual representation of text and utilize text-to-speech support (**bit.ly/inclusive365-131b**).

Google Keep is a note-taking application that invites learners to take a picture of printed text,

convert it into digital text, and then use built-in text-to-speech or some other browser-based text-to-speech application to listen to the text read aloud.

EXTENSION OPPORTUNITIES

Invite learners to explore different options to interact with text. Encourage learners to identify which solution works best for them and why.

Invite learners to brainstorm times when they might need to use an app that converts text to audio on the fly. Ideas could include using it to access a menu or listen to text on object labels.

RELATED RESOURCE

Does Use of Text-to-Speech and Related Read-Aloud Tools Improve Reading Comprehension for Students With Reading Disabilities? A Meta-Analysis (**bit.ly/inclusive365-131c**)

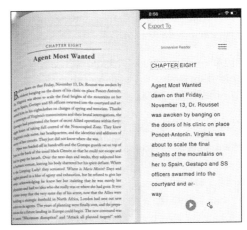

Figure 131. Convert printed text to a digital version with Microsoft Lens.

ISTE STANDARDS FOR STUDENTS
1a, 1c, 1d, 6a

ISTE STANDARDS FOR EDUCATORS
2b, 5a, 5b, 6a

STRATEGY 132

Self-Selecting Font Options for Reading

Font itself can be a barrier to decoding text. The size, color, and shape of characters along with the distance between them can all impact how the brain takes in and interprets the information. When learners can self-select the font of the text they're reading, readability can be improved.

INCLUSIVE USES

Learners should test drive different font options to decide which one is preferred when reading digital materials. Learners working to improve decoding skills, reading comprehension skills, and visual processing skills may find self-selecting the font helps improve overall readability of digital text.

SAMPLE TOOLS

A variety of Google Fonts are available when using Google Drive (**fonts.google.com**).

Open Dyslexic is an open-source font, which gives everyone the freedom to use it for any purpose (**opendyslexic.org**).

The Simplify Page feature of Read&Write for Chrome allows users to make font selections (**bit.ly/inclusive365-132a**).

EXTENSION OPPORTUNITY

Invite learners to explore at least five different fonts and font sizes while reading a passage. Ask each learner to rate the experience using a ten-point rating scale. For any learner who gives a font choice a high rating, invite them to use that font when reading any digital material.

RELATED RESOURCES

Formatting Font for Readability (**bit.ly/inclusive365-132b**)

Open Dyslexia Font, Chrome Extension (**bit.ly/inclusive365-132c**)

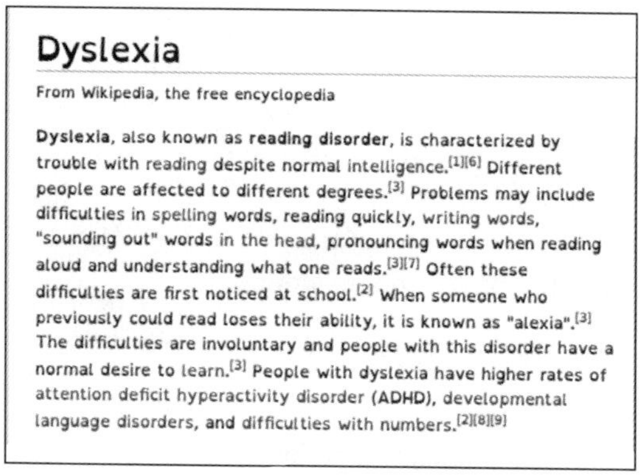

Dyslexia

From Wikipedia, the free encyclopedia

Dyslexia, also known as **reading disorder**, is characterized by trouble with reading despite normal intelligence.[1][6] Different people are affected to different degrees.[3] Problems may include difficulties in spelling words, reading quickly, writing words, "sounding out" words in the head, pronouncing words when reading aloud and understanding what one reads.[3][7] Often these difficulties are first noticed at school.[2] When someone who previously could read loses their ability, it is known as "alexia".[3] The difficulties are involuntary and people with this disorder have a normal desire to learn.[3] People with dyslexia have higher rates of attention deficit hyperactivity disorder (ADHD), developmental language disorders, and difficulties with numbers.[2][8][9]

Figure 132. Web page modified with the Open Dyslexic font to provide a more inclusive reading experience.

ISTE STANDARDS FOR STUDENTS
1a, 1d

ISTE STANDARDS FOR EDUCATORS
2b, 3a, 4d, 5a, 5b, 5c, 6a

Dual-Color Highlighting For Reading

Text-to-speech tools highlight sentences and individual words on screen as the text is read aloud, helping learners track the text visually. Many text-to-speech tools also allow the learner to display the sentences in one color and individual words in a different color that provides a contrast for added assistance with visual tracking.

INCLUSIVE USES

Learners working on decoding, fluency, and comprehension can use dual-color highlighting to help improve their reading skills, giving them an extra clue as to the specific word that is being read aloud.

SAMPLE TOOLS

Read&Write is a tool available on multiple platforms that provides text-to-speech with dual-color highlighting (**bit.ly/inclusive365-133a**).

Snap&Read is a tool available on multiple platforms that provides text-to-speech with dual-color highlighting (**snapandread.com**).

EXTENSION OPPORTUNITIES

Invite learners to try different colors and contrasts to determine preferences while using dual-color highlighting.

Muting the volume and turning the speed down is an additional strategy to support reading fluency. As each word is highlighted, learners can attempt to read along. Adjust the speed to match a learner's rate. The speed can also serve as a form of feedback and measurement. A learner can look at the rate and challenge themselves to read at the next fastest setting.

RELATED RESOURCE

Text-to-Speech as a Support for Personalizing the Reading Experience (**bit.ly/inclusive365-133b**)

Consider how the government works to facilitate transportation in the US. As part of the nation's infrastructure, the government contracts out the companies to build roads. The government doesn't contract out to companies to build cars that go on these roads. The government provides regulations for the construction of the cars but doesn't manufacture them.

Could the same model be applied to open educational resources? Like the building of roads, the government could contract out to a company to build a searchable structure tying all open education resources together. When a user is looking for a resource, they could just go to this one place. The user could search the database and results could come back with all the file formats available. The user could then select the file format to open in the app of her or his choice (Open in...). To ensure accessibility and compatibility, the government could provide regulations about the criteria necessary for that file to be found in the search, just like what currently exists for the creation of automobiles regarding safety and environmental regulations. "If you're going to sell a car in the US, it needs to meet these safety and environmental parameters. If you're going to share a resource in the National (Open) Educational Resource Database (NERD, for short! Yes! How great is that?!?!) it needs to meet these accessibility standards."

Figure 133. A sentence displayed using dual-color highlighting, indicating that this section is being read aloud using a text-to-speech tool.

ISTE STANDARDS FOR STUDENTS

1a, 1b, 1c, 1d, 4b, 4c

ISTE STANDARDS FOR EDUCATORS

2b, 5a, 5c, 6a, 6d

Adjusting the Readability Level of Text

All readers have occasions when they encounter text that is above their reading level. Even for those who have mastered reading, this might occur when they are doing research and finding sources that have vocabulary and language that is beyond their current skills. Using digital tools to adjust the reading level of the text provides an embedded solution for learners. The original text can be rewritten, using more or less text or different words with similar meanings, to decrease the reading level or text complexity.

INCLUSIVE USES

Learners who struggle with comprehension may not be engaged by reading materials written at their reading level. Often they want to read age-appropriate materials and work alongside their peers. Providing embedded support for difficult vocabulary may learners to attack these more difficult passages.

Learners with intellectual disabilities, those learning to decode, and those who are multi-language learners benefit from content that is scaffolded and adapted for their level of understanding. The presentation of the material that has been rescaled for readability can look similar to other versions of the same text. This may help learners who feel self-conscious about experiencing text at different levels than peers.

SAMPLE TOOLS

Rewordify is a free tool that simplifies difficult words. Text pasted into a yellow box is instantly simplified as the tool matches the original text's parts of speech, verb tense, and singular or plural form. The simplified version includes additional supports for reading (**rewordify.com**).

Newsela invites learners to access more than 10,000 articles, aligned to multiple genres and scaled to various reading levels (**newsela.com**).

Simple English Wikipedia provides simplified words and grammar to improve readability of Wikipedia articles (**simple.wikipedia.org/wiki**).

EXTENSION OPPORTUNITIES

Invite learners to keep a log of words that a text-leveling tool has modified, with both the original word and the replacement text. This helps learners expand their vocabulary and gain confidence in reading ability.

If the text is accessible, a text-to-speech function can be used, allowing learners to listen to text presented at one level and decode text written at another. In this way, learners are not limited to their level of decoding and have access to text at their level of understanding.

RELATED RESOURCES

Rewordify Educator Central Walkthrough (**bit.ly/inclusive365-134a**)

Getting Started with Simple English on Wikipedia (**bit.ly/inclusive365-134b**)

A.T.TIPSCAST Episode #144: Three Tools to Support Reading (**bit.ly/inclusive365-134c**)

Figure 134. Rewordify adjusts the reading level of pasted text.

ISTE STANDARDS FOR STUDENTS
1c 3c

ISTE STANDARDS FOR EDUCATORS
5a, 6a

Screen Masking with a Focus Bar When Reading

A focus bar shades a portion of the screen while highlighting the portion of the screen the user is immediately viewing. The user controls the placement of the bar to focus on the pertinent text. The focus bar reduces distractions and enhances readability.

INCLUSIVE USES

A focus bar helps maintain attention on particular parts of a screen helping learners who are working on maintaining attention while completing tasks. Learners who are working to improve visual processing might also find the focus bar bypasses some challenges and reduces anxiety caused when presented with too much visual information. A focus bar might help improve proficiency for a learner working on reading fluency.

SAMPLE TOOLS

Visor is a Chrome extension that provides a focus bar. The size of the bar and background colors can be adjusted according to user preference (**bit.ly/inclusive365-135a**).

Line Focus is a built-in feature of the Microsoft Edge browser that provides a focus bar (**bit.ly/inclusive365-135b**).

EXTENSION OPPORTUNITY

Invite learners to make adjustments to the size and color of the focus window to find which settings work best for each individual.

RELATED RESOURCES

How to Enable Line Focus in Microsoft Edge Chromium (**bit.ly/inclusive365-135c**)

Eduwalks #6: Google Extensions (**bit.ly/inclusive365-135d**)

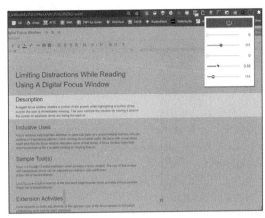

Figure 135. The Visor focus bar.

ISTE STANDARDS FOR STUDENTS
1b, 1d, 3a, 3b, 3c, 3d

ISTE STANDARDS FOR EDUCATORS
2b, 4d, 6a

Varying Text Color Intermittently to Improve Reading

Customizing the visual presentation of online text is an effective tool for some readers. One method for customizing text is to provide intermittent color changes via gradients to the text. These changes in gradients can help draw a reader's eyes from word to word and sentence to sentence. The changes in color may help maintain focus and support learners in increasing reading stamina over longer periods of time.

INCLUSIVE USES

Any learner working on improving reading fluency may find intermittent text color variation useful in increasing reading rate and endurance.

SAMPLE TOOL

Beeline Reader is a web-based tool which works on multiple platforms and provides intermittent text color variation (**beelinereader.com**).

EXTENSION OPPORTUNITY

Invite learners to experiment with different color schemes and compare results to determine if a particular combination of colors is optimal for their unique needs. They might attempt to read the same or similar passages while collecting data on how fast the passage was read and how many errors were made using various intermittent color schemes. Analyze the results to determine each learner's preferences.

RELATED RESOURCE

How to Use Beeline Reader
(**bit.ly/inclusive365-136**)

Text that changes colors intermittently can help draw a reader's eyes from word to word and sentence to sentence. This varied change in color can help maintain focus and help learners sustain for longer periods of time when attempting to read text.

Figure 136. Text with intermittent color changes.

ISTE STANDARDS FOR STUDENTS
3a, 3c

ISTE STANDARDS FOR EDUCATORS
2b, 4d, 5a, 5c, 6a

Modifying Screen Colors to Accommodate Vision Needs

Eye strain related to continued and prolonged exposure to bright digital displays is a concern. Steps can be taken to reduce eye strain and provide a more visually comfortable learning situation, especially during virtual experiences. Modifying the color scheme of the screen may be a first step towards reducing eye strain. The ability to soften the light by customizing the colors can have a dramatic effect on productivity, including the duration for which a learner or educator can work on a device.

INCLUSIVE USES

For some individuals with vision impairments, it may be necessary to modify the screen-colors to increase the ability to independently see information. Learners can perform this task independently, retaining the ability to customize colors throughout a learning session.

Some individuals with dyslexia or other reading difficulties report that the use of screen color overlays improves readability.

SAMPLE TOOLS

The Visor extension for Chrome allows the learner to place a virtual color overlay directly over a browser tab. Customizable features include the ability to individually adjust the red, green, and blue color settings to create a customized scheme. The point-of-focus feature benefits learners who have a tendency to skip lines when reading due to difficulties with eye tracking (**bit.ly/inclusive365-137a**).

iOS Color Filter is located in the accessibility settings of an iOS device, in Display and Text Size. Within this category there are multiple settings that can be activated to customize the visual presentation. This includes the ability to place a color filter over the screen to change the color palette (**bit.ly/inclusive265-137b**).

EXTENSION OPPORTUNITY

Encourage learners to explore different color combinations to support learning while on a connected device. Using Visor, modify the color settings to find a setting that is visually comfortable. Invite learners to explore the transparency slider option to modify the density of the color on the screen.

RELATED RESOURCES

Custom Screen Dimming with the Visor Chrome Extension (**bit.ly/inclusive365-137c**)

The Benefits of Dark Mode: Why You Should Turn Off the Lights (**bit.ly/inclusive365-137d**)

Figure 137. Browser window shaded with color to support learner vision needs.

ISTE STANDARDS FOR STUDENTS
1a, 1b, 5d, 6a

ISTE STANDARDS FOR EDUCATORS
3c, 5a, 5c

Reading Text with Syllable Markers

Decoding text is a skill that takes practice. The ability to divide words into chunks or syllables helps speed the process of decoding, and understanding the rules of syllabication helps learners read more accurately and fluently. One strategy that can help learners develop this skill is to provide the learner with a visual indicator of how the word can be broken down into syllables.

INCLUSIVE USES

Learners with reading challenges, including those with dyslexia, may find seeing the syllabification of words helpful in learning to decode.

SAMPLE TOOLS

Immersive Reader is a feature built into multiple tools provided by Microsoft and their partners that provides visual indicators of parts of speech over words in text (**bit.ly/inclusive365-138a**).

Immersive Reader for Chrome is an extension that provides similar functionality of Microsoft's Immersive Reader in the Chrome browser (**bit.ly/inclusive365-138b**).

Avaz Reader is a multi-featured iOS and Google Play reading app that includes syllabication as one of its features in the premium version (**avazapp.com/mda-avaz-reader**).

EXTENSION OPPORTUNITY

Invite learners to clap or tap out the syllables for individual words. Adding this auditory and kinesthetic movement can provide a multi-sensory experience to practicing decoding.

RELATED RESOURCES

The Big Five: Phonics-Teaching Syllabication (**bit.ly/inclusive365-138c**)

A.T.TIPSCAST Episode #128: App Review and Multisyllabic Word Reading Strategies (**bit.ly/inclusive365-138d**)

Syllable Games (**bit.ly/inclusive365-138e**)

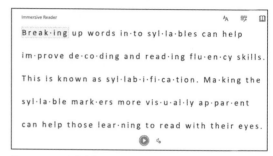

Figure 138. Syllables separated in words using Immersive Reader.

ISTE STANDARDS FOR STUDENTS
3a, 3b, 3c, 5c, 7a, 7b

ISTE STANDARDS FOR EDUCATORS
2b, 4d, 6a

Reading Text with Visual Cues for Parts of Speech

Decoding and comprehending text are two skills essential to the development of effective reading. One strategy that can help learners develop these skills is for the learner to use a visual identifier labeling the parts of speech. Visual identifiers could include color coding the words and/or adding text labels above the words. Using these visual labels in conjunction with a legend defining them helps the learner determine what part of speech each word is, giving the learner a clue about its possible meaning.

INCLUSIVE USES

Learners working to improve their reading and writing abilities may find labeling the parts of speech useful in learning the meaning of the words. It may also provide a clue as to how to decode and comprehend the word. For example if the word *red* is labeled as an adjective, the reader is signaled that it is not the word *read*, which would be labeled as a verb. It should be noted that some learners may find adding the text labels over the words, as opposed to color coding, distracting because it adds visual complexity to the word, while other learners may find they prefer text labels over the words due to difficulties in distinguishing colors.

SAMPLE TOOLS

Microsoft's Immersive Reader is a feature built into multiple tools that provides a visual indicator of parts of speech over words in text (**bit.ly/inclusive365-139a**).

Immersive Reader for Chrome is an extension that provides similar functionality of Microsoft's Immersive Reader in the Chrome browser (**bit.ly/inclusive365-139b**).

EXTENSION OPPORTUNITIES

Invite learners to use digital highlighters to identify different parts of speech. Adding this auditory and kinesthetic movement to the reading process can provide a multi-sensory experience for understanding and identifying parts of speech.

Invite learners to review labels for parts of speech as part of an editing phase of writing. Learners can review labels to confirm structural integrity or the use of a particular targeted part of speech. For example, learners might check to make sure a sentence has both a noun and a verb or, if practicing adjectives, that they exist in the composition.

RELATED RESOURCE

The Importance of Grammar Reading Comprehension (**bit.ly/inclusive365-139c**)

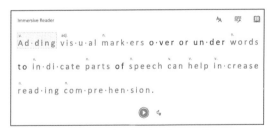

Figure 139. Immersive Reader showing words in a sentence, with markers for parts of speech.

ISTE STANDARDS FOR STUDENTS
1a, 1d, 3c, 6d

ISTE STANDARDS FOR EDUCATORS
2b, 4d, 6a

Tracking Reading Progress through Voluntary Digital Logs

Reading logs are journals or lists learners use to track books, articles, and other content they've read. Evidence suggests tasks with extrinsic motivations, such as the obligatory use of a reading log, can have a detrimental effect and undermine one's desire to learn (Deci et al., 2001). Instead, reframe the use of reading logs. Encourage learners to create their own reading logs tracking the information that is important to them. They might decide to log only the title of the book and the date they completed it, adding a rating or recommendation. They may choose to set their own goals, leave commentary, and analyze their own data. Reading logs kept digitally can help automate the analysis and provide a more accessible version than a paper-based log, and they are available anywhere with an internet connection. Inviting the use of reading logs as a voluntary exercise ensures learners use them in a manner that is significant to them and does not inhibit their love for reading.

INCLUSIVE USES

Some learners who are learning to decode and comprehend text feel empowered by reflecting on their own progress. Inviting learners to decide what data they'd like to keep about what they've read, to track that data, and then to analyze that data with accompanying graphical information, can visually show growth. Self-actualizing how much progress is made over time can shatter a learner's negative perception and boost self-confidence.

SAMPLE TOOLS

Google Sheets can be used to create digital logs (**bit.ly/inclusive365-140a**).

Goodreads invites users to track, review, and share books they've read (**goodreads.com**).

EXTENSION OPPORTUNITIES

Invite learners who decide to use a reading log to develop a rating scale and score the titles they've read. Learners can analyze results for trends in genres and authors.

When goal setting, ask the individual a series of reflective questions such as, "What information might be helpful to collect?" and "What information might help you see how much more you are reading?" to help that person decide what data to collect. Reflective questioning can help the learner take ownership of the strategy rather than see it as an imposition.

Invite learners to decide upon waypoints for when to analyze the data from the log to make conscientious decisions about whether to continue its use. Some learners may elect to use this strategy temporarily and then abandon use once the goal has been achieved.

RELATED RESOURCES

Can Reading Logs Ruin Reading for Kids? (**bit.ly/inclusive365-140b**)

Rethinking Reading Logs for Beginning Readers (**bit.ly/inclusive365-140c**)

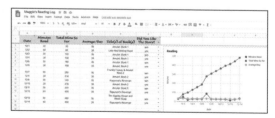

Figure 140. A portion of a voluntary reading log completed by a learner.

ISTE STANDARDS FOR STUDENTS
1a, 1b, 1c, 1d

ISTE STANDARDS FOR EDUCATORS
1c, 3b, 6a, 7a, 7c

Dual Coding Using Comics and Graphic Novels

Dual coding is the presentation of two different forms of media concurrently, such as pairing text with images or pairing verbal and visual information. Dual coding supports improved comprehension and retention of information (Douglas, 2020). Comics and graphic novels provide such an experience. Learners can use the imagery in frames or panels to help provide context for the words they are working to decode and comprehend. Furthermore, comics and graphic novels often generate a high level of interest and engagement from learners. Educators can also create their own comics and graphic novels as a way to represent content, and learners can use them as a form of expression.

INCLUSIVE USES

Learners with goals related to decoding, comprehending text, and writing may find reading and creating comics and graphic novels useful and a positive outlet for creative expression.

Learners who are challenged by writing, but enjoy drawing or creating content with digital images, may be better able to demonstrate their understanding of a topic by creating comic strips or graphic novels.

SAMPLE TOOLS

StoryboardThat is a free, web-based comic and graphic novel generator (**storyboardthat.com**).

Pixton is a free, web-based comic and graphic novel generator (**edu.pixton.com**).

MakeBeliefsComix is a free, web-based comic and graphic novel generator (**makebeliefscomix.com**).

EXTENSION OPPORTUNITIES

Invite learners to create their own comics and graphic novels as an artifact to demonstrate what they have learned.

Invite learners to visit libraries to explore the graphic novels available for loan.

RELATED RESOURCES

Free Comic Book Day (**freecomicbookday.com**)

5 Ways Comic Books Can Improve Literacy Skills (**bit.ly/inclusive365-141a**)

Book Study Using a Comic Book Generator (**bit.ly/inclusive365-141b**)

How Does Dual Coding Improve Learning? (**bit.ly/inclusive365-141c**)

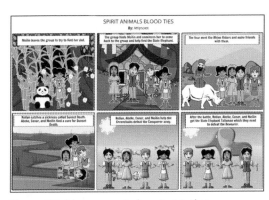

Figure 141. A learner-created comic strip that demonstrates understanding of the topic.

ISTE STANDARDS FOR STUDENTS
1c, 6b, 6c, 6d

ISTE STANDARDS FOR EDUCATORS
2b, 5a, 5b, 6d, 7a

Building Literacy through Pairing Supplemental Resources

As learners progress through middle school and high school, their exposure to more complex literature increases. Providing supplemental resources that align with the novels being read can help to build background knowledge, provide context, and increase understanding of the content in the story. Designing effective pairings helps learners better understand themes and make connections between different texts to enhance their literary skills.

INCLUSIVE USES

Learners who benefit from scaffolded supports to better understand the content of a story will benefit from the instructional method of providing supplemental resources.

Text-to-speech is available for learners whose abilities to decode are still developing.

SAMPLE TOOL

CommonLit offers a free collection of fiction and nonfiction texts. It includes supplementary resources for a large number of frequently-read texts to enhance comprehension, and also includes suggestions for instruction. The Book Pairing Filter helps educators and learners make connections between different complex texts (**commonlit.org**).

EXTENSION OPPORTUNITY

Invite learners to conduct their own internet searches to locate additional articles that help them understand themes, character development, or the time period during which a story took place.

RELATED RESOURCES

CommonLit Video Tutorial for Teachers (**bit.ly/inclusive365-142a**)

CommonLit Built for All Learners (**bit.ly/inclusive365-142b**)

CommonLit Book Pairings Tutorial (**bit.ly/inclusive365-142c**)

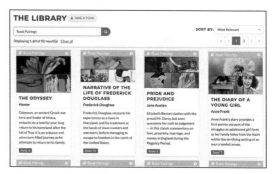

Figure 142. Example from the Book Pairings Section of CommonLit.

ISTE STANDARDS FOR STUDENTS
1b, 1c

ISTE STANDARDS FOR EDUCATORS
1a, 5a, 5b, 6a, 6b, 7a

Building a Bank of Multimodal Supplemental Materials to Enhance Understanding of Literature

In the US, state standards for reading and literacy set high expectations. Learners are expected to analyze, interpret, predict, infer, evaluate, and summarize increasingly more complex text as they progress through high school. They are expected to demonstrate a clear understanding of the author's intent for literary texts and often must compare two literary works. To enhance understanding of complex literature, it is important to provide all learners with supplementary materials. Offering multimodal materials allows learners to choose the materials that work best for them.

INCLUSIVE USES

When learners are provided with curated resources specific to the assigned text, all learners benefit. These supplemental materials may include read aloud versions, multimedia supports, and digital text, which can be visually customized to enhance reading fluency.

SAMPLE TOOLS

Wakelet is a content curation platform for links, posts, videos, and images. Use the Immersive Reader feature within Wakelet to promote independent access to text (**wakelet.com**).

Padlet is an online virtual bulletin board to display and organize information (**padlet.com**).

EXTENSION OPPORTUNITY

Invite learners to evaluate the quality of the curated supplemental materials using a Google Form.

RELATED RESOURCES

Wakelet and Immersive Reader bring text to life (**bit.ly/inclusive365-143a**)

How to Read and Understand Classic Literature (**bit.ly/inclusive365-143b**)

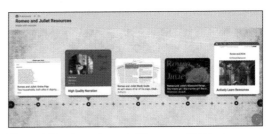

Figure 143a. A supplemental *Romeo and Juliet* resource created in Padlet.

Figure 143b. A supplemental *Romeo and Juliet* resource created in Wakelet.

ISTE STANDARDS FOR STUDENTS

1c, 3c

ISTE STANDARDS FOR EDUCATORS

5a, 5b, 6a, 6b

Comprehending Text Passages Using Word Clouds

Word cloud generators allow users to create an image made of the reoccurring words used in a block of text. Words used more frequently are displayed larger than words used less frequently. Learners can analyze the larger words to identify a theme or critical idea in the text. This visual, in conjunction with experiencing the full text, can help build understanding. Learners could use a word cloud as a pre-reading or post-reading instructional tool to assist with comprehension of the passage.

INCLUSIVE USES

Word cloud generators provide another option for learners who might have difficulty highlighting words when looking for the themes or main points of a passage. Learners can visualize the main points of a passage without necessarily being asked to decode an entire passage or as a preview before reading to support them in attending to the most critical parts of a passage.

SAMPLE TOOLS

ABCYA provides a free, web-based word cloud generator (**bit.ly/inclusive365-144a**).

Word Clouds is a free, web-based word cloud generator (**wordclouds.com**).

EXTENSION OPPORTUNITIES

Invite learners to create a shared repository for word clouds created from the same passage to further illustrate the main theme of a passage. This repository can be shared with the world to teach others about the theme of the passage.

Some word cloud generators provide amorphous images. Others can be designed to create a silhouette of an object. Depending on the theme and tool used, invite learners to create a silhouette of an object that fits with the theme of the passage.

When sharing a word cloud, invite learners to create a caption or alt tag describing the image for learners who require audio supports. The caption or alt tag can be read aloud by text-to-speech and screen reading applications.

RELATED RESOURCES

A.T.TIPSCAST Episode #135: ScreamEd (**bit.ly/inclusive365-144b**)

How to Quickly Create a Word Cloud in Google Documents (**bit.ly/inclusive365-144c**)

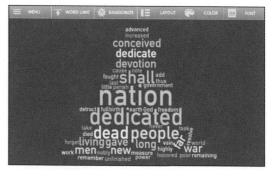

Figure 144. A word cloud generated from the Gettysburg Address using ABCYA.

ISTE STANDARDS FOR STUDENTS
1c, 4a, 5b, 6a, 6b, 6c, 6d

ISTE STANDARDS FOR EDUCATORS
3b, 5a, 5b, 5c

Creating a Personalized Dictionary Using Multimedia Slides with the Frayer Model Graphic Organizer

Learners can maintain a personalized vocabulary dictionary using a consistent graphic organizing template known as the Frayer Model. The Frayer Model consists of five cells organized in a quadrant with a center cell for the vocabulary word. The first quadrant displays the definitions of the word. The second quadrant displays pictures or symbols that illustrate the word. The third quadrant displays synonyms for the target word. The final quadrant displays examples of word usage in the context of a sentence.

Each slide in a slide deck should be set to use the same template to provide a consistent look to the dictionary. Learners can put different vocabulary terms in the dictionary based on instructional targets. These targets might include terms related to academic content, unfamiliar terms, difficult words to spell, or any other terms a learner might need to practice or recall.

INCLUSIVE USES

Learners who have goals related to learning and using new vocabulary can use this consistent structure to provide a patterned way for learning how to spell words, what they mean, and how they are used.

SAMPLE TOOL

Google Slides is a multimedia presentation tool that can be used to create a template of the Frayer Model (**bit.ly/inclusive365-145a**).

EXTENSION OPPORTUNITIES

Invite learners to complete their own pages while creating their personalized dictionaries. Invite learners to complete some or all of the quadrants using previously completed pages as a template.

Invite learners to share their own personalized dictionaries with family members to review at home.

If preferred, invite learners to print portions of their dictionaries to reference and share at home.

Invite learners to use words from their personalized dictionaries as a word bank while writing.

RELATED RESOURCE

Frayer Model + Google Slides = Vocabulary Slide Deck! (**bit.ly/inclusive365-145b**).

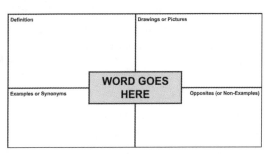

Figure 145a. A Frayer Model sample in Google Slides.

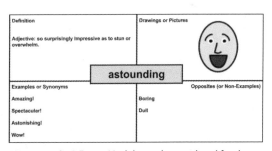

Figure 145b. A Frayer Model sample completed for the word astounding.

ISTE STANDARDS FOR STUDENTS
1a, 1c, 5b, 5c

ISTE STANDARDS FOR EDUCATORS
5a, 5c, 6a, 6d, 7a

Building Literacy through Captioned Video

Videos are a multi-sensory, engaging way to experience academic content. When the captions are turned on, synced text, audio, and video create a multimodal experience that improves literacy skills. Turning the captions on is a proven strategy for helping learners, including those with intellectual disabilities and those who are learning English as a second language, improve their ability to decode and comprehend text (Evmenova, A. S., 2008; Huang, H. C., & Eskey, D. E., 1999)

INCLUSIVE USES

Regardless of a learner's ability to hear, when watching video content with emergent readers, turn the captions on. Help to create a culture where your learning environment has a default mode where the captions are on whenever videos are shown. Invite parents to turn on the captions at home as well.

SAMPLE TOOLS

Apple Clips is a video recording app that uses speech-to-text to create captions while recording the audio, saving the step of adding captions in post-production (**apple.com/clips**).

Microsoft Stream is an online tool that automatically transcribes uploaded video (**bit.ly/inclusive365-146a**).

EXTENSION OPPORTUNITIES

Sometimes video content does not have captions. Some video services, such as YouTube, provide a function where the community can add captions.

Invite learners who belong to service organizations to earn community service hours by adding captions to existing video content. Learn how to add captions to YouTube. (**bit.ly/inclusive365-146b**).

When learners are creating video content, invite them to add captions so they learn at an early age to create content that is born more accessible.

RELATED RESOURCES

The Described and Captioned Media Program is funded and supported by the United States Department of Education. It provides media designed for learners with disabilities and is a leading resource for families and educators (**dcmp.org**).

Captions for Literacy (**captionsforliteracy.org**)

Disability-led Innovations for the Masses (**bit.ly/inclusive365-146c**)

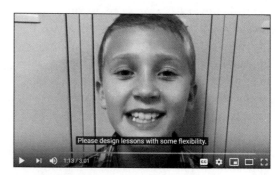

Figure 146. Captions on a YouTube video.

ISTE STANDARDS FOR STUDENTS
1c, 2b, 3c, 3d, 6a, 6c, 6d, 7a

ISTE STANDARDS FOR EDUCATORS
3a, 3c, 4d, 5a, 5c, 7b

Animating Book Characters

Judy Willis, MD, a neurologist who became a middle school educator, advocates for joyful learning and unexpected, unique learning experiences in her article "The Neuroscience of Joyful Education" (2007). Joyful learning engages and motivates learners so that information flows through the amygdala to be processed by the prefrontal cortex, where higher-order thinking occurs. With this in mind, educators can design joyful experiences that foster creativity when learning about characters in books. Educators and learners can use technology to draw or take a picture of a character and then bring that character to life through the power of video animation. Video animation can provide a fun experience that can help learners better understand the character's qualities, interactions, behaviors, and choices.

INCLUSIVE USES

Novelty engages all learners and motivates them to sustain attention. Learners working to improve how they maintain attention may find the use of video animation helpful in improving this skill. Those working to increase short term memory skills may also find that creating video animations of characters helps them better remember the character and what happens in a story.

SAMPLE TOOL

Puppet Master is an iOS application that invites users to animate any image by acting things out in front of the camera or by using touch gestures. Users can record their voice to create an animated video (**shmonster.com/ puppetmaster**).

EXTENSION OPPORTUNITIES

Take a picture of the cover of the book that will be read and ask learners to make a prediction about what the book is about. Then introduce the PuppetMaster animated character that you have prepared ahead of time, who describes the book. Invite learners to compare the differences between their prediction and the one provided by the animated character.

Invite learners to create their own puppets to animate dialogue and meaningful quotes from the shared book.

RELATED RESOURCES

"The Neuroscience of Joyful Education" (**bit.ly/inclusive365-147a**)

Puppet Master: The Education Animation App Created by a Mom (**bit.ly/inclusive365-147b**)

Puppet Master Lesson Plans (**shmonster.com/ puppetmaster-lesson-plans**)

Figure 147. A cartoon animated using the PuppetMaster app.

ISTE STANDARDS FOR STUDENTS
1a, 6a, 6b

ISTE STANDARDS FOR EDUCATORS
2b, 5a, 5b, 5c

Composing and Sharing Authentic Commentary When Reading

Commenting on or reviewing an author's work is an empowering experience for learners. After reading a text, or any other type of media with text, learners can discuss the work by leaving comments or reviews in a shared location. The comments themselves can be an engaging way to experience text and spark ongoing discussions. Comments could be reflections on elements enjoyed by the reader, questions about the parts of the narrative, or a review or critique of the work. When comments are shared with other readers, including a public audience, such as on blogs or websites such as Amazon, learners can discuss the work with anyone else who is reviewing the same text.

INCLUSIVE USES

Reluctant readers and writers may discover that reading and sharing comments about a work helps them maintain interest and motivation. Offering the opportunity to leave comments, whether via writing, video, or audio, helps learners realize their opinion and analysis matters.

SAMPLE TOOLS

A commenting feature is available for many blogging platforms, including Wordpress (**wordpress.org**).

Amazon invites people to leave reviews on products and literature (**bit.ly/inclusive365-148a**).

EXTENSION OPPORTUNITIES

Set up notifications or invite learners to period-ically check their statistics to how many people have viewed or engaged in the review.

RELATED RESOURCES

A.T.TIPSCAST Episode #142: Authentic Writing (**bit.ly/inclusive365-148b**)

It's Amazing How Authentic Writing Can Motivate K–12 Writers (**bit.ly/inclusive365-148c**)

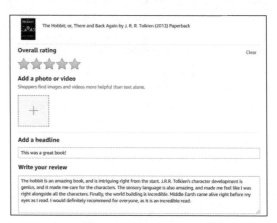

Figure 148. A review of *The Hobbit* written by a learner on Amazon.com.

ISTE STANDARDS FOR STUDENTS

2a, 2b, 3b, 6a, 6b, 6c, 6d, 7a, 7b

ISTE STANDARDS FOR EDUCATORS

3a, 5b

Linking Literature Reviews to Books with QR Codes

There are a wide variety of literature options available to learners. A common practice is to read reviews from others to help make decisions on how to spend time and money. One factor learners can use to help them decide if they should invest time and effort into a piece of literature is to read reviews created by others. QR codes on a piece of literature linking to one or more reviews of that work are a great way to access content to help decide what to read.

INCLUSIVE USES

Learners who need support selecting literature might find reviews created by those with similar backgrounds or interests helpful in deciding upon a particular piece.

Writing a text-based literature review, or a script for an audio or video-based review, is an authentic experience for learners working on writing goals.

Place QR codes on the front or back covers of books or add as annotations to digital books. Literature displays in common areas could also contain QR codes. Learners working on spatial reasoning goals may find that deciding where to place the QR code on a book or display is an authentic way to practice these abilities.

SAMPLE TOOLS

QR Monkey is a free, web-based QR code generator (**qrcode-monkey.com**).

Google Sites, Google Slides, and Google Docs provide a web-based way to house multiple reviews and additional derivative works (**gsuite.google.com**).

Leave video reviews using Flipgrid; use a QR code to link to the reviews (**info.flipgrid.com**).

EXTENSION OPPORTUNITIES

Invite learners to create their own literature reviews. Scaffold reviews based on length,

complexity, and format to meet the individual needs of the creator and potential reader.

Invite learners to create reviews for a title in one digital space such a website, word processing document, or multimedia slideshow. Add multiple reviews to the same space and link to them with one QR code.

Invite learners to keep a personalized portfolio of reviews. Potential readers often find that if one review from a certain individual is helpful, they might look to reviews by the same individual to find other literature to consume.

RELATED RESOURCES

QR Codes 101 (**bit.ly/inclusive365-149a**)

How to Make QR Codes for Classroom Libraries (**bit.ly/inclusive365-149b**)

Figure 149. This book display is augmented by QR codes that link to video book trailers.

ISTE STANDARDS FOR STUDENTS
2b, 2c, 3b, 6a, 6b, 6c, 6d, 7a, 7b, 7c

ISTE STANDARDS FOR EDUCATORS
2b, 3b, 4a, 4c, 5b, 5c, 6d, 7a

Sequencing Events Using Slide Sorter Views and Photo Albums

Putting events in sequential order is a fundamental skill necessary for reasoning, decision making, and storytelling. The order in which things occur across content areas, including science and history, affects the outcome. Many multimedia slide show tools have a feature which allows the user to see multiple pages or slides at once in a thumbnail view. Similarly, learners can also use shared digital photo albums to see multiple thumbnails. Learners can practice sequencing events by dragging these pages, slides, or images to put them in a logical sequence.

INCLUSIVE USES

Learners practicing the understanding and use of temporal concepts can place items in sequential order by dragging and dropping slides or photos.

Magnification features may allow for the size of the thumbnail views to change. The number and size of the items can be adjusted to accommodate for different learning needs.

SAMPLE TOOLS

The slide sorter view of PowerPoint allows users to see many slides at once and provides the ability to drag and drop them into a different order (**bit.ly/inclusive365-150a**).

The grid view of Google Slides allows users to see many slides at once and provides the ability to drag and drop them into a different order (**bit.ly/inclusive365-150b**).

Photo album in iPadOS allows users to open a shared photo album on iOS devices (**bit.ly/inclusive365-150c**).

EXTENSION OPPORTUNITIES

Invite learners to take photos of events during field trips. These images can then be placed into a shared photo album or onto slides. Learners can then sequence the events to recreate the order and share the story with their family, friends, or the community.

Invite learners to sequence slides with images or other information from a historical time period or some other important event to demonstrate their understanding of that event or time period.

RELATED RESOURCE

A.T.TIPSCAST Episode #45: Sequencing with PowerPoint (**bit.ly/inclusive365-150d**)

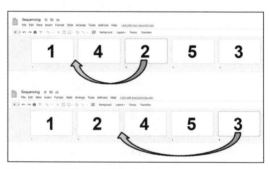

Figure 150. Slides in slide sorter view.

ISTE STANDARDS FOR STUDENTS

1c, 6a, 6b, 6c, 6d

ISTE STANDARDS FOR EDUCATORS

2b, 5a, 6d, 7a

Supporting Multilingual Learners' Access to Text with Digital Translation Tools

Emergent multilingual learners benefit from hearing and reading text in their dominant language to better process meaning and respond to the text effectively. Digital translation tools convert text into multiple languages to promote learning and understanding while learners are receiving instruction to develop their English language skills.

INCLUSIVE USES

Translation reduces the cognitive load on a learner who is both learning content and the English language. Having translation tools readily available allows emergent multilingual learners to experience content and demonstrate their knowledge without the added linguistic barrier. To further support emergent multilingual learners who may also have reading challenges, learners can utilize text-to-speech to hear and see text in their preferred language.

SAMPLE TOOLS

Word for Office 365 offers multilingual text conversion and text-to-speech under the review tab on the toolbar (**microsoft.com/en-us/translator**).

Snap&Read Universal Extension is an online text-to-speech tool that also converts text into multiple languages with read-aloud capabilities (**snapandread.com**).

The Chrome browser has translation capabilities (**bit.ly/inclusive365-151a**).

EXTENSION OPPORTUNITY

Support emergent multilingual learners by providing captioning in their language for distance learning experiences. Microsoft Translate and Captioning in Google Slides provide this option.

RELATED RESOURCE

How do you translate text in the Snap&Read universal extension? (**bit.ly/inclusive365-151b**)

Figure 151. Translation feature in Google Docs.

ISTE STANDARDS FOR STUDENTS

1b, 1d

ISTE STANDARDS FOR EDUCATORS

2b, 4a, 4d, 5a, 5b, 5c, 6a, 6b

Annotating Text Digitally

Text annotation is a critical skill for learners to develop as they engage in detailed analysis through multiple readings, also known as *close reading*. Learners markup text to track key ideas, indicate important aspects, or highlight something they don't understand. Typical annotations include circling a word, underlining a phrase, or highlighting a sentence. Annotations may also include thoughts or questions as notes in the margins. When learners read a digital text, traditional annotation symbols can be replicated digitally with a variety of tools.

INCLUSIVE USES

Any learner may benefit from making, saving, and reviewing text annotations, especially those working on decoding and initial reading automaticity. Returning to a smaller amount of annotated text helps minimize how much needs to be reread, which can decrease frustration and improve productivity.

SAMPLE TOOLS

Kami allows for annotation of any PDF document. Learners can highlight, use shapes including boxes and circles, and type text or freehand write on a touchscreen-compatible device. Documents opened and annotated in Kami can be saved and shared in Google Docs (**kamiapp.com**).

Diigo is a bookmarking tool, with annotation features, including the ability to highlight using four colors and add notes to any part of a web page or PDF document. Annotations can be shared with peer collaborators and with educators (**diigo.com**).

ClaroPDF Pro can be used to annotate and mark up any PDF file. ClaroPDF has built-in text-to-speech, synchronized highlighting, and can convert handwriting and inaccessible text in an image into a format capable of being read by screen-reading technology (**clarosoftware.com/portfolio/claropdf**).

EXTENSION OPPORTUNITIES

Invite learners to highlight the main idea in digitized text in one color and supporting details in another while engaging in close reading. Depending on the tools, learners can insert notes or annotation marks to indicate questions they may have or vocabulary they need to research.

Use highlighting and color-coding features of annotation tools to teach the main idea, supporting details, and conclusions. Invite learners to share their highlights with peers to see what they thought was the most important idea and generate discussion around differences.

RELATED RESOURCES

Nonfiction Annotations: Taking Notes While Reading (**bit.ly/inclusive365-152a**)

What Exactly Do We Mean by Close Reading? (**bit.ly/inclusive365-152b**)

Using Diigo in the Classroom (**bit.ly/inclusive365-152c**)

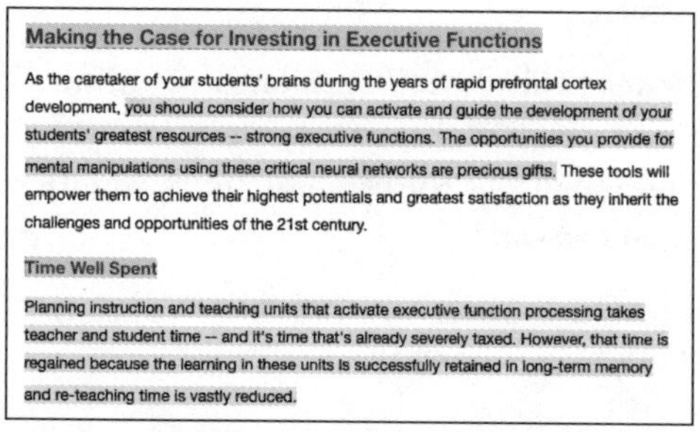

Making the Case for Investing in Executive Functions

As the caretaker of your students' brains during the years of rapid prefrontal cortex development, you should consider how you can activate and guide the development of your students' greatest resources -- strong executive functions. The opportunities you provide for mental manipulations using these critical neural networks are precious gifts. These tools will empower them to achieve their highest potentials and greatest satisfaction as they inherit the challenges and opportunities of the 21st century.

Time Well Spent

Planning instruction and teaching units that activate executive function processing takes teacher and student time -- and it's time that's already severely taxed. However, that time is regained because the learning in these units is successfully retained in long-term memory and re-teaching time is vastly reduced.

Figure 152. Digital annotations using Diigo.

ISTE STANDARDS FOR STUDENTS
1b, 3a, 3c, 5c, 6c

ISTE STANDARDS FOR EDUCATORS
4b, 5a, 5b, 6a, 7a

Camel-Casing Hashtags to Improve Readability

Hashtags provide a way to organize online conversations around a theme or topic. They function as a hyperlink to ease navigation to all the posts related to that specific hashtag. For example, the hashtag for the conversation around this book is #Inclusive365. If you were to see that hashtag appear in a social media platform, you could select it to be taken to the conversations people around the world are having about this book. Hashtags start with the octothorpe symbol (#) and continue with a string of characters. Hashtags with more than one word can be difficult to read without spaces between the words. A solution is to capitalize each separate word in the hashtag, which is a technique known as camel casing (because the captilizations give the hashtags humps, much like a camel). A hashtag with multiple words that uses camel case can be more easily read and understood than one without: #AnyQuestions #UseCamelCase.

INCLUSIVE USES

Individuals learning to decode text and some learners with visual impairments appreciate hashtags that are written using camel case. Screen reader software is better able to read camel case.

SAMPLE TOOL

Twitter.com is a common social media tool that uses hashtags that can be written using camel case (**twitter.com**).

EXTENSION OPPORTUNITY

Hashtags can be used to make jokes or commentary. Invite learners to create hashtags for content they are learning. When they create the hashtag for the content, invite them to use camel case to improve readability.

RELATED RESOURCE

Why Letter Casing is Important to Consider During Design Decisions (**bit.ly/inclusive365-153**)

Figure 153. A tweet comparing hashtags with and without camel case.

ISTE STANDARDS FOR STUDENTS

1b, 2b, 6a, 6d

ISTE STANDARDS FOR EDUCATORS

2b, 3a, 3c, 5a

Visualizing Characters' Traits

Reading novels with numerous characters can prove to be a memory nightmare. How is it possible to remember and differentiate characters while also remembering plot details and detecting literary devices? Keeping track of all the elements of a story can prove a daunting task for some learners. Digital resources that help learners visualize characters can enhance the ability to distinguish between the various characters and enhance memory for specific character traits.

INCLUSIVE USES

Visualizing character traits can help those working to improve memory skills, especially as more characters are introduced in a story. The greater number of characters, the more difficult it becomes to remember the traits of each individual.

Learners who are not yet proficient with decoding or who are working to improve fluent reading might find themselves focusing more on those skills, making it difficult to remember character details.

SAMPLE TOOLS

Sixty Second Recap provides short videos reviewing forty-five literary classics. When accessing the site, find the specific book title, explore the full playlist for that title, and select the Characters video(s) to view a multimedia guide to the main characters in the story (**bit.ly/inclusive365-154a**).

Shmoop includes hundreds of study guides that include character descriptions using teen-friendly language. Some of the character summaries include Character Cards with a graphic of the character and a brief description (**shmoop.com/study-guides**).

No Fear Shakespeare provides graphic-novel-style character summaries (**sparknotes.com/shakespeare**).

Character trait graphic organizers can help learners identify key character traits and analyze characters to enhance understanding and memory.

EXTENSION OPPORTUNITY

Invite learners to create their own visualizations of character traits by taking notes, drawing pictures, or creating their own digital graphic organizers.

RELATED RESOURCE

Top 19 Graphic Organizers to Help Students Learn about Character Traits (**bit.ly/inclusive365-154b**)

being a good shot with a rifle, and claiming her independence.

Figure 154. A 60_Second Recap video showing the main character in *Their Eyes Were Watching God* (with closed captions on).

ISTE STANDARDS FOR STUDENTS
1a, 1b, 3a, 3b

ISTE STANDARDS FOR EDUCATORS
2a, 3b, 6a

Visualizing Vocabulary with Digital Picture Dictionaries

Using a dictionary (both print and digital) is a standard strategy for vocabulary support. However, what happens when the learner is unable to gain an understanding of the target word from the print definition? The use of a picture dictionary may empower learners with the support needed to effectively understand a difficult word. Using the multimodal supports (visual paired with text and audio) can produce a higher level of reading independence for every learner.

INCLUSIVE USES

Learners are more likely to pause to look up a word when all they have to do is press on it, rather than having to alphabetically find the word in a print dictionary. When using a tool equipped with a picture dictionary, visual support provides a clue to the meaning of the word, along with the use of audio to hear both the pronunciation and definition.

SAMPLE TOOLS

Immersive Reader from Microsoft provides picture dictionary support (**bit.ly/inclusive365-155a**).

Read&Write for Chrome from TextHelp provides a picture dictionary function (**bit.ly/inclusive365-155b**).

Snap&Read Universal provides a picture dictionary (**snapandread.com**).

EXTENSION OPPORTUNITIES

Invite learners to illustrate their own writing by adding picture supports from a picture dictionary. Learners can compose text and then add a picture from the dictionary that clarifies a point, illustrates a perspective, or further demonstrates an understanding of a word.

Not every word may be illustrated or represented in a picture dictionary. Invite learners to draw or create their own visual representation for a word to demonstrate understanding.

RELATED RESOURCE

From Paper to Electronic Dictionaries, Evolving Dictionary Skills (**bit.ly/inclusive365-155c**)

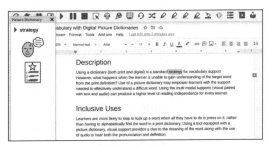

Figure 155. Highlighting a single word and using the TextHelp Read&Write for Google extension to provide picture support.

ISTE STANDARDS FOR STUDENTS

1a, 3a

ISTE STANDARDS FOR EDUCATORS

5a, 5b, 6a

Timelining to Understand a Sequence of Events

Timelines can be an effective instructional tool across a number of content areas, including social studies and science, or with both literary and informational texts. Timelines help learners organize information in a chronological sequence to better understand context; change; cause and effect; and key events in literature or history. This can be especially helpful when learners are engaged in texts that do not proceed in a linear fashion, including those that use flashbacks or memories, or when the sequence of events in a historical or scientific text are critical to understanding. Digital timeline tools help learners and educators to create a multimedia experience. Providing a timeline for a learner may support their ability to keep track of the events in a text. The timeline can then be shared publicly or privately with others.

INCLUSIVE USES

Images and text together in a timeline may be particularly helpful for learners who need a linear, visual framework to keep the sequence of events clear as they read. This strategy can also support multilingual learners in building background knowledge for events. Educators and learners can use accessible images, text, and video to retell the main events of a story.

SAMPLE TOOLS

TimeGraphics is an easy-to-use, web-based timeline tool that allows the user to save timelines in a variety of formats, including PDF, JPG, PowerPoint, Word, and Excel. Public timelines have a setting that allows editing by multiple users (**time.graphics**).

Adobe Spark is a free, web-based tool that provides multiple timeline templates, including a digital timeline option (**bit.ly/inclusive365-156a**).

Sutori is a timeline-generating website (**sutori.com**).

EXTENSION OPPORTUNITIES

Invite learners to create their own timelines to demonstrate understanding of the historical event or novel they are studying, and review their work to clarify any confusion or areas that need reteaching.

Invite learners to create a collaborative timeline of a historical event or a novel and record different chapters or time periods.

Compare details in shared timelines invite learners to double-check information in shared timelines to determine accuracy.

RELATED RESOURCES

Teaching with Timelines
(**bit.ly/inclusive365-156b**)

How to Make a Timeline Infographic
(**bit.ly/inclusive365-156c**)

Adobe Spark Timeline Instructions
(**bit.ly/inclusive365-156d**)

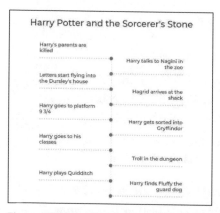

Figure 156. A timeline generated using Adobe Spark for *Harry Potter and the Sorcerer's Stone*.

ISTE STANDARDS FOR STUDENTS
1c, 5b, 5c, 6a, 6c, 6d

ISTE STANDARDS FOR EDUCATORS
5a, 5b, 5c, 7a, 7b

Customizing the Visual Presentation of Text for Written Expression

Font, font size, and line spacing can be a barrier to decoding text when it is not customized to reflect learner preferences. Manipulating the visual presentation of the text can greatly improve readability. Learners should be given the opportunity to optimize the settings that work best according to their learning profile. The default font, size, and spacing may not be appealing or the most readable font for all learners. It is possible to change the default settings to the individual preferences of learners when they are logged in to their accounts, and they open a new document.

INCLUSIVE USES

The ability to customize the visual presentation via font size changes, increased white space, and changes to colors within word processing tools can promote quality written expression, especially when editing and revising work. Editing and revision, important steps in the writing process, are easier to complete when the visual presentation facilitates review and readability. When the font size is too small and there is minimal white space, learners may be reluctant to spend quality time reviewing their compositions. All learners benefit when we demonstrate how to customize the default settings in their word processing programs.

SAMPLE TOOLS

Google Docs defaults to the Arial font, font size 11, and 1.15 line spacing, which can be difficult to read for some learners. Google Slides font style, size, and spacing defaults depend on the selected Slide Theme. To understand how to change the default settings, watch the video tutorial (**bit.ly/inclusive365-157a**). Microsoft Word offers the ability to customize the default settings.

EXTENSION OPPORTUNITY

Encourage learners to determine the most optimal settings that work best depending on what they are asked to compose. Try a variety of combinations until they identify what works.

RELATED RESOURCES

Changing the Font Size in Microsoft Word (**bit.ly/inclusive365-157b**)

8 Tips for Better Readability (**bit.ly/inclusive365-157c**)

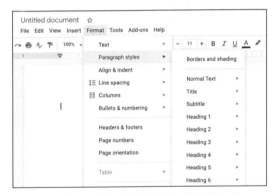

Figure 157. Customizing the default styles in Google Docs.

ISTE STANDARDS FOR STUDENTS

1a, 1d

ISTE STANDARDS FOR EDUCATORS

5a, 6a, 6b

Disabling Automatic Grammar and Spell Check

Many word processing programs enable their automatic grammar and spell check features by default. These checkers provide a visual indicator that there is a potential spelling or grammar error in the composition. For some learners, this real-time, in-the-moment feedback helps them to correct mistakes immediately. For others, however, the real-time visual indicators can be demoralizing distractions that impede self-confidence in the task of writing. Additionally, for some learners, the appearance of the visual indicator interrupts their train of thought about the text they were composing. Disabling the automatic grammar and spell check features eliminates the real-time visual indicators. The learner can use the strategy of running a spelling and grammar check once they've completed their composition, as part of the editing phase of writing.

INCLUSIVE USES

Learners who have frequent spelling or grammar errors may find it more productive and efficient to disable automatic spelling and grammar checks. Likewise, it facilitates a learner's self-confidence and self-esteem when they separate composing and editing into two distinct phases when writing.

Learners with fine motor impairments may find automatic grammar and spelling checkers burdensome as they often increase the number of keystrokes to make corrections. The visual indicator usually only appears after typing a word or phrase. To make the correction, users must navigate to the point of the error. Whether using the backspace key, trackpad, or other means, correcting the error in real-time rather than during an editing phrase requires additional motor movements.

SAMPLE TOOLS

Microsoft Word Users Can Disable Automatic Spelling and Grammar Checks by Going to File > Options > Proofing.

Google Docs Users Can Disable Automatic Spelling and Grammar Checks by Going to Tools > Spelling and Grammar (**docs.google.com**).

EXTENSION OPPORTUNITY

Encourage learners to count and track the number of errors they've made during the editing phase of writing. Determine the percentage of errors using the total number of words compared to the number of errors. As the learner improves their spelling and other mechanics, the number of errors decrease. A learner can visualize this progress, which can bolster self-confidence and self-esteem.

RELATED RESOURCE

A.T.TIPSCAST Episode #92: Thri Mor Speling Strategeez (**bit.ly/inclusive365-158**)

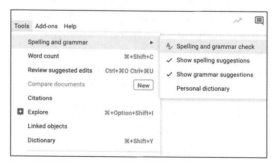

Figure 158. How to turn off spelling and grammar suggestions in Google Docs.

ISTE STANDARDS FOR STUDENTS
1c, 6a, 6b, 6c, 6d, 7b, 7c

ISTE STANDARDS FOR EDUCATORS
5a, 5c, 6a, 6d

Identifying the Optimal Method for Written Expression Considering the Learning Task

In written composition, the selected writing instrument can influence the quality of the product. Limiting learners to only paper or pencil tasks may affect the quality and quantity of what the learner is able to produce. Inviting and offering a choice of writing methods assists learners in identifying the tool that works best for the task at hand. Writing tool options, in addition to traditional tools, include keyboarding, word prediction, voice typing using speech recognition, or voice recordings.

INCLUSIVE USES

Learners who are developing their fine motor skills may find that alternative output methods promote written expression performance, since they are not limited by handwriting legibility. Learners who benefit from vocabulary and spelling support may find that alternatives to paper and pencil provide the scaffolded help they need to improve the quality of their written expression. Opportunities to try out a variety of options helps build self-advocacy and strategic competence.

SAMPLE TOOLS

The Decoste Writing Protocol is a screening and progress monitoring tool that guides decisions about writing tool preferences (**bit.ly/inclusive365-159a**).

The Online Assessment of Writing Methods is part of the Typing Training website and compares various writing methods to guide decisions about choosing the optimal tool for written expression (**typingtraining.com/writing_methods.html**).

EXTENSION OPPORTUNITIES

Invite learners to evaluate the quality of their writing and develop their own assessments to monitor progress over time. What would they change? What would they add?

Based on the task, learners may choose different tools for writing. For instance, sending a card to a family relative might require a different tool than taking notes from a recorded video. Invite learners to reflect on the tool they selected to determine if it was effective, if they'd make alterations, or if a different selection altogether would be preferred the next time they are presented with a similar task.

RELATED RESOURCES

Online Assessment of Writing Methods, Step-by-Step Tutorial (**bit.ly/inclusive365-159b**)

Introducing the New DeCoste Writing Protocol (**bit.ly/inclusive365-159c**)

Date/Time ▾	Exercise
10/15/20 11:26:29 AM	Topic: Broader Topics / Learning - Typing
10/15/20 11:24:06 AM	Topic: Broader Topics / Learning - Handwriting
10/15/20 11:19:31 AM	Open Writing / Open Writing - Typing
10/15/20 11:18:08 AM	Open Writing / Open Writing - Handwriting
10/15/20 11:14:30 AM	Open Writing / Open Writing - Typing
10/15/20 11:12:31 AM	Open Writing / Open Writing - Handwriting

Figure 159. Some of the data that is collected by the OAWM for determining the optimal written expression tool.

ISTE STANDARDS FOR STUDENTS
1a, 1c, 5b

ISTE STANDARDS FOR EDUCATORS
5a, 5b, 7a, 7b, 7c

Producing Text with Speech

Learners can produce text using their own voices. Speech-to-text tools instantly transcribe words produced verbally. The learner activates the speech-to-text function available in a variety of tools, and the tool listens to the words being spoken and then transforms the audible sounds to digital text. Speech-to-text allows learners to have their speech transcribed digitally without interrupting the flow of writing with spelling or keyboard access issues.

INCLUSIVE USES

Learners who have difficulty controlling fine or gross motor movements may find using speech-to-text useful in producing digital text.

Learners who have difficulties with spelling accuracy may find speech-to-text a useful tool for producing digital text.

SAMPLE TOOL

Voice Typing is a feature available on many G Suite applications including Google Docs, Google Slides, and Google Sheets. It is also built into the operating system of Chromebooks (**bit.ly/inclusive365-160a**).

EXTENSION OPPORTUNITIES

Invite learners to make decisions about when it is best to use speech-to-text. Certain settings, such as taking notes when someone is giving a presentation or when working independently in a quiet environment, might not be conducive to using speech-to-text. Invite learners to brainstorm a list of times and places when using speech-to-text would be appropriate or inappropriate.

Invite learners to identify what factors increase or decrease their speech recognition accuracy.

RELATED RESOURCES

How to use voice typing in Google Docs (**bit.ly/inclusive365-160b**)

Voice Typing: Four Tips (**bit.ly/inclusive365-160c**)

How to Dictate Your Book with Voice Typing in Google Docs (**bit.ly/inclusive365-160d**)

Figure 160. Voice Typing in the Tools menu in Google Docs.

ISTE STANDARDS FOR STUDENTS
1c, 1d, 6a, 6b

ISTE STANDARDS FOR EDUCATORS
2b, 3a, 4d, 5a, 5c, 6a, 6b, 6d, 7a, 7b

Supporting Multilingual Learners When Writing Using Digital Translation Tools

Emergent multilingual learners benefit from expressing what they know in their dominant language rather than requiring them to share in a less familiar language. What they produce using their dominant language often better reflects their understanding. Requiring learners to use the language they are learning increases the cognitive load and is more challenging. Learners can dictate or write in their dominant language and use digital translation tools to translate the text into English. Digital translation tools provide the opportunity to convert text into multiple languages, which is a powerful strategy for emergent multilingual learners.

INCLUSIVE USES

Automatic translation tools reduce the cognitive load for learners who are developing their written expression skills while learning the English language. Once the dictation has been recorded, the learners can use text-to-speech in both their dominant language and the language they are learning to demonstrate what they know.

SAMPLE TOOLS

Word for Office 365 offers speech-to-text, translation, and text-to-speech in multiple languages under the review tab on the toolbar.

Google Translate offers speech-to-text, translation, and text-to-speech. The text can be copied and pasted into a word processing document (**translate.google.com**).

EXTENSION OPPORTUNITY

Invite learners to perform a quarterly review of their text compositions to chronicle their progress with written expression. Encourage learners to analyze the quality and quantity of their products, including the number of words written, the vocabulary used, and the complexity of the language and sentence structure.

RELATED RESOURCES

Translating: Using Microsoft Word to Dictate, Translate, and Read Aloud (**bit.ly/inclusive365-161a**)

Dictation in Word, OneNote, and PowerPoint 365 (**bit.ly/inclusive365-161b**)

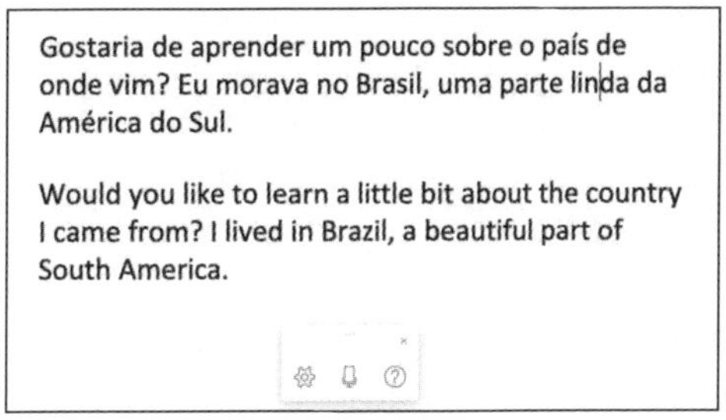

Gostaria de aprender um pouco sobre o país de onde vim? Eu morava no Brasil, uma parte linda da América do Sul.

Would you like to learn a little bit about the country I came from? I lived in Brazil, a beautiful part of South America.

Figure 161. A dictation in Portugeuse, showing the dictation microphone and the English translation in Word.

ISTE STANDARDS FOR STUDENTS
1a, 1b, 1c, 6a

ISTE STANDARDS FOR EDUCATORS
2b, 5a, 5b, 6a, 6d, 7a

Promoting Writing Using Virtual Keyboards

Virtually every touchscreen device we access today comes with a built-in, on-screen keyboard. This virtual representation of the keyboard requires moving the cursor across the screen and clicking letters to select them to type, or using fingers to select letters. One feature of most on-screen keyboards is the inclusion of word prediction. As the learner types, words are provided as the device tries to predict what the learner is writing. If the correct word appears, the learner can select the word to drop it into the composition, saving keystrokes.

INCLUSIVE USES

Accessing this keyboard may encourage writing for some learners who are not comfortable with their keyboarding skills on a traditional physical keyboard, but instead would prefer to use the trackpad or tap directly on a touch screen to enter text. Virtual keyboards can provide a level of accessibility beyond the physical keyboard. For learners with specific fine or gross motor challenges, the virtual keyboard may be the most efficient way for them to type, as these keyboards can often be configured in a manner that is most efficient for a particular individual. For other learners, it may be a preference depending on the task at hand.

Learners can often recognize correct spellings when they see them but have more difficulty generating accurate spelling on their own. For learners working on improving spelling and vocabulary skills, having words appear before they have had to spell them in their entirety can build confidence.

SAMPLE TOOLS

Chrome OS On-Screen Keyboard is a feature on Chromebooks.

Windows On-Screen is a feature of Windows devices.

iOS offers a wide range of optional third-party on-screen keyboards.

EXTENSION OPPORTUNITY

Encourage learners to activate the on-screen keyboard and type using only the trackpad. Invite learners to reflect upon their experience. How did the virtual keyboard impact their ability to capture their writing? Did it slow the process down, speed it up, or was it about the same? Did they find value in the word prediction option for quickly adding words into their writing?

RELATED RESOURCES

Use the On-Screen Keyboard in Chrome (**bit.ly/inclusive365-162a**)

How to Use the On-Screen Keyboard in Windows 7, 8, and 10 (**bit.ly/inclusive365-162b**)

5 of the Best Third-Party Keyboard Apps for iPhone and iPad Users (**bit.ly/inclusive365-162c**)

Figure 162. On-Screen Chrome OS keyboard.

ISTE STANDARDS FOR STUDENTS
1c, 6a, 6d

ISTE STANDARDS FOR EDUCATORS
5a, 6a

Personalizing 1:1 Devices with Customized Keyboards

One of the first actions taken by learners when provided with their own device is to personalize it. Stickers that speak to personalized interests often adorn the back of devices. Beyond decoration and expression, these adornments can have utility as well. For example, keyboards can be customized with stickers to provide color-coding; larger letters; upper or lower cases; and tactile cues such as raised bumpers or rougher surfaces. These personalizations can provide learners with unique customizations that fit individual needs without necessarily drawing attention to those needs. It should be noted that when customizations are being crafted, safety and maintenance of the device should be a consideration. Many devices have lids that close. Some customizations might seem reasonable with the lid open but then be destructive when the lid is closed.

INCLUSIVE USES

Learners who need or prefer a rougher tactile surface on a keyboard may find adding texture to a physical keyboard useful. A single drop of glue, once hardened, on some of the keys, such as vowels, might help provide the learner with the customization necessary to improve the keyboarding experience.

Learnings with visual challenges, either organically or neuro-cognitively, may find the experience of keyboarding improved when rows or individual keys are color coded. Stickers for shift keys, which change the case letter keys can also help to provide contrast for visual needs.

Boundaries constructed around keys can provide both a visual and tactile guide for learners with visual-spatial and/or fine motor difficulties.

SAMPLE TOOLS

Stickers can be used to customize the appearance (colors, fonts, cases, etc.) of letters on a keyboard (**bit.ly/inclusive365-163a**).

Braille stickers provide a raised yet pliable surface that can be used to add a tactile differentiator for any learner, not just those learning or using Braille (**bit.ly/inclusive365-163b**).

Wikki-Stix are strings covered in wax making them both pliable and adhesive. These sticks can be used to create colored borders around rows or individual keys (**wikkistix.com**).

EXTENSION OPPORTUNITY

As a small or whole group experience, invite every learner to discuss their keyboarding needs. Following the discussion, provide the materials to make those customizations.

RELATED RESOURCES

DIY Keyboard Stickers (**bit.ly/inclusive365-163c**)

A.T.TIPSCAST Episode #56: Typing Tutors, Part 2 (**bit.ly/inclusive365-163d**)

Figure 163. Tactile guides affixed to keyboards.

ISTE STANDARDS FOR STUDENTS
1a, 1b

ISTE STANDARDS FOR EDUCATORS
2b, 4d, 5a, 6a, 6d

Entering Text with Slide Typing

Traditional keyboards require users to lift and lower their fingers to enter text. This requires a level of fine motor strength, control, and accuracy. Some touchscreen keyboards allow for a function where individuals can enter text by sliding their fingers over the keyboard, never lifting their fingers against gravity. The keyboard senses the unique motor pattern created to compose a word and creates the word as one slides a finger from letter to letter.

INCLUSIVE USES

Learners with fine motor difficulties may find traditional typing time consuming, laborious, or frustrating. Frequent errors can take a toll on an individual's self-confidence and lead to avoidance. Slide typing may help individuals gain confidence in their ability to compose text without needing to fight gravity. Likewise, slide typing allows individuals to enter text without using fingers at all. Text is entered through any conductive surface, including a touch screen stylus. This provides a means of entering text without the need for use of fingers.

SAMPLE TOOLS

QuickPath is a feature of iOS that allows users to enter text by sliding from letter to letter (**bit.ly/inclusive365-164a**).

GBoard, a keyboard available from Google for Android and iOS mobile devices, allows users to enter text by sliding from letter to letter (**bit.ly/inclusive365-164b**).

EXTENSION OPPORTUNITY

Invite learners to create or use a stylus to assist in slide typing. Craft a stylus using household materials (a cotton swab, aluminum foil, tape and a pen) and customize it to fit the needs and preferences of the learner.

RELATED RESOURCE

What Is Gesture Typing? The Time-Saving Texting Technique We Might Soon All Be Using (**bit.ly/inclusive365-164c**)

Figure 164. Slide typing.

ISTE STANDARDS FOR STUDENTS
6b, 6c, 6d

ISTE STANDARDS FOR EDUCATORS
5a, 5c, 6b, 6d

Converting Handwriting to Typed Digital Text

Some learners have grown accustomed to handwriting notes. Evidence suggests that handwriting may help some people better remember the content they write (James & Engelhardt, 2014). Typed digital text, however, is searchable and works with other supportive technologies, like text-to-speech. One way to combine the best of both strategies is for a learner to automatically convert their handwriting into typed digital text. Learners then benefit from additional technologies that can interact with the digital text.

INCLUSIVE USES

Learners with organization or spelling challenges may find converting handwriting into typed digital text beneficial, as they can more effectively organize notes and fix spelling errors in digital text.

SAMPLE TOOLS

Microsoft OneNote allows a user to convert handwritten text into typed digital text (**onenote.com**).

The Apple Pencil, in conjunction with an iPad, allows for handwriting to be converted to typed digital text (**apple.com/apple-pencil**).

The grab image text feature of Google Keep converts handwritten text into typed digital text (**keep.google.com**).

EXTENSION OPPORTUNITIES

Invite learners to create a chart outlining when they might use different tools to produce typed text. The chart might include a list of possible tools, including typing on a keyboard, texting, typing with word prediction, texting with word prediction, speech-to-text, and handwriting which will be converted into typed digital text.

Depending on the task and the environment where the learner will be writing, different tools might be more appropriate than others. When a learner has prepared a table or list that can be referred to prior to starting a writing task, the learner can choose the best strategy for the task, and keep track of what tool was used.

Invite a learner to use text-to-speech to check the accuracy of the conversions once completed. Depending on the neatness of the handwriting, the accuracy of the conversion may be variable. Listening to the text helps learners know the conversion was accurate.

RELATED RESOURCES

How to Convert Handwritten Text into Typed Digital Text Using Microsoft OneNote (**bit.ly/inclusive365-165a**)

The Effects of Handwriting Experience on Functional Brain Development in Pre-Literate Children (**bit.ly/inclusive365-165b**)

Figure 165. A handwritten word converted to digital text in OneNote.

ISTE STANDARDS FOR STUDENTS
6a

ISTE STANDARDS FOR EDUCATORS
5a, 5b, 5c, 6a, 6b, 6d

Pre-Writing with Sticky Notes

Jotting writing ideas on digital or traditional sticky notes helps learners plan and organize their ideas in advance of writing. Learners put individual ideas, sentences, and statements onto individual sticky notes. Notes can be color-coded based on the topic. Once sufficient ideas have been generated, including a topic sentence, supporting details, and closing statements, the learner then can arrange and rearrange the sticky notes to find the order that best conveys the information. Then, depending on the tool used to generate the sticky notes, the learner can copy the sticky note outline to their draft document to write their paragraph or report.

INCLUSIVE USES

Learners who are developing writers can use this strategy to make paragraph or multi-paragraph writing less intimidating. This strategy can help wean a learner from depending on a scribe, and it expects smaller chunks of writing at one time, which reduces the cognitive load on learners. Additionally, learners can use color-coded sticky notes, with different colors for main ideas and supporting details, helping them to organize their writing.

SAMPLE TOOLS

Jamboard allows learners to generate multiple sticky notes on a page. Sticky notes can easily be rearranged, and multiple pages can be representative of multiple paragraphs for a paper. Learners paste the text from their Jamboard pages into their draft document (**jamboard.google.com**).

PowerPoint allows learners to use individual slides as sticky notes, with the ability to rearrange the slides and then export them into Word as an outline.

Google Keep allows learners to create notes that can then easily be imported into a Google Doc. Notes can be tagged and color-coded (**keep.google.com**).

EXTENSION OPPORTUNITY

Invite learners to work collaboratively on a shared sticky note writing task. Jamboard, Google Keep, and PowerPoint all can be collaborative documents. Peers can give each other feedback and make suggestions when one member of a group is struggling.

RELATED RESOURCE

How to Save Microsoft PowerPoint Presentation Outlines to Word (**bit.ly/inclusive365-166**)

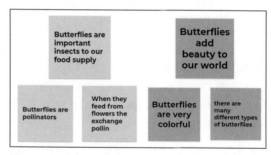

Figure 166. Color-coded notes created in Jamboard.

ISTE STANDARDS FOR STUDENTS
1a, 1b, 6a

ISTE STANDARDS FOR EDUCATORS
5a, 7a

Recording Audio to Compose Thoughts for Pre-Writing

Transforming thoughts into text is a complex process. Often the challenges of spelling, along with typing or writing, can interfere with the flow of ideas. Recording thoughts on audio before transcribing these thoughts into a written or typed format allows a writer to have a free flow of ideas without writing barriers. Tools that allow audio files to be inserted directly into a document along with text allow the learner to toggle back and forth between written expression and oral expression of ideas. The learner can listen to the audio files and transcribe the audio into text. Whenever the learner loses their place, gets distracted, becomes frustrated with spelling, or otherwise fatigues, they can take a break knowing the audio of the composition is readily available. Recording audio files may work well for pre-writing in spite of poor audio quality, lower volume, and background noises; speech-to-text technologies may be pickier about sound quality.

INCLUSIVE USES

Learners who have demonstrated that verbal communication is a preferred method of expression as compared to writing may find recording audio forpre-writing beneficial.

Learners with evolving handwriting or spelling skills may find it less frustrating to make audio recordings for each sentence and then listen back while typing. Generating thoughts and turning them into text at the same time is a heavier cognitive load.

Learners whose speech articulation causes interference with speech-to-text technologies may find recording audio and listening back to it a more efficient method of producing text.

SAMPLE TOOLS

Voice Note is a function of the premium version of Read&Write for Chrome extension, which allows users to record audio comments (**bit.ly/inclusive365-167a**).

The Voice Recorder in OneNote allows users to record audio files and compose text in the same document (**bit.ly/inclusive365-167b**).

EXTENSION OPPORTUNITY

Invite learners to use a graphic organizer to generate a template for their composition. The learner can record audio as their pre-writing process, then transcribe one sentence in each cell to help visualize the separation between individual ideas and easily manipulate them into the order that reflects their thinking.

RELATED RESOURCE

Making Time for Voice Recordings (**bit.ly/inclusive365-167c**)

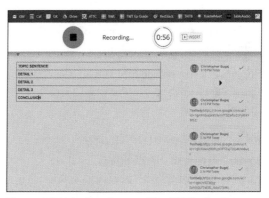

Figure 167. Voice Note feature of Read&Write for Chrome.

ISTE STANDARDS FOR STUDENTS
6a, 6b, 6c, 6d

ISTE STANDARDS FOR EDUCATORS
2b, 4d, 5a, 5b, 5c, 6a, 6d, 7a, 7b

STRATEGY 168

Structuring Writing Using Free-Form Digital Graphic Organizers

Graphic organizers are visual tools that help learners brainstorm, organize, and sequence ideas as part of the writing process. They are often provided in a static, printed format with learners asked to fill in blank cells with limited space available to write in, which can stifle creativity and motivation to write. Free-form digital graphic organizers allow learners the freedom to record their thoughts and then easily manipulate and rearrange ideas.

INCLUSIVE USES

Any modality for generating text can be used with digital graphic organizers.. The size of a cell in a digital graphic organizer expands with the text added, allowing learners to have as much space as needed.

Digital graphic organizers are mistake-tolerant, promote risk-taking, and allow learners to reorganize and rethink relationships, which is beneficial to all learners.

SAMPLE TOOLS

Bubbl.us is a free-form, online, collaborative graphic organizer tool (**bubbl.us**).

Popplet is a free online tool and an iOS app that create free-form graphic organizers (**popplet.com**).

EXTENSION OPPORTUNITY

Invite learners to share and review their graphic organizers with peers as a small group experience that is part of the prewriting process. Peers can provide feedback before the actual draft begins.

RELATED RESOURCE

Graphic Organizers to Help Kids with Writing (**bit.ly/inclusive365-168**)

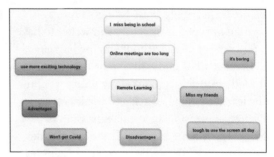

Figure 168. Brainstorming using Bubbl.us.

ISTE STANDARDS FOR STUDENTS
1a, 1c, 6b, 6c

ISTE STANDARDS FOR EDUCATORS
2b, 3b, 5a, 5b, 6a, 6b

Collaborative Brainstorming through Multiple Modalities

Brainstorming is an effective way to generate ideas and catapult thinking into action. It is a critical step to take before doing research or starting a project. Brainstorming using online tools can promote collaboration and allow learners to provide input and contribute to the ideation of a shared product.

INCLUSIVE USE

Digital brainstorming tools allow learners to use other functions of technology that might support learning, such as text-to-speech and word prediction. Some learners might choose to type their brainstorming input, others might use speech-to-text, while others might use audio or video comments. Inviting learners to share ideas using their preferred method helps encourage and reinforce the idea that everyone's voice should be heard.

SAMPLE TOOLS

Padlet is a digital bulletin board for notes, hyperlinks, videos, and images. These can then be rearranged, connected to other ideas, commented on, liked, starred, voted on, or marked on a numerical scale. A Padlet page can be made private (only invited contributors) or public (anyone with the link) (**padlet.com**).

Popplet is a mind mapping tool that is available online or on iOS devices. Collaborators can color-code ideas and add images, videos, and weblinks. It has a bright, clean visual design that makes it accessible for a broad range of age groups. Popplet mind maps can be viewed in presentation mode as a slide show, and educators and collaborators can also see a timeline view that shows the evolution of the mind map. Settings allow collaborators to be identified, or names can be hidden (**popplet.com**).

AnswerGarden is a web-based tool that has a brainstorm mode where learners can post brainstormed answers to a question and have those answers appear instantly. Educators can set up the question in moderator mode, which requires approving each post before it is visible. There is an option to export the responses for later review (**answergarden.ch**).

EXTENSION OPPORTUNITIES

Learners can brainstorm ideas for possible projects or goals. Others can then provide feedback by voting suggestions up or down to help come to a consensus.

Invite learners to find and use a brainstorming template such as those found at **bit.ly/inclusive365-169a** to help guide them through the brainstorming experience.

RELATED RESOURCE

Brainstorming Techniques to Visually Generate Ideas for Teams (**bit.ly/inclusive365-169b**)

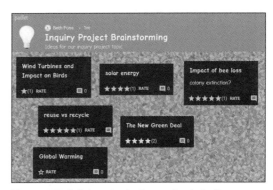

Figure 169. Collaborative brainstorming in Padlet.

ISTE STANDARDS FOR STUDENTS
1b, 1c, 3c, 3d, 7b , 7c

ISTE STANDARDS FOR EDUCATORS
5a, 5b, 5c

Ensuring Accessibility Using Premade Templates for Documents

Word processors often provide premade document templates from which to work. These templates can not only improve the overall aesthetic quality of the final product but greatly improve the accessibility of a document. Templates are often pre-formatted to comply with accessibility standards mitigating the need to retroactively correct errors made when not using a template. Learners might also find it easier to plug text, images, and other content into predetermined areas of a template rather than creating a document from scratch. This can decrease frustration and improve overall productivity.

INCLUSIVE USES

As learners collaborate with others who have diverse needs it is important to work within documents that are accessible to everyone. It may not be apparent or obvious that other collaborators require a particular accommodation or have a particular need. Templates help ensure universal access, no matter a person's abilities. Templates born accessible also mean less time retrofitting documents to make them accessible.

Document templates can help ensure accessibility when learners compose text for public consumption in an attempt to make meaningful contributions to the world.

SAMPLE TOOLS

Templates can be found in Word by going to the File menu and selecting New (**bit.ly/inclusive365-170a**).

Templates can be found in Google Docs by going to File > New > From Template. (**bit.ly/inclusive365-170b**).

EXTENSION OPPORTUNITIES

Templates are usually organized by categories for quick access. Learners can be invited to browse these categories to increase familiarity with what is available for future projects.

Depending on the rules of your particular educational institution, it may be possible for learners to create their own templates and place them in a shared environment for others to access and use. Encourage learners to create a template they would use to help with their own learning and submit it to the shared gallery to help others.

RELATED RESOURCE

Using Style Guides for Accessibility (**bit.ly/inclusive365-170c**)

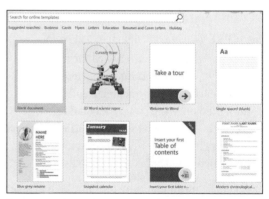

Figure 170. Some document templates available in Word.

ISTE STANDARDS FOR STUDENTS

1c, 2b, 6a, 6b, 6c, 6d, 7a, 7b

ISTE STANDARDS FOR EDUCATORS

2b, 2c, 3b, 3c, 4b, 5a, 5c, 6d

Accessing Vocabulary with Word Banks

A word bank is a list of academic words related to the content that a learner is learning. The word bank provides learners access to key vocabulary necessary for reading or writing about a particular topic. Word banks can be text only, text with a definition, or text with a picture. Word banks typically assist learners with understanding or using vocabulary that they have had explicit instruction about and now need to apply as they read or write about the topic. Word banks can be provided digitally or in a variety of low-tech ways. To create a simple word bank, create a digital table using any tool that allows table creation. Create two columns, filling the first with key content words and the second with definitions (or pictures).

Digital versions can include the ability to click on a word to hear it spoken, read the definition, or add it to a document.

INCLUSIVE USES

Word banks allow learners to overcome language or literacy barriers by providing access to academic vocabulary that they may have difficulty writing, spelling, or typing independently or efficiently. Word banks can be customized to include more or fewer words, color code words based on function or category, or include picture or symbol supports.

SAMPLE TOOLS

Clicker Writer is an iPad app or Chromebook extension with customizable word banks available to a learner during writing tasks. Additional scaffolded support is available, including forced order writing, picture-supported writing, text-to-speech,and word prediction (**cricksoft.com/us/clicker/apps**).

Create shared word banks in Google Keep and pin the word bank, enabling the learner to refer to it as they are composing text in Google Docs (**keep.google.com**).

Use a table in a word processing program or rows and columns in a spreadsheet program to create word banks. Learners can copy and paste words, or use the word bank as a reference.

Word Bank Universal allows learners to create their own word banks. Vocabulary from any web page or digital document can be easily added to a word bank with just a click (**bit.ly/inclusive365-171a**).

EXTENSION OPPORTUNITY

Invite learners to use a word bank when writing in response to something they are reading. Educators or learners can create the word bank in any suitable application by importing or adding keywords from the text. Learners who need more support may benefit from a sentence frame (Figure 171) to help kickstart the writing process. Color coding the types of words in the word bank (e.g., character names versus traits) can provide additional support.

RELATED RESOURCE

How Word Banks Support Learners in Expanding Their Vocabulary (**bit.ly/inclusive365-171b**)

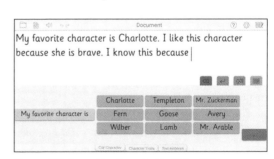

Figure 171. A word bank created in Clicker Writer.

ISTE STANDARDS FOR STUDENTS
1b, 1c, 6a, 6c, 6d

ISTE STANDARDS FOR EDUCATORS
5a, 5,b, 5c, 6a, 6b, 6d, 7a

Providing Digital Word Walls

Word walls are commonly displayed in elementary learning spaces and provide reference support during reading and writing tasks involving explicitly taught sight words. Transforming this instructional method to a digital format allows learners access to the visual whenever it is needed. Digital word walls can exist as a file within a Learning Management System or shared digital space that learners can access as an ongoing resource for any writing task, just as they would use a physical word wall.

INCLUSIVE USES

Customize digital word walls for learners who might benefit from limiting the number of words displayed or who may need access to higher-level vocabulary. Save custom word walls for any learners to their device, their Google Drive, or any other digital storage system.

Learners can also access text-to-speech if needed with digital word walls.

SAMPLE TOOL

Create customized digital word walls in Google Sheets or Excel, which will allow words to be sorted alphabetically as they are added.

EXTENSION OPPORTUNITIES

Invite learners to add challenging words or new words of interest or complexity to a personalized digital word wall, allowing them to take ownership of their learning and create a resource that supports their learning.

Invite learners to use word walls to provide a quick and easy reference for vocabulary used in science, social studies, or math.

RELATED RESOURCES

Word Walls (**bit.ly/inclusive365-172a**)

How to Use Digital Word Walls and Dictionaries in Google Drive (**bit.ly/inclusive365-172b**)

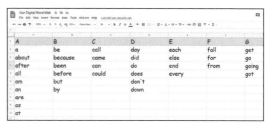

Figure 172. A first-grade digital word wall created in Google Sheets.

ISTE STANDARDS FOR STUDENTS

1a, 1c

ISTE STANDARDS FOR EDUCATORS

2b, 3b, 5a, 5b, 6d

Building Vocabulary Using Alphabet Brainstorming

Alphabet brainstorming helps learners expand the vocabulary that they are using in their writing. Learners brainstorm a list of words or phrases related to their writing topic, for as many letters of the alphabet as possible. Generating ideas for more than one word or phrase per letter is encouraged. Learners are also invited to generate words using different parts of speech such as adjectives, adverbs, nouns, verbs, etc.

INCLUSIVE USES

Multilingual learners and those who are working on building their language or vocabulary skills might benefit from opportunities to find the words they may need to include in their writing as part of their pre-writing tasks.

SAMPLE TOOLS

Learners can add words and phrases to each letter section using a table in Google Docs as a template (**bit.ly/inclusive365-173a**).

Clicker Writer allows the creation of alphabetized topic word banks that can be generated from pre-existing text sources. Educators can load word banks from which learners can choose words that match each letter of the alphabet (**bit.ly/inclusive365-173b**).

EXTENSION OPPORTUNITY

Invite learners to work collaboratively and consider words that relate to a topic as they read a text or listen to a video about that topic. This supports building background knowledge along with developing vocabulary skills.

RELATED RESOURCE

Alphabet Brainstorm (**bit.ly/inclusive365-173c**)

Figure 173. Brainstorming topic words for writing about butterflies in Clicker Writer.

ISTE STANDARDS FOR STUDENTS
1b, 2a, 6a

ISTE STANDARDS FOR EDUCATORS
5a, 5b, 6d

Improving Word Choice with a Digital Thesaurus

As learners go through the writing process and edit their work to make improvements, they often need to examine word choice. They may overuse a word or wish to find a more ~~clear~~ precise word that better conveys the nuances of their thoughts and ideas. Digital thesauruses provide the learner with access to synonyms, antonyms, and at times examples of how a word can be used in a sentence. Digital versions are available for younger learners with text-to-speech for pronunciation and images to help comprehension. Thesauruses are available as built-in tools in Word and Google Docs, while there are a variety of online tools: thesaurus extensions for browsers, thesaurus apps, or thesaurus websites. Voice assistants can also have digital thesaurus functionalities.

INCLUSIVE USES

Digital thesauruses can be accessed easily within certain writing tools—such as Word and Google Docs—by highlighting and right-clicking on a word. Thesauruses that include images and ~~precise~~ clear definitions in addition to synonyms can be particularly useful for those with emerging reading and writing skills.

SAMPLE TOOLS

Power Thesaurus is a crowdsourced thesaurus that provides synonyms, antonyms, definitions, and examples. Being crowdsourced there are often popular words, slang, current uses of words, and unique uses of words (**powerthesaurus.org**).

Kids Wordsmyth provides definitions, parts of speech, synonyms, and antonyms, along with pictorial representations of words (**kids.wordsmyth.net**).

EXTENSION OPPORTUNITY

Encourage learners not only to use a thesaurus when writing, but also when they encounter a word they are not sure of when reading.

RELATED RESOURCE

Using a Dictionary or Thesaurus Effectively (**bit.ly/inclusive365-174**)

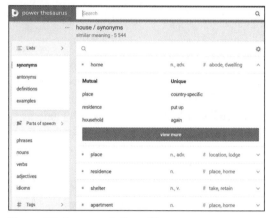

Figure 174. Synonyms in Power Thesaurus.

ISTE STANDARDS FOR STUDENTS
1c, 3a, 6a

ISTE STANDARDS FOR EDUCATORS
4b, 5a, 5b, 6a

Varying Word Choice Using Word Clouds

All of the words in the body of a text, copied and pasted into a word cloud generator, creates a visual representation of the words included in the text (with articles, prepositions, and pronouns excluded). The size of individual words in the cloud indicates the frequency with which that word is repeated in the text. When learners paste their own text into a word cloud generator, they can identify words that they may have overused. The word cloud allows learners to quickly identify any overused words and substitute more varied or effective alternatives, which will lead to better writing and vocabulary skills.

INCLUSIVE USES

Learners who are developing their written expression skills or who multilingual learners often have difficulty with varying vocabulary, particularly in their writing. Word cloud generators provide an engaging way to help all learners identify what words they use most frequently in their writing and expand word choices.

SAMPLE TOOLS

Tagxedo is a word cloud generator that also offers shape and style options (**tagxedo.com**).

Word Cloud Generator is a free generator that includes font, color, shape, and theme options (**wordclouds.com**).

Word Cloud Add-On is a Google Docs add-on that provides a chart with the frequency rate of individual wordswithin a given text (**wordtagcloud.com**).

EXTENSION OPPORTUNITY

Invite learners to compare word clouds with their peers, identify overused words, and suggest alternatives. Introduce digital thesaurus tools to help learners choose synonyms.

RELATED RESOURCE

Improve Writing and Reading Comprehension Using Word Clouds (**bit.ly/inclusive365-175**)

Word	Frequency
word	9
students	6
words	5
clouds	4
text	4
writing	4
identify	3
overused	3
thesaurus	3
tool	2

Figure 175. A word cloud with word counts.

ISTE STANDARDS FOR STUDENTS
1c, 3c, 5b, 6a, 6c

ISTE STANDARDS FOR EDUCATORS
2b, 4b, 5a, 6d, 7a

Guiding Appropriateness of Word Choice with Automatic Text Substitutions

Some learners may need guidance as to what is appropriate and inappropriate to share in a collaborative working document. Learners might use inappropriate language, not realizing their word choice is disruptive or potentially upsetting to others. Automatic text substitutions allow educators to provide guidance in real-time when typing a word. When they type an inappropriate word, a substitute word or phrase replaces it automatically. For instance, if a learner were to use a profane word, it would be substituted with the phrase, "That word is not appropriate for use in this shared document. Please choose a different word."

INCLUSIVE USES

Some learners who are working on social skills or pragmatic language may not realize certain words are offensive or inappropriate in academic writing. Giving guidance through text substitutions is non-threatening and reduces the potential for embarrassment.

SAMPLE TOOL

Google Docs users can create automatic text substitutions by going to Tools>Preferences.

EXTENSION OPPORTUNITY

Invite learners to create their own text substitutions for frequent mistakes. They can target common spelling errors or frequently occurring typographical errors, with the learner entering in the correct spelling so that the error is autocorrected. Use caution when employing this strategy, as automatically correcting words does not necessarily give the learner an opportunity to identify, learn from, and then correct the mistake. For some learners, however,

decreasing frustration by correcting the mistake can be more meaningful than learning the accurate spelling of a word.

RELATED RESOURCES

How to Edit or Add Automatic Text Substitutions in Google Docs (**bit.ly/inclusive365-176a**)

Replace Text and Punctuation in Documents on Mac (**bit.ly/inclusive365-176b**)

Auto Text in Google Docs (**bit.ly/inclusive365-176c**)

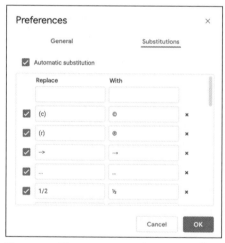

Figure 176. The pop-up menu for automatic substitutions in Google Docs.

ISTE STANDARDS FOR STUDENTS
1b, 1c, 2a, 2b, 6a, 6b, 6c, 6d, 7d, 7c

ISTE STANDARDS FOR EDUCATORS
3a, 3c, 6b, 6d

Shared Writing to Support Emergent Literacy

Shared writing is a scaffolded writing experience in which the educator leads emergent writers in constructing a collaborative text using a common sentence structure or sentence frame. The educator thinks aloud to model the writing process, with learners contributing their own ideas to finish the sentence. The shared writing experience can be part of a larger set of emergent writing and reading tasks known as Predictable Chart Writing. Predictable Chart Writing is a series of shared group writing and reading activities in which the educator leads emergent writers in exploring a co-constructed text repeatedly over the course of one week (see also Strategy 180).

INCLUSIVE USES

Shared writing experiences by their nature support learners of all ages who are emergent writers.

SAMPLE TOOL

Tar Heel Reader is an extensive collection of free, easy to read, switch-accessible books with read-aloud features. Tar Heel Reader provides a digital resource for a shared writing experience with images that are pulled from Flickr's Creative Commons licensed photographs to support writing (**flickr.com/creativecommons**). When the shared writing project is completed, it is saved onto the Tar Heel Reader website, where it can be enjoyed by any other reader using the website. Books in Tar Heel Reader are switch accessible for individuals with significant physical challenges who cannot operate a standard mouse or keyboard. There are settings that provide text-to-speech and options for individuals with visual disabilities (**tarheelreader.org**).

EXTENSION OPPORTUNITY

Groups can create a set of books using Tar Heel Reader that can be shared with others to showcase their skills as writers. Invite learners to engage in shared reading experiences with the text they have written using the complementary Tar Heel Shared Reader website.

RELATED RESOURCES

Predictable Chart Writing (**bit.ly/inclusive365-177a**)

Necessary Components of Successful AAC Implementation (**bit.ly/inclusive365-177b**)

Figure 177. The Tar Heel Reader writing interface.

ISTE STANDARDS FOR STUDENTS
6b, 6d

ISTE STANDARDS FOR EDUCATORS
5a, 5,b, 5c, 6a, 6b, 6d, 7a

Capitalizing on Learner Interests to Develop Written Expression Skills

Written expression is a multi-faceted skill requiring the ability to synthesize a number of foundational skills, including how to compose text for a variety of audiences and purposes. Too often, educators provide a generic prompt to learners to write about a topic or curriculum content area, which may lead to disengagement, task avoidance, or a writing quality that does not reflect a learner's abilities. Instead, learners often achieve greater success when they are invited to write about topics based on their personal interests. Interest-driven written expression reduces the cognitive load for writers and promotes their ability to independently compose persuasive, narrative, or expository writing.

INCLUSIVE USES

Those working to master the skill of writing may find using high-interest, highly motivating, personalized writing exercises helpful in learning how to formulate words into sentences to convey intended meanings, change someone's mind, tell a compelling story, or explain how something works. See the tools below for online platforms that support these exercises.

SAMPLE TOOLS

No Red Ink is an engaging, digital writing and grammar instruction platform with assessment and data collection tools based on learners' interests (**noredink.com**).

Write About This is an iOS and Android app with hundreds of engaging visual and text prompts to promote a love of writing, even for learners who are reluctant writers. Add your own custom prompts or use the audio recording feature as a form of text composition (**writeaboutapp.com**).

EXTENSION OPPORTUNITIES

Invite learners to review data generated by their performance and identify additional skill development areas.

Invite learners to generate their own custom writing prompts.

RELATED RESOURCES

Using No Red Ink's Interactive Tutorials (**bit.ly/inclusive365-178a**)

Write About This in the Classroom (**bit.ly/inclusive365-178b**)

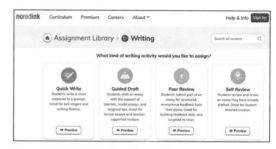

Figure 178. No Red Ink writing options.

ISTE STANDARDS FOR STUDENTS
1a, 1b, 1c

ISTE STANDARDS FOR EDUCATORS
5a, 6a, 6b, 7a, 7b, 7c

Supporting Emergent Writers with Digital Scribbling

Erickson and Koppenhaver (2020) describe emergent writing as the "explorations, experiments, and inventions of learners who do not yet fully understand all of the conventions that make written communication possible because of their inexperience with writing tools." As keyboards emerge as one of the most common writing tools used by conventional writers, emergent writers need the opportunity to scribble with a keyboard much the way they do with pencils, crayons, and markers. Digital scribbling is the opportunity for emergent writers to explore key hits and the resulting letters, numbers, and symbols they produce. As with conventional scribbling, writers are then able to attribute meaning to their scribbles that they can share with the educators supporting their writing. This is a critical part of the developmental writing continuum.

INCLUSIVE USES

Learners who are unable to hold conventional writing utensils due to physical disabilities can be provided the opportunity to write with a traditional or adapted keyboard. Additionally, when text-to-speech is utilized as a part of the writer's feedback, any writer who is not hearing impaired can hear what they have written and consider what their scribbles might communicate to others.

SAMPLE TOOLS

WriteReader is a free writing tool for the emergent writer. An educator "translates" the writer's text into conventional text that provides an accurate model for the learner. It also provides audio recordings, text-to-speech, the ability to add images as illustrations, and the ability to add captions, speech bubbles, and thought bubbles to the illustrations. Multiple pages can be combined to make a book (**app.writereader.com**).

Clicker Writer is a simplified word processing program for the Chromebook or iPad that provides word banks, conventional keyboard access, an onscreen keyboard, and alternative access through switches with text-to-speech (**cricksoft.com/us/clicker/apps**).

EXTENSION OPPORTUNITIES

Invite learners to narrate their digital scribbling and transcribe their narration to go along with their text.

Invite learners to keep a digital portfolio of their writing and reflect on their progress periodically.

RELATED RESOURCE

Getting Started with WriteReader (**bit.ly/inclusive365-179**)

Figure 179. Digital scribbling by a learner along with the educator's translation of the scribbling in WriteReader.

ISTE STANDARDS FOR STUDENTS

1b, 6a, 6b, 6d

ISTE STANDARDS FOR EDUCATORS

2b, 5a, 5b, 5c, 6a, 6d, 7a

Predictable Chart Writing for Emergent Readers and Writers

Predictable Chart Writing is a series of shared group writing and reading experiences in which the educator leads emergent writers in exploring a co-constructed text repeatedly over the course of one week. Learners begin with a shared sentence stem, with each learner generating a sentence as part of an educator lead group experience, creating a chart or list of sentences. On the second day, the chart is reread, first using a model by the educator. Then learners are given the opportunity to read the chart aloud as well. On subsequent days, the chart is reread again, and individual sentences from the chart are taken apart and reconstructed, word-by-word, by learners. Ultimately, the learners create a book from the text to bring home and to share with other learners.

INCLUSIVE USES

Predictable Chart Writing supports learners of all ages and all abilities who are emergent writers. Learners using augmentative and alternative communication (AAC) systems can construct their sentences using their devices.

SAMPLE TOOLS

Tar Heel Reader is a digital resource offering a shared writing experience with images that are pulled from Flickr's Creative Commons licensed photographs to support writing. When the written text is completed, it is saved onto the Tar Heel Reader website, where it can be enjoyed by any other reader using the website. Books in Tar Heel Reader are switch accessible for individuals with significant physical challenges who cannot operate a standard mouse or keyboard. There are settings that provide text-to-speech and options for individuals with visual disabilities (**tarheelreader.org**).

Book Creator is a web-based resource and an iOS app used by learners to create text using speech recognition or keyboarding. It is easy to add images labeled for reuse through the integrated Google Image search. Created books can be added to a user's digital library shelf and shared with others (**app.bookcreator.com**).

EXTENSION OPPORTUNITIES

Invite learners to write for an authentic audience by sharing their co-constructed texts with families and other readers around the world using Book Creator or Tar Heel Reader.

Discuss with learners why both technology platforms use images licensed for reuse and the importance of not using images found online without permission.

RELATED RESOURCES

Predictable Chart Writing (**bit.ly/inclusive365-180a**)

Necessary Components of Successful AAC Implementation (**bit.ly/inclusive365-180b**)

Figure 180. Pages from a Predictable Chart Writing experience created in Book Creator.

ISTE STANDARDS FOR STUDENTS
2a, 6b, 6d, 7a, 7b

ISTE STANDARDS FOR EDUCATORS
5a, 5,b, 5c, 6a, 6b, 6d, 7a

Writing Succinctly with Word Length Boundaries

The writing process can be daunting for beginning writers. Written expression requires idea generation, vocabulary and spelling skills, the ability to organize and sequence ideas, and memory skills. Applying a word length boundary as a guideline provides an opportunity for beginning writers to learn how to write a message with maximum impact using minimal words. Creating writing that could actually be posted on social media, or even used within the learning space but with the same character limit, encourages learners to consider word choice, to eliminate passive voice (which generally produces longer sentences than active voice), and explore how they can write an impactful yet brief message.

INCLUSIVE USES

Those working to improve their writing abilities may find the invitation to write shorter messages with limited word counts incentivizes writing. Additionally, having an authentic audience to write for may prove to be empowering for those otherwise reluctant to write.

SAMPLE TOOL

Twitter has a character count limit of 280 characters (**twitter.com/home**).

EXTENSION OPPORTUNITIES

Invite learners to create a specific hashtag as part of a writing prompt for a Twitter-length writing task.

Invite learners to edit long messages down to attempt to reach a certain word count while maintaining the integrity of the original message.

RELATED RESOURCE

Use of Twitter Across Educational Settings: A Review of the Literature (**bit.ly/inclusive365-181**)

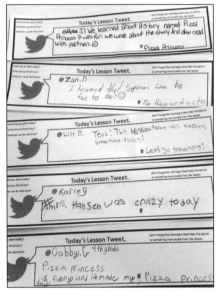

Figure 181. Learner examples of a Twitter-length writing task.

ISTE STANDARDS FOR STUDENTS
1c, 2a

ISTE STANDARDS FOR EDUCATORS
5a, 5b, 5c

Encouraging Poetry Writing with Templates

Poetry is included across English Language Arts standards, yet it is often challenging for learners to apply the conventions of different poetry forms into their own writing. The use of premade templates to encourage and guide poetry writing can be a stepping stone for learners to reframe how they see themselves: as confident, creative poets.

INCLUSIVE USES

Poetry templates can be scaffolded as needed for different learners. Scaffolds can range from a structured fill-in-the-blank form to more complex graphic organizers that support poetry forms that require a set number of syllables, words, lines, or stanzas. Poetry templates remove the cognitive load and make writing engaging and fun.

SAMPLE TOOLS

The Poetry Templates Google Site is filled with pre-made graphic organizers and Google Docs, available for download, that provide structured support for creating poetry (**bit.ly/inclusive365-182a**).

The poetry section on Language is a Virus has a variety of digital poetry generators for everything from mixed up Shakespeare sonnets to haiku and options for making concrete or visual poems (**bit.ly/inclusive365-182b**).

The Poetry Machine has examples of poems and specific information about each poem format. It prompts a learner through writing a poem, line by line (**bit.ly/inclusive365-182c**).

EXTENSION OPPORTUNITIES

Invite learners to develop their own poetry generator by selecting impactful words and phrases to add to a customizable spinner. Invite them to share their poetry generator with a

peer and see what they can write with online spinners (**superteachertools.us/spinner** and **wheeldecide.com**).

Invite learners to submit their poetry to the Foyle Young Poets of the Year competition (**bit.ly/inclusive365-182d**).

RELATED RESOURCE

Top Tips for Teaching Poetry (**bit.ly/inclusive365-182e**)

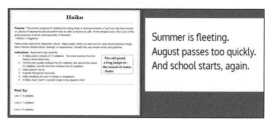

Figure 182. Haiku poem using a Haiku template.

ISTE STANDARDS FOR STUDENTS
6a, 6b, 6d

ISTE STANDARDS FOR EDUCATORS
2b, 5a, 5b,5c, 6a, 6c, 6d, 7a

Developing Grammar Skills from Personalized Interests

It is universally agreed that the best writers have a clear understanding of grammar principles. What are effective ways to teach grammar skills? Targeted mini-lessons and extensive reading and writing opportunities based on personalized interests are effective instructional methods. As learners improve their written expression skills through drafting, editing, and refining their compositions, they learn the correct use of grammar.

INCLUSIVE USES

Learners who are developing their understanding of grammar may find using high-interest, highly motivating, personalized exercises helpful in learning and practicing grammar principles.

SAMPLE TOOL

No Red Ink is an engaging, digital grammar instruction platform with pre-assessment and data collection tools based on learners' interests. Educators can gauge pre-assessment skills and provide practice tasks to gain mastery with applying grammar rules. Interest-based experiences and adaptive exercises replace rote paper-based instruction (**noredink.com**).

EXTENSION OPPORTUNITY

Invite learners to review data generated by their performance and identify additional areas needing skill development.

RELATED RESOURCES

Necessity of Grammar Teaching (**bit.ly/inclusive365-183a**)

Effectively Teaching Grammar: What Works and What Doesn't (**bit.ly/inclusive365-183b**)

Figure 183. Grammar options in No Red Ink.

ISTE STANDARDS FOR STUDENTS
1a, 1b, 1c

ISTE STANDARDS FOR EDUCATORS
5a, 6a, 6b, 7a, 7b, 7c

Prompting Sensory Details in Writing

Skilled authors add sensory details to help readers envision and experientially connect with events in a story. When learning to write creatively, learners can use multimodal prompts to help to remember to incorporate sensory details.

INCLUSIVE USES

Traditional paper graphic organizers limit the flexibility and accessibility that digital forms offer. Ideas can be brainstormed, explored, manipulated, and changed much more readily using a digital tool. Learners working on improving their writing abilities may find the use of multimodal reminders to include sensory details helpful.

SAMPLE TOOLS

A Sensory Details Chart created using Google Docs allows embedded audio instructions to provide supports for success and independence (**bit.ly/inclusive365-184a**).

Audio Notes is a feature of Read&Write for Chrome that is free for educators. It allows users to leave audio comments in a Google Doc (**bit.ly/inclusive365-184b**).

The Kaizena Audio Notes add on for Google Docs provides educators and learners with an option for leaving audio comments in a document (**kaizena.com**).

EXTENSION OPPORTUNITIES

Invite writers to compare the two sentences or paragraphs with and without sensory details to help them understand how adding details engages the reader.

Invite learners to choose a picture to describe using sensory details without sharing the picture. Then post the pictures with the descriptions online, and have learners try to match those that go together.

RELATED RESOURCE

Descriptive and Sensory Detail (**bit.ly/inclusive365-184c**)

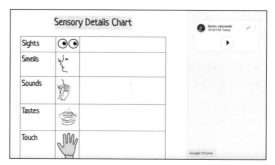

Figure 184. Sensory details chart created in Google Docs, with audio instructions.

ISTE STANDARDS FOR STUDENTS
6a, 6b, 6c

ISTE STANDARDS FOR EDUCATORS
5a, 5c, 6a

STRATEGY 184

Recording Audio to Improve Voice and Tone in Writing

Voice and tone express the personality of a writer and reflect their attitude toward a topic. Use of a digital audio recording as a part of the writing process helps learners hear the tone and voice they need to convey with words for their audience. When used as a step between brainstorming and drafting, recording ideas for language to be used can help learners hear how word choice, rate of speech, and the pitch of their voice convey emotions and ideas. They can then translate this into the text that they generate. When used as a part of the revision process, recording helps learners hear if the vocabulary they have chosen, and the phrasing of their writing, is communicating the message in the way they intended.

INCLUSIVE USES

Learners with writing challenges may find that dictating their ideas allows them to bypass spelling barriers that could inadvertently move them to use less sophisticated vocabulary and less complex sentence structure than when they type or handwrite. Additionally, when learners read aloud their own writing and then listen to it via an audio recording they are better able to pick out any errors or changes they want to make to improve their writing.

SAMPLE TOOLS

Read&Write for Chrome from TextHelp allows learners to insert voice comments within any Google Doc (**bit.ly/inclusive365-185a**).

OneNote allows sound recording to be inserted anywhere into a notebook (**onenote.com**).

EXTENSION OPPORTUNITY

Invite peers to read aloud and record each other's writing during the revision process. This allows learners to know whether the voice and tone they attempted to convey was evident to their audience.

RELATED RESOURCE

4 Ways Audio Recording Can Boost Classroom Learning (**bit.ly/inclusive365-185b**)

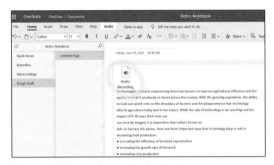

Figure 185. A saved recording in OneNote.

ISTE STANDARDS FOR STUDENTS

1c, 6a

ISTE STANDARDS FOR EDUCATORS

6a, 7a

Sparking Creative Writing with Pictures And Word Banks

Pictures are a powerful way to generate ideas for writing. Word walls or banks can also spur ideas about what to write. Why not combine both into one idea-generating experience for creative writing? Learners can choose a picture which represents a topic they might be interested in writing about. They can then drag words from the bank onto the picture to create their message. Organizing words by parts of speech might help learners put them in order.

INCLUSIVE USES

Learners who are learning parts of speech, creative writing, and idea generation might find combining picture and word prompts helpful.

Using correctly-spelled words to generate sentences while writing might help learners who are working on improving spelling. Learners may more accurately spell words sooner by seeing the correct spelling repeatedly.

Learners with certain impairments which impact fine or gross motor control may find dragging or clicking on words to create sentences less burdensome than typing.

SAMPLE TOOLS

PIC-LITS is a free website that provides a catalog of pictures and corresponding word banks. Once a picture is selected, a writing workspace appears. Individualized banks of words provide writing support categorized by parts of speech, including nouns, verbs, adjectives, and adverbs. Core vocabulary is available to support sentence generation (**piclits.com**).

Use Google Drawings to embed pictures to facilitate creative writing. Word walls can be created with text boxes and placed outside the workspace for learners to drag into the picture (**docs.google.com/drawings**).

EXTENSION OPPORTUNITIES

Encourage emerging writers to pull in words that might be descriptive of the picture, worrying less about formulating a complete sentence and more about making connections. Once completed, invite the learner to record audio talking about the picture they created. The picture and corresponding audio can be embedded in another tool, such as a Google Doc or Google Slides presentation.

Invite learners to create poems using pictures and word banks.

Invite learners to write for an authentic purpose, sharing their work with the world to inspire others with the writing they've created.

RELATED RESOURCES

Using Pictures for Creative Writing Prompts (**bit.ly/inclusive365-186a**)

A.T.TIPSCAST Episode #135: ScreamEd (**bit.ly/inclusive365-186b**)

Figure 186. The PIC-LITS work space ready for a learner's creative writing.

ISTE STANDARDS FOR STUDENTS
1c, 3c, 6a, 6b, 6d

ISTE STANDARDS FOR EDUCATORS
3b, 4b, 5a, 5b, 6a, 7a

Writing Creative Narratives with Video

Narrative writing can give learners an opportunity to flex their creative muscles and demonstrate storytelling abilities. This type of writing also gives them an opportunity to demonstrate story structure, parts of speech, setting and scene, and conflict and resolution. Learners may have all these skills, but if they are unable to translate them into writing, these amazing stories will be lost. Using video to tell a story gives learners another way to express themselves.

INCLUSIVE USES

Video as an alternative to traditional writing supports can be useful for evolving writers, allowing them to generate a story without the barriers that handwriting or typing may pose. Utilizing video for storytelling also taps into oral storytelling traditions that are an integral part of many cultures around the world, where stories were passed down from storyteller to storyteller without ever being written down.

SAMPLE TOOL

Flipgrid is a free video response tool that works on mobile devices or computers. Create a grid, share the connection code, and watch the videos pour in (**info.flipgrid.com**).

EXTENSION OPPORTUNITY

Invite learners to create a collaborative video story by adding one sentence at a time until the story is completed.

RELATED RESOURCES

Creative Writing 101: A Beginner's Guide to Creative Writing (**bit.ly/inclusive365-187a**)

Flipgrid Tutorial: Creating Video Assignments (**bit.ly/inclusive365-187b**)

Flipgrid for ALL! 50+ Ways to Use Flipgrid in the Classroom (**bit.ly/inclusive365-187c**)

Figure 187. A Flipgrid collaborative story.

ISTE STANDARDS FOR STUDENTS
1c, 2b, 5c, 6a, 6b, 6d

ISTE STANDARDS FOR EDUCATORS
5a, 5b, 6d

Writing with Emojis

Emojis are prevalent in the lives of learners of all ages. Educators can leverage their use as a method to engage learners in writing. Using pictures to promote and complement writing is not a new concept, but using emojis as a prompt may be a new way to generate ideas and emphasize tone.

Effective communication not only includes long-form writing, but short, precise, impactful messages that convey emotions, humor, and personality. Whether sending a single emoji, a string of emojis, or a combination of text and emojis, these images can make all the difference in how the person receiving the message interprets it and how one perceives the sender.

INCLUSIVE USES

Learners working on improving writing skills can brainstorm ideas using emojis. The use of pictures may be a helpful and effective method to help learners formulate messages in writing. Educators can also use emojis to provide feedback to learners throughout the writing process.

Those working on relating to the emotions and perspectives of others, regulating social-emotional skills, and pragmatic language skills may find using emojis as an effective tool to help them practice these skills.

Additionally, emojis are created using ASCII code which allows them to be read aloud by screen readers (**bit.ly/inclusive365-188a**).

SAMPLE TOOLS

Emojipedia is a web-based catalog of emojis. Users enter a search term to find related emojis. Once the desired emoji is found, it can be copied and pasted into other applications (**emojipedia.org**).

EmojiCopy allows emojis to be displayed on a single screen. Users scroll through the webpage to find a desired emoji. When a selection is made it drops into the copy bar along the bottom of the screen, allowing it to be pasted into other applications (**emojicopy.com**).

EXTENSION OPPORTUNITIES

Learners can use emojis to brainstorm writing prompts. Once the thought has been conveyed with emojis, learners could type or use voice dictation to describe the string of icons.

Learners and educators alike can use emojis to leave comments and provide feedback.

Invite learners to play a game where they guess the message displayed in a string of emojis. Learners could participate as players, as message creators, or both.

RELATED RESOURCE

Worth a Thousand Interpersonal Words: Emojis as Effective Signals for Relationship-Oriented Digital Communication (**bit.ly/inclusive365-188b**)

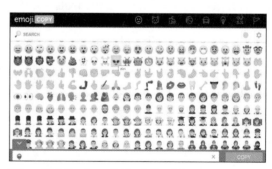

Figure 188. Emojis available via Emoji Copy.

ISTE STANDARDS FOR STUDENTS
1c, 3c, 6a, 6b, 6c, 6d

ISTE STANDARDS FOR EDUCATORS
5a, 6a, 6d

Writing Creative Narratives Using 3D Animation

Crafting a compelling story is a uniquely human endeavor. For some, it even becomes a livelihood. Well-crafted narratives about real or imagined events are rich with setting, character development, story structure, conflict, and resolution. The complexity of the details can depend on the skill level of the learner. The narrative arc, including the setting, the conflict, the challenge, the climax, and the resolution, can be taught using engaging 3D animations that the learner generates.

INCLUSIVE USES

3D animation facilitates imagination and creativity for beginning writers of all skill levels. Creating a story using technology can support learner variabilities in the areas of fine motor skills, spelling, idea generation, and memory skills.

SAMPLE TOOL

Toontastic 3D is an innovative storytelling animation application for iOS and Google Play designed to teach elements of storywriting with animated supports. The built in instruction within the app reduces reliance on adult support (**toontastic.withgoogle.com**).

EXTENSION OPPORTUNITIES

Invite learners to create a variety of stories—adventures, mysteries, science fiction, historical—to explore a variety of genres and publish their creations for others to enjoy.

Invite learners to not only animate their stories but also design their own characters with either photos of themselves and friends or from original drawings.

Beyond storytelling, invite learners to use 3D animation to demonstrate knowledge on topics of study and to create instructional stories to teach those learned concepts to others.

RELATED RESOURCE

A Step-by-Step Plan for Teaching Narrative Writing (**bit.ly/inclusive365-189**)

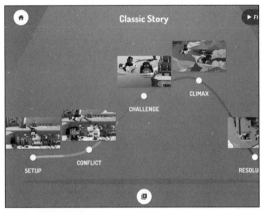

Figure 189. The Narrative Arc as illustrated in Toontastic 3D.

ISTE STANDARDS FOR STUDENTS

4a, 4b, 6a, 6b, 6c, 6d

ISTE STANDARDS FOR EDUCATORS

5d, 6d

Writing for an Authentic Audience with Social Media

Writers pay more attention to the quality of their message when they are writing for an authentic audience. Learners are no different. The use of social media to engage in microblogging with the possibility of involving a global audience helps learners understand the power of their words and the importance of communicating effectively in writing. Educators can set up whole or small group social media accounts to provide a forum for learners to write for an authentic audience while still protecting learner privacy and abiding by minimum age requirements for the use of specific platforms. Learners can use educator and parent approved aliases and avatars (see also Strategy 29) to further maintain privacy.

INCLUSIVE USES

Writing a social media post provides motivation for those working on improving their writing skills to share their ideas. Additionally, when using platforms that have a built in maximum character limit, such as Twitter or Instagram, learners can feel less intimidated by the amount of writing they need to do.

SAMPLE TOOLS

Twitter allows for short posts of up to 280 characters, along with up to 4 images. Once posted, a tweet can not be edited, although it can be deleted. Twitters requires that all users be at least thirteen years old (**twitter.com**).

Instagram allows for longer, editable posts and multiple images. Instagram requires that users be at least thirteen years old (**instagram.com**).

Facebook allows for longer, editable posts and multiple images. Group pages with privacy filters can be set up allowing multiple individuals to create a post as long as posters have their own Facebook account. Facebook requires users to be at least thirteen years old (**facebook.com**).

EXTENSION OPPORTUNITIES

Invite learners to set up accounts as individuals from history or literature. Learners can write to answer a specific question or address a topic from that individual's perspective. Examples might be discussing the writing of the constitution using the personas of George Washington, Alexander Hamilton, or John Hancock, or writing as a companion to Martin Luther King.

Invite learners to set up accounts for objects or concepts about which they are learning. Learners can answer a specific question or address a topic from that object's perspective. Examples might be writing from the perspective of an element, planet, animal, or geographic structure like a volcano or ocean.

RELATED RESOURCE

Use of Twitter across Educational Settings: A Review of the Literature (**bit.ly/inclusive365-190**)

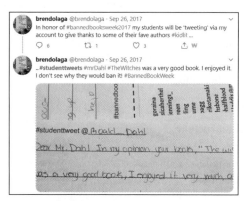

Figure 190. Educator Twitter posts featuring learner book reviews.

ISTE STANDARDS FOR STUDENTS
1c, 2a

ISTE STANDARDS FOR EDUCATORS
3a, 3c, 3d

Creating and Sharing Audio Stories

Oral storytelling has been a tradition across cultures and going far back in time. Engaging learners in oral storytelling is a culturally responsive pedagogical practice that can be used across age levels. Learners can participate in oral storytelling with a digital twist by using applications and software that provide easy access to audio recording features. Learners can start with an image as an anchor for the story and then generate their tale. Stories can be played back using the same tool that was used to record, downloaded to become an artifact in a digital portfolio, and shared with an authentic audience in the community. Stories can be recorded spontaneously or as the final part of a writing project that addresses speaking and listening outcomes.

INCLUSIVE USES

Learners who have expressed a dislike for writing may find dictating a story a more enjoyable, less frustrating experience than handwriting or typing text. Learners who demonstrate difficulty with oral language may find the option to record and re-record less intimidating than giving a live oral presentation.

SAMPLE TOOLS

ChatterPix and ChatterPix Kids are available for iOS and Google Play. Both start with an image that is then given an animated moving mouth. The learner can record up to thirty seconds of a story, which the animated image then speaks aloud (**bit.ly/inclusive365-191a**).

VoiceThread allows learners to add both text and audio (from a computer microphone or telephone) comments to an added image. Learners can also work collaboratively in VoiceThread (**voicethread.com**).

PowerPoint allows learners to use slides with images along with recorded narration. Learners can collaborate online in PowerPoint 365 (**bit.ly/inclusive365-191b**).

EXTENSION OPPORTUNITIES

Invite multiple learners to build a story collaboratively using VoiceThread or PowerPoint.

Invite learners to create an ongoing podcast featuring original stories. The podcast could be standalone episodes featuring a different short story in each episode, or it could be a longer serial narrative that tells an ongoing story over several episodes.

RELATED RESOURCES

Oral Storytelling as a Pedagogical and Learning Tool for Cultural and Cross-Cultural Understanding (**bit.ly/inclusive365-191c**)

Teaching with Stories as the Content and Context for Learning (**bit.ly/inclusive365-191d**)

Figure 191. An image from the *The Three Little Pigs* as part of a VoiceThread audio story.

ISTE STANDARDS FOR STUDENTS
6a, 6b, 6d

ISTE STANDARDS FOR EDUCATORS
4c, 4d, 5a, 5c, 6a

Self-Editing Written Work Using Text-to-Speech

Audio support may be an essential editing feature for some learners to effectively and independently review and improve their own writing work. The ability to ear-read is a valuable skill to connect with information typically presented in print. Text-to-speech is a useful function built into the accessibility features of many contemporary technologies. It allows a user to listen to text displayed on the screen. When rereading composed text, learners often read what they believe they have included in the document. Using text-to-speech helps them identify missing words, incorrect grammar, and other composition errors. This accessibility feature can provide an audio reading experience for learners to independently complete the editing steps of the writing process.

INCLUSIVE USES

Turning on the text-to-speech feature of digital text enables learners to interact with written materials, regardless of reading ability or preference.

SAMPLE TOOLS

Chrome OS has a powerful suite of built-in accessibility features that are designed to customize the Chromebook experience for each learner and provide needed support. Located within the settings of Chrome OS, once activated, the Select to Speak button is placed in the system tray at the bottom of the Chromebook screen. The icon is a small speaker. To listen to text aloud, click the button, then select text on the screen. A pink box surrounds the text to be read. The device begins to read the text aloud, accompanied with word-by-word highlighting.

iOS has Speak Selection and Speak Screen features that can be found in the settings under accessibility.

EXTENSION OPPORTUNITIES

Encourage learners to review their compositions using text-to-speech to identify grammatical and content-related errors. The dual sensory support (visual and audio) may help them identify areas for improvement.

Offer text-to-speech to learners to give them the opportunity to decide if it is a function that will work for them. Learners can choose to either highlight specific words to have them spoken aloud, or have the entire page read aloud.

RELATED RESOURCES

Hear Text Read Aloud (**bit.ly/inclusive365-192a**)

How to Use Select to Speak on Your Chromebook (**bit.ly/inclusive365-192b**)

Adjust Voices for VoiceOver, Speak Screen, and Speak Selection on Your iPhone, iPad, or iPod Touch (**bit.ly/inclusive365-192c**)

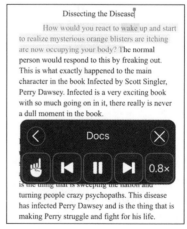

Figure 192. Learner using Speak Screen to edit a book review.

ISTE STANDARDS FOR STUDENTS
1d, 3c

ISTE STANDARDS FOR EDUCATORS
1a, 2b, 4b, 5a, 7a

Creating Editing Checklists to Improve Written Expression

Editing is an essential component of the writing process. Once a first draft is completed, editing begins. Educators can guide learners to create checklists to facilitate the editing process. These checklists can provide the sequential, linear, differentiated support needed by many writers to learn how to edit on their own. When checklists are developed and created digitally, learners can use the checklist in ways that work best for them, and educators can suggest adaptations to meet specific learner needs.

INCLUSIVE USES

Editing checklists can be customized to the needs of the learner depending on the amount of support they require. They can be easily translated into multiple languages to support multilingual learners.

SAMPLE TOOLS

Project-based learning customized editing checklists are available in both English and Spanish (**bit.ly/inclusive365-193a**).

Google Keep is an application that allows learners to save their checklist and pin it to the top of the screen to refer to when composing and editing text in Google Docs (**keep.google.com**).

EXTENSION OPPORTUNITIES

Invite learners to create their own customized checklists. Ownership promotes use.

Invite learners to reflect on the effectiveness of the checklist. Are there items they should change or add? For example, would it be beneficial to add an item about listening to their writing using a text-to-speech tool?

RELATED RESOURCE

Why Is Editing Important in Writing? (**bit.ly/inclusive365-193b**)

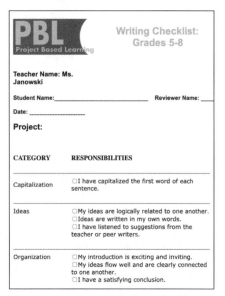

Figure 193. A customized editing checklist created in PBL Checklists.

ISTE STANDARDS FOR STUDENTS

1a, 1c, 4a, 4b

ISTE STANDARDS FOR EDUCATORS

5a, 5b, 5c, 6a, 7b

Providing Feedback to Improve Written Expression

To be effective, feedback needs to be clear, purposeful, meaningful, and compatible with prior knowledge, and it needs to provide logical connections (Hattie & Timberly, 2009). As learners develop written expression skills, educator feedback provides needed support and helps them improve the quality of their writing. When text is composed in word processing tools, it is possible to insert comments as feedback to support the development of writing skills.

INCLUSIVE USES

Individuals working on improving their independent writing skills benefit from educators providing constructive and specific feedback through digital comments. Digital comments can be referenced repeatedly, which can help learners take as much time as they need to read, process, and reflect on the feedback.

SAMPLE TOOLS

Use the insert comments feature in Google Classroom with Google Docs (**bit.ly/inclusive365-194a**).

Use the insert comments feature in Word for Office 365 (**bit.ly/inclusive365-194b**).

EXTENSION OPPORTUNITIES

Encourage learners to reflect on the type of feedback that most helped them improve the quality of their written work.

Encourage learners to take the initiative and ask for feedback when they are struggling with composing text.

RELATED RESOURCES

The Power of Feedback (**bit.ly/inclusive365-194c**)

How to Respond to Student Writing: 10 Ways to Give Feedback That Sticks (**bit.ly/inclusive365-194d**)

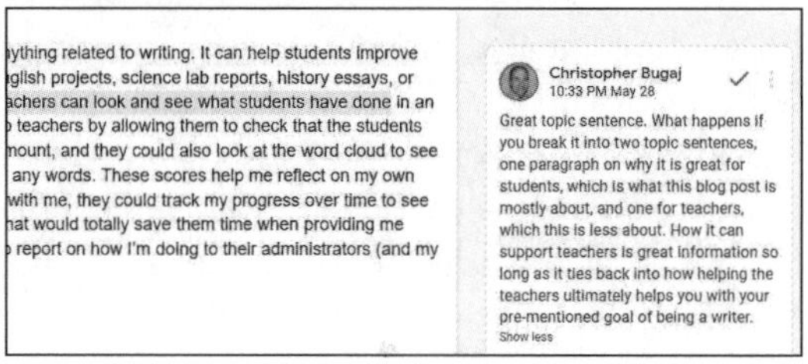

Figure 194. A learner's draft blog post with feedback via comment.

ISTE STANDARDS FOR STUDENTS

1a, 1c, 6a

ISTE STANDARDS FOR EDUCATORS

5a 5b, 5c, 6a, 6b, 6d, 7a, 7b

Providing Feedback Banks

Learning how to provide constructive, purposeful, specific, and kind feedback is a necessary skill to learn, practice, and master in contemporary society. Learners may need explicit guidance about how to phrase feedback when collaborating with others. A bank of options provides learners with a reference housing many possibilities. A bank organized into categories which include affirmations ("This statement is written in a way that makes me think"), probing questions ("What fact can you use to support this claim?"), reflective questions ("What would happen if you worded this differently?"), and suggestions ("Consider changing this wording"), helps learners thoughtfully consider how to give feedback.

INCLUSIVE USES

Learners with goals to practice social skills may find feedback banks useful during peer editing. A feedback bank provides a visual cue for reference. Once proficient, the learner can become more autonomous.

Colors, symbols, or icons can be used to help identify the purpose of the phrases in the bank. Affirmations might be accompanied with a thumbs up icon 👍. Probing questions could have a question mark or an emoji of someone shrugging 🤷. Reflective questions might contain a mirror or magnifying glass 🔍. Suggestions might be represented by an arrow or person rubbing their chin as if thinking 🤔.

SAMPLE TOOL

Google Keep is a note-taking application that allows users to create a customized feedback bank that can be easily placed in a document (**keep.google.com**).

EXTENSION OPPORTUNITIES

Invite learners to participate in an experience in which they develop their own feedback banks, providing phrases in each category. Developing personalized banks helps learners internalize, remember, and own the phrases.

Invite learners to practice providing feedback during a collaborative writing project and during a face-to-face project. The feedback bank can be used to help learn skills in both situations. Providing feedback in live situations often requires more practice than during collaborative writing since face-to-face situations require more immediate response times.

RELATED RESOURCE

20 Ways to Provide Effective Feedback for Learning (**bit.ly/inclusive365-195**)

Figure 195. Google Keep notes with color-coded feedback prompts.

ISTE STANDARDS FOR STUDENTS
1c, 2b, 7b, 7c

ISTE STANDARDS FOR EDUCATORS
1b, 2b, 3a, 4c, 4d, 5a, 5b, 6a, 6d

Editing Writing to Minimize Passive Voice

Using passive voice can make writing less compelling. Use of active voice is typically preferred in formal writing. Active voice often uses fewer words, making writing more concise, and it creates a faster-flowing narrative, which makes for more engaging reading. An example of active versus passive voice follows: "Thousands of travelers visit the Grand Canyon every year," versus "The Grand Canyon is visited by thousands of travelers every year." While it is important for learners to be able to identify passive voice in their writing independently, even experienced writers can struggle to identify passive voice. Grammar tools that include both passive voice checkers and editing for active voice are useful for writers of all abilities.

INCLUSIVE USES

Learners who are working to become proficient in English or who have writing challenges benefit from grammar tools that can catch use of passive voice. The learner can then focus on their ideas and not on more complex grammatical constructions.

SAMPLE TOOLS

Word includes a Grammar Check tool.

The Hemingway Editor is available online and as a downloadable application. When used online, learners copy and paste sections of their writing and receive color-coded feedback about passive voice and readability (**hemingwayapp.com**).

EXTENSION OPPORTUNITIES

Invite learners to copy sections of a novel or other text that they are reading and check it for passive voice. Ask them then to evaluate how they could change any passive voice to active voice.

Invite learners to compare different passages before and after editing with a passive voice checker. Learners can discuss the differences in voice and the impact the change might have on the reader.

RELATED RESOURCE

Passive Voice Grammarly Blog (**bit.ly/inclusive365-196a**)

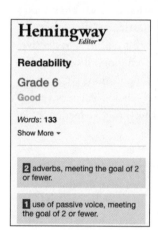

Figure 196. The Hemingway Editor.

ISTE STANDARDS FOR STUDENTS

1c, 3c, 6a, 6d

ISTE STANDARDS FOR EDUCATORS

5a, 5c, 6a, 6d, 7a

Assessing Progress Using Version History

Version history, available in both the G Suite for Education and Office 365 tools, allows users to see the changes made in a document, spreadsheet, or slide deck over time. This provides a means for educators to see how a learner has self-corrected, responded to feedback, and made revisions to their work, providing valuable insight into how that learner reflects on their work and makes improvements. Using version history also allows educators to see the work that individual members of a group have done, allowing for assessment of progress on group tasks when otherwise it would be difficult to see individual contributions.

INCLUSIVE USES

Viewing version history can give a great deal of insight into the writing process that an evolving writer is going through, allowing an educator to apply targeted support and feedback to a learner.

SAMPLE TOOLS

Google Slides, Docs, and Sheets all offer version history under the file menu (**bit.ly/inclusive365-197a**).

Office 365 for Word, PowerPoint, and Excel all offer a version history feature (**bit.ly/inclusive365-197b**).

EXTENSION OPPORTUNITIES

Invite learners to review version history to self-reflect on their own growth and learning over the course of their work in a document or to consider the processes that they use in writing or creating.

Invite learners to self-reflect on how much they have contributed to collaborative writing tasks by reviewing version history.

RELATED RESOURCE

What is Version History and How to Use It in Google Docs? (**bit.ly/inclusive365-197c**)

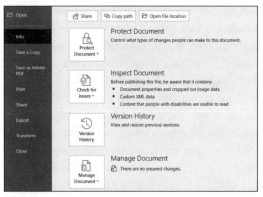

Figure 197. Version history in Word.

ISTE STANDARDS FOR STUDENTS

1c

ISTE STANDARDS FOR EDUCATORS

7b, 7c

Self-Monitoring with Word Count

One way learners can monitor their growth as writers is to use the word count function available in most word processing tools. While the number of words in a composition is not the only measure of writing proficiency, learners who are developing their writing skills can push themselves to write more and more often. Using word count statistics, learners can chart their own progress toward a goal of writing so many words within a period of time. While length does not necessarily improve the quality of a learner's writing, generating text and writing more efficiently is necessary to become an effective writer. Additionally, this can ultimately increase on-task performance and stamina for writing.

INCLUSIVE USES

Learners who are evolving as writers benefit from seeing their own growth over time. Setting a goal to increase the word length of a composition can be helpful for learners who may find writing laborious, and can help them view themselves as writers. Increasing the quantity of writing should go hand in hand with strategies for increasing the quality of writing, however.

SAMPLE TOOLS

Google Docs has word count statistics that can easily be accessed from the tools menu (**google.com/docs**).

Wriq provides a writing productivity tracker, and also tracks other statistics over time (**bit.ly/inclusive365-198a**).

EXTENSION OPPORTUNITY

Invite learners to chart their word counts and the amount of time they spend writing, and reflect on the impact that information has on their confidence as a writer. Do they notice progress over time?

RELATED RESOURCE

Why Writers Should Use a Secret Sauce, Tracking (**bit.ly/inclusive365-198b**)

Figure 198. Word count in Google Docs.

ISTE STANDARDS FOR STUDENTS
1a, 5b

ISTE STANDARDS FOR EDUCATORS
5a, 6a, 6b, 7a

Analyzing Online Book Reviews to Improve Written Expression

Book reviews may guide decisions about which books to read. Many individuals turn to online reviews as the basis for recommendations. The power of the book review can be leveraged as a tool for learning about persuasive writing, opinion pieces, and evaluating the reviews of others. Amazon book reviews are examples of crowdsourced writing. Learners can be invited to read reviews of books they've read. They can then critique the writing, evaluate the quality of the review, analyze how well it is written, determine whether it is helpful, and think about what they would write instead.

INCLUSIVE USES

A blank piece of paper or computer screen can be daunting for some learners. They often feel intimidated by the blank space and feel like filling that space would be a monumental task. When teaching writing, learners can be shown examples of different writing genres and taught how to evaluate quality. The use of online book reviews can be an excellent option, as they are evaluating people who are unknown to them. Once they are more comfortable evaluating the writing of others and making editing suggestions, they can reframe how they see themselves as writers. Any learner working on improving writing skills might find analyzing online book reviews helpful.

SAMPLE TOOLS

Amazon book reviews include curated reviews by topic (**bit.ly/inclusive365-199a**).

Goodreads is a website where people track which books they've read and share reviews (**goodreads.com**).

EXTENSION OPPORTUNITIES

Invite learners to leave their own reviews on websites to share their voice, their opinions, and their recommendations.

Invite learners to leave an audio response review, one of the features that is available on the Amazon website.

RELATED RESOURCE

How to Write a Good Book Review (**bit.ly/inclusive365-199b**)

Figure 199. An Amazon book review.

ISTE STANDARDS FOR STUDENTS

1c, 1d, 2a, 3b, 6a

ISTE STANDARDS FOR EDUCATORS

3b, 3c, 3d, 6a, 6b, 6d

Collecting Highlighted Text

As learners read, they often highlight salient points such as the main idea and key details. Using different colors for different components of the text allows learners to visually distinguish between the highlighted elements and refer back easily in the future. When highlighting digital text, learners can use technology to extract that highlighted text and organize it based on the text color. In this way, learners can categorize highlights.

INCLUSIVE USES

Learners working on organization, vocabulary, and writing skills might find highlighting and then collecting those highlights useful when studying, learning words, and composing written material.

SAMPLE TOOLS

Read&Write for Chrome is an extension with a Collect Highlights feature that allows users to collect highlights of different colors (**bit.ly/inclusive365-200a**).

Highlight Tool is a Google Docs add-on that allows users to customize highlight colors and collect them either in sequence or by color. Create and share personalized, self-created highlighter libraries with peers and educators (**bit.ly/inclusive365-200b**).

EXTENSION OPPORTUNITY

Invite learners studying parts of speech to highlight words: nouns in one color, verbs in another, and adjectives in yet another, while reading a piece of text. The learner can then collect the highlights grouping all the nouns, verbs, and adjectives together as a check for understanding.

Invite learners to highlight different portions of text while doing research by using separate colors based on different categories. For example, for research about volcanoes, a learner might read text and highlight items about where volcanoes are located using one color, items about how volcanoes are formed using another color, items about famous eruptions using another color, and items about people who study volcanoes using another. When ready to review the facts, the learner can extract the highlights, which can be instantly grouped by topic, while also citing the source.

RELATED RESOURCES

Read&Write for Chrome: Collect Highlights (**bit.ly/inclusive365-200c**)

Highlighting Tool: A Great Google Add-On Resource (**bit.ly/inclusive365-200d**)

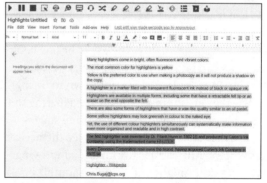

Figure 200. Highlights collected according to color in a Google Doc.

ISTE STANDARDS FOR STUDENTS
2c, 3a, 3c

ISTE STANDARDS FOR EDUCATORS
2c, 3b, 3c, 6a

Keyboarding Practice with Silly Stories

Learning to keyboard effectively and proficiently takes practice. Learners engaging in keyboarding instruction can use websites that stress correct finger placement, but depending on the site, some might find this less than engaging. Learners might develop their typing proficiency when they discover and use a captivating tool that holds their interest. Creating silly stories, word-by-word, can help build letter location proficiency, establish motor memory patterns, and build confidence in typing skills, all while having fun.

INCLUSIVE USES

Learners who find maintaining attention for arduous tasks difficult, who experience fatigue with repetitive fine motor tasks, or who have other fine motor difficulties may find practicing keyboarding by creating funny, silly stories engaging.

SAMPLE TOOL

Glow Word Books invites learners to type individual words to complete a silly story with a Mad Libs-style tool (**bit.ly/inclusive365-201a**).

Mad Takes is another option to type individual words and generate a silly story (**madtakes.com**).

EXTENSION OPPORTUNITIES

Invite multiple learners to alternate word entries to collaborate in making a wacky story.

Invite learners to listen to the story created using text-to-speech.

RELATED RESOURCE

Keyboarding Skills: When Should They be Taught? (**bit.ly/inclusive365-201b**)

Figure 201. A silly story generated using Mad Takes.

ISTE STANDARDS FOR STUDENTS

1a, 6a, 6b

ISTE STANDARDS FOR EDUCATORS

5a, 6a, 6b

Participating in Self-Paced, Self-Directed STEAM Learning Experiences

Quality learning experiences are freely available to those who take the initiative to use them. Learners can participate in interactive experiences to learn about a wide array of topics that satiate their curiosity, suit their interests, or contribute to the achievement of goals, including those that involve STEAM topics. These self-paced, self-guided experiences allow learners to explore the content, taking all the time they need to consume and understand.

INCLUSIVE USES

Learners who require a structure for the content they are consuming and information presented in a linear, sequential format may find a self-paced, self-guided learning experience appealing and beneficial.

Learners who have a particular interest which may or may not align with an offered course or curriculum could find participating in a self-study on that topic of interest motivating and helpful.

SAMPLE TOOLS

Earth School is a web-based experience created by TED and a variety of different organizations to create thirty quests related to learning about natural sciences (**ed.ted.com/earth-school**).

Khan Academy provides self-paced learning courses on a variety of topics, including math and science (**khanacademy.org**).

Swift Playgrounds is a free, self-paced course provided by Apple that offers an opportunity to learn how to code (**apple.com/swift/playgrounds**).

EXTENSION OPPORTUNITIES

Invite learners to keep a digital portfolio or journal of what they are learning during self-directed learning. This could be a blog, website, scrapbook, or online journal. The creation of digital artifacts of what they have accomplished provides an opportunity for self-reflection and demonstrates evidence of learning. Learners could also be invited to share this resource to inspire others.

Invite learners to partner with another individual or a small group of individuals to participate in the structured experience as a collaborative team, helping each other with interactive discussion and reflective feedback.

RELATED RESOURCES

5 Surprising Results of a Self-Paced Classroom (**bit.ly/inclusive365-202a**)

Why Middle-Schoolers Thrive in a Self-Paced Classroom (**bit.ly/inclusive365-202b**)

Figure 202. Learning coding in Swift Playgrounds.

ISTE STANDARDS FOR STUDENTS
1a, 1d, 3d

ISTE STANDARDS FOR EDUCATORS
2b, 5a, 5b 6a, 6b, 6c, 6d, 7a, 7b, 7c

Building Mathematical Understanding with Digital Concrete Resources as a Part of the CRA Continuum

The Concrete-Representational-Abstract (CRA) continuum is a three-part instructional strategy, with each part building on the previous instruction to promote learning and retention and to address conceptual knowledge (Bouck et al., 2017). The CRA instructional sequence consists of three stages: concrete, representational, and abstract. In the concrete stage, math manipulatives are used to concretely represent and help learners understand abstract mathematical concepts. Learners can move along the continuum from concrete to representational (typically drawings) to abstract as they gain understanding and master increasingly complex mathematical skills.

INCLUSIVE USES

CRA is an evidence based strategy for individuals with learning disabilities (Bouck et al., 2017). All learners benefit from the use of math manipulatives, but learners with emerging math skills in particular benefit from having concrete representations as they learn. Digital math manipulatives may also be easier to use than physical manipulatives for learners with impairments which impact fine motor control.

SAMPLE TOOLS

Math Learning Center apps are available for download on iPad, Chromebook, and as web-based tools that can be used online. Their tools include number racks, number lines, geoboards, and more (**mathlearningcenter.org/resources/apps**).

Mathicon's Polypad has bright, colorful polygon shapes, number tiles, algebra tiles, pentominoes, and tangrams, and offers activities and lessons that go up through geometry, algebra, and even physics (**mathigon.org/polypad**).

Didax provides digital unifix cubes, number lines, counters, and much more (**bit.ly/inclusive365-203a**).

EXTENSION OPPORTUNITY

Invite learners to explore the same types of manipulatives on different websites and choose the ones they prefer. Their choices may be based on ease of access, visual displays, or tools provided within the website.

RELATED RESOURCES

Concrete-Representational-Abstract (CRA) Instruction (**bit.ly/inclusive365-203b**)

Using Virtual Manipulatives to Teach Math (**bit.ly/inclusive365-203c**)

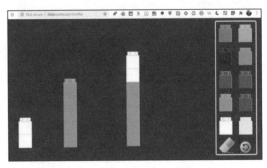

Figure 203. Digital Unifix Cubes from Didex.

ISTE STANDARDS FOR STUDENTS
1a, 1b, 1c, 5a, 5b, 5c

ISTE STANDARDS FOR EDUCATORS
5a, 5b, 5c, 6a, 6b, 6c

Building Mathematical Understanding with Digital Representational Resources as a Part of the CRA Continuum

The Concrete-Representational-Abstract (CRA) continuum is a three-part instructional strategy, with each part building on the previous instruction to promote learning and retention and to address conceptual knowledge (Bouck et al., 2017). At the representational stage of teaching a concept, the educator advances from using manipulatives into a representational level, which may involve drawing pictures, circles, dots, and tallies; or using stamps to create pictures for counting. Learners draw to represent the concrete objects previously used. This same concept can be employed in the digital space as well by looking to digital drawing tools to draw or otherwise create images for counting.

INCLUSIVE USES

CRA is an evidence-based strategy for individuals with learning disabilities (Bouck et al., 2017). For learners who are unable to physically draw using a traditional pencil and paper to support the completion of math equations, providing that workspace in a digital environment gives them a way to complete this task independently.

SAMPLE TOOLS

Google Drawings is a rarely-used addition to your G Suite—but so powerful. Dig into Google Drawings and unleash the power of creativity to solve visual problems. Drawing and shapes can be added to the workspace. Consider ways to divide the workspace to represent parts of math equations (**docs.google.com/drawings**).

Jamboard provides a digital whiteboard space with autodraw tools that aid learners in drawing shapes, plus a shape creation tool (**jamboard.google.com**).

EXTENSION OPPORTUNITY

Encourage learners to create their own virtual math workspace in a tool such as Google Drawings or Jamboard to solve equations and other mathematics problems using digital drawings as representations of concepts, and to support problem solving.

RELATED RESOURCE

The Google Drawings Manifesto for Teachers (**bit.ly/inclusive365-204a**)

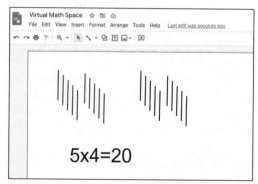

Figure 204. A virtual math space drawn in Google Drawings.

ISTE STANDARDS FOR STUDENTS
1b, 1c, 5a, 6c.

ISTE STANDARDS FOR EDUCATORS
5a, 5b, 5c, 6a, 6b, 6c

Building Mathematical Understanding with Digital Abstract Resources as a Part of the CRA Continuum

The Concrete-Representational-Abstract (CRA) continuum is a three-part instructional math strategy, with each part building on the previous instruction to promote learning and retention and to address conceptual knowledge (Bouck et al., 2017). The CRA instructional sequence consists of three stages: concrete, representational, and abstract. In the abstract stage, learners represent mathematics equations, algorithms, and formulas using typical math symbols and solve problems without the use of manipulatives. Learners can move along the continuum from concrete to representational to abstract as they gain understanding and master increasingly complex mathematical skills, but as learners explore new concepts they benefit from going back to the use of manipulatives and other representations. There are a number of tools available that support the ability to write math problems digitally and to move seamlessly along the CRA continuum.

INCLUSIVE USES

CRA is an evidence-based strategy for individuals with learning disabilities (Bouck et al., 2017). Writing equations with digital tools, including through dictation, as well as the use of text-to-speech functions provide support to individuals with disabilities as they develop conceptual understanding of mathematics.

SAMPLE TOOLS

EquatIO allows learners to add mathematical equations and formulas to documents, supporting the abstract understanding of mathematical concepts, including standard algorithms. EquatIO allows learners to incorporate manipulatives and representation drawing into their problem solving as needed.

EquatIO supports dictation and provides text-to-speech as well (**bit.ly/inclusive365-205a**).

OneNote allows learners to type or handwrite math equations using their Math Assistant tool (**onenote.com**).

EXTENSION OPPORTUNITY

Invite learners to explore a variety of resources for creating mathematical expressions on different websites and choose the ones they prefer. Their choices may be based on ease of access, visual displays, or the tools provided within the website.

RELATED RESOURCES

Concrete-Representational-Abstract (CRA) Instruction (**bit.ly/inclusive365-205b**)

Create Math Equations Using Ink or Text with Math Assistant in OneNote (**bit.ly/inclusive365-205c**)

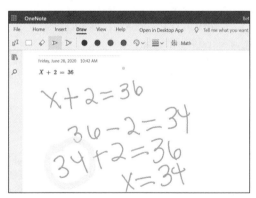

Figure 205. An equation written in OneNote.

ISTE STANDARDS FOR STUDENTS
1a, 1b, 1c, 5a, 5b, 5c

ISTE STANDARDS FOR EDUCATORS
5a, 5b, 5c, 6a, 6b, 6c

Interviewing Professionals Virtually

Enhanced educational experiences such as field trips and invited guest speakers have become increasingly more difficult to schedule due to costs and logistics. Virtual interviews with professionals are a way to share real life experiences, complement content from other media sources, and expose learners to different career options. Author and illustrator virtual visits can be an engaging addition to a genre, book, or author study. Using video conferencing platforms, scientists, authors, illustrators, and other professionals are available at low or no cost to educational institutions to share their work, answer questions, and help learners see how they can pursue these careers in the future.

INCLUSIVE USES

Virtual visits eliminate physical barriers that may come with field trips and also are easier for learners who may experience sensory overload in a large assembly or out in the community. Lee and Low, a large, multicultural publishing company, provides guest speakers from diverse cultures; underrepresented learners gain the opportunity to see themselves as successful authors and illustrators.

SAMPLE TOOLS

Skype a Scientist provides connections between educators and scientists for the purposes of video conferencing (**skypeascientist.com**).

Lee and Low helps foster virtual author and illustrator visits (**bit.ly/inclusive365-206a**).

EXTENSION OPPORTUNITIES

Create a virtual career day in which learners can sign up for sessions with professionals whose careers are of particular interest.

Invite learners to work in small groups or individually to generate questions that can be sent to the professionals before a live event. Learners can then use these questions as guides when asking questions during the live virtual interview.

Invite learners to brainstorm a list of professionals with whom they'd like to meet or otherwise interact. An authentic writing task might be to draft an email that could be sent by the educator requesting the interview.

RELATED RESOURCE

How to Set up a Skype Author Visit (**bit.ly/inclusive365-206b**)

Figure 206. Fifth-grade learners videoconferencing with a scientist.

ISTE STANDARDS FOR STUDENTS
7b, 7d

ISTE STANDARDS FOR EDUCATORS
4c, 5b

Facilitating Problem Solving with Reflective Questions

Cultivating learners' abilities to problem solve is critical to their understanding of science and mathematics concepts. Developing their ability to ask questions and reflect on how they engage in problem solving supports learners in making sense of increasingly complex problems. When educators pose questions that are applicable to a wide range of problem solving tasks and do not prescribe specific mathematical steps for solving a particular type of problem, learners can consider a variety of paths to a solution. Using a random question generator or rolling a dice to receive an educator-selected reflective question assists learners in thinking critically in a fun and game-like manner.

INCLUSIVE USES

Random question generators, including spinners and dice, infuse an element of play into a learning task, rather than making questions feel like an assessment or a test. Elements that gamify the experience may help engage learners who resist or avoid tasks which invite reflective questions or problem solving.

SAMPLE TOOLS

LessonPix Play Tools allow an individual to create a set of targeted questions that are then generated randomly when the learner draws a card from a hat or spins the spinner (**lessonpix.com**).

The random name generator available at ClassroomScreen can be used to create a set of questions instead of a set of names, and learners can spin to pick a question to consider (**classroomscreen.com**).

EXTENSION OPPORTUNITY

Invite learners to collaborate with a peer to answer a question. This can alleviate anxiety as well as produce more reflection. This can be done in conjunction with a Think, Pair, Share activity (see Strategy #21).

RELATED RESOURCES

6 Essential Questions for Problem Solving (**bit.ly/inclusive365-207a**)

Using Questions to Stimulate Mathematical Thinking (**bit.ly/inclusive365-207b**)

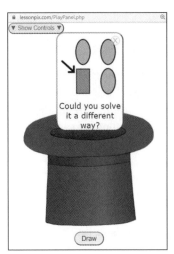

Figure 207. Random questions generated using the Play Tools in LessonPix.

ISTE STANDARDS FOR STUDENTS
5b, 7b, 7d

ISTE STANDARDS FOR EDUCATORS
4c, 6c, 7a

Developing Number Sense Skills with Digital Number Racks

Math manipulatives are engaging and beneficial tools to transform abstract math concepts into something more concrete. There are a variety of math manipulatives available. One type of math manipulative is a digital number rack, also known as a rekenrek, an instructional resource to facilitate the development of number sense. Typically organized in rows of tens, with five beads of one color and five beads of another color, number racks encourage learners to think in groups of fives and tens while exploring a variety of addition and subtraction strategies.

INCLUSIVE USES

Digital number racks allow learners who may have fine motor skills issues access to opportunities to explore with a digital manipulative. Digital number racks also allow learners to practice these skills when access to concrete tools is not possible.

SAMPLE TOOL

The Math Learning Center Math Number Rack app is available for iOS, online, and for Chrome. The app features include:

- Display 1 to 10 rows of beads, with 10 beads per row.

- Use the resizable shade to hide beads and model subtraction problems.

- Bead colors are reversed on rows 6 to 10 to distinguish groupings of 50 beads.

- Drawing tools allow users to annotate their work.

- The text tool allows users to write equations and expressions (**bit.ly/inclusive365-208a**).

EXTENSION OPPORTUNITIES

Invite learners working in makerspaces to use the materials available to create physical number racks for learners with varying physical needs.

Invite learners to make their own number racks using pipe cleaners strung with beads and mounted on cardboard or a piece of flat foam.

RELATED RESOURCES

How to Use a Rekenrek (**bit.ly/inclusive365-208b**)

For directions on how to make a variety of DIY 3-dimensional math racks, check out (**bit.ly/inclusive365-208c**).

Using Questions to Stimulate Mathematical Thinking (**bit.ly/inclusive365-208d**)

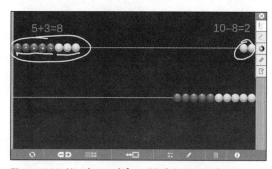

Figure 208. Number rack from Math Learning Center.

ISTE STANDARDS FOR STUDENTS
1c, 5a

ISTE STANDARDS FOR EDUCATORS
4b, 5a, 6a, 6b

Counting and Number Sense with Digital Ten Frames

The number ten is the building block of the base ten number system. Using ten frames to support understanding of number sense and place value is a common practice in early mathematics instruction. A ten frame provides learners with an opportunity to explore different arrangements of counters to prompt a variety of mental images of numbers grouped in amounts of ten. These counters promote different mental strategies for manipulating numbers, all in association with the number's relationship to ten. The use of digital ten frames supports this understanding in an engaging and accessible manner, and is available to learners in virtual or physical learning spaces.

INCLUSIVE USES

Virtual manipulatives, such as a digital ten frame, provide learners who may not have the fine motor abilities to draw a ten frame or to move counters on a paper an opportunity to use the strategy. Learners may also find the digital tool more engaging when invited to customize the color or shape of the counters.

SAMPLE TOOLS

The interactive ten frame from the National Council of Teachers of Mathematics allows learners to choose from a variety of counters and play a ten frame game, have open exploration, or work on simple addition skills. Audio supports are built in (**bit.ly/inclusive365-209a**).

The Number Frame app from the Math Learning Center allows learners to choose from premade 5, 10, 25, or 100 frames or make a custom frame to work on the understanding of multiplication of any number. Learners use the frames to count, represent, compare, and compute with numbers in a particular range (**bit.ly/inclusive365-209b**).

EXTENSION OPPORTUNITY

Make learning life-sized and kinesthetic by creating ten frames using painters tape on the floor or on a large table. Use items such as books, stuffed animals, or even learners themselves as counters for the ten frame.

RELATED RESOURCES

A Sense of "ten" and Place Value (**bit.ly/inclusive365-209c**)

Using Questions to Stimulate Mathematical Thinking (**bit.ly/inclusive365-209d**)

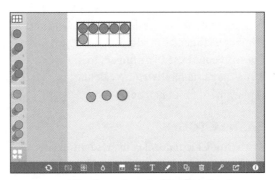

Figure 209. A Ten Frame from the Math Learning Center.

ISTE STANDARDS FOR STUDENTS

5a, 5c

ISTE STANDARDS FOR EDUCATORS

6a, 6c, 7a, 7b

Calculating Equations Using a Handwriting Calculator

A handwriting calculator converts written numbers into text and then calculates the results. Learners use their fingers or a stylus to handwrite numbers on the screen of the device. The application then converts the handwritten numbers and math symbols into digital numbers and symbols. The digital problems or equations are then calculated to provide the learner with the result of the calculation.

INCLUSIVE USES

Any learner accustomed to completing mathematical calculations using a pencil and paper might find handwriting calculators useful to help them derive or confirm results. Learners who have difficulty holding a writing utensil but who could use their fingers to draw or write may find handwriting calculators a good replacement for pencil and paper.

SAMPLE TOOLS

My Script Calculator 2 converts handwritten mathematics into digital numerals and symbols (**myscript.com/calculator**).

Microsoft Math Solver converts handwritten mathematics into digital numerals and symbols (**math.microsoft.com**).

EquatIO is an extension for Chrome that converts handwritten mathematics into digital numerals and symbols (**equatio.texthelp.com**).

EXTENSION OPPORTUNITY

Learners can use handwriting calculators when working to solve authentic problems in project-based learning lessons. In addition to using more traditional calculators or pencil and paper, handwriting calculators provide learners with another option to sketch out calculations on the fly. Educators can encourage the use of handwriting calculators by modeling their use to confirm results when providing instruction.

RELATED RESOURCES

This Calculator App Solves Handwritten Math Problems (**bit.ly/inclusive365-210a**)

Using Questions to Stimulate Mathematical Thinking (**bit.ly/inclusive365-210b**)

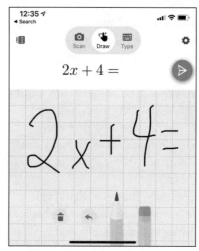

Figure 210. Handwritten math equation converted to digital numbers and symbols using the Math Solver app.

ISTE STANDARDS FOR STUDENTS
1c, 3b, 5a, 5b, 5c, 5d

ISTE STANDARDS FOR EDUCATORS
2b, 5a, 5c, 6a, 6b, 7a, 7b, 7c

Listening to Math Using Text-to-Speech

Mathematics and science educators at all levels have long created materials that include formulas, equations, and graphs. Traditionally, this content has been presented to learners as paper and pencil tasks and textbook content. More recently, this content has been made available digitally, but if a screen reader can't recognize and properly present the information, a segment of the population is excluded from ready access to digital formulas, equations, and graphs. When materials are created with accessibility in mind, those who have disabilities related to visual acuity, perception, and/or processing can access them and, ultimately, learn the content.

INCLUSIVE USES

Use the right tools to create mathematical and scientific expressions that can be read aloud. Provide these accessible materials to learners and invite them to respond in their preferred modality including writing, typing, or dictating.

Some math and science teachers might have traditional educational materials that were originally created in inaccessible formats. Educators and learners can use a mobile version of EquatIO to scan an existing document and then use optical character recognition (OCR) to convert it into a more accessible format. A document scanned to digital format using OCR allows a digital screen reader to read it aloud for learners who need that support.

SAMPLE TOOL

EquatIO is a Chrome extension that supports the creation of accessible mathematical equations, formulas, and more on a computer or Chromebook. The extension also works with Google Forms and the graphing site Desmos. The extension is free for educators to create accessible resources to share with learners. It can be used on an interactive whiteboard. Additionally, there is a mobile version (**bit.ly/inclusive365-211a**).

EXTENSION OPPORTUNITY

Invite learners to explore the additional features in EquaIO such as handwriting and voice recognition, and to identify features that support their learning.

RELATED RESOURCE

This playlist provides a series of videos related to the operation and successful implementation of EquatIO (**bit.ly/inclusive365-211b**).

Figure 211a. EquatIO workspace.

Figure 211b. Math symbols in EquatIO.

ISTE STANDARDS FOR STUDENTS
5a, 5b

ISTE STANDARDS FOR EDUCATORS
2b, 5a, 7b

Improving Math Accessibility with Interactive Digital Calculators

Digital math resources enhance the learning experience. Learners often have access to a hand-held graphing calculator. Deeper understanding, especially of complex math concepts, results when combined with online graphing and four-function calculator software.

INCLUSIVE USES

Desmos has been designed with accessibility in mind for learners with vision impairments. Font size, sufficient contrast, and features that communicate with screen readers to improve screen reading accuracy have been added to the design. It is Web Content Accessibility Guidelines 2.1 compliant (**desmos.com/accessibility**).

The ability to review online videos and simulations at one's own speed for understanding benefits all learners. Meaningful feedback is provided to help learners adapt their math thinking.

SAMPLE TOOL

Desmos is a free, interactive graphing calculator software with full-featured accompanying resources (**desmos.com**).

EXTENSION OPPORTUNITY

Invite learners to explore their peers' thinking and ask questions of each other to support learning.

RELATED RESOURCES

Getting Started with Desmos Activities (**bit.ly/inclusive365-212a**)

Desmos Step-by-Step Guide (**learn.desmos.com**)

Desmos Classroom Activities (**teacher.desmos.com**)

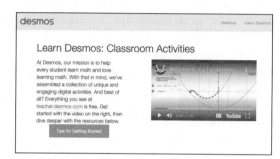

Figure 212. Desmos.

ISTE STANDARDS FOR STUDENTS

1a, 1b, 1c, 5a, 6c

ISTE STANDARDS FOR EDUCATORS

1a, 5a, 5b, 5c, 6a, 6b, 6c

Recording Calculations to Illustrate Thinking

Performing accurate calculations is a part of developing proficiency in mathematics. At times, learners may need guidance from educators about why their calculations are not working out as they expected. When mistakes occur, it is useful for educators guiding learners to know what they were thinking when they made the mistake. When learners video record themselves doing calculations while narrating their thoughts, it allows educators to better understand the cause of breakdowns and errors.

INCLUSIVE USES

Learners working to improve their mathematical abilities may find recording video of their work a useful practice to demonstrate their thinking to an educator.

Learners with fine or gross motor impairments may find repetitive completion of similar calculations challenging or fatiguing. When a learner demonstrates competency, that learner may not need continued practice on that skill, and could move on to practicing the next skill, without the fatigue of the extra practice. By viewing a recording of a learner's work and problem-solving strategies, the educator has the documentation needed to determine proficiency.

SAMPLE TOOLS

Seesaw is both a web-based and mobile application with drawing and recording tools that can be used when writing mathematical calculations (**seesaw.com**).

Flipgrid provides the ability to record short videos, combined with a whiteboard feature (**flipgrid.com**).

EXTENSION OPPORTUNITY

Create a shared library of videos produced and shared by learners that accurately demonstrate the completion of a specific type of calculation. Share this library with others learning the same skill.

Create a shared library of video produced and shared by learners that does not accurately demonstrate the completion of a specific type of calculation. These videos could be organized in a location labeled "common errors." Inviting learners to share their mistakes helps build the understanding that everyone makes mistakes, that making mistakes is completely acceptable, and that growth comes from learning from these mistakes.

RELATED RESOURCES

Rebranding "Show Your Work" (**bit.ly/inclusive365-213**)

How to Solve Math Problems with Flipgrid (Whiteboard Mode) (**bit.ly/inclusive365-213b**)

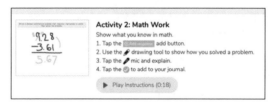

Figure 213. Showing your thinking in Seesaw.

ISTE STANDARDS FOR STUDENTS
1a, 1b, 1c, 4a, 6c

ISTE STANDARDS FOR EDUCATORS
5a, 5b, 5c, 6a, 6b, 6c, 7a, 7b

STRATEGY 213

Checking Calculations Automatically

A calculation checker provides learners with an opportunity to confirm the accuracy of their calculations. Learners hover a mobile device or tablet over a calculation to compare their own result with the one produced by the application. Depending on the application used, learners can experience step-by-step breakdowns of how a result was reached. The learner can then find and correct mistakes when the results are different. Learners can then proceed with confidence as they work on more challenging problems.

INCLUSIVE USES

Any learner working on mastering mathematical skills might find calculation checkers useful. Learners who do not yet feel confident in their math skills may find that calculation checkers provide a layer of security that can be used to bolster self confidence in their calculation abilities.

SAMPLE TOOLS

Photomath is an application that allows users to scan calculations to conduct automatic checks for accuracy (**photomath.net/en**).

Snapcalc is an application that allows users to scan calculations to conduct automatic checks for accuracy (**bit.ly/inclusive365-214a**).

Mathway is a free, web-based tool that allows users to type or upload a picture of algebraic equations to automatically check accuracy (**mathway.com/Algebra**).

EXTENSION OPPORTUNITIES

When working collaboratively on a group project, learners may find it useful to designate a person to check the mathematical calculations completed by the group using a calculation checker.

Educators can encourage the use of calculation checkers by modeling their use to confirm results when providing instruction.

RELATED RESOURCE

What If We Didn't Teach What a Calculator Can Do? (**bit.ly/inclusive365-214b**)

Figure 214. Using a calculation checker on a mobile device.

ISTE STANDARDS FOR STUDENTS
1c, 3b, 5a, 5b, 5c, 5d

ISTE STANDARDS FOR EDUCATORS
2b, 5a, 5b, 5c, 6a, 7a

STRATEGY 214

Sharing Science Lab Results Using Multimedia

Discovery and "aha" moments are hallmarks of science labs, which provide hands-on opportunities to explore concepts, develop questions, and test hypotheses. This type of lab experience is a prime example of self-directed learning. However, documenting the results of a lab can be a daunting process for some learners, turning them off to the entire process and denying them the opportunity to experience the inherent value of self-discovery. Offering learners collaborative ways to record their results and conclusions may be an effective way to help learners experience the joy of making discoveries. Learners can use multimedia applications to record their voice, to include images and video, and to interact and collaborate with other learners in order to share science lab results.

INCLUSIVE USES

Offering novel alternatives for documentation instead of using traditional hand-written science lab templates may engage learners who find completing a written report uninspiring. Learners who are challenged by writing may be more successful using a multimedia application to record results.

SAMPLE TOOLS

Flipgrid is a free video-recording tool that allows learners to record a response to a lab prompt, and to view and respond to responses from peers (**info.flipgrid.com**).

VoiceThread allows learners to record a video response to a prompt and to view and respond to responses from their peers (**voicethread.com**).

EXTENSION OPPORTUNITY

Invite learners to design the lab questions themselves and use the technology for each step of the process, including establishing the hypotheses, recording the experiment, detailing the results, and summarizing the conclusion. Learners can work in small groups and one person to be designated as the recorder for the different steps of the lab.

RELATED RESOURCE

Get Creative with Lab Reports Alternatives (**bit.ly/inclusive365-215a**)

Figure 215. Learner demonstrating a science experiment.

ISTE STANDARDS FOR STUDENTS

3a, 3b, 4a, 5a, 5b, 6a, 6b, 6c

ISTE STANDARDS FOR EDUCATORS

5a, 5b, 5c, 6a, 6b, 6d, 7a, 7b

Developing Practical Money Skills

Learners need to develop financial literacy skills to live and work independently in the community. An often-overlooked area in mathematics curriculum is teaching these practical money management skills, including how to organize and maintain a bank account, managing credit/debit cards, and using financial transaction applications. Games and simulation experiences can help learners practice and build their financial literacy skills.

INCLUSIVE USES

Learning personal finance skills are critical for all learners. As learners transition from the K–12 setting into the adult phase of their lives (college, work, community living) these skills become critical for independence.

SAMPLE TOOLS

Practical Money Skills is a free website, developed by Visa, that provides financial skill building, lesson plans, and more. According to the website, the program "strives to link consumers, educators, banks and governments to the tools and resources they need, helping individuals and communities develop their money management skills. Visa believes that greater financial knowledge can empower people to better manage their money and improve their quality of life" (**practicalmoneyskills.com**).

Junior Achievement USA offers simulated financial experiences for learners (**bit.ly/inclusive365-216a**).

EXTENSION OPPORTUNITIES

Invite learners to determine what additional information they need to learn about personal finance and money skills and to collaborate to develop resources that meet their needs. Invite learners to create and share their own video tutorials to empower them with the financial knowledge they need as they transition to live beyond high school.

RELATED RESOURCES

Lesson Plans to Teach Practical Money Skills (**bit.ly/inclusive365-216b**)

Free Financial Literacy Lesson for High School Teachers (**bit.ly/inclusive365-216c**)

Teach Me How to Money: A Personal Finance Podcast (**bit.ly/inclusive365-216d**)

Figure 216. Learner practicing money management skills at an ATM.

ISTE STANDARDS FOR STUDENTS
1a, 1d, 2b, 3d, 5a

ISTE STANDARDS FOR EDUCATORS
2b, 3a, 4b, 5a, 7a

Building Community Partnerships to Implement STEAM Programs

How can educators engage learners in the world of science, technology, engineering, art, and mathematics (STEAM) while highlighting real-world problems and solutions? One way is by making connections with individuals with disabilities who need technology tools to become more independent. Makerspaces and robotics and engineering clubs provide a way for learners to come together, not only to learn about and engage in STEAM projects and develop their skills, but to benefit their larger community.

INCLUSIVE USES

Connecting learners to the larger maker community and working collaboratively to solve real-world problems promotes an inclusive community. People with disabilities need assistive technology devices to maintain independence in the community. STEAM programs have learners who are developing skills to build unique devices from scratch. Everyone wins when a person with a disability gets a one-of-a-kind tool they need and learners get real world experience designing and building items. Additionally, interacting with community members with disabilities provides learners with an opportunity to develop empathy for others and build lifelong friendships.

SAMPLE TOOL

ATMakers.org is an online community that exists to connect makers, educationally based STEAM/Robotics teams, and people with disabilities who need assistive technology. These partnerships benefit all. People with disabilities obtain the devices they need for independence and the maker teams have opportunities to design and build devices that highlight their skills (**atmakers.org**).

EXTENSION OPPORTUNITY

Invite learners to explore the projects listed on the ATMakers website and Facebook group page. Find an opportunity for collaboration and facilitate a connection between the learners and ATMakers community members. Set up a videoconference call so all interested parties can connect and discuss the need. Start the design process and work collaboratively to solve this problem.

RELATED RESOURCES

What Does ATMakers.org Do? (**bit.ly/inclusive365-217a**)

ATMakers Facebook Group (**facebook.com/groups/ATMakers**)

Figure 217. ATMakers Facebook page.

ISTE STANDARDS FOR STUDENTS
4a, 4b, 4c, 4d, 7a, 7b, 7c, 7d

ISTE STANDARDS FOR EDUCATORS
4a, 4b, 4c, 5b, 5c, 6b, 6c

STRATEGY 218

Building Understanding of Transformations in Mathematics with Digital Tools

A transformation is a mathematical process involving manipulation of a two-dimensional object, such as a polygon on a plane or a coordinate system. Learners begin to study transformations as early as pre-kindergarten by gaining an understanding of how an object, such as a pattern block, can be manipulated in space. Understanding of transformations extends up through high school level geometry and beyond. Digital resources, such as manipulatives and interactive courses, can support the stages of conceptual understanding about transformations, from concrete to representational to abstract.

INCLUSIVE USES

Manipulatives are an important resource for the evidence-based Concrete-Representational-Abstract (CRA) strategy. Digital manipulatives provide learners of all skill levels the opportunity to move polygons and other objects in a virtual space. Learners with physical impairments may find digital manipulatives easier to translate, rotate, reflect, or dilate (the four types of transformations) than handheld manipulatives. Learners can supplement their mathematics instruction with online courses, particularly when they are having challenges with a particular concept.

SAMPLE TOOLS

Mathigon's interactive online courses provide engaging instruction for a range of mathematical topics, including transformations (**bit.ly/inclusive365-218a**).

Mathigon's Polypad app helps learners explore transformations by providing a range of digital manipulatives including polygons, tangrams, and pentominoes (**mathigon.org/polypad**).

Mathplanet offers Creative Commons-licensed digital math courses that include video demonstrations of math concepts, including transformations (**mathplanet.com**).

EXTENSION OPPORTUNITIES

Invite educators to explore the courses on Mathigon or Mathplanet as a refresher prior to teaching content to their learners.

Invite learners to participate in a design challenge where they transform an object using a set of shapes into something new, using their imaginations to think creatively.

RELATED RESOURCE

Transformations—They're Not Just for Functions! (**bit.ly/inclusive365-218b**)

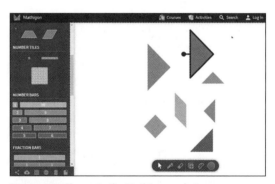

Figure 218. Shapes in the Mathigon website.

ISTE STANDARDS FOR STUDENTS
1a, 1b, 1c, 5a, 5b, 5c

ISTE STANDARDS FOR EDUCATORS
5a, 5b, 5c, 6a, 6b, 6c

Using Digital Geoboards to Explore Mathematics Concepts

Geoboards are commonly used as hands-on instructional tools where learners manipulate rubber bands around the pegs on a square board to make mathematical discoveries and build their understanding of measurement concepts, such as perimeter and area; geometry concepts including shapes, angles, and congruence; and number and operations concepts including fractions. While this can be done on traditional geoboards, digital geoboards are more flexible and offer additional options for engagement and annotation.

INCLUSIVE USES

Learners with disabilities related to fine-motor control may find working with digital geoboards preferable to using physical manipulatives. Learners who require concrete representations to understand measurement and fractional concepts may benefit from the ability to hide or show grid lines.

SAMPLE TOOL

Geoboard, available for free online, or as an Android or iOS app, provides a digital geoboard experience (**bit.ly/inclusive365-219a**).

EXTENSION OPPORTUNITIES

Invite learners to use the geoboard on an interactive whiteboard during whole group learning experiences or as an interactive math center.

Invite learners to take screenshots of their digital geoboard creations and record their thinking using an audio recording tool.

RELATED RESOURCE

18 Clever Ways to Use Geoboards in the Classroom (**wearteachers.com/geoboards**)

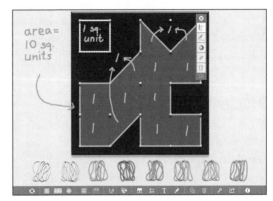

Figure 219. Sample virtual geoboard.

ISTE STANDARDS FOR STUDENTS

5b, 5c

ISTE STANDARDS FOR EDUCATORS

5a, 5b, 5c, 6a, 6b, 6c, 6d, 7a

STRATEGY 219

STRATEGY 220

Manipulating Virtual, Interactive 3D Models For Math

Virtual, interactive, three-dimensional (3D) models allow learners to understand math concepts in a way that is impossible with traditional instructional methods. Digital manipulatives promote deeper learning as the learner can view the mathematical objects from a variety of planes and perspectives. Exploring 3D graphs and functions, and constructing solids and shapes using interactive 3D tools bring mathematical concepts alive.

INCLUSIVE USES

3D visualization software benefits all learners who need interactive visual supports to understand math concepts. Digital resources allow learners to explore and review the concepts as many times as necessary to truly understand mathematical concepts.

SAMPLE TOOL

GeoGebra is a dynamic math app that features the ability to create 3D mathematical objects. It can be downloaded or used within the website itself (**geogebra.org**).

EXTENSION OPPORTUNITY

Invite learners to become the experts. Encourage learners to create instructional videos demonstrating the creation of 3D mathematical objects. Learners could also created a collaborative website to highlight these instructional videos.

RELATED RESOURCES

GeoGebra 3D: Beginner Tutorials with Lesson Ideas (**bit.ly/inclusive365-220a**)

Workshop: Using the 3D Features of GeoGebra (**bit.ly/inclusive365-220b**)

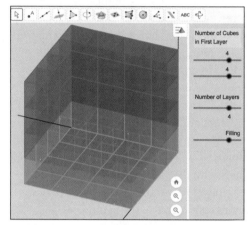

Figure 220. Interactive 3D model in GeoGebra.

ISTE STANDARDS FOR STUDENTS
1a, 1b, 1c, 5a, 6c

ISTE STANDARDS FOR EDUCATORS
5a, 5b, 5c, 6a, 6b, 6c, 7a, 7b

Manipulating Virtual Interactive 3D Models For Science

Virtual, interactive 3D objects allow a learner to manipulate the object on screen to explore it from different angles. It provides the learner with an opportunity to experience the depth of an object, which can be difficult to perceive using only 2D pictures. Moving the object around also provides the learner with a kinesthetic experience. Interactive 3D objects can be particularly useful for exploring a wide variety of objects related to science and scientific principles, such as astronomical objects, fossils, organs of the body, and the structures of atoms and cells.

INCLUSIVE USES

Manipulating virtual 3D objects may be engaging to all sighted learners. Educators might find that interactive 3D objects are particularly engaging to learners who have otherwise shown disinterest with traditional learning experiences.

SAMPLE TOOL

Lifeliqe is a website that provides a variety of 3D objects related to science, along with lesson plans that include step-by-step instructions for how to use the objects (**bit.ly/inclusive365-221a**).

EXTENSION OPPORTUNITIES

Invite learners to record short videos that show them engaging with a 3D object in order to explain what they've learned about the object.

Invite learners to record short videos in which they use the object as a prop to tell a story that can be shared with others.

RELATED RESOURCE

Harness the Power of 3D Models in the Classroom (**bit.ly/inclusive365-221b**)

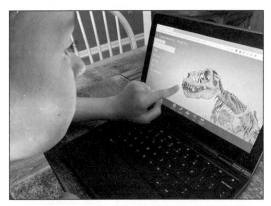

Figure 221. Learner interacting with a 3D representation of a dinosaur fossil.

ISTE STANDARDS FOR STUDENTS

1b, 3a, 3c

ISTE STANDARDS FOR EDUCATORS

5a, 5b, 6b

STRATEGY 222

Supporting Mathematics Understanding with Digital Graph Paper

Graph paper can assist in making math problems concrete for learners. Online graph paper offers more options for completing math exeriences. It provides a digital canvas on which to enter math problems, track data, or graph coordinates, just like on traditional graph paper.

INCLUSIVE USES

For learners with fine motor challenges, while traditional graph paper can help keep math problems lined up, the size of the individual graphing squares can be problematic. Using digital graph paper eliminates fine motor control issues, while still providing the ability to easily line up math equations. Learners can easily create straight lines without a ruler. Digital graph paper also provides a streamlined platform for entering information and keeping it organized.

SAMPLE TOOL

Free Online Graph Paper is a free web resource that offers an array of graph paper sizes and styles. Many of the files are downloadable and printable , but learners can use the Virtual Online Graph Paper right on the screen (**print-graph-paper.com**). Digital graph paper can mitigate fine motor control issues while still providing the ability to easily line up math equations.

EXTENSION OPPORTUNITY

Invite learners to create their own graph paper reflecting on color and thickness of the lines.

RELATED RESOURCES

Graph Paper as a Math Accommodation (**bit.ly/inclusive365-222a**)

Graph Paper Coding (**bit.ly/inclusive365-222b**)

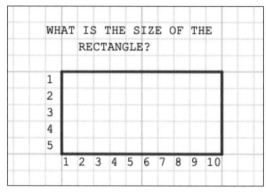

Figure 222. Solving a measurement problem using digital graph paper.

ISTE STANDARDS FOR STUDENTS

1c, 1d, 3c, 5a

ISTE STANDARDS FOR EDUCATORS

2b, 3b, 4b, 5a, 5b, 5c, 6b, 6c

Visualizing STEAM with Premade, Interactive Concept Maps

Concept maps are graphical representations of the relationships between ideas that help learners organize and analyze information. Using premade, interactive concept maps is a powerful instructional tool for learning new information, enhancing study skills, and building higher-level cognitive skills. Premade concept maps contain supplementary information including articles and videos to build science and math knowledge. Because they are premade, they save educators time when designing or supplementing content.

INCLUSIVE USES

Premade interactive concept maps can help learners better understand science, math, or interdisciplinary concepts. They include scaffolds, such as vocabulary terms links to articles and videos that support all learners and independent learning.

SAMPLE TOOL

CK-12 Concept Map is a free resource that helps learners visualize math and science concepts with interactive concept maps (**ck12.org/conceptmap**).

EXTENSION OPPORTUNITY

Encourage learners to customize the interactive concept maps. They can add or delete concepts to make them more personally meaningful.

RELATED RESOURCE

Introduction to CK-12 Interactive Concept Maps (**bit.ly/inclusive365-223a**)

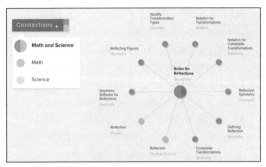

Figure 223. Concept map generated with CK-12.

ISTE STANDARDS FOR STUDENTS
1a, 1c, 5b, 6b, 6c

ISTE STANDARDS FOR EDUCATORS
2b, 3b, 5a, 5b, 6a, 6b

STRATEGY 223

Teaching Mathematical Concepts Using a Digital Sandbox

Children playing with real sand in a real sandbox have an opportunity to build and create, but they face real limitations. Digital sandbox tools allow users to freely create objects in a virtual world where their only limitations are their imaginations. Educators and learners can use digital sandbox tools to produce virtual manipulatives to demonstrate and illustrate mathematical concepts. Sandbox tools often provide blocks or other units to create the environment. These blocks can be used as virtual manipulatives that can be used to help represent numerical concepts.

INCLUSIVE USES

Engage learners who find traditional methods of learning mathematical concepts a challenge by having them use digital sandbox tools.

SAMPLE TOOL

Minecraft: Education Edition from Microsoft allows users to create in a digital sandbox (**education.minecraft.net**).

EXTENSION OPPORTUNITY

Invite learners to use digital sandbox tools to create educational materials for their peers.

RELATED RESOURCE

Mathcraft: Fractions On a Number Line (**bit.ly/inclusive365-224a**)

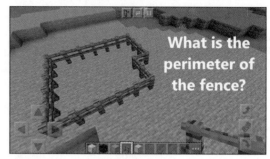

What is the perimeter of the fence?

Figure 224. Blocks in Minecraft representing mathematical concepts.

ISTE STANDARDS FOR STUDENTS
1b, 4a, 4b, 4c 4d, 6a, 6b, 6c, 6d

ISTE STANDARDS FOR EDUCATORS
4c, 5a, 5c, 6b, 6c, 6d, 7a

Making Art through Computational Sketching

Some graphing calculators allow learners to create pictures and animations through the use of equations and inequalities. This is known as computational sketching. Learners apply what they know about mathematics to create drawings using line segments, ellipticals, curves, and circles using the functions of the calculator. Depending on the skill and creativity of the learner, these drawings can range from simple lines to complex animations with colors and shading. Educators can address specific mathematical concepts, such as equations to create lines, by having learners design a drawing that requires them to write equations that draw a slope and line intersection.

INCLUSIVE USES

Computational sketching combines math with art, which taps into the strengths of learners who prefer to demonstrate their learning through art.

Some graphing calculators provide text that can be read aloud using screen-reader software, which helps to make the experience accessible for learners with low vision or who are blind.

SAMPLE TOOL

The Desmos Graphing Calculator can be used to create computational art and has accessible text (**desmos.com/calculator**).

EXTENSION OPPORTUNITY

Invite learners to review the past winning entries to the yearly Desmos Global Math Art Contest for learners 13–18 years old, and then submit their own creations (**desmos.com/art**).

RELATED RESOURCES

Desmos Art: The Definitive Guide to Computational Sketching (**mathvault.ca/desmos-art-guide**)

Graphing Calculator Art: How to Make a Face (**bit.ly/inclusive365-225a**)

Accessing Features in the Desmos Graphing Calculator (**bit.ly/inclusive365-225b**)

Figure 225. Award-winning artwork created by a learner using Desmos.

ISTE STANDARDS FOR STUDENTS
5a, 5c, 6a, 6b, 6c

ISTE STANDARDS FOR EDUCATORS
2b, 4b, 5a 6c

STRATEGY 226

Doodling with Graphs

Graph paper can be used for much more than just solving math problems. Drawing on graph paper highlights the mathematical nature of art and the important relationship between these two content areas. Using traditional or digital graph paper allows learners to explore concepts, such as symmetry, proportions, lines, and geometry.

INCLUSIVE USES

For learners who have difficulty controlling fine motor movements, or who lack confidence in their artistic ability, using traditional or digital graph paper provides a guide for proportionality to create with increased accuracy. Learners working to improve spatial reasoning skills may also find drawing using graph paper as a guide beneficial. Digital tools that allow a grid to be filled in with the click of a mouse or the tap of a stylus or finger offer even more support.

SAMPLE TOOLS

Free Online Graph Paper is a website that has an array of graph paper sizes and styles. Many of the files are printable but there is also Virtual Online Graph Paper, which can be used right on the screen. With the virtual graph paper, learners can use graphing coordinates to create art with intersecting lines (**print-graph-paper.com**).

Brik Build is a free resource that allows learners to click on colors to fill squares in a grid to create designs. The designs can be translated into 3D brick-style creations using Brik or other commercially available building brick pieces (**brik.co/pages/brikbuild**).

The Desmos Graphing Calculator allows for a variety of both simple and complex art creations (**desmos.com/art**).

EXTENSION OPPORTUNITY

Invite learners to create a design using traditional or digital graph paper and translate that into a 3D sculpture using building brick pieces.

RELATED RESOURCES

Using Graph Paper to Make Art (**bit.ly/inclusive365-226a**)

Graph Paper Doodles (**bit.ly/inclusive365-226b**)

Graph Paper Coding (**bit.ly/inclusive365-226c**)

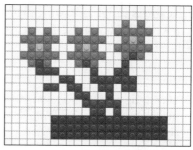

Figure 226. Picture of flowers created with the Brik Build design tool.

ISTE STANDARDS FOR STUDENTS
1c, 1d, 3c, 5a

ISTE STANDARDS FOR EDUCATORS
2b, 3b, 4b, 5a, 5b, 5c, 6b, 6c

Collaborating in a Shared Learning Space with Augmented Reality

Augmented reality (AR) provides learners with an opportunity to combine virtual space with the real world. Many of the tools that provide AR experiences are focused on a single learner interacting individually with the combined space. But providing learners with a collaborative space to interact with the AR provides deeper connections and opportunities for learning.

INCLUSIVE USES

Using AR apps can provide inclusive learning experiences for all learners. Bringing learners into a virtual environment or situation can be very engaging, and the immersive nature of this environment can deepen learning. Collaborative AR tools can help build problem-solving skills and support cooperative learning by providing learners with a platform for working together and sharing responsibilities to complete a task.

SAMPLE TOOL

Just a Line app, available for both iOS and Android mobile devices, uses AR to enable learners to virtually interact with the real world. Learners can also collaborate with others in real time and interact in the same workspace. The app is available from Apple (**bit.ly/inclusive365-227a**) and Google Play (**bit.ly/inclusive365-227b**).

EXTENSION OPPORTUNITY

Invite learners to participate in a collaborative AR experience by playing a virtual game of tic-tac-toe.

RELATED RESOURCE

Just a Line: The First Cross-Platform Collaborative ARApp (**bit.ly/inclusive365-227c**)

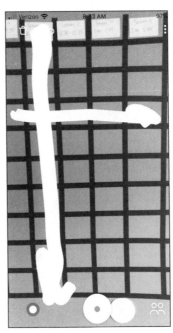

Figure 227. Marking up a map and identifying continents using the Just A Line app.

ISTE STANDARDS FOR STUDENTS
1a, 1b, 1c, 1d, 4b, 4c, 6b, 6c, 7a

ISTE STANDARDS FOR EDUCATORS
2b, 2c, 5a, 5b, 5c, 6d, 7a

STRATEGY 227

Making to Solve an Authentic Problem

The world has no shortage of problems. Problems can be personal, local, global, simple, or complex. When educators pose a problem to learners and invite them to devise solutions, they introduce authenticity into learning. With access to a 3D printer, learners can design and make a tangible item to solve the problem. Invite learners to make objects to help peers, younger learners, or others learn specific skills. The next time learners wonder, "What should we make?" invite them to ask, "Who can we help?"

A step in any solution-seeking project is to research if anyone else has already found a solution. Learners might search databases where others share designs.

INCLUSIVE USES

Some learners may become intimidated by an abundance of options. Working to solve a problem can provide a distinct purpose, drive persistence when hurdles arise, and sets up a pay off where learners know their actions improved lives. Project databases provide ideas for those who might struggle with solving the problem on their own. 2D representations of 3D models help people visualize a final product.

SAMPLE TOOLS

Make: Projects is a community that offers *Maker Faires*, a magazine, and an online database (**makeprojects.com**).

Thingiverse is a community database of designs for 3D printers (**thingiverse.com**).

Instructables hosts a catalog of projects, organized into categories, such as circuits, workshop, craft, living, and outside (**instructables.com**).

EXTENSION OPPORTUNITY

Engage learners in a discussion around a problem someone they know is having. This could be a younger learner, peer, family member, or anyone else important to the individual. For example, a sibling may know their brother or sister is working to learn language using augmentative/alternative communication. The learner might find a print based on a common interest and then work together to create it. Each piece could be printed and assembled while modeling words on the AAC, such as "Put on," "This way," "What next?," "My turn," and "We did it!"

RELATED RESOURCES

Making Project-Based Learning Authentic (**bit.ly/inclusive365-228a**)

Talking With Tech Episode #2—Bill Binko: DIY Assistive Technology, "Makers," & the Convergence of Assistive Technology and Universal Design (**bit.ly/inclusive365-228b**)

Road Tested / Solving Authentic Problems in Makerspaces (**bit.ly/inclusive365-228c**)

Figure 228. Maker projects purposed to assist with completing daily tasks, listed on Thingiverse.com.

ISTE STANDARDS FOR STUDENTS
4a, 4b, 4c, 4d

ISTE STANDARDS FOR EDUCATORS
2a, 2b, 3a, 5a, 5b, 5c, 6c, 6d

Keeping Dice on the Table during Games

Not every inclusive strategy needs to involve digital technology, right? Maybe you want to engage learners in a board game designed to reinforce a topic. But we don't want the game to get cancelled because the dice have gone missing since they were thrown *just* a bit too hard! Placing dice in containers makes it so they don't get lost and are easier to roll! Happy gaming!

INCLUSIVE USES

Modifying the environment can go a long way towards creating an inclusive environment for gameplay. For some learners, gripping and throwing dice may be difficult, which can result in an inability to participate. Finding inclusive ways to enable full participation involves a little creativity and the solutions can be thrilling for all involved.

SAMPLE TOOL

Empty water bottle + Dice = Gaming success!

Step 1: Drink water from a bottle! Step 2: Insert dice into an empty bottle and seal with cap. Step 3: Play games!! It's that easy. Now you have a dice shaker that can aid with a number of issues that could arise during gameplay. First, dice being thrown across the room is a thing of the past because they are encased in the bottle. Second, for learners who physically find it difficult to pick up, shake, and throw dice, the bottle provides an easier grip. Third, you can now play the game anywhere. You don't even need a flat surface for the dice to roll on. Shake the bottle and rest it on your leg. The dice will lay flat in the bottom of the bottle.

EXTENSION OPPORTUNITIES

Invite learners to create their own dice roller with options for different types of games, including those that require multiple dice. These dice may be different sizes and/or shapes.

As part of a makerspace, encourage learners to gather up the materials needed to create dice shakers for educators and learners in the community. Shaker bottles can be customized to match the specific game and/or theme.

RELATED RESOURCES

17 Fun Dice Games to Play with Family and Friends (**funattic.com/dice-games**)

LessonPix Live: Games People Play (**bit.ly/inclusive365-229a**)

Figure 229. A clear bottle with flat sides makes it easier to view dice.

ISTE STANDARDS FOR STUDENTS
1a

ISTE STANDARDS FOR EDUCATORS
5a, 5b, 6c, 6d

3D Printing Assistive Devices

Many institutions of learning are now equipped with 3D printers and science, technology, engineering, art, and mathematics (STEAM) focused programs. But what experiences are learners participating in with those devices? Are learners gaining real-world design skills and using them to solve real-world problems? Taking a design approach and creating assistive devices can provide an avenue for community involvement with learners solving real-world problems while learning the skills of 3D printing.

INCLUSIVE USES

When educators connect 3D printing skills to creating devices that can increase independence for individuals with disabilities in their own community, learners also develop empathy and an understanding of the power of technology in the world around them. For community members with disabilities, a handle to grip a house key could be the difference between living independently or not. Our learners have the power to make real change in our communities.

SAMPLE TOOL

Assistive Device Academy is a free course, designed by Makers Making Change and the PrintLab, consisting of lessons and documents to support the 3D printing of five different types of assistive devices. Starting with an introduction to assistive technology and people with disabilities, learners begin to understand the power of creating assistive devices. Plans are included as part of the course to design five items: a plastic bag holder, a shirt buttoning tool, a handle for a house key, a tool to open soda cans, and a bottle opener (**weareprintlab.com**).

EXTENSION OPPORTUNITY

As a group, participate in the first section of the course highlighting people with disabilities and assistive technology. Discuss ways the learners could connect with individuals in their community to design and build everyday items to increase independence. Now go through the lessons and build the five items. Learners can print multiple devices and donate them to disability organizations within the community.

RELATED RESOURCE

Assistive Device Academy (**bit.ly/inclusive365-230a**)

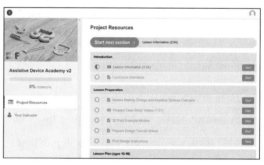

Figure 230. Assistive Device Academy.

ISTE STANDARDS FOR STUDENTS

4a, 4b, 4c, 4d, 7a, 7b, 7c, 7d

ISTE STANDARDS FOR EDUCATORS

4a, 4b, 4c, 5b, 5c, 6b, 6c

Memorizing Mathematical Facts with Music

Have you ever experienced an earworm? It is the phenomenon of having the melody of a song stuck in your head. You might even find yourself singing or humming the tune aloud! Earworms can be used to help learners remember foundational math facts. Putting math facts to a melody can help learners recall the fact faster and use it more expeditiously when engaging in a task that necessitates the need for it.

INCLUSIVE USES

Music engages most learners, but learners who have difficulties remembering or recalling information might find math facts easier to remember when they are sung with a repetitive melody or rhythm.

SAMPLE TOOLS

GoNoodle provides humorous videos and other experiences to help learners recall math facts (**bit.ly/inclusive365-231a**).

Mr. DeMaio, an educator, has a playlist on his YouTube channel dedicated to learning math facts through music and song (**bit.ly/inclusive365-231b**).

EXTENSION OPPORTUNITY

Invite learners to compose and record their own songs for math concepts and share them out to the world to help other learners.

RELATED RESOURCES

Music and Learning: Why Teachers Should Consider Music in the Classroom (**bit.ly/inclusive365-231c**)

Can Songs Help Students Learn? (**bit.ly/inclusive365-231d**)

Figure 231. Early learners dancing to a music video featuring math facts.

ISTE STANDARDS FOR STUDENTS
1a, 1b, 1c

ISTE STANDARDS FOR EDUCATORS
5a, 5b

Playing Multiple Musical Instruments with Your Voice

Playing a musical instrument typically requires a sophisticated level of coordination of various muscle groups. This can present a challenge for those with impairments related to motor control and coordination. However, musical exploration can occur without knowing how or having the ability to play a specific instrument. Music that can be created digitally can provide an alternative way to access and play music. Using digital tools, individuals can compose music with their voices, adding layers of musical instruments into a unique masterpiece. Individuals can use their voice to access a variety of instruments including drums, electric guitar, and maybe some cowbell! Learners can express themselves and connect to learning experiences through the power of music.

INCLUSIVE USES

Learners with impairments that impact fine and gross motor control and coordination can explore their creative sides using digital tools to play music.

SAMPLE TOOL

Google Mix Lab allows individuals to create music by talking to the computer. Saying "Give me a drum beat" lays the foundation for the song. Using voice commands, additional instruments can be layered into the piece until it sounds amazing (**mixlab.withgoogle.com**).

EXTENSION OPPORTUNITIES

Invite learners to create a musical score to accompany a discussion topic or project. Encourage collaboration where each learner is responsible for one instrument track, leading to a finished score.

Invite learners to record and share their musical masterpiece with the world!

RELATED RESOURCE

50+ Lesson Ideas for the Chrome Music Lab (**bit.ly/inclusive365-232a**)

Figure 232. Create your own musical score with Mixlab.

ISTE STANDARDS FOR STUDENTS
1d, 4a, 4c, 5d, 6b

ISTE STANDARDS FOR EDUCATORS
4b, 5a, 5b, 6a, 6b, 6d

Making Tunes with a Virtual Music Lab

Expression is at the heart of the Universal Design for Learning guidelines and should be the goal of all our interactions with learners by poviding opportunities for learners to express themselves in writing, communication and even music. We need to provide learners with opportunities to express themselves in writing, communication, and even music! Music can connect individuals to the topic about which they are learning while providing opportunities to practice writing, listening, communicating, and coding. There are many opportunities to create music using a virtual music lab. When the learners create music, we all get to hear the results.

INCLUSIVE USES

Learners who feel they are not musically talented using handheld instruments can explore their creative side using digital tools. Learners don't have to worry about being physically unable to hold or play an instrument. Now everyone can play the drums! All you need is a computer and internet access and you can create.

SAMPLE TOOL

Chrome Music Lab lets learners explore their own creativity through music experimentaton. An array of choices are available to create your audio masterpiece (**musiclab.chromeexperiments.com**).

EXTENSION OPPORTUNITY

Task learners with creating a score to accompany a reading passage from a work of fiction. Each learner can score a different portion of the text. Once the music is created, have a dramatic reading (this can happen either in person or virtually) where the educator acts as the narrator and the learners each play their score at the appropriate time in the story.

RELATED RESOURCES

Chrome Music Lab: Create Your Own Songs with Song Maker (**bit.ly/inclusive365-233a**)

Chrome Music Lab: How to make cool music and sounds (**bit.ly/inclusive365-233b**)

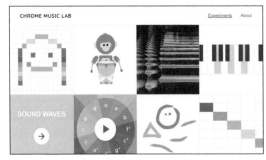

Figure 233. Multiple options for how to create using the Chrome Music Lab.

ISTE STANDARDS FOR STUDENTS
1d, 4a, 4c, 5d, 6b

ISTE STANDARDS FOR EDUCATORS
2b, 4b, 5a, 6b, 6c

Orchestrating a Virtual Musical Performance

Have you ever wanted to conduct an orchestra? Well grab your conductor stick and fire up your Chrome browser. Using the camera on a device, learners can conduct a virtual orchestra simply by moving their arms.

INCLUSIVE USES

Learners with impairments impacting fine motor control and coordination might have difficulty accessing traditional instruments or controlling digital instruments through keyboards. These learners may enjoy orchestrating the music through the use of gross motor movements. Moving in space in front of the camera provides an opportunity for creative self-expression.

SAMPLE TOOL

Google's Semi-Conductor allows individuals to conduct a virtual orchestra through arm movement. Moving arms up and down controls the virtual musicians and simulates a concert environment. Raising or lowering an arm controls volume. Side-to-side arm movement controls which section of the orchestra plays (**semiconductor.withgoogle.com**).

EXTENSION OPPORTUNITIES

Invite learners to lead a virtual orchestra as an opportunity to build in kinesthetic movement during both in-person and distance learning. Learners might enjoy a musical break and rotate through playing a musical interlude between discussion topics or projects.

Invite learners to record their musical compositions and performances and share them with the world.

RELATED RESOURCE

AI Experiment: Semi-Conductor
(**bit.ly/inclusive365-234**)

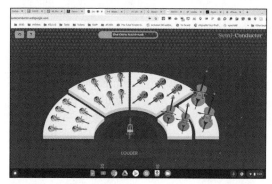

Figure 234. Lead an orchestra from the comfort of your home using Semi-Conductor.

ISTE STANDARDS FOR STUDENTS

1d, 4a, 4c, 5d, 6b

ISTE STANDARDS FOR EDUCATORS

4b, 5a, 5b, 6a, 6b, 6d

Coding to Practice Problem Solving in Early Childhood

Learners benefit by engaging in self-guided exploration where opportunities arise from their own actions to deepen problem-solving skills. This is especially true for very young learners. Coding takes learners through the process of considering and creating step-by-step instructions that a computer application needs to move through a sequence of actions as intended. Coding websites and apps provide learners the opportunity to problem solve through trial and error as well as experience success from experimentation. Engaging in coding experiences at an early age provides an opportunity to learn foundational skills that can be built upon as they mature.

INCLUSIVE USES

Coding provides young learners with language delays or those who are multilingual learners, the opportunity to practice critical vocabulary and sight words, including *up, down, turn, jump*, and more, depending on the coding experience.

Depending on the platform used, some coding applications can be accessed using switches and/or voice control, which can be useful for learners with fine and/or gross motor impairments.

SAMPLE TOOLS

Tommy the Turtle Learns to Code from Zyrobotics teaches basic coding through the use of commands, sequences, and loops (**bit.ly/inclusive365-235a**).

Starfall Geometry 3D does not explicitly use coding language, but instead takes young learners through a problem-solving experience in which they need to use logic to move an object through a maze, simulating the experience they would get while coding (**bit.ly/inclusive365-235b**).

EXTENSION OPPORTUNITY

Invite learners to engage in a low-tech, offline coding experience where they use the same language and rules that coding requires in a physical rather than digital space. For example, learners could provide directions to a staff member using arrows, colors, shapes, or any other materials. The staff member then acts like a robot who follows the code set by the learners.

RELATED RESOURCES

Accessibility Information for Starfall (**bit.ly/inclusive365-235c**)

Creating Coding Stories and Games (**bit.ly/inclusive365-235d**)

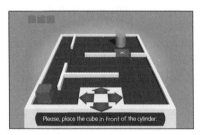

Figure 235. Starfall's Geometry 3D.
Image copyright © by Starfall Education Foundation. Reproduced with permission.

ISTE STANDARDS FOR STUDENTS
4a

ISTE STANDARDS FOR EDUCATORS
5a, 5b, 5c, 6c

Coding with Raspberry Pi

The Raspberry Pi is a single board, inexpensive computer (around $40 US) that can be programmed to perform an array of tasks. With resources stretched thin across education, using Raspberry Pi computers for coding could be a cost-effective, engaging way to dive into coding and physical computing. Learners plug the Raspberry Pi into a monitor, keyboard, and mouse, and voila! You have a computer! Take that old box of stray equipment and put it to good use! As systems get refreshed, keyboards, microphones, and monitors from those old computers can be repurposed with a Raspberry Pi to become a fully functional machine on which learners can engage in learning experiences related to computer science. Raspberry Pi computers run a simple operating system that supports various coding experiences. Learner-built Raspberry Pi machines can be allocated to different learning spaces. Each room could have one or several. Learners might choose to create an entire lab of Raspberry Pi machines.

INCLUSIVE USES

A powerful feature of Raspberry Pi computing is the hands-on aspect of creating the device. Learners who gravitate towards hands-on experiences thrive with the Raspberry Pi because the device needs to be wired together to enhance the functionality.

EXTENSION OPPORTUNITY

Invite learners to create a Raspberry Pi weather station to track temperature, barometric pressure, and more! A learning challenge like this not only has a coding component (learners determine the parameters they want to measure and code the computer to generate that information) but it also has the physical experience of setting up the weather station.

RELATED RESOURCES

Raspberry Pi Education Resources (**raspberrypi.org/education**)

Raspberry Pi Weather Station How-To (**bit.ly/inclusive365-236a**)

Figure 236. Learner engaged in music coding with Raspberry Pi (to left of keyboard).

ISTE STANDARDS FOR STUDENTS
4a, 5b, 5c, 5d, 7b, 7c

ISTE STANDARDS FOR EDUCATORS
5a, 5b, 5c, 6a, 6b, 6c, 6d

Practicing Mathematics with Robots

As mastery of computer science standards continues to be integrated into learning requirements, robots have become a staple in educational settings. Incorporating robots into curricular experiences can be an engagement windfall. Educators and learners alike love robots! Some robots can be programmed using a web-based or Bluetooth-enabled device or with code. Others require learners to code them by pressing physical buttons on their exterior. Regardless of the manner of programming, robots provide opportunities to practice mathematics in a fun way. Use robots to work on foundational math skills like counting, operations, measurement, time, and more. They can also be used for higher-level math, such as algebra, calculus, and geometry. Educators can design ways to move math concepts from the abstract to the concrete by designing opportunities for learners to get on the floor and explore.

INCLUSIVE USES

Learners who are apprehensive or reluctant to participate in math exercises that to them have no apparent connection to their lives or immediate application, might find engaging with robots fun and motivating.

Learners who are working to build their visual-spatial skills may find the hands-on aspect of working with robots useful.

SAMPLE TOOLS

Sphero robots come in all shapes and sizes. Learners can explore math concepts in multiple ways, such as controlling a robot via block coding (dragging around color-coded puzzle pieces to generate commands) or through a driving app (like a remote control car) (**sphero.com**).

The Code and Go Robot Mouse is programmed through specifying a series of arrows that determine a path of travel. Pressing the forward arrow three times, the right arrow once, and the forward arrow three times again would make the mouse move three units forward, turn to the right, and then move three more units forward. (**bit.ly/inclusive365-237a**)

EXTENSION OPPORTUNITY

Learners can determine a path the robot must travel to win a race, navigate a maze, or answer math facts. Learners can employ math skills to direct the robot to traverse a grid, avoid obstacles, or even draw geometric shapes. This may require learners to make calculations to determine distances and input directional codes, and to alter those codes if the robot did not behave as initially expected.

RELATED RESOURCE

Sphero Edu Math Activities (**bit.ly/inclusive365-237b**)

Figure 237. Code and Go Robot Mouse in action.

ISTE STANDARDS FOR STUDENTS
1b, 5a, 5c, 5d

ISTE STANDARDS FOR EDUCATORS
5a, 5b, 5c, 6a, 6b, 6c, 6d

Making Art with Robots

Many learning institutions have robots as part of their STEAM programs. Finding a way to incorporate these tools into other curricular experiences can be an engagement jackpot. Learners love robots (educators love robots too, who are we kidding!). By combining the coding aspect of these robots with some physical supports within the learning environment, we have a surefire way to engage learners in the curricular materials. Brushes and pencils can now be replaced with robots that walk or roll over a piece of paper, leaving behind a design. Look at your art supplies and brainstorm a way to connect them to a robot to facilitate artistic expression.

INCLUSIVE USES

Learners with fine motor or physical challenges may find using robots to create art beneficial and engaging. Educators can design ways to incorporate robots into the mix to act as a platform for the creativity of the learner.

SAMPLE TOOL

Sphero Robots are app-enabled robots that come in a variety of shapes and sizes, including Star Wars choices! Controlling them via block coding or through driving apps enables learners to use these tools to support learning across curricular areas (**sphero.com**).

EXTENSION OPPORTUNITIES

Let's paint! First, create a robot corral using a cardboard box. Now squirt some paint on a canvas that is placed within the box. Drop in the Sphero robot and you have a rolling paintbrush. Learners can move the Sphero around through the paint and across the canvas to unleash their creative genius. When done, take a wet towel and wipe the paint from the surface of the Sphero.

Want to draw? Tape a marker to a robot that walks and place the robot directly on top of the paper. Draw a picture by navigating the robot across the surface. Think of it like a real-life Etch A Sketch!

RELATED RESOURCE

Sphero Edu Art Activities (**bit.ly/inclusive365-238a**)

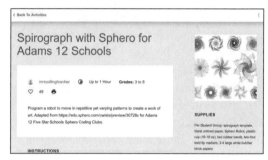

Figure 238. A learner using a tablet and Sphero robot to independently paint a picture. *Photo courtesy of educator, Wendy Thompson.*

ISTE STANDARDS FOR STUDENTS
1b, 5a, 5c, 5d.

ISTE STANDARDS FOR EDUCATORS
5a, 5b, 6a

Teaching Language Concepts Using Robots

Computer science skills are becoming increasingly necessary to be an active participant in the world in which we live. Many parts of the world have adopted computer science standards to help guide learners and educators toward building these skills. These skills, however, do not need to be taught in isolation. Instead, they can be integrated with existing content; for example, with learning language concepts, such as position prepositions (under, over, in, out, through, and between), ordinal words (first, second, and third), temporal words (before, after, and next), and action verbs (go, stop, eat, and play). Learners can code robots to both represent language concepts and express what they mean. Robots then follow their programming to perform commands that illustrate whichever language concepts are the focus of the instruction. For example, learners can program the robots to go under a table, through a tunnel, or navigate a maze following a specific sequence, which demonstrates multiple language concepts.

INCLUSIVE USES

Individuals learning language, including those who use augmentative/alternative communication devices, may find learning with robots an engaging way to gain an understanding of specific concepts and also to demonstrate that they can use them expressively.

SAMPLE TOOLS

WonderWorkshop has a number of different programmable robots including the Dot, Dash, and Cue, which can be used to teach language (**wonderworkshop.com**).

Sphero has a variety of programmable robots useful for teaching language concepts (**sphero.com**).

EXTENSION OPPORTUNITY

Provide a list of language concepts to learners. This list could be early sight words or one generated from words used on the home screen of augmentative/alternative communication devices. Invite learners to choose a word, program a robot to demonstrate that word, and create a video of the robot performing actions to teach a language concept to others.

RELATED RESOURCES

Get with the Program(ming) (**bit.ly/inclusive365-239a**)

Talking With Tech Episode #117 Using Robots and Coding to Teach Core Words and Support Peer Collaboration" (**bit.ly/inclusive365-239b**)

Teaching Language with Coding, Robots, & AAC—AAC in the Cloud 2020 (**bit.ly/inclusive365-239c**)

Figure 239. Dash robot navigating maze to teach the word turn.

ISTE STANDARDS FOR STUDENTS
1d, 3d, 4a, 4b, 4c, 5a, 5b, 5c, 5d, 6c, 6d, 7a, 7c, 7d

ISTE STANDARDS FOR EDUCATORS
2b, 2c, 5a, 5b, 6b, 6c, 6d, 7a

Converting Hard-Copy Documents into Accessible, Digital Resources

Individuals need a system to manage the information they gather while learning, especially for research tasks. Part of research may include taking information in hard-copy form and bringing it into a digital space. Optical character recognition (OCR) is a technology that retrieves information and converts it to usable, editable, searchable, and accessible text.

INCLUSIVE USES

Learners working to build research and writing skills may find using searchable, annotated, digitized versions of text a more efficient way to locate and use text when crafting a project. Text-to-speech may be crucial for evolving readers, so text needs to be digitized in an accessible format in order to utilize text-to-speech.

SAMPLE TOOLS

The Grab Image Text feature of Google Keep is an OCR feature. The text and image can both be saved and color-coded in an accessible digital format (**keep.google.com**).

The Microsoft Lens app can be used to take a picture of text. When the file is opened in OneNote, the Immersive Reader feature can be used to access the text (**bit.ly/inclusive365-240a**).

Google Drive can automatically recognize text. When a clear picture of text is taken using the Drive app, users can right-click on the file in Drive to open it in Google Docs. The original picture will appear with the accessible, digitized text below. Some editing may be needed to ensure accuracy (**drive.google.com**).

EXTENSION OPPORTUNITIES

Invite learners to explore a print-based resource while doing research. Demonstrate how to take the picture and use an OCR tool to convert to text. Ask learners how they might use the technology to enhance, organize, and further their research. Invite learners to discuss how this feature might be used when creating a final written product to give credit to the source material.

Educators can take pictures from paper-based materials, such as flyers, brochures, and posters, and convert them into accessible, digital, searchable text that can be used to further learning or streamline productivity.

RELATED RESOURCES

How to Convert Image to Text in Google Keep (**bit.ly/inclusive365-240c**)

Microsoft Lens How-To (**bit.ly/inclusive365-240d**)

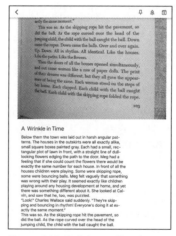

Figure 240. Grab Image Text from Google Keep.

ISTE STANDARDS FOR STUDENTS
1c, 2b, 3c, 6b

ISTE STANDARDS FOR EDUCATORS
5a, 6a

Citing Sources with Format Consistency

As responsible digital citizens, learners must learn to cite their sources and create a bibliography or works cited list as part of a research or writing project. However, even the most seasoned researcher admits that keeping up with the formats for any common citation styles (APA, MLA, Chicago, etc.) is a challenge. Online citation generators or those built as a feature of the software help learners easily create citations as part of a finished product.

INCLUSIVE USES

Citation generators simplify the process of creating citations. They decrease spelling and typing demands and also lower the executive function load necessary for following a particular style's format.

SAMPLE TOOLS

Citation Machine takes researchers step by step through the process of building a citation in the most common format styles (**bit.ly/inclusive365-241a**).

Microsoft Word's Citations function, which is under the Reference tab, provides a built-in means to create citations within a document, and also creates a bibliography or works cited page at the end of a document (**bit.ly/inclusive365-241b**).

Snap&Read, a browser extension and an iOS app, automatically creates a citation that can be pasted into a document when information is gathered from a website (**snapandread.com**).

EXTENSION OPPORTUNITY

Invite learners to compare the citations they have generated with examples of citations formatted in the same style from Purdue's OWL website to see if the citation generator they are using is providing an accurate citation (**bit.ly/inclusive365-241c**).

RELATED RESOURCE

APA, MLA, Chicago—Automatically Format Bibliographies (**bit.ly/inclusive365-241d**)

Figure 241a. Citations and Bibliography tool in Microsoft Word.

Figure 241b. Citation created in Snap&Read.

ISTE STANDARDS FOR STUDENTS
2c

ISTE STANDARDS FOR EDUCATORS
3a, 3c

Following Directions Using Picture-in-Picture Video

Video tutorials allow learners to experience step-by-step directions for how to perform a variety of tasks. Navigating between different tabs, windows, or screens to view the tutorial while simultaneously trying to go through the steps in a task can be cumbersome for learners. Picture-in-picture tools allow a learner to anchor a video in the top layer of the screen. This allows learners to quickly view the directions relayed in the video while simultaneously performing the task, without needing to toggle back and forth between multiple screens or manipulate window sizes.

INCLUSIVE USES

Learners who have fine motor control challenges may find resizing or toggling between windows difficult. Single command operations to open picture-in-picture video may provide access to the content easier with less frustration.

SAMPLE TOOLS

Picture-in-Picture by Google is a Chrome extension that allows users to play videos using a picture-in-picture view (**bit.ly/inclusve365-242a**).

Picture-in-Picture in Apple iOS plays video using a picture-in-picture view. (**bit.ly/inclusve365-242b**)

EXTENSION OPPORTUNITIES

Invite learners to create their own videos that provide directions for how to complete digital tasks.

Most picture-in-picture tools allow the user to move the video window around. Invite learners to determine the best placement of the picture-in-picture video by trying it in different locations and, if possible, adjusting the size.

RELATED RESOURCE

How To Use Picture-in-Picture on iPhone iOS 14 (**bit.ly/inclusve365-242c**)

Figure 242. Three-panel template on Storyboard That with a video of a boy explaining storyboarding using picture-in-picture view.

ISTE STANDARDS FOR STUDENTS

1a, 1d, 3a, 3d

ISTE STANDARDS FOR EDUCATORS

3b, 3c, 4a, 5c, 6a, 6b

Creating a Map of a Historical or Literary Journey

Learning to read maps and manage geographic data helps people become familiar with how to navigate the world in which they live. Maps can also be used to visualize both historical and literary events. Learners can create a customized digital map by dropping pins to indicate specific locations, then adding layers of text, multimedia, and links to document the journey. Using Google Maps, learners can measure the distance between two points, helping them visualize the scope of a journey that a real person or literary character has taken. The learner can use the map as a repository for information they have gathered through research. Pins can be used to create different layers, and layers can be turned on or off, depending on the information the learner wants displayed.

INCLUSIVE USES

Those working to improve their writing abilities can demonstrate understanding of an event by adding text to pinned events and locations on a map. Individuals who have demonstrated a need or preference for processing information with visual supports may find data presented on maps a useful modality.

SAMPLE TOOL

My Maps, part of the Google Suite of tools, allows users to create and share maps (**bit.ly/inclusive365-243a**).

EXTENSION OPPORTUNITIES

Invite learners to work independently or collaboratively to create locations on a map to support events in their own stories or narratives.

Invite learners to generate a map with a global theme. Learners can identify a place they would like to visit or have visited, adding descriptions to the location. If possible, include learners from around the world to share their location and information about where they live. Invite learners to think of additional topic ideas of interest.

RELATED RESOURCES

My Maps Help and Directions (**bit.ly/inclusive365-243b**)

Google My Maps for Activities in Your Classroom (**bit.ly/inclusive365-243c**)

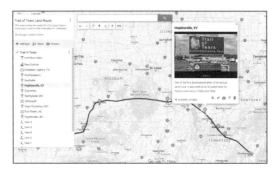

Figure 243. Trail of Tears Land Route created in My Maps (bit.ly/inclusive365-243d).

ISTE STANDARDS FOR STUDENTS

3c., 6a , 6b, 6c, 6d

ISTE Standards for Educators

6a, 6b, 6d, 7a

Pausing Videos Intermittently to Prompt Learner Engagement

Videos are an effective way to teach content. To enhance the experience, educators can embed questions, comments, and/or prompts intermittently to invite learners to reflect on the content or to draw attention to a particular point being made in the video. These questions, comments, and prompts can be inserted along the timeline of the video. When the viewer gets to that point, the question or comment appears on the screen and the video is automatically paused. Learners can then engage with the content to continue watching the video

INCLUSIVE USES

Learners with goals related to expanding attention and memory may find intermittently pausing a video to reflect on comments or respond to questions helps in learning the content.

SAMPLE TOOLS

Edpuzzle allows users to add audio support, comments, and multiple-choice or short-answer questions to a video. Learner progress can be tracked using an educator dashboard (**edpuzzle.com**).

PlayPosit is a website that allows users to add comments and questions to video content (**playposit.com**).

EXTENSION OPPORTUNITIES

Invite learners to enhance a video designed to educate others about a topic by adding comments and creating their own questions.

Intermittent comments and questions can be added to videos as a form of asynchronous coaching to learn a skill. No matter the skill, whether it be a professional development methodology for a colleague, a technique for coaching parents, or an academic strategy for a school-aged learner, adding moments of reflection to video content can enhance its effectiveness as a teaching tool.

Individualizing the amount and type of questions, comments, and/or prompts helps personalize the video viewing experience for each learner.

RELATED RESOURCES

How Students Review Feedback and Comments in Edpuzzle (**bit.ly/inclusive365-244a**)

How to Use Edpuzzle to Create Video-Based Lessons (**bit.ly/inclusive365-244b**)

Figure 244. Embedded question in a video created by using Edpuzzle.

ISTE STANDARDS FOR STUDENTS
1c, 1d, 3c, 6a, 6b, 6c

ISTE STANDARDS FOR EDUCATORS
6a, 6b, 6c, 6d, 7a, 7b, 7c

Highlighting Digital Text

For years, learners have used different colors to highlight important information, categorize content, and call out confusing portions of text on paper. Similarly, learners can use highlighters to mark up digital text. Different colored digital highlighters can be used to make content stand out when revisiting the content.

INCLUSIVE USES

Learners building organizational, vocabulary, and writing skills might find highlighting and revisiting those highlights useful when studying, learning words, and composing written material.

SAMPLE TOOLS

Read&Write for Chrome is an extension with a digital highlighter feature with different colors (**bit.ly/inclusive365-245a**).

Highlight Tool is a Google Docs add-on that allows users to customize their highlight colors. Users can create and share personalized, self-created highlighter libraries with peers and educators (**bit.ly/inclusive365-245b**).

EXTENSION OPPORTUNITY

Invite learners to highlight different portions of text while doing research by using separate colors for different categories. For example, if researching volcanoes, a learner might use a different highlight color for each of these topics: where volcanoes are located, how volcanoes are formed, famous eruptions, and people who study volcanoes.

RELATED RESOURCE

Highlighting Tool: A Great Google Add-On Resource (**bit.ly/inclusive365-245c**)

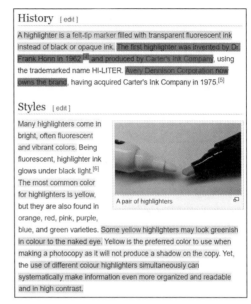

Figure 245. Example of highlighted text in multiple colors to support learning.

ISTE STANDARDS FOR STUDENTS
2c, 3a, 3c

ISTE STANDARDS FOR EDUCATORS
2c, 3b, 3c, 6a

Implementing See, Think, Wonder

The See, Think, Wonder thinking routine was developed by Project Zero, a research center at the Harvard Graduate School of Education. The strategy provides a routine for exploring works of art and other interesting visuals. The routine begins with learners expressing what they see in an image, then reflecting on what they think about the image and what they see, and finally considering what the image makes them wonder about. When used with works of art or other images that connect to a topic or unit of study, this routine stimulates reflection and discussion about why something looks the way it does or is the way it is. While traditionally done as a face-to-face discussion, in a digital environment, the use of technology to engage in a collaborative discussion allows the routine to be used either asynchronously or synchronously in a distance-learning environment.

INCLUSIVE USES

See, Think, Wonder has no wrong answers, allowing learners to contribute freely and without anxiety around being correct. Using works of art, photos, or even interesting objects engages learners in a topic. Depending on the tool used to display the visual, learners can add audio notes or video notes in addition to text.

SAMPLE TOOLS

Jamboard can be used to post works of art or other visuals and learners can respond to the questions with different colored digital sticky notes in the collaborative tool (**jamboard.google.com**).

VoiceThread can be used to post images and learners can respond with audio, video, or text posts (**voicethread.com/products/k12**).

EXTENSION OPPORTUNITY

Invite learners to use the routine with an image or artwork that connects to a topic of study near the end of a unit to assess learners' ability to synthesize their learning.

RELATED RESOURCE

See, Think, Wonder (**bit.ly/inclusive365-246a**)

Figure 246. See, Think, Wonder experience in Jamboard.

ISTE STANDARDS FOR STUDENTS
6c, 7a, 7b

ISTE STANDARDS FOR EDUCATORS
2b, 5a, 5b

Experiencing Art Exhibit Field Trips through Augmented Reality and Artificial Intelligence

Augmented reality (AR) and artificial intelligence (AI) provide options for interactive virtual field trips for aspiring artists. Beyond virtual art exhibits, AR and AI allow learners to examine the art and consider how it influences and reflects lived experiences. When learners can be within a piece of art virtually, they can notice unique elements, envision the artist's purpose, and be more connected to the expression.

INCLUSIVE USES

AR allows learners to interact with art from galleries and museums across the globe and experience it up close in 3D. Google Arts and Culture includes multiple languages and many of the works and exhibits have described captions for the visually impaired.

SAMPLE TOOLS

Google Arts and Culture is available as an app for iOS and Android, and as a website (**bit.ly/inclusive365-247a**). It uses AI and AR to provide the following experiences:

- **Art Projector:** See how artworks look in real size.

- **Pocket Gallery:** Wander through immersive galleries.

- **Art Camera:** Explore high-definition artworks.

- **360° videality tours:** Step inside world-class museums.

- **Street View:** Tour famous sites and landmarks.

- **Explore by Tim:** Point your device camera at artworks to learn more, even when offline (at select museums only).

The Met 360° Project is a series of videos created using spherical 360° technology that allows virtual visitors to immerse themselves in the artwork and architecture of the Metropolitan Museum of Art (**bit.ly/inclusive365-247b**).

The Merge Cube allows learners to hold a 3D AR image of a work of art, such as a sculpture (**bit.ly/inclusive365-247c**) and the 3D Museum Viewer app allows them to hold and explore museum pieces (**bit.ly/inclusive365-247d**).

EXTENSION OPPORTUNITY

Invite learners to give a guided virtual tour of an art museum or exhibit, describing why they selected the particular museum or exhibit.

RELATED RESOURCES

Google Art and Culture YouTube Channel (**bit.ly/inclusive365-247e**)

The Museum Art and Culture Consortium At Home Activities (**bit.ly/inclusive365-247f**)

Figure 247. Sampling of exhibits available through Google Arts and Culture.

ISTE STANDARDS FOR STUDENTS

3a, 6b, 6c

ISTE STANDARDS FOR EDUCATORS
5a, 5b, 5c

STRATEGY 248

Asking Voice Assistants to Check Facts, Spelling, and Math

Voice assistants exist on mobile devices and in personal learning environments, including learners' homes. Learners can ask voice assistants to check facts they encounter in media sources, confirm the spelling of words before or after they are written, and verify mathematical formulas and calculations. Voice assistants can add a level of confidence to the validity of the content being consumed and produced by the learner.

INCLUSIVE USES

Learners who have difficulty controlling fine or gross motor movements may find using voice assistants beneficial. Learners with reading challenges may prefer listening to information provided by a voice assistant as an alternative way to be presented with content.

SAMPLE TOOLS

Siri is a voice-operated assistant built into the operating system on Apple devices (**apple.com/siri**).

Google Assistant is an app on mobile devices and it also works with the Google Home device (**assistant.google.com**).

Alexa is a voice-operated assistant available on Amazon Echo and various mobile devices (**developer.amazon.com/alexa**).

EXTENSION OPPORTUNITIES

Invite learners to create their own applications that run on voice assistants. What sorts of problems could be addressed by learners who work to solve them by creating skills learned by voice assistants?

Invite learners to collaboratively create and maintain a shared repository of voice-assisted skills they've discovered and found useful. Other learners can explore the list/database to find skills useful to them.

RELATED RESOURCES

Alexa, Do You Belong In The Classroom? (**bit.ly/inclusive365-248a**)

Create Alexa Skills in Minutes (**bit.ly/inclusive365-248b**)

Figure 248. Learner typing on a computer in a kitchen with an Echo Show in the background displaying the spelling for the word empowered.

ISTE STANDARDS FOR STUDENTS
3a, 3b

ISTE STANDARDS FOR EDUCATORS
2b, 2c, 3d, 5a, 6b, 7a

Learning Asynchronously from Experts

How do we connect our young learners to the larger world and engage them in deeper conversations? Once again, YouTube to the rescue! This time through TED Talks. TED (Technology, Entertainment, Design) is an organization that hosts speakers throughout the world and invites them to share their knowledge with everyone. Can't get a guest speaker to talk about a specific curriculum topic? There is probably a TED Talk about it. Want to create a flipped lesson with a video component? You are in luck, there is probably a TED Talk video you could use.

INCLUSIVE USES

By providing this modality for learning about new, interesting topics, learners can stop, pause, and take notes at their own pace as they process this information. Use of captions promotes access for all and provides literacy support for evolving readers.

SAMPLE TOOL

The TED Talk YouTube Channel has over 2500 videos available for free. This catalog of learning opportunities expands learning and engages learners with new ideas and an evolved worldview (**youtube.com/user/TEDxTalks**).

EXTENSION OPPORTUNITY

Think about how you want to embed this type of learning experience. A shorter clip could be used during a group discussion, either live or during a virtual discussion. If you are creating a distance-learning lesson, consider one of the longer clips as an anchor. Encourage learners to turn on the captions to promote literacy skills.

RELATED RESOURCES

Six Ways to Use TED Talks in the Classroom (**bit.ly/inclusive365-249a**)

35 Must Watch TED Talks that Students will Love (**bit.ly/inclusive365-249b**)

Figure 249. TEDx YouTube channel.

ISTE STANDARDS FOR STUDENTS
2b, 7a, 7b, 7d

ISTE STANDARDS FOR EDUCATORS
1b, 1c, 2a, 2c, 3a, 3b, 4a, 5c

STRATEGY 250

Effective Note-Taking with Audio Syncing

Successful note-taking involves identifying a key concept and succinctly describing it while continuing to consume the information being presented, repeating the process for the next important concept. When notes are created using a single modality, like writing, learners will likely review those notes through reading. When notes are created using multiple modalities, such as writing while audio recording, learners have more than one way to review. Syncing written or drawn notes to recorded audio enables learners to jump to any place in the notes and listen to the content. They can listen as many times as necessary, which eliminates the pressure learners might feel in the moment to collect quality information.

INCLUSIVE USES

Learners with emerging reading, writing, drawing, typing, and/or listening skills may find reviewing content using multiple modalities helpful in learning the concepts. This increases the effectiveness of note-taking and promotes academic independence.

SAMPLE TOOLS

Mic Note is a Chrome application that provides a note-taking space that allows the learner to type in notes while they are recording the audio. The notes are all time-stamped so that they are automatically synced to the audio. Learners can go back into those notes at any point to select their typed notes, which plays the corresponding audio (**micnote.audio**).

OneNote allows learners to record audio and sync it with typed notes (**onenote.com**).

Audio Note 2 links notes typed or written to the simultaneously-recorded audio (**bit.ly/inclusive365-250c**).

Notability is an iOS app that combines typed or written notes with audio (**gingerlabs.com**).

EXTENSION OPPORTUNITIES

Invite learners to use timestamps as reference points in audio-synced notes. Rather than typing complete thoughts, or even words, learners could type a single letter. This inserts a timestamp that the learner can return to. Learners can then listen again and take their time to complete the written notes.

Invite learners to record audio notes while working independently.

Invite learners to draw or sketch while taking notes with recorded audio, connecting different parts of the drawing to the audio recorded during that portion of the drawing.

RELATED RESOURCES

How to Record Audio on Your Chromebook with Mic Note (**bit.ly/inclusve365-250a**)

Record Audio or Video Notes in OneNote (**bit.ly/inclusve365-250b**)

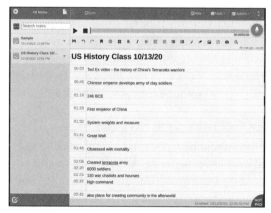

Figure 250. Learner-generated, timestamped notes synced to an audio recording using Mic Note.

ISTE STANDARDS FOR STUDENTS
1a, 1d, 3c, 5c, 6a

ISTE STANDARDS FOR EDUCATORS
5a, 6a

Semantic Mapping to Improve Vocabulary

When learners are expanding their vocabularies, a thesaurus can help them find just the right word to make a point or lead them to more descriptive word choices. Digital thesauruses can also offer interactive semantic maps, graphical representations that help learners more easily see the connections between words. Learners can refer to a digital thesaurus whenever they encounter new vocabulary word, which will help them build on prior knowledge and allow them to explore word relationships.

INCLUSIVE USES

The use of a visual and interactive thesaurus with graphical semantic maps and dictionary tools promotes word and vocabulary exploration for those who are expanding their use of language and vocabulary.

SAMPLE TOOLS

Visuwords is an interactive dictionary and thesaurus that creates graphical word maps to show relationships between words to help understand language in new ways. It includes color-coded parts of speech and color-coded word relationships. Visuwords uses Princeton University's WordNet, an open-source database built by language researchers to show word associations. Every time a link is selected, a new word with its graphical word map appears (**visuwords.com**).

EXTENSION OPPORTUNITY

Invite learners to explore a word of the day in an online thesaurus as a way to build vocabulary.

RELATED RESOURCES

About Visuwords (**bit.ly/inclusive365-251a**)

Connecting Word Meaning through Semantic Mapping (**bit.ly/inclusive365-251b**)

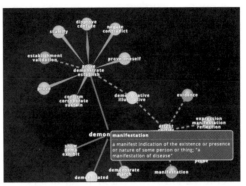

Figure 251. Graphical word map for the word demonstrate.

ISTE STANDARDS FOR STUDENTS

1a, 1b, 3a, 3b, 5b

ISTE STANDARDS FOR EDUCATORS

3b, 5a, 5b, 6a, 6b

Transferring Notes between Tools Based on Purpose

Learners frequently search digital content when building background knowledge or conducting research. When learners take notes or save references for research, the process is facilitated when they can quickly transfer notes directly into an online document or presentation. These might be more frequently used for publication.

INCLUSIVE USES

The ease of moving notes to a working document supports learners building their organizational skills. Learners who struggle with managing multiple resources at the same time may find it beneficial to work with tools that work together. This integration reduces the distractions and short-term memory demands related to copying and pasting.

SAMPLE TOOL

Collecting artifacts within Google Keep allows easy integration into Google Docs or Slides. Learners have easy access to their notes and can transfer notes, citations, and images by clicking and dragging content into their document or presentation. Google Keep is a full-featured note-taking resource that works across all devices and platforms (**keep.google.com**).

EXTENSION OPPORTUNITY

Invite learners to use Google Keep integration when working on group projects. They can use common labels to easily collaborate.

RELATED RESOURCE

How to Access Google Keep through Google Docs (**bit.ly/inclusive365-252a**)

Figure 252. Notes from Google Keep alongside a Google Doc.

ISTE STANDARDS FOR STUDENTS

3c

ISTE STANDARDS FOR EDUCATORS

3a, 3b, 3c, 4c, 5a, 5b, 5c, 6a, 6b

Creating Tutorials Using Screen Recordings

Spoken directions for how to accomplish a task are often ephemeral. Listeners often have only one attempt to listen, comprehend, and process those directions. In person, if a listener asks for the directions to be repeated, the person giving the directions will likely repeat the directions using a different set of words, which can add to the complexity of the original directions. Video provides a multimodal experience where auditory, text, and visual information are provided simultaneously. A screencast is a digital video recording of a computer screen while a task is being completed. It captures the user's input, including mouse clicks and text input, and it usually includes audio narration of the actions on the screen. Depending on the tool used, the video can also be annotated to provide additional support, including zooming, highlighting, or text overlaid on the video. Educators can create step-by-step screencasts to help learners sequence tasks and follow multistep directions. Recordings can be paused, replayed, and watched at different speeds to provide the customized, consistent repetition and review each learner needs.

INCLUSIVE USES

Screen recordings can connect concepts to background knowledge and promote self-paced learning. Learners who benefit from experiencing content more than once might find controlling the video to rewatch and hear the directions again useful.

SAMPLE TOOLS

Screencastify is a Chrome extension that allows users to produce videos. No internet connection is needed to record, only to upload the video file to Google Drive and/or YouTube. Record and share up to five minutes of video content with the free version (**screencastify.com**).

Loomis is a Chrome extension, and desktop or iOS app that allows users to create video recordings of the screen, voice, and face (**bit.ly/inclusive365-253a**)

Screen Recording, built into iOS devices, is located in the Control Center. By default, the system only records the audio played within the system. A force press on the record button activates the microphone to narrate the action. When finished, the video is saved automatically to the Camera Roll.

EXTENSION OPPORTUNITY

Educators can show off their personalities and build relationships by including favorite pop culture references, quotes, memes, or animations that can help learners understand a concept or follow a direction.

RELATED RESOURCES

Add Audio & Video Instructions to Help Students Navigate Work While Learning Remotely (**bit.ly/inclusive365-253b**)

How to Record the Screen on Your iPhone, iPad, or iPod Touch (**bit.ly/inclusive365-253c**)

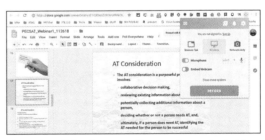

Figure 253. Using Screencastify to produce a short video tutorial.

ISTE STANDARDS FOR STUDENTS
1b, 2c, 3c, 6a, 6b, 6d

ISTE STANDARDS FOR EDUCATORS
2b, 3b, 4a, 5a, 5c, 7a

Evaluating Resources for Authenticity Using Fact-Checkers

Evaluating found resources for their authenticity has become an essential skill for living in contemporary society. Determining the validity of information is a necessary step in any decision-making process. Websites that provide fact-checking features can help learners verify whether the content they are consuming is true, false, or somewhere in between.

INCLUSIVE USES

Misinformation can fool anyone. Content can be created with a bias that causes confusion for the reader as to the validity of the information. Empowering all learners to verify information helps promote independence and self-agency. Fact-checkers that provide clear information in accessible formats can help any individual verify information independently.

SAMPLE TOOLS

Snopes is an independent, nonpartisan website dedicated to confirming the validity of claims using a rating system with corresponding symbols (**snopes.com**).

AllSides is a website that curates stories from right-, center-, and left-leaning media sources so readers can compare biased reporting. This website doesn't necessarily check facts but it does provide multiple angles of the same pieces of information (**allsides.com**).

The aim of FactCheck.org is to be a nonpartisan, nonprofit website that aims to "reduce the level of deception and confusion in U.S. politics" by monitoring the accuracy of information presented by politicians and shared in media campaigns (**factcheck.org**).

EXTENSION OPPORTUNITIES

Learners can use specific frameworks when verifying information. Two popular ways to evaluate information are the RADAR framework (rationale, authority, date, accuracy, relevance) and the CRAAP test (currency, relevance, authority, accuracy, purpose). These frameworks help learners by inviting them to ask a series of questions to determine the biases and veracity of a piece of information.

Invite learners to create a rubric that they can use to help themselves verify information. A rubric based on the RADAR or CRAAP frameworks and used to score information can help the learner quantify the content.

RELATED RESOURCES

Evaluating Sources with RADAR
(**bit.ly/inclusive365-254a**)

Evaluating Sources with the CRAAP Test
(**bit.ly/inclusive365-254b**)

Figure 254. CRAAP test infographic.

ISTE STANDARDS FOR STUDENTS
3a, 3b, 3c, 3d

ISTE STANDARDS FOR EDUCATORS
3b, 3c

Sketchnoting for Taking Notes

There are many different note-taking techniques. Sketchnoting is a note-taking technique that invites learners to create a work of art or diagram from the concepts they are learning. When a person draws an image, this helps them better recall the information embedded within the image. Drawing pictures also helps learners understand concepts.

INCLUSIVE USES

Inviting learners to explore different note-taking techniques allows them to discover which ones they prefer to use to accomplish any given task. Learners who demonstrate difficulty with spelling or orthographics might find they prefer to sketch their notes, creating a personalized diagram to help with comprehension and recall.

SAMPLE TOOLS

Sketchbook is a free application that can be used to create sketchnotes (**sketchbook.com**).

Google Drawing is a free, web-based drawing application (**docs.google.com/drawings**).

Sketch.IO is a free, web-based drawing application (**sketch.io**).

EXTENSION OPPORTUNITIES

Invite learners to create a shared repository for sketchnotes on a particular concept. Experiencing others' sketchnotes can help further one's own understanding and recall of the concept. Learners can provide feedback on the notes to improve and refine their own techniques.

Invite learners to work on a shared sketchnote by using a tool that allows for either synchronous or asynchronous collaboration.

Invite learners to create a caption and/or alt-text tag describing the sketchnote image so that it can be shared with learners who require audio supports. The caption and/or alt tag can be read aloud by text-to-speech and screen reading applications.

RELATED RESOURCES

Sketchnoting by ISTE (**bit.ly/inclusive365-255a**)

Talking with Tech, Episode #39: Carrie Baughcum: Using Drawing to Teach Language (**bit.ly/inclusive365-255b**)

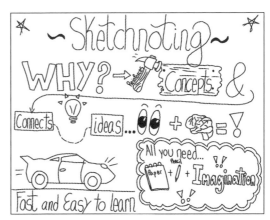

Figure 255. Sketchnote on Sketchnoting, created by Kiera McMahon, sophomore in a high school in Virginia.

ISTE STANDARDS FOR STUDENTS

1b, 1c, 3a, 3c, 5a, 5c, 6a, 6b, 6c, 6d

ISTE STANDARDS FOR EDUCATORS

2b, 5a, 5b, 5c, 6a, 6d, 7a, 7b, 7c

Playing Virtual, Online Games to Explore the Earth

This planet is a wondrous place filled with interesting locations, creatures, cultures, and artifacts. Playing games is a fun way to learn about different aspects of the world. Online games can virtually transport the learner to different locations and increase engagement by immersing the learner in the experience. Virtual, online games use tools like interactive maps, live webcams, and 3D structures to help learners discover and explore a region or topic. Learners can play games and quizzes to assess what they have learned.

INCLUSIVE USES

Virtual explorations offer novelty and engagement for all learners. Learners working on improving their visual-spatial abilities and those learning to maintain attention may find playing games while exploring interactive maps a fun way to improve these skills.

SAMPLE TOOL

Google Earth is a virtual, 3D mapping system that provides close-up access to locations learners might never get to experience in real life. It is compatible with a variety of text-to-speech applications so learners can listen to text embedded in the experience. Within Google Earth is the Voyager feature. Learners can take a guided virtual tour on a variety of topics, some tours even include virtual games (**earth.google.com/web**).

EXTENSION OPPORTUNITY

Invite learners to find and explore a topic of interest in Google Earth's Voyager. Learners could explore the topic and then participate in a related interactive quiz. Topics range from Animals of the World, Ocean Safari, and World War II, to Football Trivia and Summer Blockbusters. There are three Where on Earth is Carmen San Diego adventures, made possible due to a partnership between Google Earth and Houghton-Mifflin. There is something for everyone.

RELATED RESOURCE

How to Find Games and Quizzes in Google Earth (**bit.ly/inclusive365-256a**)

Figure 256. One of the games available in Google Earth.

ISTE STANDARDS FOR STUDENTS
1a, 1b, 1c, 7a

ISTE STANDARDS FOR EDUCATORS
2b, 3b, 5a, 5b, 5c, 6a, 6b

Listening to Diverse Voices through Audio Stories

Fiction and nonfiction audio stories can help learners experience heroes of any race, gender, or cultural heritage. Whether looking to learn more about people who have similar backgrounds or different backgrounds, listening to audio stories can help people broaden their own perspectives or help inspire the setting of educational goals. Be sure that audio stories, as with all resources, feature under-represented groups as a range of characters and experiences, not simply as tokens or through stereotypes. When learners from all backgrounds hear from authors with diverse backgrounds telling the stories of characters with diverse backgrounds they see themselves represented authentically.

INCLUSIVE USES

For some learners, audio stories might provide less of a barrier than printed text. Learners with visual impairments or print-related disabilities may find listening to audio stories more accessible than other forms of media. If access to text is difficult, either due to print-related, economic, or geographic challenges, audio stories might provide learners with an option to experience stories of diversity.

SAMPLE TOOLS

The Good Night Stories for Rebel Girls podcast is a free podcast that provides audio stories of female heroes from a variety of countries and cultures (**rebelgirls.com**).

The Timestorm podcast is a free podcast that tells stories about twins who travel through time to discover Puerto Rican history (**timestormseries.com**).

The Very Best Code Switch Episodes for Kids is a collection of educational podcasts about a variety of diverse topics (**bit.ly/inclusive365-257a**).

EXTENSION OPPORTUNITIES

Invite learners to record and share their own audio stories through individual or group podcasts.

Invite learners to listen to stories communally at listening stations and then engage in discussion about the stories afterward.

Invite learners to share audio stories with their families at home or while traveling together.

RELATED RESOURCE

8 Podcasts That Help You Talk To Kids About Race (**bit.ly/inclusive365-257b**)

Figure 257. Learner listening to audio stories on mobile device.

ISTE STANDARDS FOR STUDENTS
7a, 7b, 7d

ISTE STANDARDS FOR EDUCATORS
2b, 3a, 3b, 4d, 5a, 5c, 6a, 6b

STRATEGY 258

Visualizing Quotations from Real or Fictional Individuals

"I have not yet begun to fight." —John Paul Jones

"I have a dream that my four children will one day live in a nation where they will not be judged by the color of their skin, but by the content of their character." —Martin Luther King, Jr.

"A house divided against itself cannot stand." —Abraham Lincoln

"Do or do not. There is no try." —Yoda

Life is filled with quotes to live by. A powerful quote is something people remember. Quotes can reinforce learning about fictional characters or remembering significant contributions from historical figures.

Learners can find quotations relevant to a topic of study, share them in an interesting way, and collaborate on creating an artifact where the quotations are shared such as an audio file or podcast, infographic, gallery, poster, video, animation, or any other meaningful way.

INCLUSIVE USES

Learners who are practicing reading, writing, and/or social skills may find locating meaningful quotes from other individuals helpful, inspirational, and fun. Creating a collaborative resource allows learners to create together in an engaging, non-stressful way.

SAMPLE TOOLS

Use Canva to create a professional-looking poster of selected quotes (**canva.com**).

Highlight memorable quotes by turning them into a meme with Meme Generator (**bit.ly/inclusive365-258a**).

EXTENSION OPPORTUNITY

All learners could find a quote that is meaningful to them and then animate a character saying it. Then the animations could be assembled on a website and published as a collaborative creation online.

RELATED RESOURCE

Getting Started with Canva (**bit.ly/inclusive365-258b**)

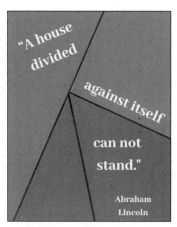

Figure 258. Quotation poster created in Canva.

ISTE STANDARDS FOR STUDENTS
2a, 6b, 6c, 7b, 7c

ISTE STANDARDS FOR EDUCATORS
3b, 5a, 5b, 5c, 6a, 6b, 6d

Choosing Editable Open-Source Reading Materials for Secondary Learners

Traditional textbooks are costly, quickly outdated, and have usage restrictions imposed by copyright regulations. Open-source texts are created by authors who are experts in their content areas, but who allow users to reuse, revise, remix, and redistribute the content. Secondary-level courses, such as biology, chemistry, psychology, sociology, physics, and business can be studied using open-source textbooks.

INCLUSIVE USES

Open-source content can be redistributed in a way that makes it consumable in different modalities. This flexibility allows educators or learners themselves to make adjustments for the varied needs of learners. Changes can be made to the complexity of the text and modality of the content, including audio, video, or picture supports. Open-source content is more easily accessed by screen readers and can be more easily annotated or highlighted than some publishers' online editions.

SAMPLE TOOLS

OpenStax is an online library for accessible, open source, peer-reviewed textbooks from a nonprofit charity at Rice University (**openstax.org**).

OERCommons is a public library of open-source educational resources that educators can explore, implement, or collaborate on with other educators around the globe (**oercommons.org**).

EXTENSION OPPORTUNITY

Invite learners to demonstrate what they have learned about a topic by creating a new open-source resource about it. Learners could make

a video, record a podcast, generate a multimedia slideshow, or create a product that helps others to better understand the targeted concept. Learners could share their newly created content by labeling it with an open-source license, encouraging others to use, share, and remix it.

RELATED RESOURCES

#GoOpen is a social media hashtag is used by educators sharing how they are implementing open educational resources (**bit.ly/inclusive365-259a**).

Information from the U.S. Department of Education on Open Education Resources (**bit.ly/inclusive365-259b**)

Figure 259. OpenStax website. Image used with a Creative Commons Share Alike 4.0 license.

ISTE STANDARDS FOR STUDENTS
3a, 3b, 3c, 6b, 7a

ISTE STANDARDS FOR EDUCATORS
2b, 2c, 3a, 3b, 6a

STRATEGY 260

Transcribing Audio for Note-Taking

Effective note-taking requires a combination of skills: intact active working memory, legible handwriting or proficient keyboarding, ability to summarize main points, and ability to sustain focus and attention are some of the skills successful notetakers possess. Audio transcription resources automatically transcribe audio and save both the text and the audio recording for later and repeated review.

INCLUSIVE USES

Learners working to improve their working memory and attention skills benefit from audio transcription options. Learners developing keyboard proficiency or working to improve their handwriting legibility may find audio transcription resources bypass output challenges and promote success.

SAMPLE TOOL

Word in Office 365 includes recording audio transcription in a side window within the document, as well as the ability to edit and insert the transcribed text and recording (**bit.ly/inclusive365-260a**).

EXTENSION OPPORTUNITY

Invite learners to use the note-taking method that they believe works well for them and then use the transcription to "fill in the gaps" for important information they may have missed.

RELATED RESOURCES

Record and Transcribe Audio, Video Tutorial (**bit.ly/inclusive365-260b**)

Microsoft's Transcribe in Word Feature, Designed for Students, Reporters, and More (**bit.ly/inclusive365-260c**)

Figure 260. Example of transcription from a video.

ISTE STANDARDS FOR STUDENTS
1a, 1b

ISTE STANDARDS FOR EDUCATORS
5a, 5b, 6a

Encouraging Curiosity Using the See, Think, Wonder Routine

Wondering encourages learners to make careful observations and consider how they interpret information, which sets the stage for inquiry. Educators guide learners by asking thoughtful questions, which may inspire additional wonder. The See, Think, Wonder thinking routine was developed by Project Zero, a research center at the Harvard Graduate School of Education. Use the sentence stems "I see…", "I think…", and "I wonder…" with visuals such as photos or artwork to stimulate responses. "I see" could be interchanged with "I hear" for audio experiences. The "I wonder" stem elicits learners' questions.

INCLUSIVE USES

Posing questions in a graduated manner allows learners of all abilities to use information that is right in front of them to propel them into higher-level thinking, including asking meaningful questions about what is not right there. Providing accessible resources to facilitate inquiry supports learners who may have yet to fully develop their reading abilities.

SAMPLE TOOLS

Wonderopolis is a website devoted to children's questions. A Wonder of the Day is posted daily, with extension experiences and resources, and children are encouraged to submit their own questions. The site provides several accessibility features and all articles include text-to-speech through Microsoft's Immersive Reader. Vocabulary support and definitions are provided for highlighted vocabulary words. Some articles include videos with available closed captioning (**wonderopolis.org**).

Wonderopolis collaborated with Flipgrid to create a Flipgrid Wonder of the Day where learners can explore and record their thoughts about the embedded prompts (**bit.ly/inclusive365-261a**).

Google Arts and Culture is a repository of artwork from museums all over the world and can be a source of images for See, Think, Wonder routines (**artsandculture.google.com**).

EXTENSION OPPORTUNITIES

Invite learners to individually seek answers to questions they are wondering about and track their inquiries. Compare their results with others to stimulate discussion. Learners can then take turns sharing what they learned during small group discussions or using a video recording tool like Flipgrid.

Invite learners to find an image or audio resource that they would like to use as a part of a See, Think, Wonder routine.

RELATED RESOURCES

Nurturing a Sense of Wonder (**bit.ly/inclusive365-261b**)

See, Think, Wonder Routine from Project Zero (**bit.ly/inclusive365-261c**)

Figure 261. Wonderopolis home page.

ISTE STANDARDS FOR STUDENTS
1a, 1b, 3a, 3d

ISTE STANDARDS FOR EDUCATORS
5b, 6c, 6d

Augmenting Reality to Visualize STEM and History

Early development relies on individuals manipulating objects to learn. Toddlers grab, pull, twist, and turn objects to learn more about them. As learners grow and are exposed to more and increasingly complex objects, it becomes less practical to learn through physical manipulation. Augmented reality (AR) brings 3D objects to life, allowing individuals to continue to learn through interactions with objects they wouldn't otherwise be able to explore. Imagine holding a model of a planet in your hand, exploring details of a sculpture locked away in a museum, or examining every angle of a mythical creature that never existed. AR gives educators an opportunity to engage learners in a way that was previously unimaginable.

INCLUSIVE USE

AR exemplifies engagement. Reinvigorate those uninterested in learning by inviting them to manipulate objects using AR.

SAMPLE TOOLS

Merge Cube is a foam cube, about the size of a Rubik's Cube, with QR-style codes printed on every side. Those codes transform the cube into a 3D object when viewed through a mobile device loaded with specific apps. The Merge Object Viewer app has a library of pre-made AR objects (**mergeedu.com/cube**).

The Quiver Augmented Reality app provides an interactive mixed reality experience. Color a picture, then take a picture of it using the mobile app and watch the picture come alive (**bit.ly/inclusive365-262a**).

EXTENSION OPPORTUNITIES

Learners might design a model, print it on a 3D printer, and only then discover the model needs a slight tweak. Invite learners to instead create a virtual 3D version using AR to examine their

prototype. Learners can upload the .STL file (a common file type used for 3D objects) to the Object Viewer website for the Merge Cube. The app displays a code for the object. Enter that code directly into the Object Viewer app and the 3D model appears! Learners can examine the model from all angles for mistakes before printing, saving time, money, and frustration!

Invite learners to create a gigantic 3D object. Learners can draw the markings on the Merge Cube or use a copier to print a larger version. These drawings and/or copies can be placed on objects of any size. When users hover the app over the markings, the object will scale, making for huge 3D representations.

RELATED RESOURCES

Print Your Own Merge Cube
(**bit.ly/inclusive365-262c**)

Merge Cube Mania in Middle School—
The 10 Minute Teacher Podcast
(**bit.ly/inclusive365-262d**)

Figure 262. Explore a Mayan pyramid using the Merge Cube.

ISTE STANDARDS FOR STUDENTS
1d, 4a, 4b, 4c, 4d

ISTE STANDARDS FOR EDUCATORS
5a, 5b, 5c, 6a, 7a

Building Collaborative Resource Lists with Digital Curation Tools

Bookmarking using digital curation tools not only allows learners to locate resources that they want to visit again, but it also allows them to share what they have curated with others. Multiple learners can work collaboratively to build a set of shared resources for group projects by using digital curation tools. Creating shared resources allows learners to see other perspectives on a topic, consider previously unknown sources, and divide the workload when researching.

INCLUSIVE USES

When inclusive groups are heterogeneously created, learners working on collaboration and executive functioning skills may benefit from seeing the contributions of others to help them consider resources they may not have considered. This also creates opportunities to pool together a larger set of resources than one individual might find alone.

SAMPLE TOOLS

Wakelet allows users to invite contributors to a collection by sharing a numerical code, a QR code, or a collaboration link (**wakelet.com**).

Diigo allows collaborators to join a common group to share resources. Resources curated in Diigo can be annotated by any collaborator (**diigo.com**).

Google Keep allows collaborators to share a specific note (**keep.google.com**).

EXTENSION OPPORTUNITIES

Invite learners to locate resources for a group project, each addressing a different component, and then use an agreed-upon shared curation tool. Individuals can then review the shared

resources collectively to use them to build the project.

Invite other educators to collaborate on building a shared, curated list of resources when planning together, working on a professional project, or to provide as a resource to families or communities.

RELATED RESOURCES

Collaborate on Wakelet, Blog Post (**bit.ly/inclusive365-263a**)

Learn More about How to Collaborate with Diigo (**bit.ly/inclusive365-263b**)

Figure 263. Collection of pictures, maps, photos, and websites of Australia collected collaboratively by a group of learners in Wakelet.

ISTE STANDARDS FOR STUDENTS
7b

ISTE STANDARDS FOR EDUCATORS
2c, 4b, 5a, 5b, 7a

Listening to Media with Variable Playback Speeds

One of the benefits of learning from recorded audio and video content is the ability to pause, rewatch, or relisten to specific segments, and to experience the content at variable playback speeds. Learners can experience content at faster rates, allowing for consumption in less time than when content is presented in real time. Alternatively, for some, decreasing the playback speed can assist in comprehension.

INCLUSIVE USES

Although it may seem that faster speeds equate to decreased attention to detail, experiencing content at a faster rate can actually focus attention and decrease how long someone needs to maintain focus. Likewise, for some learners, slowing down the rate of presentation can increase comprehension. For example, reducing the playblack speed while listening to someone with an unfamiliar accent or who has a quicker rate of speech might help the learner more clearly understand what is being communicated.

SAMPLE TOOLS

YouTube allows users to adjust the playback speeds of a video (**youtube.com**).

The Podcast app from Apple allows users to adjust the playback speed (**bit.ly/inclusive365-264a**).

Most audiobook interfaces allow for adjustable playback speed, including Audible (**audible.com**) and Overdrive's Libby app, which is used by many public libraries (**bit.ly/inclusive365-264b**).

EXTENSION OPPORTUNITIES

Invite learners to practice adjusting playback speeds based on preferences related to their own needs or factors surrounding the qualities of the original recording.

Play a video of someone talking quickly at typical speed and again at a slower speed, inviting learners to document the words being said each time. Then compare the results to illustrate the benefits of varying playback speeds.

Play a video at 1.25 speed and note elapsed time when it ends. Compare that to the running time of the video played at normal spped to determine how much time was saved. Extrapolate the outcome by figuring the time saved if the learner was experiencing ten videos of the same length, then 20, and then 50. This illustration might help a learner who is reluctant to engage with the content, by showing them it takes less time.

RELATED RESOURCES

A.T.TIPSCAST Episode #47: x2 (**bit.ly/inclusive365-264c**)

How to Speed Up or Slow Down YouTube Videos (**bit.ly/inclusive365-264d**)

Figure 264. YouTube video with Playback Speed menu open.

ISTE STANDARDS FOR STUDENTS
1b, 1d, 3a, 3c

ISTE STANDARDS FOR EDUCATORS
1c, 2b, 2c, 3b, 5a, 5b, 5c, 6a

Toggling between Linear and Diagram Views of Content

Outlining is a method for taking notes, structuring writing, and organizing information into topics and subtopics. Outlining provides a linear, visual representation of information. Mind mapping is also a method of taking notes, structuring writing, and organizing information into topics and subtopics. Mind mapping presents information in a web or diagram view, which provides a very different visual experience for the user. Some tools provide both outlining and mind-mapping tools and include a feature that allows users to toggle between the views as they input or review the information.

INCLUSIVE USES

Invite learners to toggle between views or to primarily work in one view, based on individual preferences, while they are using a note-taking tool. Learners who prefer to organize information linearly could use the outline function while learners who prefer the diagram style of presentation can choose to use the mind map. Invite learners to toggle between both to see which works best for them to organize, recall, and apply information.

SAMPLE TOOLS

Transno is a note-taking website and mobile application that allows users to toggle between an outline and mindmapping view (**transno.com**).

Inspiration Maps is a mobile application that allows users to toggle between diagram and outline views as they organize information (**diagrammingapps.com**).

EXTENSION OPPORTUNITIES

Invite learners to use outlines and mind maps as final products to demonstrate their understanding of learned concepts.

Invite learners to compare and contrast the effectiveness of studying from outlines and mind maps to determine which view helps them recall the information best.

RELATED RESOURCES

The Theory Behind Mind Mapping (**bit.ly/inclusive365-265a**)

How and Why to Create a Useful Outline (**bit.ly/inclusive365-265b**)

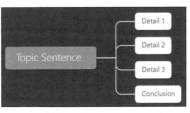

Figure 265a. Outline view of a topic sentence followed by three details and a conclusion.

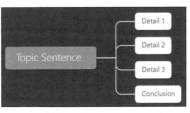

Figure 265b. Mind mapping view of a topic sentence followed by three details and a conclusion.

ISTE STANDARDS FOR STUDENTS

1a, 1d, 3a, 3c, 5c, 6a, 6b, 6c, 6d

ISTE STANDARDS FOR EDUCATORS

2b, 5a, 5b, 5c, 6b, 6d, 7a

STRATEGY 266

Taking Notes From Web-Based Video

Learners need strategies when conducting research and organizing important notes. One media learners may explore during research is the use of video, a powerful resource to engage learners in educational content. Learners can take notes from video content in multiple ways, however, notes synced with timestamps provide individuals with the opportunity to jump back to specific video content. This can expedite the research process by helping learners know which moments of the video related to specific notes.

INCLUSIVE USES

For some learners, reading articles is less effective than watching video clips when researching information. Learners who are learning to read may find that experiencing video content is a more effective way to learn new content while they are developing more sophisticated decoding and reading comprehension skills.

SAMPLE TOOLS

YiNote is a browser extension that will connect directly to a web-based video on YouTube. Notes are automatically timestamped to the video, allowing learners to return to specific sections of the video for future viewing. Each time the video is opened, and the extension is activated, those notes appear. After annotating, the learner can send those notes to Google Docs, OneNote, or Evernote (**yinote.co**)

ReClipped is a browser extension that allows the creation of timestamped notes on videos (**reclipped.com**).

Rocket Note is a browser extension that allows users to create timestamped notes on YouTube videos (**getrocketnote.com**).

EXTENSION OPPORTUNITY

Invite learners to collaborate on notes by sharing and comparing specific notations with their peers. Learners can analyze their notes to see if there are relevant aspects of a specific video they'd like to add or adjust.

RELATED RESOURCE

How to Take Notes from a Video: 5 Strategies that Work (**bit.ly/inclusive365-266a**)

Figure 266. Web video annotated with YiNote.

ISTE STANDARDS FOR STUDENTS
1b, 3a, 3b, 3c, 6a

ISTE STANDARDS FOR EDUCATORS
5a, 6b

Digital Note-Taking with Cornell Notes

Cornell Notes is a note taking strategy that guides the learner in taking notes efficiently, so that the notes are effective for studying or for using to outline a written response. The aim is to reduce your notes to essential ideas to improve recall. To use Cornell Notes, divide your page or document into three main sections:

1. Cue Section: left column taking up 1/3 of the page. Key points (vocabulary, important details, main ideas, questions) to remember.

2. Notes Section: right side of the page. Important information for each cue section item, including short phrases, important ideas, and where to find information in the text.

3. Summary section: bottom 1/5 or 1/4 of the page. Answer to "Why is this information important?"

Moving from handwritten notes to digital notes takes away space and handwriting concerns. It also allows for easy access to links or information that may need to be copied directly into a writing draft.

INCLUSIVE USES

When learners with any emerging skill are provided the option to take notes digitally, they can then use any of their regularly available support tools, such as text-to-speech, speech-to-text, word prediction, or a digital dictionary. Learners who struggle with organizing papers have fewer, if any, to keep track of. Digital notes can be organized in a folder with all of the other resources for a unit of study. Digital notes can also be found more quickly using search functions.

SAMPLE TOOL

Google Sheets provides a layout for Cornell Notes. Learners can use a color-coded template, or they can create their own on the fly without having to create a table, as they would in Docs or Word (**bit.ly/inclusive365-267a**).

EXTENSION OPPORTUNITY

Invite learners to customize their own Cornell Notes template with the cues, colors, and directions that best meet their needs. Educators can model how to keep the template easily accessible in their own Google Drive or other folder, and how to ensure that the original template can't be written over so that they have a clean copy to work from every time.

RELATED RESOURCE

The Best Way to Take Notes (**bit.ly/inclusive365-267b**)

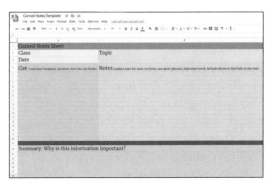

Figure 267. Cornell Notes template in Google Sheets.

ISTE STANDARDS FOR STUDENTS

1a, 3a, 5c

ISTE STANDARDS FOR EDUCATORS

4b, 5a, 5b, 6b, 7b

Transcribing Audio to Searchable Text

Listening to recorded audio, such as podcasts, can be a rewarding way to learn. It can be a hands-free experience, allowing learners to be mobile or engaged in other activities while learning. However, returning to the audio to find a specific moment or point can be arduous, requiring scrubbing back and forth to find the desired content. Transcribing the audio to searchable text allows learners to find specific content more expeditiously while simultaneously making the content accessible to those who have difficulty hearing.

INCLUSIVE USES

Learners with hearing impairments may require transcriptions of audio to experience the content. Learners who are working on improving their decoding and reading comprehension may find reading transcribed text while listening to the recorded audio and an effective methodology for improving their literacy skills.

SAMPLE TOOL

Otter.ai is a transcription tool that works on mobile devices and web browsers. Using the built-in microphone of your device, Otter collects audio and provides real time transcription. The transcriptions are autogenerated, searchable, and provide identification of different speakers (**otter.ai**).

EXTENSION OPPORTUNITY

Use Otter.ai to record a group discussion or conversation. When finished, the group can review the notes for accuracy. Learners can use the searchable tags to quickly scan the document for key phrases. Learners can assign identities to speakers within the note by selecting a user and editing the name. Keep the transcription and audio note in a shared location for all the learners to review at a later date.

RELATED RESOURCES

How to Automatically Transcribe Audio or Video Recordings (**bit.ly/inclusive365-268a**)

Transcribe Your Recording in Microsoft 365 (**bit.ly/inclusive365-268b**)

Figure 268a. The NPR podcast, featuring a button for accessing the transcript.

Figure 268b. Otter.ai transcription.

ISTE STANDARDS FOR STUDENTS
1b, 1d, 3d, 5d, 6a

ISTE STANDARDS FOR EDUCATORS
5a, 6a

Make Concepts Stick using Singing and Music

Ever hear a song that you loved so much and that was so catchy you couldn't help singing it over and over again in your head? Hearing information presented through music and song can help learners understand and remember concepts. Listening to audio files or video clips of people singing can help make introductions, explanations, and representations of topics more memorable. Music is often used as a strategy in early learning (e.g., the ABC song). Learners and educators alike can continue to use and offer music as an option for older learners as well. Zaretta Hammond refers to the use of music and singing as a culturally responsive strategy that helps to "make learning sticky" (2015).

INCLUSIVE USES

Some learners may find it difficult to decode and comprehend text in written articles. Songs from genres of music aligned to the preferences of the individual learner can help them comprehend and recall the information.

SAMPLE TOOL

Flocabulary is a website that provides educational music videos that cover a wide variety of topics (**flocabulary.com**).

EXTENSION OPPORTUNITIES

Invite learners to use audio loops to create and record their own songs, which can be shared with other learners to assist them in learning historical or current events. These could be audio-only files or made into music videos to express what they've learned.

Invite learners to create song parodies, using music from contemporary artists, to demonstrate their learning.

RELATED RESOURCES

Educational Rap Playlist (**bit.ly/inclusive365-269a**)

Rapping Teacher Turns Social Studies Lessons into Songs (**bit.ly/inclusive365-269b**)

Mr. Doggett's YouTube Channel (middle school educator) (**bit.ly/inclusive365-269c**)

3 Tips to Make Any Lesson More Culturally Responsive (**bit.ly/inclusive365-269d**)

Figure 269. Flyer for a hip-hop lyric-writing and performance program for middle school learners, created by Maryland middle school educator Michael Doggett.

ISTE STANDARDS FOR STUDENTS
3a, 3b, 3c, 3d

ISTE STANDARDS FOR EDUCATORS
2c, 3a, 3b, 3c, 4d, 5a, 5b, 5c, 6b, 6d, 7a

Making Connections with Digital Concept Maps

Concept maps are graphical representations of relationships between concepts that help learners organize and analyze information. When using and creating concept maps, learners make connections to previous knowledge, making it easier to assimilate and remember new but connected information. Concept maps help individuals learn new information, enhance study skills, and build higher-level cognitive skills. Color-coding within the map provides visual supports for understanding connections and relationships between concepts, such as main ideas and supporting details.

INCLUSIVE USES

Online concept maps are mistake-tolerant and allow learners to recreate their work or reorganize the relationships if errors are made. Cells can be color-coded to show different levels and connections, making it easier to understand the relationships. The visual presentation can enhance memory skills for later recall.

SAMPLE TOOLS

Bubbl.us is a free, online, collaborative concept-mapping and graphic organizer tool (**bubbl.us**).

Popplet is a free online tool and iOS app for creating concept maps and graphic organizers (**popplet.com**).

EXTENSION OPPORTUNITIES

Invite learners to collaborate on a concept map in small groups, with one person as the driver to develop the concept map online.

Encourage learners to share their concept-map creations with peers and to explain their thinking to solidify their understanding.

RELATED RESOURCES

Using Graphic Organizers To Make Sense of the Curriculum (**bit.ly/inclusive365-270a**)

Concept Maps (**bit.ly/inclusive365-270b**)

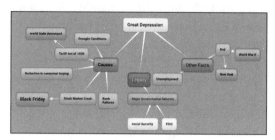

Figure 270. Concept map demonstrating connections between events and occurrences related to the Great Depression.

ISTE STANDARDS FOR STUDENTS
1a, 1c, 5b, 5c

ISTE STANDARDS FOR EDUCATORS
2b, 3b, 5a, 5b, 6a, 6b

Pairing Digital Pictures with Notes for Reference and Task Completion

Taking pictures of learning materials allows learners to capture and reference a visual reminder of necessary information much more expeditiously than handwriting, typing, audio, or video. At first, learners could be encouraged to take a variety of pictures and then work on deciding which are relevant. In time, the learner will develop the skills to determine when pictures should be taken. Pictures can be used in tandem with color-coding, tagging, and calendar reminders to provide a comprehensive organizational strategy.

INCLUSIVE USES

Those learning to manage deadlines and complete to-do list items and tasks on time may find value in visual reminders.

Learners with emerging writing skills may find collecting information through pictures more expeditious and advantageous than only handwriting or typing notes.

SAMPLE TOOLS

Google Keep provides a way for learners to take pictures and connect them to a digital note. Within that digital note, learners can use color-coding and labels to provide additional ways to categorize the information. Users can also attach a date/time reminder to a note to trigger a notification (**keep.google.com**).

Microsoft OneNote provides a platform to create digital notebooks that include images. Color-coding and setting reminders can assist with remembering tasks (**onenote.com**).

EXTENSION OPPORTUNITIES

Invite learners to take pictures of any materials they believe support their learning. Educators can help learners craft a checklist with questions to later help organize or sort the images.

Questions might include: Why did I take this picture? What is in the picture that I thought would help me learn? What words describe this picture? What categories or labels correlate to this picture? Given the opportunity again, would I take the same picture or might there be a better picture? Would I recommend the picture to others and, if so, how would I share it? Based on the answers, learners could create a note, attach the picture to it, and then create labels for organization.

Educators might find it useful to take pictures of materials from professional learning experiences and organize them using searchable note-taking applications.

RELATED RESOURCES

15 Ways for Students to Use Google Keep infographic (**bit.ly/inclusive365-271a**)

Student Planner Using Google Keep and Calendar (**bit.ly/inclusive365-271b**)

Create a To-Do List with OneNote (**bit.ly/inclusive365-271c**)

Figure 271. Notes paired with pictures in Google Keep.

ISTE STANDARDS FOR STUDENTS
1a, 3c, 5b

ISTE STANDARDS FOR EDUCATORS
5a, 6a, 6c

Researching with Digital KWL Charts

What I *know*, what I *want* to know, and what I *learned* charts, commonly referred to as KWL charts, help learners access background knowledge on a topic, generate questions about what they want to learn about a topic, and then reflect after a learning experience on what they have learned. While traditionally these graphic organizers are created on paper, digital tools provide an opportunity for learners to organize and efficiently use the information to guide research and support writing on a topic.

INCLUSIVE USES

The use of digital KWL charts provides an anchor for learners to set a purpose for reading or researching. Setting this purpose helps to focus the learner's attention on what is relevant within a source that answers the questions they posed. Furthermore, when learners use digital tools to write in their own KWL charts they can access supports like text-to-speech or speech-to-text. It is easier to manipulate or change ideas within a KWL chart when it is digital, compared to paper-based charts.

SAMPLE TOOLS

Snap&Read has a KWL outline template that allows learners to pull information from digital texts and other resources. The layout of Snap&Read's templates position the graphic organizers alongside any website or PDF that they are using (**snapandread.com**).

Google Forms allows users to create a KWL chart that includes images or multimedia to support or activate background knowledge. When information is added to the form, it can be sorted and referenced in the generated spreadsheet (**docs.google.com/forms**).

Holt Interactive KWL Chart is an online, fillable KWL chart that requires no special software (**bit.ly/inclusive365-272a**).

EXTENSION OPPORTUNITIES

Invite learners to use variations on the KWL, including:

- KWHL—What I *know*, what I *wonder* about, *how* will I find out, what I *learned*.

- KWLUM— What I *know*, what I *want* to know, what I *learned*, how will I *use* what I learned, what *more* do I need to learn.

RELATED RESOURCES

KWL example. This link takes you to a forced copy of a KWL made in Google Forms (**bit.ly/inclusive365-272b**).

Harnessing the Power of KWL Charts in Education (**bit.ly/inclusive365-272c**)

Figure 272a. KWL chart created using Google Forms.

ISTE STANDARDS FOR STUDENTS
1a, 3a, 5c, 6c

ISTE STANDARDS FOR EDUCATORS
4b, 5a, 5b, 6d, 7a

Incorporating Multiple Modalities to Improve Note-Taking

Successful note-taking involves identifying a key concept and then succinctly formulating a message that describes that concept using text and/or images, while continuing to consume the information being presented. Then one needs to prepare to repeat the process for the next important concept. When notes are created using a single modality, such as writing, learners likely have only one way, such as reading, to review those notes. When notes are created using multiple modalities, like writing while audio recording, learners have multiple ways to review those notes, like reading and listening. Syncing written or drawn notes to recorded audio provides learners the opportunity to employ multiple modalities to review information by both seeing and listening to the content. Learners can also listen repeatedly to ensure understanding. This strategy eliminates the pressure learners might feel in the moment to collect quality information. The use of note-taking apps on mobile devices provides a platform with constant access, regardless of the learning environment.

INCLUSIVE USES

Learners with emerging reading, writing, drawing, typing, and/or listening skills may find reviewing content using multiple modalities simultaneously helpful. Finding ways to combine multiple modalities increases the effectiveness of notes and helps to provide academic independence.

SAMPLE TOOLS

AudioNote is a cross-platform, note-taking solution that provides audio synced with typed notes (**bit.ly/inclusve365-273a**).

Notability is an iOS app that combines multiple modalities into a single note-taking solution.

Write, type, draw, and add pictures and audio to create seamless supports to promote independence (**gingerlabs.com**).

EXTENSION OPPORTUNITIES

Invite learners to use timestamps as reference points in audio synced notes. Rather than attempting to type complete thoughts, sentences, or even words, learners could type a single letter, word, or key idea. This will engage the timestamp, allowing the learner to return to that point later, listen to the audio, and then complete the written note, taking as much time as needed.

Learners can then return to the notation they have left for themselves later, listen to the audio, and complete the written note, taking as much time as needed.

RELATED RESOURCE

How to Use Notability (**bit.ly/inclusve365-273b**)

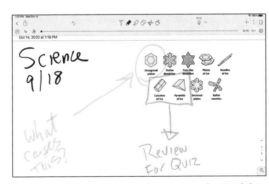

Figure 273. Learner-generated notes using the Notability app on an iPad, with synced audio, inserted pictures, and a drawing to create a comprehensive multimodal note.

ISTE STANDARDS FOR STUDENTS

1a, 1d, 3c, 5c, 6a

ISTE STANDARDS FOR EDUCATORS

5a, 6a

STRATEGY 274

Integrating Digital Notes across Applications

Educators often use shared slide decks or shared notebooks when presenting content to learners. When learners use a note-taking tool in conjunction with the shared resources, it is possible to easily save and organize resources into a digital note for easy reference later. Learners can continue to take notes beyond what the educator has provided.

INCLUSIVE USES

Being able to have the original educator materials side by side with a digital note taking tool supports learners who may be challenged by having multiple tabs open and moving between different documents for note-taking. This also supports learners with executive function challenges by minimizing distractions and improving organization.

SAMPLE TOOLS

Google Slides and Google Keep integrate beautifully together. By opening the Keep Viewer in Google Slides, the learner can easily move back and forth between the slides and a note in Keep, right within the Google Slides environment (**docs.google.com/presentation**, **keep.google.com**).

PowerPoint and OneNote provide integration as well. By choosing OneNote under the print option for PowerPoint, learners can upload a set of PowerPoint slides directly into OneNote and can take additional notes while viewing the original educator-provided slides (**microsoft.com**).

EXTENSION OPPORTUNITIES

Invite learners to share their notes with a peer to collaboratively compare and supplement their notes.

Invite learners to share their notes with educators. An educator can then provide feedback to the learner on the notes and what they may have overlooked in the original document.

RELATED RESOURCE

Integrating Digital Notes across Applications— Google Slides and Google Keep (**bit.ly/inclusve365-274a**)

Figure 274. Google Slides with Google Keep Viewer on the side.

ISTE STANDARDS FOR STUDENTS
1a, 1b, 3c

ISTE STANDARDS FOR EDUCATORS
2b, 3b, 5a, 5b, 6a

Self-Identifying Executive Function Strengths and Challenges

A two-pronged approach to promote the development of executive function skills is advocated by Dawson and Guare (2018). They posit that intervention must include environmental supports and explicit strategy instruction. They have created an executive function skills questionnaire to help learners identify their own executive function strengths and areas to strengthen. With this information, educators can analyze results to then design appropriate interventions, considering questions such as, *What areas do we need to strengthen? What environmental supports will be provided? How will the skill be taught? How will we assess effectiveness?* In answering these questions, educators can examine what no-tech, low-tech, and high-tech resources can be used to support learners in developing their executive function skills.

INCLUSIVE USES

A structured approach to developing executive function skills supports all learners. Using a questionnaire that helps identify areas of strength and opportunities for growth allows educators to examine resources, supports, and instructional strategies that can be used by individual learners and/or applied universally to all learners.

SAMPLE TOOL

Executive Skills Questionnaire (Dawson and Guare) (**bit.ly/inclusive365-275a**).

EXTENSION OPPORTUNITIES

Invite learners to complete the executive skills questionnaire to identify the priority areas they would like to strengthen and the skills they would like to develop. Invite learners to then develop goals around the results and brainstorm ways to measure growth.

Invite learners to share the questionnaire with family members, compare results, and develop group goals based on commonalities.

RELATED RESOURCE

Executive Skills in Children and Adolescents, Second Edition: A Practical Guide to Assessment and Intervention (The Guilford Practical Intervention in the Schools Series) (**bit.ly/inclusive365-275b**)

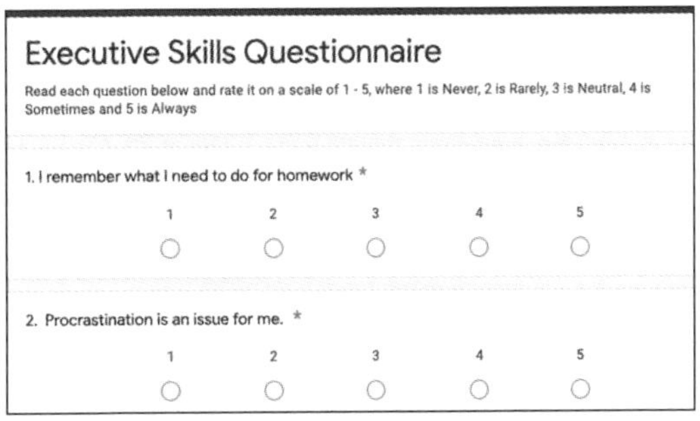

Executive Skills Questionnaire

Read each question below and rate it on a scale of 1 - 5, where 1 is Never, 2 is Rarely, 3 is Neutral, 4 is Sometimes and 5 is Always

1. I remember what I need to do for homework *

    1   2   3   4   5

2. Procrastination is an issue for me. *

    1   2   3   4   5

Figure 275. Questions on a sample executive skills questionnaire.

ESQ-R Self-Assessment Tool (**bit.ly/inclusive365-275c**)

ISTE STANDARDS FOR STUDENTS
1a, 1b

ISTE STANDARDS FOR EDUCATORS
1c, 5a, 5b, 6a, 6c

Recognizing Logical Fallacies in Arguments

Groups working to come to a shared understanding may enter into a discussion where one or more people attempt to make a point meant to persuade the other(s) into accepting an alternative viewpoint. When making the decision whether to be persuaded and adopt the other viewpoint, it might be important to know whether the argument being used is logical. Practiced computational thinkers can learn to recognize illogical arguments and make counterpoints based on sound reasoning. Individuals can practice recognizing logical fallacies by being exposed to them and witnessing examples.

INCLUSIVE USES

People with disabilities are victimized at a higher rate than others (Bureau of Justice Statistics, NCJ 250200). Nefarious individuals may prey on people with disabilities and attempt to persuade them to take actions they would otherwise not. Explicitly practicing how to recognize when someone is making an argument that is not based on logic might help learners make decisions based on sound reasoning.

SAMPLE TOOL

Your Logical Fallacy Is shares twenty-four logical fallacies along with a corresponding symbol to help people recognize when an argument being made is illogical (**yourlogicalfallacyis.com**).

EXTENSION OPPORTUNITIES

Invite learners to participate in a role-play experience where each participant acts out a logical fallacy.

Invite learners to make a poster, story, video, or other media to illustrate a logical fallacy.

Educators can use the logical fallacies to spot flaws in rational thinking when making decisions about policy and practices.

RELATED RESOURCE

YourLogicalFallacyIs.com is described in the introduction of the Talking with Tech Podcast Episode #118: Christine Tripoli and Ellen Mazel—Assessment and Treatment of Cortical Visual Impairment (**bit.ly/inclusive365-276a**).

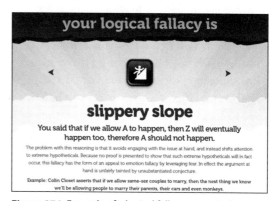

Figure 276. Example of a logical fallacy presented at YourLogicalFallacyIs.com.

ISTE STANDARDS FOR STUDENTS
2b, 3a, 3b, 3c, 3d, 5a, 5b, 6c, 7a, 7b, 7d

ISTE STANDARDS FOR EDUCATORS
2a, 2b, 2c, 3b, 6c

Employing a Checklist to Identify Tools for Task Completion

Given a specific task, there may be a variety of tools available to complete that task. Choosing the most useful tool among the options available can be tricky. Answering a series of guiding questions from a checklist can help a learner make decisions about which tool or tools are the right ones for the job. A learner can document answers on the checklist using a survey or poll. Engaging in self-reflection while answering the questions and analyzing the results helps the learner understand what tools are most effective and efficient to complete the task at hand.

INCLUSIVE USES

Using a question checklist reduces barriers for learners who are building skills related to organization, task initiation, and/or work completion.

SAMPLE TOOL

A tools checklist written as a series of questions can be developed using a survey or polling tool such as Google Forms (**bit.ly/inclusive365-277a**).

EXTENSION OPPORTUNITIES

Invite learners to look for patterns as they analyze their responses collected over time. Are there particular tools that they tend to use repeatedly? If so, the learners could then be asked to make decisions about when to stop using the survey or poll and, instead, just start using some of their go-to tools.

After completing a task, invite learners to analyze the effectiveness of the tool selected by returning to the survey or poll and assigning the decision a quantitative score. Was it the correct tool for the job? Was it effective in getting the job done? By quantifying and

ranking the effectiveness of the tool, the learner can make decisions about how effective the survey itself is at helping select appropriate tools.

RELATED RESOURCE

A.T.TIPSCAST Episode #119: Assistive Technology Movie Review—Man of Steel (**bit.ly/inclusive365-277b**)

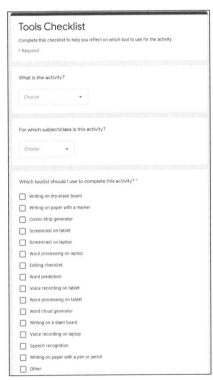

Figure 277. Sample tools checklist in Google Forms.

ISTE STANDARDS FOR STUDENTS
1a, 1d, 4b, 6a

ISTE STANDARDS FOR EDUCATORS
2b, 2c, 3b, 5a, 6a, 7a

STRATEGY 278

Organizing Resources and Tools by Task

Time is a precious commodity to all learners. Learners can preserve time by organizing resources and the tools they frequently use to complete a given task in a way that allows the learner to quickly access them. Rather than hunting for a particular website, or feeling frustrated by being unable to recall a previously used tool or resource, learners can organize items by the task they are attempting to complete. Learners could have a list of tools and resources they use for writing, reading, math, or other tasks related to learning.

INCLUSIVE USES

Learners who have difficulty managing tools and resources may find it useful to maintain a list organized by task. Being able to open those tools and resources quickly helps them become accustomed to their use and limits the amount of time it takes to begin working on that task. Learners who are accustomed to waiting to act until being provided explicit instructions may demonstrate increased independence when utilizing lists that organize tools and resources by task. Seeing a list of tools and resources per task may help a learner get started on a task without waiting for a prompt from an educator.

SAMPLE TOOLS

OneTab is a Chrome browser extension that enables learners to group open tabs into a list. Saved tabs can be re-opened when needed, either individually or as a group. Saved tab lists can also be shared with others via a URL or QR code (**one-tab.com**).

The Session Buddy Google Chrome extension allows users to group tabs by different purposes or functions and quickly access them when working on a particular task. Clusters of tabs can be labeled by task (**sessionbuddy.com**).

EXTENSION OPPORTUNITY

Beyond content related to academics, learners may find it useful to organize other content based on purpose as well. It might be helpful for learners to organize resources related to extracurriculars, hobbies, and other interests so that they can be expeditiously accessed.

RELATED RESOURCES

How to Use OneTab (**bit.ly/inclusive365-278a**)

How to Organize Your Online Tutoring Materials Using Session Buddy (**bit.ly/inclusive365-278b**)

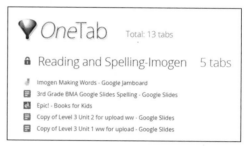

Figure 278. Reading and spelling resources compiled using OneTab.

ISTE STANDARDS FOR STUDENTS
1d, 3c, 5c

ISTE STANDARDS FOR EDUCATORS
2c

Color-Coding for Digital Organization

According to research at MIT (Trafton, 2014), our brains process images, including color, within milliseconds. When learners use color to organize their digital files, it supports their ability to quickly locate information that they need. Some file-storage tools allow users to select a color for any folder. Folders can be customized to match the colors for different events in a digital calendar and of notes based on subjects in a note-taking application. Learning to develop a personalized color-coding scheme across tools can help individuals increase productivity and remain organized.

INCLUSIVE USES

Color-coding supports learners working to improve reading or executive function skills as they can more quickly locate a folder, calendar item, or note based on color rather than having to read text labels for the items.

SAMPLE TOOLS

Google Drive/Google Calendar/Google Keep allows color-coding of folders, calendar items, and digital notes, respectively (**bit.ly/inclusive365-279a**).

Microsoft OneNote/Outlook allows color-coding of tabs and calendar items (**bit.ly/inclusive365-279b**).

Folder Marker for MS Windows 10 is an add-on to color-code folders (**bit.ly/inclusive365-279c**).

EXTENSION OPPORTUNITIES

Expand color-coding for paper resources, including using tabs in three-ring binders and colored manilla folders for organizing paper resources. Sticky notes are also available in different colors to coordinate with digital notes.

It might be important to create a color-coding key for some learners for temporary use until they become more familiar with and accustomed to the color scheme.

RELATED RESOURCES

Color-Coding to Keep Kids Organized (**bit.ly/inclusive365-279d**)

MIT News—*In the blink of an eye: MIT neuroscientists find the brain can identify images seen for as little as 13 milliseconds* (**bit.ly/inclusive365-279e**).

Figure 279. Color-coded folders in Google Drive.

ISTE STANDARDS FOR STUDENTS

1a, 1d

ISTE STANDARDS FOR EDUCATORS

6a, 6b

Employing Flexible Seating Options to Develop Executive Function Skills

Learners' engagement increases and unproductive behaviors decrease when the environment includes flexible seating choices. When offering seating choices, help learners identify which options promote on-task actions for them. When learners become cognitively aware of what works best for them, they are developing their executive function skills, such as impulse control and metacognitive skills.

Provide learners with an opportunity to choose seating based on what they determine to be necessary to complete the task at hand. Options could include both soft and hard surfaces upon which to sit and work. Options could include surfaces that provide for vestibular and kinesthetic movement, such as bouncy balls, swivel chairs, and durable cushions.

INCLUSIVE USES

All learners benefit when allowed to make choices. Offering flexible seating choices is another way to empower learners, as it acknowledges learner variability. Some learners prefer to work at a desk, others may choose to work on wiggle cushions, balls, or wobble stools.

Learners practicing to regulate attention may find they can maintain focus longer, when they experience spontaneous motor movements.

SAMPLE TOOL

Wobble stools, exercise balls, floor cushions, and beanbag chairs all offer flexible seating.

EXTENSION OPPORTUNITIES

Encourage learners to try a variety of seating options and think about which arrangement is optimal for them as a learner. Invite them to record their responses and collect and analyze class data about learner preferences.

Invite learners to adapt current furniture using commonly found materials. For instance, halved tennis balls could be placed under two chair legs, on opposing corners. When seated in this chair, learners can wobble back and forth.

Individuals participating in family and consumer science experiences could make non-slip, secure cushions for furniture.

RELATED RESOURCES

Jackson, Amber and Feng, Jay, (2019). Learning comfortably: Flexible seating and student performance in the elementary classroom. *Georgia Educational Research Association Conference.* (**bit.ly/inclusive365-280a**)

The Kinesthetic Classroom: Teaching and Learning through Movement, Michael Kuczala, TEDxAshburn (**bit.ly/inclusive365-280b**)

Exercise—Brain Rules by John Medina (**bit.ly/inclusive365-280c**)

Figure 280. Learning spaces with seating surfaces that promote kinesthetic movement.

ISTE STANDARDS FOR STUDENTS
1a, 1b, 1c, 4a, 4c

ISTE STANDARDS FOR EDUCATORS
2b, 3a, 4b, 5a, 5b, 5c, 6a, 6b

Naming Digital Folders with Images

Digital file folders can be difficult to organize and differentiate. They can often look the same, with the only differentiator being the text-based folder name. Learners can name or rename file folders using images to help them navigate the files and increase their productivity.

INCLUSIVE USES

Color-coding file folders by purpose can be an organizational strategy, but those who have difficulty seeing color may not find that useful. Learners who have yet to master decoding skills may find using folders that pair images with text not only helps improve navigation but also helps them learn the spelling of the words.

SAMPLE TOOL

Emojipedia.org is a free-to-use database of emojis that can be searched, then easily copied and pasted to use as an icon for a file folder. It can be used with storage tools such as Google Drive (**emojipedia.org**).

EXTENSION OPPORTUNITY

Invite learners to search for emojis as a large or small group experience. Collectively, they can decide on an emoji to use in the naming of shared file folders.

RELATED RESOURCE

EduWalks #5: Strategies to Stay Organized (**bit.ly/inclusive365-281a**)

Figure 281. File folders named with text and emojis.

ISTE STANDARDS FOR STUDENTS

1b, 7a

ISTE STANDARDS FOR EDUCATORS

2b, 4d, 5a, 6d

Tagging to Organize and Find Notes

In a traditional file folder structure, learners need to make a decision about how to name folders, organize them into categories and subcategories, consistently make decisions about where to place individual files, and then remember how they made those decisions to locate the file again. Tagging digital content with multiple labels eliminates the need to make a decision about where to put the content. Labeling content, including notes, using multiple tags allows a learner to quickly find the notes when they are needed. One can also search or filter by tag to find any piece of content labeled with that tag.

INCLUSIVE USES

Learners working on organizational skills may find it useful to use content tags with digital tools. It is easier to navigate digital tags than a paper folder or indexing system.

SAMPLE TOOLS

Google Keep is a note-taking tool that allows a user to apply multiple labels to each note and then access all the notes with that label (**keep.google.com**).

Microsoft OneNote is a note-taking tool that allows users to label content with multiple tags (**onenote.com**).

Evernote is a note-taking tool that allows users to tag notes with multiple labels (**evernote.com**).

EXTENSION OPPORTUNITIES

Invite learners to brainstorm specific tags they might use for organizing notes. Learners who use terms that are too broad may find that those tags are not useful. For instance, tagging notes with general words like *technology* or *education* tends to be less helpful than tagging with specific words like *biology* or *graphic organizers*.

Learners could tag items using multiple specific terms including the subject, unit of study, block of day, and/or an educator's name, for example *Earth Science*, *Volcanoes*, *Block 3*, and *Mr. Sheehan*. Having multiple tags can help the learner find the notes again quickly by selecting the tag that makes most sense for the task at hand.

Invite educators to create tags related to professional development events, such as conferences they've attended or courses they've taken, such as *ISTE <insert year>*.

RELATED RESOURCE

A Sure Fire Way to Help Students Never Forget Another Assignment—Google Keep (**bit.ly/inclusive365-282a**)

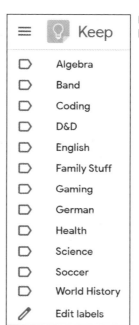

Figure 282. Examples of labels in Google Keep.

ISTE STANDARDS FOR STUDENTS
1a, 3a, 3c

ISTE STANDARDS FOR EDUCATORS
2b, 2c, 4b

Bookmarking Effectively

Internet searches lead to a wealth of information, yet saving important information from the searches can be a daunting task. Saving curated links as bookmarks in a browser can be difficult to manage over time. However, dedicated bookmarking tools provide a range of full-featured options to manage important curated websites, videos, and resources. Depending on the tool, these features include being able to tag resources, share curated lists easily, add text annotations, and include summaries and images from a bookmarked page to provide context for the saved resource.

INCLUSIVE USES

Learners with executive function challenges can use bookmarking tools to help logically organize saved web pages. Bookmarking tools may also provide visual support and collect highlighted annotations, simplifying the organization of sources for research. Bookmarking tools can also provide a one-click means of collecting resources, decreasing the need to copy and paste links into a separate document.

SAMPLE TOOLS

Wakelet is a content-curation platform for links, posts, videos, and images (**learn.wakelet.com**).

Diigo is a social bookmarking tool with annotation features (**diigo.com/education**).

EXTENSION OPPORTUNITY

Encourage learners to evaluate different bookmarking options and determine which tool works best considering their own learning style. Learners can even critique different options and share video feedback using a tool like Flipgrid (**flipgrid.com**).

RELATED RESOURCES

The Educator's Guide to Wakelet (**bit.ly/inclusive365-283a**)

Using Diigo in the Classroom (**bit.ly/inclusive365-283b**)

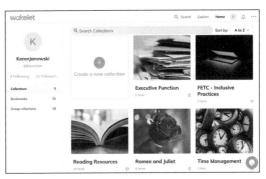

Figure 283. Wakelet bookmarking organization.

ISTE STANDARDS FOR STUDENTS

1a, 1b, 1d, 2b, 3a, 3b, 3c, 4b, 6a,

ISTE STANDARDS FOR EDUCATORS

5a, 5b, 6a, 6b

STRATEGY 283

Organizing Web Links with the Bookmarks Bar

Learners feel the need, the need for speed! They need to quickly access an important, frequently accessed website to complete a task but can't seem to find the link. Where did they put it? There are many tools available to import links but using the functions built into the browser itself may be the least restrictive. Learners can use the Bookmarks bar built into their browser to organize and locate resources.

INCLUSIVE USES

Managing digital resources can be a struggle for learners if they don't use a system. These organizational systems must be personalized and functional in order to be used. Using the Bookmarks bar within the Chrome browser may work because it's always there! Every time a learner opens Chrome, the information is there. No need to access another web-based storage tool or search through a long list of links. Learners can set up folders on the Bookmarks bar to create organizational structure.

SAMPLE TOOL

The Bookmarks bar has always been a part of the Chrome browser. Select Bookmarks from the drop down menu and click Show Bookmarks Bar. Now customize that toolbar with items needed by that learner. Consider folders (and maybe even folders within folders!) to provide the structure necessary for them to complete their tasks (**google.com/chrome**).

EXTENSION OPPORTUNITY

Speak to learners and identify their current system for saving web links for later review. Do they have a system? Is it working for them? Would they be open to trying a new system? Have them activate the Bookmarks bar and start setting it up. Ask them to consider what folders they could set up to organize their links. They can create the folders by right-clicking in any open space on the Bookmarks bar and choosing Add Folder. Show them how to save to these folders each time they locate a new resource.

RELATED RESOURCE

How to Manage Chrome Bookmarks Like a Pro (Website Tips) (**bit.ly/inclusive365-284a**)

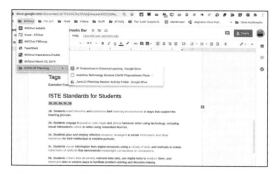

Figure 284. Bookmarks saved in the Chrome browser.

ISTE STANDARDS FOR STUDENTS
1b, 2b, 3a, 3c, 5b

ISTE STANDARDS FOR EDUCATORS
2b, 4b, 5a, 6a,

Managing Browser Tabs for Productivity

When researching or completing research online, it is not unusual to have multiple browser tabs open simultaneously. The fear of closing a tab on a needed resource often leads to leaving all tabs open, whether or not they are helpful to the project. This often leads to visual chaos and inefficiency for learners. The ability to reduce tab clutter or selectively close tabs and have them reopen automatically at a set time can increase efficiency and organization when working online.

INCLUSIVE USES

Learners who are working to build their organization skills benefit from a less cluttered screen. Tools with automatic reminder functions bypass working memory and organizational challenges.

SAMPLE TOOLS

The Tab Snooze extension for Chrome and Firefox allows the learner to close a tab and schedule it to reopen later that day, the next day, or at an assigned time (**bit.ly/inclusive365-285a**).

OneTab is a tab management extension for Chrome and Firefox that reduces open tabs to a list format. Tabs can be restored all at once or individually, as needed (**bit.ly/inclusive365-285b**).

Chrome browser tabs can be grouped and color-coded! Right-click on any open tab and select Add Tab to Group. Name the group and assign a color. Now these tabs can be collapsed to simplify the display.

Key commands can also be used to bring back tabs that were closed accidentally. The key command CTRL+Shift+T restores closed tabs in the Chrome browser. Chrome also offers a menu that lists recently closed tabs and windows. To access it, go to Chrome's menu, select History to see the list, then click the desired tab or window to reopen it.

EXTENSION OPPORTUNITY

Invite learners to try Tab Snooze, OneTab, and the Chrome Browser to manage their tabs, and to reflect on which tool they deem most effective in meeting their learning needs.

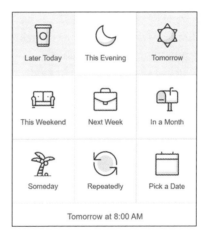

Figure 285. Choices for when to reopen a tab in Tab Snooze.

ISTE STANDARDS FOR STUDENTS
1a, 3a

ISTE STANDARDS FOR EDUCATORS
5a, 5c, 6a, 6c

STRATEGY 286

Managing Browser Extensions Independently

Browser extensions allow learners to customize their web experience to support their specific needs. As individuals add more extensions to their web browser, organization and management of installed extensions becomes challenging. The number of extensions one has active and running at any given time may impact browser performance. A necessary life skill is to learn how to manage resources and to create an efficient digital learning environment. An extension manager allows both learners and educators to activate and deactivate browser extensions by quickly toggling them on and off.

INCLUSIVE USES

Learners who are working on skills to improve productivity, limit distractions, and maximize workflow may find managing extensions helps in these areas. Educators can help guide learners when selecting which resources should be activated or deactivated to support the learning task.

SAMPLE TOOLS

Extensity is a Chrome extension that provides support to manage all the learner's extensions. Select the icon on the URL bar and all installed Chrome extensions appear in an alphabetical list. Bolded extensions mean they are currently active. Grayed-out extensions are currently inactive. Select the desired extension to activate or deactivate it (**bit.ly/inclusive365-286a**).

Chrome Extensions Manager is a default feature of the Chrome browser with an icon of a white puzzle piece that displays a list of active and inactive extensions. Users can quickly activate and deactivate extensions by selecting this icon or by going to **chrome://extensions**.

EXTENSION OPPORTUNITY

Limiting extensions to only those necessary to complete the task reduces the power consumption of the browser and improves system efficiency. At the onset of a learning task, invite learners to open the entire list of extensions available in the extension manager. Learners can review the list, considering each extension, and make decisions as to which is necessary, possibly necessary, or unnecessary. Once the task is completed, the learners can return to the extension manager to make changes for the next task.

RELATED RESOURCES

Tuesday Tech #53: Extensity (**bit.ly/inclusive365-286b**)

Talking with Tech Episode #63: Interviews from ATIA and FETC: Christine Baudin of AAC for the SLP, Michael Dicpinigaitis, and Mike Marotta (**bit.ly/inclusive365-286c**)

Figure 286. Extensity extension for Chrome browser.

ISTE STANDARDS FOR STUDENTS
1b, 1d, 6a

ISTE STANDARDS FOR EDUCATORS
5a, 6a

Decluttering Web Pages to Limit Distractions

Distractions abound while working online. Extraneous links can entice learners to visit irrelevant or inappropriate sites while banners, video clips, ads, and comments can clutter the page. Simplifying the visual presentation of a web page to display only pertinent information can be an invaluable way to promote learner autonomy and improve the usefulness of an otherwise overwhelming site.

INCLUSIVE USES

Learners working to improve executive functioning, those who are easily distracted, and some learners with visual impairments benefit from decreased amounts of information presented on a website. The uncluttered presentation can be an effective reading solution for learners who need or prefer to use text-to-speech. Learners who are working on developing their decoding, reading comprehension, and reading fluency skills might find it useful to practice these skills using a visual presentation that emphasizes text.

SAMPLE TOOLS

Mercury Reader filters web pages and removes distractions like banners and ads to produce a version of the page that is focused on the text. You can send the simplified page to your Kindle or other device for reading (**mercury.postlight. com/reader**).

Snap&Read Universal is a Chrome extension and an iOS app that provides the ability to remove ads, images, and distractions from websites (**bit.ly/inclusive365-287a**).

Distraction Free Mode is a Google extension that minimizes distractions while working on a Google Doc (**bit.ly/inclusive365-287b**).

Reader View is a built-in feature of the Safari web browser that will remove all items from the web page except for the main text and embedded pictures (**bit.ly/inclusive365-287c**).

EXTENSION OPPORTUNITY

Offer learners an opportunity to compare the original web page with a simplified web page and discuss how the change impacts their ability to attend to the text.

RELATED RESOURCES

How to Use the Remove Distractions Feature in Snap&Read (**bit.ly/inclusive365-287d**)

How to Use Reader View in iOS Devices (**bit.ly/inclusive365-287e**)

Figure 287a. Website with original content.

Figure 287b. Same website as viewed with Mercury Reader.

ISTE STANDARDS FOR STUDENTS
1a, 3a, 3c, 6a

ISTE STANDARDS FOR EDUCATORS
4b, 5a, 6a

STRATEGY 288

Self-Managing Time through Technology Analytic Trackers

Time management is a skill every learner needs to master. Collecting data about how much time one spends using different resources and learning how to analyze that data can help learners make productivity and efficiency decisions. Just as wearing a pedometer provides insights into mobility, different technologies can track analytics related to device usage. Depending on the tool, the data could also include a breakdown of time spent using technology per function of the application.

INCLUSIVE USES

Providing learners with visual representations of how much time they spend on different applications can help them become more self-aware. Quantifying the experience with numbers can help learners analyze their own actions and set goals to spend more or less time in certain applications. Learners who have goals regarding self-awareness, time management, and compulsive behaviors might find analyzing the data meaningful to intrinsically motivating change.

SAMPLE TOOLS

Screen Time is a feature of iOS devices that tracks time spent using different applications and calculates percentages by function, such as games, social networking, creativity, productivity, and more. It also calculates daily use averages. Additionally, it provides access to features that can help guide learners by self-imposing downtime, limits, and content and privacy restrictions (**bit.ly/inclusive365-288a**).

Rescue Time is automatic time-tracking software available as a desktop download or a browser plug-in that shows graphical representations of time spent on various applications (**rescuetime.com**).

EXTENSION OPPORTUNITY

Invite learners to chart elements of their technology use using a survey tool or spreadsheet. Learners can then analyze the data and reflect on performance. They can ask themselves if the technology is supporting or detracting from the achievement of their educational goals. Learners could then be invited to make a plan to take steps to either maintain or change actions based on the analytics. They can then track changes over time to monitor progress toward achieving productivity goals.

RELATED RESOURCES

How to Start Using Screen Time for iPhone, iPad, and iPod Touch (**bit.ly/inclusive365-288b**)

How to Use Downtime in Screen Time for iPhone, iPad, and iPod Touch (**bit.ly/inclusive365-288c**)

Getting Started with Rescue Time (**bit.ly/inclusive365-288d**)

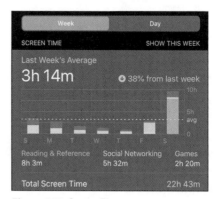

Figure 288. Screen Time.

ISTE STANDARDS FOR STUDENTS
1a, 1c, 2b, 5a, 5b, 5c, 5d

ISTE STANDARDS FOR EDUCATORS
3b, 3c, 3d, 4a, 4b, 4c, 4d, 5a, 5b, 5c, 6a, 6b, 7a, 7b, 7c

Automating Commonly Used Multi-Step Actions

Learners in the digital age may have to take multiple sequential steps to access functions of technology. These steps must be taken in a specific order to complete the task. For example, to set a timer, it might mean locating the timer, activating the timer, setting the duration, and choosing what happens when the timer ends. Then, to reset the timer, the learner might need to go through all of those steps again. Some devices and applications allow users to create shortcuts or macros that set up a sequence of events to automatically occur when triggered by the individual, at a specific time, or upon arrival or departure of a specific location. This streamlines the experience, which can both decrease frustration and increase productivity, all while illustrating the power of automation.

INCLUSIVE USES

Learners who have difficulty physically accessing devices may find shortcuts and macros useful. Learners who have difficulty remembering how to navigate multiple steps may also find automating sequences helpful.

SAMPLE TOOLS

Macros can be created in Microsoft Word to automate frequently used tasks (**bit.ly/inclusive365-289a**).

Shortcuts are a feature of iOS devices that can be used to automate tasks accessed frequently (**bit.ly/inclusive365-289b**).

EXTENSION OPPORTUNITIES

Invite learners to brainstorm and then outline repetitive tasks they perform on a device. Then, invite learners to create macros or shortcuts for these tasks. Once completed, invite the learners to share what they automated with other learners to inspire them with ideas about what else could be automated.

Invite learners to create a screen recording of how and why they created their shortcut or macro with an explanation of how the automation saves them time. Then, invite the learner to share that video with a wider audience.

RELATED RESOURCE

How to Create and Use Macros in Microsoft Word (**bit.ly/inclusive365-289c**)

Get to Know the Siri Shortcuts App (**bit.ly/inclusive365-289d**)

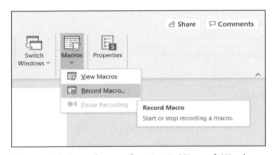

Figure 289. Record macro function in Microsoft Word.

ISTE STANDARDS FOR STUDENTS
1d, 5a, 5c, 5d, 6a

ISTE STANDARDS FOR EDUCATORS
2b, 5a, 5c, 6c

STRATEGY 290

Triggering Reminders Set to Location

Learners often travel from location to location, moving throughout busy lives from one learning environment to the next. Travel among home, school, work, leisure activities, and more means managing different tasks and materials based on where one is and what is happening in that place. Some mobile devices and apps can be set to trigger a reminder based on arrival at or departure from a given location. When the mobile device or app is brought to or away from the set location, the reminder triggers. Reminders can be set to help remember lists of items needed in that location, prompts for social language cues, steps for task completion, or anything else a person might need to be reminded to do.

INCLUSIVE USES

Triggering a reminder when someone arrives or leaves a location is useful for any learner, but it might be particularly beneficial for those living with impairments that impact memory skills. Learners working on improving vocational skills may also find reminders set for locations helpful in preparing for work.

SAMPLE TOOLS

Google Keep allows users to set reminders based on location (**bit.ly/inclusive365-290a**).

iPhones and iPads provide location-based reminders (**bit.ly/inclusive365-290b**).

EXTENSION OPPORTUNITY

Invite learners to make a table with three columns. They should list common events or tasks in the first column. Materials needed to participate in the event or complete the task go in the second column. The locations of the events or tasks are placed in the final column. Invite the learner to use this completed table to set the reminders of each location.

RELATED RESOURCE

Apps for Organization and Job Readiness (**bit.ly/inclusive365-290c**)

Figure 290. Location-based reminder in Google Keep.

ISTE STANDARDS FOR STUDENTS
1b, 5d, 6a

ISTE STANDARDS FOR EDUCATORS
5a, 6a

Spacing Out Learning Intervals Using the Pomodoro® Technique

The Pomodoro® Technique is a time management method developed and trademarked by Francesco Cirillo from Italy. He noticed that if he set a timer and worked for short bursts of time, typically about twenty to twenty-five minutes, with brief breaks, he completed more tasks in a shorter amount of time. While traditionally done with a manual timer (the name comes from the Italian word for *tomato*, as Cirillo used a tomato-shaped kitchen timer back in the 1980s), digital timers can be used as well. The method is now widely used to facilitate task initiation, sustained effort, and task completion.

INCLUSIVE USES

Individuals learning to manage time effectively benefit from using the Pomodoro® Technique to improve time on task.

SAMPLE TOOLS

Pomodoro® Timer software is developed by the originator of the technique (**bit.ly/inclusive365-291a**).

Tomato Timer is a free web-based timer that allows learners to easily set intervals and break times (**tomato-timer.com**).

Focus Keeper is an iOS app that incorporates intervals and breaks into the timer (**bit.ly/inclusive365-291b**).

EXTENSION OPPORTUNITIES

Invite learners to set a goal each day for how many interval groupings they will complete across the day and to use the timer tools to track this.

Invite learners to try the different digital timer options and identify if they have a preference when working on time-management skills.

RELATED RESOURCE

The Pomodoro® Technique (**bit.ly/inclusive365-291c**)

Figure 291. Tomato Timer app showing a work interval.

ISTE STANDARDS FOR STUDENTS

1a, 1c

ISTE STANDARDS FOR EDUCATORS

5a, 6a

Prioritizing Choices and Tasks using an Eisenhower Matrix

Learning how to prioritize tasks is an important skill. Attempting to decide which tasks to accomplish in which order can take time away from actually accomplishing the tasks. The visualization technique known as an Eisenhower Matrix helps learners make decisions about what to complete first, what they can do later, what someone else should do, or what they shouldn't do at all. An Eisenhower Matrix is a form of graphic organizer where the user places tasks into one of four quadrants. The first quadrant is for items that are important and urgent. The second quadrant is for items that are important, but not urgent. The third quadrant is for items that are not important but urgent. The final quadrant is for items that are neither important nor urgent.

INCLUSIVE USES

Learners who are challenged with managing time or making decisions about which tasks to work on first may find participating in an exercise using an Eisenhower Matrix helpful in plotting out action steps. When used in conjunction with digital tools, such as a table in a word processor, a spreadsheet, or graphic organizing software, learners can use accessibility tools, such as text-to-speech, when interacting with or completing the exercise.

SAMPLE TOOLS

A color-coded, four-quadrant table with labels can be created in Google Docs (**bit.ly/inclusive365-292a**).

A color-coded, four-quadrant table with labels can be created in Microsoft Word (**bit.ly/inclusive365-292b**).

Diagrams.net is a free, web-based graphic organizer (**diagrams.net**).

EXTENSION OPPORTUNITIES

Invite learners to work collaboratively with peers to complete an Eisenhower Matrix when deciding on roles and a timeline for work on a project.

Invite learners to reference the completed matrix regularly and to interact with it by marking off completed items and reprioritizing. Some learners may find it helpful to engage with an ongoing matrix weekly or even daily.

Invite learners to keep completed matrices. The learner can analyze the matrices for patterns or use them as evidence to demonstrate growth in the skill of decision-making.

RELATED RESOURCE

How to Overcome Procrastination with the Eisenhower Matrix (**bit.ly/inclusive365-292c**)

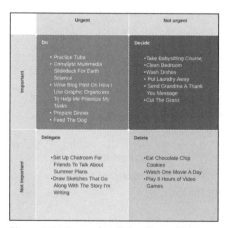

Figure 292. A completed Eisenhower Matrix by a high school learner.

ISTE STANDARDS FOR STUDENTS
1a, 1b, 1d, 4a, 4b, 4d, 5b, 5c, 6a, 6c

ISTE STANDARDS FOR EDUCATORS
1a, 2a, 5a, 5c, 6a, 6c, 6d

Managing Tasks with Virtual and Collaborative Kanban Charts

Learners are often managing several multistep projects at one time. Sometimes, learners are working on these projects with other learners. A Kanban chart (sometimes called Kanban board) is a method of keeping projects organized by putting tasks into columns. As tasks are completed, they are moved to the next column of the project until the project is completed. Kanban charts can be created using low-tech means, such as sticky notes. High-tech Kanban charts allow users to participate remotely and may provide additional accessibility options.

INCLUSIVE USES

Learners can practice managing and completing tasks with Kanban charts. Use Kanban charts to provide a visual reminder of the sequence for individual tasks, including everyday tasks, to progress through the day.

SAMPLE TOOLS

Trello is a web-based application that provides a digital Kanban chart (**trello.com**).

Microsoft Planner, a part of the Office 365 suite, is a web-based application that provides a digital Kanban chart (**tasks.office.com**).

Padlet is an online virtual bulletin board that can display and organize information in columns (**padlet.com**).

EXTENSION OPPORTUNITIES

Invite learners to create Kanban charts related to a project-based learning lesson where the learner is asked to plot out the tasks needed to complete the project.

Invite learners to break down tasks into discrete parts when creating Kanban charts.

RELATED RESOURCE

What is a Kanban Board?
(**bit.ly/inclusive365-293a**)

Figure 293. Kanban chart in Trello with three-columns: To Do, Doing, and Done.

ISTE STANDARDS FOR STUDENTS

1a, 1b, 1d, 4a, 4c, 4d, 5c, 5d, 7b, 7c

ISTE STANDARDS FOR EDUCATORS

4a, 4c, 4d, 5a, 6a, 7a

STRATEGY 294

Managing Tasks with Virtual Digital Bulletin Boards

There are many ways for learners to digitally manage tasks. The real trick is finding a system that works to meet each learner's unique needs. Digital bulletin boards can serve as a visual cue and organization station for learners, much in the same way a note on a physical bulletin board may be a prompt with a visual cue to get a task completed. Depending on the tool, digital bulletin boards can include color-coded notes and built in reminders, and can be shared with others.

INCLUSIVE USES

Those learning how to independently organize themselves benefit from digital task management tools. Color-coding and digital reminders in conjunction with the use of a virtual bulletin board provide cues needed to manage learning tasks.

SAMPLE TOOLS

The Note Board extension for Chrome allows learners to create multiple digital bulletin boards that can have pinned notes. It has a reminder function, color-coding options, and attached pictures. Each board can have multiple tabs, increasing effectiveness (**bit.ly/inclusive365-294a**).

Padlet is a web-based and app-based tool where users can create a certain number of boards before having to upgrade to a full account. Boards can be recycled and reused multiple times. In addition to text, users can also post pictures, links, drawings, video, and audio (**padlet.com**).

Google Keep acts as a web-based and app-based bulletin board with virtual sticky notes (**keep.google.com**).

EXTENSION OPPORTUNITY

Invite learners to create multiple note cards to represent each subject area along with a To Do note card. As the learner engages in different topics throughout the day, encourage them to enter tasks onto the corresponding note cards.

RELATED RESOURCES

How to Use Padlet to Manage Tasks (**bit.ly/inclusive365-294b**)

Note Board Chrome Extension (**bit.ly/inclusive365-294c**)

Figure 294. Note Board Chrome extension.

ISTE STANDARDS FOR STUDENTS
1a, 1d, 3c, 5c

ISTE STANDARDS FOR EDUCATORS
5a, 6a

Integrating Multiple Visual Supports for Learner Management

Visual supports greatly enhance the learner's experience, especially in a noisy environment where collaborative learning is occurring. When projected on an interactive whiteboard or shared on a distance-learning platform, visual instructions can decrease extraneous noise and increase learners' independence in any setting. Beneficial tools include customizable text that can include written directions, a countdown timer that shows the passage of time, a traffic light to signal the start, and symbols indicating how to work with peers, including silent, whisper, ask a neighbor, and work together.

INCLUSIVE USES

Visual supports help all learners, including those whose memory and time management skills are developing. Create an environment that provides the visual cues learners need for task completion while reducing the need for auditory repetition and review.

SAMPLE TOOL

Classroomscreen is a free all-in-one learning environment solution that includes a variety of visual supports to support learning (**classroom-screen.com**).

EXTENSION OPPORTUNITY

Include your learners in identifying which of the visual supports they need to help them complete the task. Give them ownership to initiate and sustain attention to the task.

RELATED RESOURCE

Eduwalks: Strategies for Distance Learning (**bit.ly/inclusive365-295a**)

Figure 295. Custom display from Classroomscreen.

ISTE STANDARDS FOR STUDENTS
1a, 1b, 6a

ISTE STANDARDS FOR EDUCATORS
5a, 5c, 6a, 6b

Applying Spaced Repetition to Enhance Study Skills

Spacing out study times can help learners better understand and remember content. Brief moments of study at a greater frequency may be more effective for some learners than prolonged moments of study at a lesser frequency. This method, called *spaced repetition*, enhances memory as it takes advantage of the spacing effect, which indicates that people remember more when learning is spaced out to allow new neural connections to strengthen. As learners study for a test or other task, they progressively space out the amount of time in between their study sessions. The break between study sessions gives the brain time to make connections. Ultimately, less total time is needed to remember information when the learner returns to the same information repeatedly, remembering more each time.

INCLUSIVE USES

Learners who use ineffective study skills benefit from understanding that if they space out their studying, rather than trying to do it all at one time, they may actually need to spend less total time studying. Learners working on building memory skills and those working to streamline how much time theys spend studying may find spaced repetition useful.

SAMPLE TOOLS

Brainscape is a fun, electronic flashcard tool that uses spaced repetition strategies as part of their learning algorithms (**brainscape.com/teachers**).

Anki is a free electronic flashcard tool for Mac, Windows, iOS, and Android devices and supports images, audio, and video (**apps.ankiweb.net**).

EXTENSION OPPORTUNITY

Encourage learners to evaluate the effectiveness of the technique. Compare the results of studying using their typical methods of test preparation and then employ spaced repetition combined with the use of electronic flashcards to determine which method achieve the desired results.

RELATED RESOURCES

How to Remember More (**bit.ly/inclusive365-296a**)

The Most Powerful Way to Remember What You Study, Video (**bit.ly/inclusive365-296b**)

Figure 296. Information provided when using Brainscape study skill tools.

ISTE STANDARDS FOR STUDENTS
1a, 1b, 3a, 5a

ISTE STANDARDS FOR EDUCATORS
5a, 6a, 6b

Keeping On Track with Intermittent Reminders

Keeping on track can be a difficult process for learners. Consistent, self-initiated reminders can help keep personal learning goals in focus. Learners can craft their own goals and then be prompted with messages to provide support. Using a tool that replaces the New Tab window in the Chrome browser with time management support and motivational reminders can subtly yet effectively facilitate task completion. Consistency of the display and personalized messages provide a customized solution tailored to each learner.

INCLUSIVE USES

Learners working on improving time management skills might find reminders with self-created personalized messages helpful in completing tasks in a timely manner. Learners who have grown dependent on prompts from others may find using self-initiated reminders useful in increasing intrinsic motivation.

SAMPLE TOOL

Momentum is a Chrome extension that replaces the New Tab window with a picture and the personalized greeting "Good morning, [Learner]." The replacement picture rotates each time a new tab is opened, providing additional levels of support via optional widgets, such as to-do lists, inspirational quotes and mantras, weather updates, and a bookmarks bar. There is a line for the learner to add their main focus for the day (**bit.ly/inclusive365-297a**).

EXTENSION OPPORTUNITIES

Invite learners to start their day by crafting and displaying a main focus in their learning space, whether that be digital, physical, or both. Perhaps this is completing a specific step toward a larger learning task, making sure to update their calendar with upcoming due dates,

or any other objective they'd like to work to accomplish by the end of the day.

For learners who get overwhelmed by the amount of information they need to interact with throughout the day, use the Mantra widget. Instead of the standard, "What is your main focus for today?" greeting that appears in the new window of Momentum, learners can customize a statement to provide comfort and support as they move through the day. Adding in a phrase like, "You got this!" can provide the needed spark to complete a task.

A bank of sample tasks, objectives, and/or mantras might be useful for learners who are beginning to create their own.

RELATED RESOURCES

Momentum: Quick Start Guide (**bit.ly/inclusive365-297b**)

EduWalks: Wellness (**bit.ly/inclusive365-297c**)

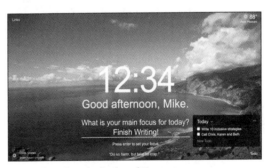

Figure 297. Sample display of Momentum.

ISTE STANDARDS FOR STUDENTS

1a, 1d, 2d

ISTE STANDARDS FOR EDUCATORS

5a. 6a

Setting Reminders Using a Voice Assistant

Remembering to complete work is one of the responsibilities of a learner. There are often multiple things a learner might need to remember. Remembering everything one needs to do can be challenging in the best of situations. Digital calendars and similar technologies that respond to voice commands allow learners to set reminders using their voice. Learners can practice the skill of setting a reminder before their attention is focused elsewhere and the work task is forgotten.

INCLUSIVE USES

Reminders made using a voice assistant can help support those with impairments related to fine motor skills. Any person can benefit from reminders to help keep themselves organized and get work accomplished.

SAMPLE TOOL

Siri is an example of a voice assistant that can be used to create reminders on iOS devices that come with calendar and reminders features (**apple.com/siri**).

EXTENSION OPPORTUNITY

Invite learners to share recording methods that work best for them as part of a study skills or learning center experience. Encourage them to discuss why certain features of the technology work well and others do not.

RELATED RESOURCE

Speaking To-Dos with Siri (**bit.ly/inclusive365-298a**)

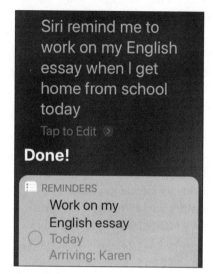

Figure 298. Siri setting a reminder.

ISTE STANDARDS FOR STUDENTS
1a, 1b, 1c

ISTE STANDARDS FOR EDUCATORS
3d, 5a, 6b, 7a

Solving Problems Using Interactive Mind Maps

Digital mind maps are visual representations of ideas and concepts and how they connect and relate. When used as an interactive, problem-solving template, a mind map can assist a learner in learning the steps needed to tackle a difficult problem. A problem-solving template takes the learner through the process of describing the problem, hypothesizing possible solutions, detailing the expected outcome, developing an action plan, and then reflecting on the actual outcome.

INCLUSIVE USES

Using a step-by-step template provides the structure and support that a learner may need to identify and solve a difficult problem. Digital mind maps allow for the flexibility of adding multiple modalites to each segment of the map. Images, audio, and/or video can be added so learners can experience the content in more than one way, helping them solve the given problem.

SAMPLE TOOL

Mindomo's problem-solving template is a digital mind map to support problem solving (**bit.ly/inclusive365-299a**).

EXTENSION OPPORTUNITY

Invite learners to explore additional mind-mapping templates to determine their usefulness for brainstorming, planning, organizing, or studying.

RELATED RESOURCE

Getting Started with Mindomo for Education (**bit.ly/inclusive365-299b**)

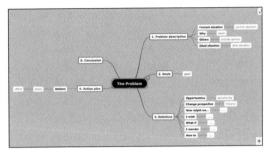

Figure 299. Example of a problem-solving template.

ISTE STANDARDS FOR STUDENTS
1a, 4a, 4b, 5c

ISTE STANDARDS FOR EDUCATORS
5a, 6a, 6b, 6c, 6d, 7a

STRATEGY 299

STRATEGY 300

Supporting Task Completion with Timers

The use of timers can assist learners in managing their time to initiate a task, sustain effort to remain on task, and complete work according to expectations. They can be customized for individual learners or used in larger groups for all learners. Timers can show learners how much time they have left to work on a task before transitioning, as well as the passage of time as they work on a task. Additionally, a timer used with a productivity technique, such as the Pomodoro Technique, can help learners structure their time in short bursts of work combined with short breaks to sustain effort to finish tasks.

INCLUSIVE USES

Learners living with ADHD or anxiety may benefit from the use of a timer, which offers a visual guide for sustaining attention and effort for set periods of time. Learners working to improve time-management and task-completion skills might also find timers useful.

SAMPLE TOOLS

The 360 Thinking iOS app from Cognitive Connections provides the option of setting separate, color-coded sections of a timer clock for the get-ready, start, mid-point goal, and end phases of a task. Each section or slice can be customized with specific directions as well as a determined amount of time the learner has to complete each section (**bit.ly/inclusive365-300a**).

Online-Stopwatch's digital classroom timers has so many options! There are sensory-based timers that look like lava lamps, funny race timers, exam timers, and more (**bit.ly/inclusive365-300b**).

The Thinking Time Tracker is available as a Chrome Extension (**bit.ly/inclusive365-300c**).

EXTENSION OPPORTUNITIES

Invite learners to set their own goals for the time it might take them to complete a task and use a timer to hold themselves accountable for meeting their goals.

When choosing a timer, invite learners reflect on the usefulness of it as a tool. Did they think it helped them be more productive and efficient? If not, why not? They might find that the type of timer they chose was distracting rather than helpful.

RELATED RESOURCES

Executive Functioning: More Time Techniques (**bit.ly/inclusive365-300d**)

The Secret to Staying Productive When You Have a Big Project (**bit.ly/inclusive365-300e**)

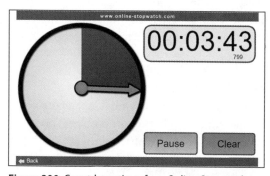

Figure 300. Countdown timer from Online-Stopwatch.

ISTE STANDARDS FOR STUDENTS
1a

ISTE STANDARDS FOR EDUCATORS
5a, 5c, 5d, 6a

Managing Time Using Nonlinear Visual Schedules

Knowing what to expect can help learners navigate their day. Linear visual schedules present a predictable sequence, reminding learners that time is not infinite. Nonlinear, or amorphous, visual schedules present items or events in a randomized field. As learners progress through their day, they identify the visual for the task to which they are transitioning. The visual can then be crossed off or moved to a linear portion of the schedule to indicate the completion of one task and the start of the next. Unexpected events sometimes occur during the day, like a fire drill, for instance. Question marks can be added to the nonlinear schedule to reflect the idea that something unanticipated happened. When something happens that was unexpected, learners can cross off the question mark or move it onto the linear portion of the schedule.

INCLUSIVE USES

Many adults manage their lives using lists and calendars. Both are examples of visual schedules. Using an amorphous visual schedule can help learners build time and resource management skills. Any learner developing a system to sequence events or follow step-by-step directions might use a non-linear schedule to practice this skill.

SAMPLE TOOLS

Padlet, an online corkboard, can be used to create nonlinear visual schedules (**padlet.com**).

Sticky notes could be used to create a nonlinear visual schedule.

EXTENSION OPPORTUNITIES

Invite learners to choose which way they'd like to manage their nonlinear visual schedules. Some might like to have a low-tech version with tactile symbols on a tangible board. Others might prefer a digital tool with visuals that can be dragged and dropped onto the linear template. Invite learners to create their own nonlinear schedule using tools they prefer.

Learners with goals to become less rigid and more flexible may need a visual for unexpected events. Use question marks or other symbols to represent unpredictability. Educators can create unexpected occurrences. These occurrences could be something as simple as the spilling of water, dropping of a book, or a visitor coming into the learning space. Placing an expected visual everyday for mundane events prepares learners to expect the unexpected so they practice flexibility when something truly unexpected occurs.

RELATED RESOURCE

A.T.TIPSCAST Episode #18: Amorphous Visual Schedules (**bit.ly/inclusive365-301a**)

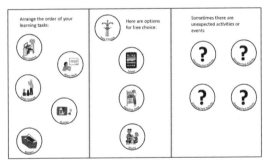

Figure 301. A nonlinear visual schedule where learners mark off what they have completed. Images used with permission from LessonPix.

ISTE STANDARDS FOR STUDENTS
1a, 1b

ISTE STANDARDS FOR EDUCATORS
2a, 4a, 5a, 6a

STRATEGY 302

Breaking Down Tasks into Component Parts with Linear Visual Schedules

Visual schedules are images, often combined with text, that are used to support task completion and increase independence. Developing visual schedules encourages task analysis by breaking it down into steps. Visual schedules allow learners to know exactly what they need to do without having to ask others, "What comes next?" Visual schedules can be digital or print and follow a linear pattern aligned either horizontally or vertically. They can also be used as a support in the learning space for groups of learners or customized per individual. Visual schedules can be used in conjunction with timers to help learners complete tasks based on self-paced goals.

INCLUSIVE USES

Linear visual schedules support learners whose executive functioning skills are developing. Learners with anxiety and those with intellectual disabilities that interfere with their ability to complete a task without frequent verbal reminders may also benefit from the use of a linear visual schedule. Visual schedules help support the understanding of the elements of a task, reduce working memory load, reduce anxiety, accommodate receptive language difficulties, and may motivate learners to work through a less favorable experience to get to one that is more preferred.

SAMPLE TOOLS

LessonPix is a digital platform that allows educators to create a variety of image and text-based visual schedules. It includes vertical and horizontal layouts, numbered schedules, and other templates (**lessonpix.com**).

Choiceworks (iOS) integrates images, text, and audio in a dynamic visual schedule that allows learners to virtually move or check off elements as they are completed. Choiceworks also supports the use of video modeling, and includes a timer and choice boards (**beevisual.com**).

EXTENSION OPPORTUNITY

Invite learners to create visual schedules, including the elements for which they need prompts to complete successfully. Engage learners in deciding on the text and images to describe and illustrate the steps in a task.

RELATED RESOURCES

Visual Supports and Autism Spectrum Disorders (**bit.ly/inclusive365-302a**)

Picture Schedules—Many Styles for Many Uses (**bit.ly/inclusive365-302b**)

Figure 302. Step-by-step visual schedule to support learners with an independent writing task.

ISTE STANDARDS FOR STUDENTS
1a, 1b

ISTE STANDARDS FOR EDUCATORS
5a, 6a

Supporting Transitions with Visual Schedules

Visual schedules are images and/or text that are used to support learners in transitioning from one task to another. Visual schedules can be in digital or print format. They can be used in learning environments to support whole or small groups as well as customized to meet the needs of individual learners. When learners have difficulty transitioning from one task to another, visual schedules provide the support learners need to understand unexpected changes in the day's schedule.

INCLUSIVE USES

Visual schedules support learners whose executive function skills are developing or whose anxiety interferes with their ability to easily transition from one experience to another. Visual schedules provide predictability, and aid in transition between tasks, helping to reduce stress and accommodate for differences in receptive language abilities.

SAMPLE TOOLS

LessonPix is a digital platform that allows educators to create a variety of image- and text-based visual schedules that can be printed out or used on a digital device. It includes vertical and horizontal layouts, numbered schedules, and schedules that allow the learner to check off events to demonstrate completion (**lessonpix.com**).

The Choiceworks app for iOS integrates images, text, and audio into a dynamic visual schedule that allows learners to virtually move or check off elements of the schedule as they are completed. Timers, choice boards, and video can be integrated into any schedule. The use of the timer can be particularly helpful in supporting transitions (**beevisual.com**).

EXTENSION OPPORTUNITY

Provide an auditory cue along with visuals to alert learners that a transition is coming. Provide a 5-minute warning and then a 1-minute warning. Invite learners to mark components on a visual schedule as done as a part of the transition from one task to another.

RELATED RESOURCES

Transition Time: Helping Individuals on the Autism Spectrum (**bit.ly/inclusive365-303a**)

Using a Visual Schedule (**bit.ly/inclusive365-303b**)

Figure 303. Visual schedule in Choiceworks for transitioning from one task to another. ©2011 Bee Visual LLC.

ISTE STANDARDS FOR STUDENTS
1a, 1b

ISTE STANDARDS FOR EDUCATORS
5a, 6a

Linking Operational and Social-Emotional Tutorials to QR Codes

Tutorials in different modalities are often useful for demonstrating how to complete a series of steps. Videos or documents with text and pictures can be used to provide details about how to complete tasks. However, finding the instructional tutorial you need when you need it can be challenging. One solution is to generate quick response (QR) codes as links to access tutorials. The QR codes can be strategically placed to provide instructions on how to complete the task.

INCLUSIVE USES

Remembering multistep directions can be difficult or frustrating for any learner. QR codes provide an on demand, in-the-moment experience for how to complete the task that can be watched or read repeatedly. Depending on the task, each step can be divided into a separate, sequential QR code.

Place QR codes in areas where various social scripts can be practiced. Learners working to achieve social-emotional and language goals can use the QR code to experience a video or text script of what to say or how to react in a given situation, such as ordering lunch or providing salutations when entering or exiting a room.

SAMPLE TOOLS

QR Monkey is a free, web-based QR code generator (**qrcode-monkey.com**).

Flipgrid Shorts has a QR code generator feature that can be used to record a video tutorial while instantly creating a corresponding QR code. The generated QR codes can be printed on labels and affixed where needed (**bit.ly/inclusive365-304a**).

EXTENSION OPPORTUNITIES

Invite learners to create their own tutorials and and associated QR codes. Learners can then discuss where to place the QR codes to be accessed by others.

QR codes can be created with different colors or images. A key can be established for a learner to know that certain colors or symbols equate to specific types of tutorials. For example, a green QR code with a symbol of a person in the middle might indicate that the QR code is for a social exchange where a blue QR code with a symbol of a device in the center might indicate a tutorial on how to operate a device.

RELATED RESOURCE

Twelve Ideas for Teaching with QR Codes (**bit.ly/inclusive365-304b**)

Figure 304. QR code attached to a 3D printer to provide support for operation.

ISTE STANDARDS FOR STUDENTS
2b, 2c, 3b, 6a, 6b, 6c, 6d, 7a, 7b, 7c

ISTE STANDARDS FOR EDUCATORS
2b, 3a, 3b, 4c, 5a, 5b, 6a, 6b

Displaying the Time until the Next Event

Learners can keep track of events and plan out tasks by maintaining a daily calendar. Learning how to gauge and manage how much time is remaining before the next event is a skill. A persistent display of the time left until the next event on the calendar can help learners plan and pace out the time they spend on a given task.

INCLUSIVE USES

Learners who find time management challenging might find a persistent display of time left helpful in learning how to manage actions necessary to make progress toward the completion of the task. A persistent display of time remaining before the next event on a calendar can serve as a reminder that there are time limitations on the current task, especially if the task they are working on is nonpreferred.

SAMPLE TOOL

The Checker Plus for Google Calendar extension for the Chrome browser provides users with a display of the time until the next event on Google Calendar occurs (**bit.ly/inclusive365-305a**).

EXTENSION OPPORTUNITY

Invite learners to add their own events to their Google Calendar and consider the times displayed between events. Adding events to a calendar and pacing them out with enough time to complete each task is a skill that takes practice and guidance.

RELATED RESOURCE

Checker Plus for Google Calendar (**bit.ly/inclusive365-305b**)

Figure 305. Events displayed using the Checker Plus for Google Calendar extension.

ISTE STANDARDS FOR STUDENTS

1a, 1b

ISTE STANDARDS FOR EDUCATORS

3c, 5a, 5c, 6a, 6b

STRATEGY 306

Assigning Tasks with Automatic Notifications for Collaborative Feedback

Collaboration often requires providing feedback to teammates on shared files as they work to complete projects. Learners can look for ways to automate the process of notifying teammates that feedback has been provided. Tools providing automatic notification features help streamline the process of group collaboration.

INCLUSIVE USES

Notifications help learners who are developing organization skills to be more aware of their responsibilities. A notification provides an automatic reminder that a task is now ready to be addressed, while also providing a prompt to complete that task. Notifications of comments assigned to learners who require or prefer to listen to text can use a corresponding text-to-speech tool to hear the text in the comments read aloud.

SAMPLE TOOL

When a user adds a "+" in the text field of a comment in a Google application they will be prompted with a list of contacts. A user can select from that list to assign the comment to a particular contact. This generates an email notification to the contact and adds the comment to a list of follow-up events made searchable in Google Drive. Users can use the search field in Google Drive to create a concise list of every action assigned to them by selecting the dropdown arrow, scrolling to Follow-Up, and selecting Any (**bit.ly/inclusive365-306a**).

EXTENSION OPPORTUNITY

Invite learners to assign tasks to themselves by selecting their own name from a list of contacts. This strategy keeps all of the items they have been assigned to do in one searchable location.

RELATED RESOURCE

How to Assign a Comment to Another Person in a Google Application (**bit.ly/inclusive365-306b**)

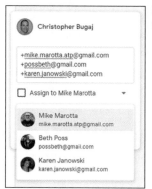

Figure 306. Assigning tasks to team members.

ISTE STANDARDS FOR STUDENTS
1c, 2b, 6b, 6c, 6d, 7b

ISTE STANDARDS FOR EDUCATORS
4a, 4c

Splitting Screens to Improve Navigation

Switching between open tabs and windows on a digital device is a common occurrence when learners are researching and writing. Managing and navigating everything on the screen can be time consuming at best and create an executive function nightmare for some learners at its worst. Learners can use split screen tools to access multiple tabs at once, allowing learners to easily read, take notes, check a reference, or look up additional information while still having their working document in front of them at all times.

INCLUSIVE USES

Using split screens reduces the cognitive load by decreasing how much information needs to be held in short term memory when shifting between pages or documents, and ultimately allows all learners to stay more focused on what it is they need to accomplish. Learners working on improving time management and/ or task completion skills may find split screen supports useful.

SAMPLE TOOLS

Tab Resize is a Chrome extension that automatically resizes open windows to appear in a side-by-side or other configuration for work completion (**bit.ly/inclusive365-307a**).

Dualless is a Chrome extension that automatically splits open tabs into multiple views (**bit.ly/inclusive365-307b**).

Using Split View on iPads allows multiple screens to be visible at one time (**bit.ly/inclusive365-307c**).

EXTENSION OPPORTUNITY

Invite learners to try different configurations of a split screen (e.g., horizontal, vertical, three panes) to consider what works best for them. Their preference may be depend on the task the learner is working to accomplish.

RELATED RESOURCE

Split-Screen is Like Having Dual Monitors (**bit.ly/inclusive365-307d**)

Figure 307. Screen split to allow learner to take notes on the left and see the original resource on the right.

ISTE STANDARDS FOR STUDENTS

1a, 1d, 3a

ISTE STANDARDS FOR EDUCATORS

5a, 6a, 6b, 6d

STRATEGY 308

Visualizing Future Thinking Using Interactive Image Hotspots

Learners can be overwhelmed by the prospect of initiating and completing a task, and unsure of where to begin. Challenging tasks could range from handling morning or end-of-day routines, completing projects, or even deciding what tools are needed to get started. A strategy called *future thinking*, developed by Sarah Ward (2016), invites learners to visualize what the finished product will look like and what must be done to achieve the desired result. Digital interactive images with embedded hotspots that link to additional media, such as text, audio, or video, can help learners visualize what the end result could be and what steps are necessary to get there.

INCLUSIVE USES

Providing tools that facilitate future thinking support learners who are developing working memory and organizational skills.

SAMPLE TOOL

ThingLink is a website that allows users to create interactive images using embedded hotspots to visualize the desired outcome of a task or routine (**thinglink.com**).

EXTENSION OPPORTUNITY

Invite learners to create Thinglinks for younger learners who may struggle with learning new routines in the learning space. Link to a QR code so they are readily available across the learning space environment.

RELATED RESOURCES

ThingLink Tutorial (**bit.ly/inclusive365-308a**)

The Brilliance of Sarah Ward and Kristen Jacobsen (**bit.ly/inclusive365-308b**)

Strategies for Improving Executive Function Skills to Plan, Organize, and Problem Solve for School Success (**bit.ly/inclusive365-308c**)

Figure 308. Focus camera on the QR code to access image in ThingLink.

ISTE STANDARDS FOR STUDENTS
4a, 4b, 6a, 6b

ISTE STANDARDS FOR EDUCATORS
5a, 5c, 6b, 6d

Participating in Esports for Social Engagement

Esports invites learners to play video games competitively within the structure of leagues and tournaments. Like with traditional sports, esports involves a team of learners collaborating and communicating together to out-strategize and out-perform others. The games take skill and practice to improve and win. Learners think critically and problem solve how to master the game, while also experiencing the added bonus of having fun.

INCLUSIVE USES

Video gaming is a popular hobby enjoyed by millions of people around the world. Esports initiatives are naturally inclusive. Learners with cognitive, social-emotional, and communication challenges can participate in a competitive team experience centered around playing a video game. Learners with physical challenges can also participate through the use of adapted equipment, such as switches and controllers.

SAMPLE TOOLS

The High School Esports League provides learners with a structured system for participation in esports (**highschoolesportsleague.com**).

The Xbox Adaptive Controller is a commercially available controller with multiple programmable switch inputs (**bit.ly/inclusive365-309a**).

The Adaptive Switch Kit by Logitech is a commercially available kit that provides a variety of switches (**bit.ly/inclusive365-309b**).

EXTENSION OPPORTUNITY

An entire ecosystem of related experiences has blossomed around traditional sports, including audio commentary, analysis of statistics and tactics, merchandise creation and sales, marketing techniques, and food service preparation and concession. Invite learners

to participate in these same experiences for esports. Esports events and games are often streamed online for spectators to consume remotely. This provides an opportunity for learners to become commentators and analysts for the gaming experience. Teams can create names, design the logo, create team apparel and other merchandise, and market those products to family, friends, and the community. At live events, learners can sell food items to coaches, players, spectators, or any other attendees. Each activity provides an opportunity for learners to understand and practice critical life skills.

RELATED RESOURCES

What Is Esports and Why Is It a Big Deal? (**bit.ly/inclusive365-309c**)

Complete Guide to Esports Scholarships (**bit.ly/inclusive365-309d**)

University of California Irvine Inclusivity Plan (**bit.ly/inclusive365-309e**)

Figure 309. Learner participating in esports league play.

ISTE STANDARDS FOR STUDENTS

1a, 1c, 1d, 2a, 2b, 2d, 3b, 5b, 5c, 5d, 6a, 6c, 6d, 7a, 7b, 7c

ISTE STANDARDS FOR EDUCATORS

2a, 2b, 2c, 4b, 4c, 4d, 5a, 5b, 6a, 6b, 6c, 7a

Meditating to Manage Stress and Anxiety

Certain situations, circumstances, and events can cause anxiety in individuals, which may hinder or impede learning. Despite designing environments and experiences with flexibility in mind, impending tasks can cause stress. Looming and converging deadlines, pressure to not let down others in a learning group, and balancing academic learning time with other interests are just a few examples of what can contribute to anxiety. Meditation can be used to identify, manage, and cope with stress and anxiety. Learners can use meditation applications and reflect upon their use of different techniques and strategies meant to help improve one's own social-emotional wellness.

INCLUSIVE USES

Any learner feeling anxious or stressed may find it useful to explore applications that provide methodologies for regulating and managing anxiety through meditation. Improving social-emotional wellness improves one's own ability to focus on learning.

SAMPLE TOOL

Headspace for Educators has a number of guided meditations along with inspiring videos, quick workouts, group meditations, and more (**headspace.com/educators**).

EXTENSION OPPORTUNITY

Invite learners to provide feedback about how anxious they were before, during, or after a meditation session. This analysis could be a simple rating scale presented with visuals. The learner, the educator who designed the experience, and anyone else supporting the learner should reflect on the effectiveness of meditation.

RELATED RESOURCES

Happiness Apps: How Schools are Joining the Fight for Better Student Mental Health (**bit.ly/inclusive365-310a**)

Teachers Use Meditation Apps in Class to Rewire Kids' Brains, Improve Performance (**bit.ly/inclusive365-310b**)

Figure 310. Learner practicing self-help calming strategies.

ISTE STANDARDS FOR STUDENTS
1a, 1c, 4d

ISTE STANDARDS FOR EDUCATORS
3a, 4d, 5a, 5c, 6a

Building Community for Distance Learning with Familiar Rituals

Building community between learners and educators is critical no matter if you are working in in-person, distance, or hybrid environments. Consistency in familiar routines and rituals can help to establish a sense of community, especially when some learners are in different environments.

One familiar routine that translates well to a digital environment is daily morning announcements, including things like the Pledge of Allegiance, school news, and vocabulary word of the day. These can be hosted on a digital learning platform or a private Facebook page or YouTube channel and streamed live. Lunchtime social opportunities can also be transferred to a digital platform, with learners at home being able to videochat with each other. Virtual spirit weeks, with opportunities for learners and educators to dress up, or a Friday event where educators use virtual backgrounds featuring the school mascot or logo provide a way to share the spirit of a learning community.

INCLUSIVE USES

Having shared rituals that allow simultaneous participation, whether learners are in the building or at home, provides an inclusive experience. These rituals, including having learners participate in morning announcements, allow distance learners to be seen as valued members and leaders of the learning community.

SAMPLE TOOLS

YouTube allows live streaming from a private channel. This means events can be broadcast to only the community members who are signed up or who have access to the link. Live streams can then be recorded and made available for viewing at any time (**bit.ly/inclusive365-311a**).

Facebook also offers private live streaming that can be restricted to just registered members of the shared community (**bit.ly/inclusive365-311b**).

EXTENSION OPPORTUNITIES

Invite all learners and members of the learning community to engage in group events, such as virtual assemblies or pep rallies, virtual concerts, and virtual plays and performances.

Reach out to learners from other learning communities to build a larger network around a common interest or theme, and build rituals that go beyond a local setting.

RELATED RESOURCES

Creating a School Community (**bit.ly/inclusive365-311c**)

Prioritizing Human Connection When Social Distancing is the New Norm (**bit.ly/inclusive365-311d**)

Figure 311. Educator reading to learners using Facebook Live.

ISTE STANDARDS FOR STUDENTS
7a, 7b, 7c

ISTE STANDARDS FOR EDUCATORS
3a

STRATEGY 311

Identifying and Labeling Emotions

Social-emotional learning is defined by the Collaborative for Academic, Social, and Emotional Learning (CASEL) as the "process through which children and adults understand and manage emotions, set and achieve positive goals, feel and show empathy for others, establish and maintain positive relationships, and make responsible decisions." (1994). Individuals can learn to identify and label their emotions as a part of understanding and managing them. Digital and no-tech tools can support learners in developing the vocabulary to name the emotions that they experience.

INCLUSIVE USES

Learners with emerging vocabulary skills benefit from direct instruction in learning how to label and define their emotions and the emotions of others.

Individuals working to improve their social-emotional skills can practice describing how they are feeling so that they can develop strategies to channel their emotions and self-regulate.

SAMPLE TOOLS

Mood Meter uses colored quadrants to help learners identify their mood based on their energy level, and then helps them narrow down a more specific feeling within each of four quadrants. It provides learners specific vocabulary to identify their feelings, a target for how they want to feel, and ideas for how they can shift to a more productive or preferred way of feeling. The app tracks self-identified emotions over time and also provides guides and videos to support learners who want to shift to a different emotion (**bit.ly/inclusive365-312a**).

The Guess the Feeling Game from PBS Kids is a tool for younger children that associates feelings with favorite cartoon characters from the Daniel Tiger television show (**bit.ly/inclusive365-312b**).

EXTENSION OPPORTUNITY

Invite learners to identify words that describe their emotions very specifically, beyond the more general mad, sad, scared, happy, and calm. They can use the Mood Meter to discover words and then use a dictionary tool to define unfamiliar words.

RELATED RESOURCES

CASEL (**bit.ly/inclusive365-312c**)

School Resources for Navigating Challenging Times (**bit.ly/inclusive365-312d**)

Center on the Social and Emotional Foundations for Early Learning (**bit.ly/inclusive365-312e**)

Teaching Emotional Intelligence in Early Childhood (**bit.ly/inclusive365-312f**)

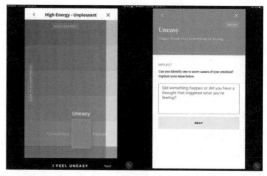

Figure 312. Emotion and definition of the emotion in the Mood Meter app.

ISTE STANDARDS FOR STUDENTS
1a, 1b, 1c

ISTE STANDARDS FOR EDUCATORS
3a, 5a

Partnering Learners with Study Buddies and Accountability Partners

Whether in physical spaces, hybrid situations, or in distance learning settings, learners can build connections with others and develop cooperative and collaborative skills. Pairing learners on a rotating basis with study buddies (great for elementary-aged learners) or accountability partners (for secondary learners) is one way to develop these relationships over time. Learners can be paired with a specific peer for a week at a time and rotated through the peers multiple times across the year. Learners would meet with their study buddy/accountability partner when there are opportunities for paired collaborative work, as thought partners, to provide feedback, and to check on progress toward work. In a physical learning space, study buddies might be paired when there is time to turn and talk, while in a virtual environment there could be opportunities to connect via breakout rooms, in collaborative documents, or in private chats. By rotating through peers throughout the year, learners have the opportunity to get to know a variety of peers that they may have otherwise not gotten to know. There should also always be opportunities for learners to collaborate and work with self-selected peers and in larger groups.

INCLUSIVE USES

Ongoing rotations of peer pairings allows learners who might not have a large social circle the opportunity to develop new relationships with others whom they might not get to work with otherwise. Peer pairings that last over an extended period of time, rather than just one instance, allow learners to get to know each other in more than simply a passing way.

SAMPLE TOOL

NowComment provides web-based commenting and collaboration on all types of files, including MS Office documents, PDFs, and HTML web content. It allows learners to connect with one or more peers for conversation (**nowcomment.com**).

EXTENSION OPPORTUNITY

Invite learners to devise their own ways of creating different pairings throughout the school year.

RELATED RESOURCE

Best Student Collaboration Tools (**bit.ly/inclusive365-313a**)

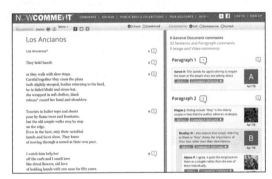

Figure 313. Interaction between various learners in NowComment.

ISTE STANDARDS FOR STUDENTS

7a, 7b, 7c

ISTE STANDARDS FOR EDUCATORS

2b, 3a, 4c, 5a, 6a

STRATEGY 313

Developing a Digital Transition Toolkit for Independence

When learners begin to plan for the next stages of their lives it is useful to catalog currently used tools and plan for tools that might be helpful for success in the next environment—college, work, or community living. Knowing what tools are useful to complete tasks and what tools might be needed for future tasks helps learners prepare for the challenges that await them in the new environments. Listing the tools used to complete current tasks, reflecting on their effectiveness, and brainstorming tools that might be needed to complete anticipated tasks prepares learners for the upcoming transition.

INCLUSIVE USES

Transition plans highlight strategies and tools that learners use to increase independence. A transition toolkit can be created to promote self-advocacy and can act as a centralized repository to keep important information related to the impending transition. After the transition has occurred, the learner can use the toolkit as a reference for self-advocacy by asking for access to specific functions of tools as accommodations in the next environments.

SAMPLE TOOL

Google Forms and Microsoft Forms can be used as a resource to document information a learner might need to independently transition to a next phase after the K–12 experience has ended (**bit.ly/inclusive365-314a**).

EXTENSION OPPORTUNITY

Invite learners to document tools they use to perform tasks successfully. Focus on the tasks and the tool features that support the successful completion of those tasks. Attach pictures, web links, and other artifacts that will assist with demonstrating task completion.

RELATED RESOURCE

IEP Transition Plans: What to Know (**bit.ly/inclusive365-314b**)

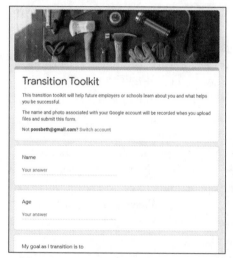

Figure 314. A Google Form for a learner to fill out documenting supports needed for transition.

ISTE STANDARDS FOR STUDENTS
2a, 2d, 3c, 6d, 7a

ISTE STANDARDS FOR EDUCATORS
3c, 3d, 6a

Promoting Independence with Audio Support

Have you ever gone on an audio tour of a museum? Just remember how helpful that was and how much more information you were able to gather with that audio support. To increase independence, learners may require additional information about the environment. Whether it is the need to read a sign, better understand the scene in front of them, or even to help with managing money—digital tools can provide this support via audio cues. A simple audio cue may be all that is necessary for a learner to effectively, independently traverse a situation.

INCLUSIVE USES

Using digital tools that provide audio cues for learners can be the difference between independently navigating a situation or not. Audio cues can provide that dual sensory experience (audio combined with the visual) that can benefit all.

SAMPLE TOOLS

SeeingAI is a free iOS app designed by Microsoft that uses the camera of a mobile device to identify items in the environment, such as people, the scene, and documents, and provides an audio description. While marketed as a tool for people who are blind or visually impaired, this tool could support a broader range of learners who could benefit from hearing audio cues about environmental items (**bit.ly/inclusive365-315a**).

Envision AI is an iOS and Android app that uses the camera of a mobile device to identify items in the environment and provides audio description support to increase independence. This app has a free trial and then requires a monthly subscription to continue to use the features (**bit.ly/inclusive365-315b**).

EXTENSION OPPORTUNITY

Encourage learners to use the SeeingAI app as they move through their environment (school, home, out in the community). Use the feature to hear a description of the scene. Did this level of support help them independently access this environment? Did they need something spoken aloud that they missed by visually scanning the environment?

RELATED RESOURCES

Navigating Systems for the Blind and Visually Impaired (**bit.ly/inclusive365-315c**)

Envision AI for iOS and Android (**bit.ly/inclusive365-315d**)

Seeing AI—Making the Visual World More Accessible (**bit.ly/inclusive365-315e**)

Figure 315. Auditory description (with text) of a scene using Seeing AI.

ISTE STANDARDS FOR STUDENTS
1b, 3d, 7b

ISTE STANDARDS FOR EDUCATORS
4b, 5a, 6a

Building Empathy through Perspective-Taking

Seeing a situation from another person's point of view is an important lifelong skill. It helps develop kindness, empathy, and successful collaboration. Promoting the development of perspective-taking leads to reduced conflict in learning communities and stretches into work and life. Facilitating authentic experiences where learners practice discussing, engaging, and/or experiencing how others would approach a situation helps to build character, centered around kindness and goodwill. Sample experiences include:

- Create a visual story showing a possible conflict situation. Place pictures of actual people or avatars in the scenes and give them empty thought or speech bubbles. Invite learners to generate responses about what could be said by each party in the story. Learners could handwrite, type, or record audio responses in the bubbles, based on their preference.

- Use short videos of real-life scenarios that show conflict. Pause the video and ask viewers about what to say or how to respond in the situation or use an online tool to create pauses and question prompts.

- Invite learners to create a bank of possible responses that they could reference while participating in the activities or use when in real-life situations.

INCLUSIVE USES

Learners who are building their social-pragmatic skills, including those with language delays, may find practicing how to see a situation from someone else's point of view particularly beneficial.

SAMPLE TOOLS

Book Creator is an online creation tool with thought and speech bubble options. Add photos, images, or clip art to work on perspective-taking scenarios (**bookcreator.com**).

EdPuzzle is an online video tool that allows content creators to add automatic pauses with question prompts at strategic points throughout the video (**edpuzzle.com**).

EXTENSION OPPORTUNITIES

Create a collective artifact of all picture and video stories that learners can review independently or with a peer, educator, or family member. Invite learners to review it repeatedly and add additional scenarios as they experience or anticipate them. Invite learners to reflect on the artifact, visualizing their responses from when they were in actual situations.

Invite learners to create their own situations and experiences and share them with other learners.

RELATED RESOURCE

Perspective-Taking (**bit.ly/inclusive365-316a**)

Figure 316. Sample page using thought bubbles in Book Creator. A prompt by an educator might be, "What do you think this person is thinking?"

ISTE STANDARDS FOR STUDENTS
1b, 1c, 6b, 6c

ISTE STANDARDS FOR EDUCATORS
3a, 5a, 5b, 5c, 6a

Setting Goals with Vision Boards

Goal-setting is an important means of motivating learners to consider what they want to accomplish over a period of time, and the steps they need to take to reach their goals. A vision board is a collection or collage of images, quotes, and other inspirational visuals that help an individual consider and visualize their goals. The elements of a vision board help inspire and remind a learner of their goals and what they can do to achieve them. The goals reflected on a vision board should be SMART goals. When learners create their vision board digitally, they can access it anywhere to check-in, refine the content, or update the board with their progress. Digital vision boards can be linked in a learner's digital portfolio for both educators and learners to access to reflect on progress.

INCLUSIVE USES

Using visuals is an evidence-based practice that supports many diverse learners. Having a visually-based resource that a learner has created themselves increases motivation and relevance for that learner. Visuals can help a learner more clearly see and focus on a goal.

SAMPLE TOOLS

Pinterest allows learners to curate a variety of images from the internet and have them displayed together on a single page (**pinterest.com**).

Padlet allows learners to add links, images, text, and more to their board (**padlet.com**).

Glogster EDU allows learners to make a digital poster that can include images, video, text, and more (**edu.glogster.com**).

Google Slides can be used to create and keep vision boards for a whole group or for multiple goals for a single learner (**google.com/slides**).

EXTENSION OPPORTUNITY

Invite learners to share their vision board with one or more peers to review their goals and to promote accountability in achieving the goals. Schedule periodic check-ins throughout the time frame for the goals, where peers discuss the progress that they have made and update their vision boards to reflect these discussions.

RELATED RESOURCE

Setting SMART Goals (**bit.ly/inclusive365-317a**)

Figure 317. Vision board created in Google Slides.

ISTE STANDARDS FOR STUDENTS
1a, 6b, 6c, 6d

ISTE STANDARDS FOR EDUCATORS
2b, 5a, 5b, 5c, 6a, 6b

Communicating Remotely with Parents and Caregivers

Fostering open lines of communication between parents and educators is essential to building successful relationships and promoting parent engagement. Phone calls are challenging for educators to make during the day, and calling or texting after hours from a personal phone jeopardizes educator privacy. There are numerous digital tools that allow parents and educators to communicate conveniently and securely about learner progress, important news from home, special events, or just day-to-day updates. These tools also allow for messages to be sent to an entire group of learners or for messages just to select parents.

INCLUSIVE USES

Many digital communication tools have built-in translation available, making communication easier for families and educators who do not speak the same language.

Tools that provide messages in text form allow parents with disabilities to access the content using the functions of their personal technology, such as text-to-speech.

SAMPLE TOOLS

Seesaw is a multifeatured tool that includes communication features, including the ability to translate text into fifty-five different languages (**app.seesaw.me**).

Class Dojo is a multifaceted tool that includes the ability to translate messages automatically into a family's preferred language, to indicate times that the educator is not available, and to send photos, videos, and much more (**classdojo.com**).

Remind provides two-way messaging without having to reveal the educator's personal phone number (**remind.com**).

EXTENSION OPPORTUNITIES

Sharing photos or videos of learners engaged in learning experiences can foster positive relationships. Encourage families to share photos and videos of their children engaged in learning in the community or in distance-learning experiences.

Invite parents and learners to use the record of communication to reflect on progress, demonstrate growth, and illustrate skill acquisition.

RELATED RESOURCES

Power Up Your Parent-Teacher Communication (**bit.ly/inclusive365-318a**)

Teacher-Parent Communication Centered on Learning in Seesaw (**bit.ly/inclusive365-318b**)

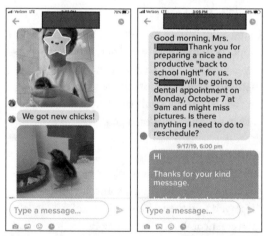

Figures 318a and 318b. Parent-educator communication from Class Dojo.

ISTE STANDARDS FOR STUDENTS
2a, 6a, 6d

ISTE STANDARDS FOR EDUCATORS
4d

Implementing Equitable Calling Strategies

In a hectic learning space, it can be challenging to ensure that all learners are provided with the same opportunity to be called on during activities. At times, educators may single out certain learners due to an unconscious bias or only call on learners who raise their hands. A common low-tech method for random calling is the use of popsicle sticks labelled with learners' names pulled out of a can. The use of digital randomizers is an instructional and equity strategy that ensures that no learners are overlooked.

INCLUSIVE USES

Consistent use of an equitable calling strategy helps establish norms for participation and encourages learner engagement. The use of this strategy keeps learners mentally alert and ready to contribute. When used routinely, the practice promotes a culture of participation. One caveat is that some learners have a great deal of anxiety around being called on to answer, so educators should have a consistent means for any learner to opt out of answering. Being able to say "pass" or "May I ask a friend?" make for best practice in implementing equitable calling strategies for all learners.

Some learners need time to process a question and find random selection stressful. For these learners, do not input their names. Instead, give them advance warning to prepare them for being called on. Every learner has something to contribute. Offer scaffolded supports to those who need the support.

Consider using random-selection tools only for non-stressful tasks, such as choosing a fun event, feeding the pet who lives in the learning space, or helping to pass out or collect supplies.

SAMPLE TOOLS

Classroom Tools' Random Name Picker can help ensure equitable selection techniques (**bit.ly/inclusive365-319a**).

Classroomscreen offers a random name function to ensure equitable name-calling (**bit.ly/inclusive365-319b**).

Wheel of Names is a random name generator. It is possible to add images in addition to text (**bit.ly/inclusive365-319c**).

EXTENSION OPPORTUNITIES

Use a random generator marked only with colors in order to group learners. Allow learners to spin the wheel and group them based on the color that they get.

Invite learners to use the random name generator for other purposes, such as choosing what task to complete next, answering yes/no/maybe questions, or picking what book to read during a group read-aloud.

RELATED RESOURCE

University Study Finds Random Student Selection Keeps Students Engaged (**bit.ly/inclusive365-319d**)

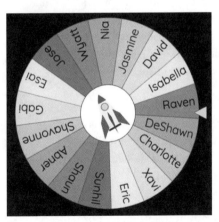

Figure 319. Wheel of Names randomizer.

ISTE STANDARDS FOR STUDENTS

1a, 4d

ISTE STANDARDS FOR EDUCATORS

4d, 5a, 5c

Accessing Esports Initiatives and Unified Gaming Programs Using Universal Controllers

School video gaming clubs and eSports initiatives provide a naturally inclusive environment where learners can practice skills related to collaboration, communication, and critical thinking. Participation in video gaming and esports provides nonthreatening, low-stress, highly enjoyable, and motivating learning opportunities. Gaming and esports also provides an opportunity to practice social-emotional regulation by sharing fun experiences with peers in a common area of interest. Provision of a universal controller provides an opportunity for learners who could not otherwise access a traditional handheld controller to participate in the gaming experience.

INCLUSIVE USES

Teams participating in esports initiatives could be made up of individuals with or without disabilities. Learners working on social skills can participate in a gaming experience, which provides an opportunity to practice learned skills. Learners with physical disabilities can use universal controllers to take part in a fun experience while being an equal contributor to team dynamics and success.

SAMPLE TOOLS

The Xbox Adaptive Controller is a commercially available controller with multiple programmable switch inputs (**bit.ly/inclusive365-320a**).

The Adaptive Switch Kit by Logitech is a commercially available kit that provides a variety of switches (**bit.ly/inclusive365-320b**).

EXTENSION OPPORTUNITY

Learners participating in makerspaces could be challenged with the authentic experience of creating a controller for a peer who has unique access requirements. With support from related service staff, such as physical and occupational therapists, learners could analyze potential access methods for an individual, design prototype controllers, test those controllers, and then make refinements, all in an effort to help a peer or other learner participate in the experience of gaming.

RELATED RESOURCES

Xbox Adaptive Controller Review (**bit.ly/inclusive365-320c**)

PlayVS is an organization that supports the set up of an esports program (**bit.ly/inclusive365-320d**).

Ablegamers.org (**bit.ly/inclusive365-320e**)

Figure 320. Learner waiting to use the Xbox Adaptive Controller as Bill Binko from AT Makers finishes connecting it to an Xbox.

ISTE STANDARDS FOR STUDENTS
1b, 1c, 1d, 5a, 5b, 5c, 5d, 7a

ISTE STANDARDS FOR EDUCATORS
2b, 3a, 5a, 5c, 6b, 6d, 7a

Breathing Techniques for Emotional Regulation

Deep breathing is an evidence-based mindfulness technique to support learners in regulating their emotions and reducing stress (Ma, X., et al, 2017). Educators can encourage short breathing exercises and also teach learners how and when to use these techniques independently when needed.

INCLUSIVE USES

Those working to manage their social-emotional and self-regulation skills might benefit from explicitly being taught strategies they can use quickly and easily to help them de-escalate, relax, and focus.

SAMPLE TOOLS

The Breathe app is preloaded on the Apple Watch and it guides the user through regular breathing exercises. It can be set to automatically prompt the user to engage in a breathing exercise (**bit.ly/inclusive365-321a**).

Breathing Zone is available on Google Play and iOS and provides guided breathing exercises (**bit.ly/inclusive365-321b**).

MyLife is an iOS app that takes learners through a series of breathing exercises based on specific scenarios (**my.life**).

EXTENSION OPPORTUNITIES

Invite learners to engage in breathing exercise breaks before and after high stress experiences, such as tests. Breathing exercises might also be helpful after recess or physical education experiences when learners may still have excess energy and need to get their bodies focused for a task that involves less physical exertion.

Educators might find engaging in breathing exercises a good way to relieve stress and anxiety. Mindful breathing exercises work for people of all ages!

RELATED RESOURCES

Evidence-Based Practices in Teaching Self-Calming to Special Needs Children (**bit.ly/inclusive365-321d**)

The MyLife website has free premium activities for educators (**my.life/mylife-for-schools/educators**).

Figure 321. The Breathing Zone app—match your breathing as the flower grows and shrinks.

ISTE STANDARDS FOR STUDENTS
1a, 1b, 1c

ISTE STANDARDS FOR EDUCATORS
2b, 5a, 6a

STRATEGY 322

Supporting Collectivist Learning Online

Culturally responsive learning pedagogy includes supporting collectivist learning, as many cultures are collectivist in nature. Collectivism, as defined by Zaretta Hammond, author of the book *Culturally Responsive Teaching and the Brain*, is when a culture has "a focus on group interdependence, harmony, and collaborative work" (2015). While the U.S. has, in general, more of an individualism approach to education, with an emphasis on the individual learner working hard to make progress and to become independent, many learners come from collectivist cultures, including most Latin and South American and African nations.

Distance learning, with learners at home and not physically working together, tends to be more individualistic. However, there are ways to support collectivist learning using the features of distance learning platforms. One such way is to encourage the use of the chat by learners during educator-led experiences, in order to support each other by answering questions. Another is to invite learners to add collaborative annotations to text or math problems using whiteboard tools or note-taking applications to support each other in solving a problem or contributing to a group project.

INCLUSIVE USES

Emphasizing collectivist online instructional practices and learner participation includes everyone in both the in-person and distance learning experience while building relationships. When emphasizing collaboration, it is less about the accuracy of answers and more about how learners support each other in building understanding. Learners who are working to hone social skills and pragmatic language skills may find collective/collaborative experiences particularly useful.

SAMPLE TOOLS

Jamboard is a collaborative learning tool that allows learners to annotate together (**jamboard.google.com**).

Google Keep allows learners to share collaborative notes (**keep.google.com**).

Whiteboard.Chat is a multi-device whiteboard space where learners can chat, draw, and colloborate (**whiteboard.chat**).

EXTENSION OPPORTUNITY

Invite learners to create rotating peer groups on a weekly basis and ask group members to use chat messages to encourage and support each other during distance learning sessions.

RELATED RESOURCES

Making CRT Manageable (**bit.ly/inclusive365-322a**)

Online Teaching Can Be Culturally Responsive (**bit.ly/inclusive365-322b**)

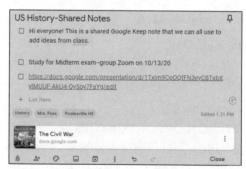

Figure 322. Collaborative note in Google Keep.

ISTE STANDARDS FOR STUDENTS
7a, 7b, 7c

ISTE STANDARDS FOR EDUCATORS
4c, 4d

Expecting Diverse Representation When Selecting Technology

Recognizing biases against underrepresented populations is imperative when choosing tools and resources to use in educational settings. Some questions to consider include:

- Do text-to-speech tools offer multiple dialects, including African American Vernacular and Latinx?

- Do images within tools include culturally diverse options for skin tones, facial features, and hairstyles? Are varied body types and genders portrayed?

- Do the examples within the resources show diverse family dynamics and cultural groups without stereotypes or tokenism?

- Are tools that rely on AI responsive to dialects and articulation differences?

INCLUSIVE USES

Provide learners flexibility in choosing voices and images that represent themselves. Avoid stereotyping gender portrayal, particularly in terms of pitch of voice, hairstyles, or clothing choices. Consider using the inclusive singular pronouns *they*, *their*, and *them*. Ask for and respect preferred pronoun use.

If you are using speech-to-text and AI voice-recognition applications, be aware that learners with accents, dialects, and what are considered to be nonstandard pronunciation may have more difficulty. Expect and provide additional time for the technology to learn to adapt to these vocal variances.

SAMPLE TOOLS

LessonPix has images that reflect a range of skin tones, facial features, and hairstyles, as well as options for religious dress. Images also show individuals with a range of disabilities and assistive devices (**lessonpix.com**).

Storyboard That (**storyboardthat.com**) and PixtonEdu (**edu.pixton.com/educators**) are comic generators that offer a range of characters with many skin tone and hair options.

Acapella Voices, available on Voice Dream Reader and other text-to-speech tools, includes Micah, a southern Black-sounding voice; Deepa, an Indian-accented English voice; and Nizer, a British English-accented voice, and others (**acapela-group.com/voices/repertoire**).

EXTENSION OPPORTUNITY

Invite learners to listen to a variety of voices available within their text-to-speech tools or voice output device, then select and change the voice they prefer depending on the context.

RELATED RESOURCES

Stanford Researchers Find that Automated Speech Recognition Is More Likely to Misinterpret Black Speakers (**bit.ly/inclusive365-323a**)

African American Language Facts (**bit.ly/inclusive365-323b**)

Figure 323. LessonPix character.

ISTE STANDARDS FOR STUDENTS
1b, 7a, 7b, 7d

ISTE STANDARDS FOR EDUCATORS
2b, 4d

STRATEGY 324

Crafting a Resume Using a Template

As learners prepare to transition to life beyond high school, they often develop a resume to highlight their skills and expertise. Learning to create a resume is an important life skill that will serve the learner throughout their professional life. Working on a resume is an authentic and motivating reason for learners to engage in reading and writing experiences. Using a digital resume template can help ensure a professional looking, well-crafted resume.

INCLUSIVE USES

Learners seeking employment may need to create a quality resume. A high quality resume affords individuals an opportunity to not only show a potential employer what makes them a good fit for a job, but it also gives them an opportunity to showcase their writing and design skills. Learners working on vocational skills and those developing their reading and writing abilities may find the use of a template to complete the resume helpful.

SAMPLE TOOL

MyPerfectResume is a free resume builder that provides a simple three-step roadmap to a winning resume by selecting a template, adding in a personalized list of skills and abilities, and downloading the final copy (**myperfectresume.com**).

EXTENSION OPPORTUNITY

Encourage learners to explore different careers to determine an area they would be interested in pursuing. With that information in hand, learners could begin the process of building a resume by brainstorming ideas for skills and abilities they would like to highlight. Use speech-to-text to dictate ideas into a word processing document. Then work to group ideas into common themes. Once they add

the information into the resume builder, set up mock interviews where each learner has the opportunity to be both the employer and the job seeker. This provides learners with a real-world taste of the interview process and gives them experience with answering questions about their value to an employer.

RELATED RESOURCES

How to Write a Resume: The Complete Guide (**bit.ly/inclusive365-324a**)

Sample High School Resumes and Cover Letters (**bit.ly/inclusive365-324b**)

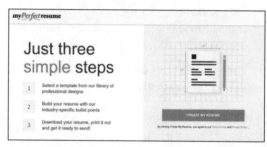

Figure 324. MyPerfectResume website.

ISTE STANDARDS FOR STUDENTS
2a, 2d, 3c, 6d, 7a

ISTE STANDARDS FOR EDUCATORS
6a

Targeting Social-Emotional Learning With Role-Playing Games

Role-playing is a strategy used by educators to help learners develop problem-solving skills in a wide range of situations. However, some learners may be hesitant to engage in role-play, feeling embarrassed, shy, or awkward. Changing the role-playing into a game where learners take on the persona of someone else, such as a character in a fantasy setting, can diminish the anxiety produced for some learners and provide an opportunity to participate in a role-playing experience in a playful and engaging way.

INCLUSIVE USES

Role-playing also provides an opportunity for learners to practice communication and problem-solving skills in a game setting. As the game master, educators promote collaboration, critical thinking, and cooperation by presenting learners with challenges within the context of a game. All learners can work together in these games to solve the puzzles or overcome the obstacles put in place by the game master.

Gaming scenarios can be designed for the individual or the role-playing party based on individual goals and personalized learning needs. For example, a learner who is working to develop their following directions skills with a multistep puzzle to get through a maze. Assign a learner working on sharing tools with an in-game challenge that can only be overcome by giving resources to another player.

SAMPLE TOOL

Dungeons and Dragons is a classic role-playing game that has a number of accessible tools that allow players of all ages to begin playing (**bit.ly/inclusive365-325a**).

EXTENSION OPPORTUNITIES

Invite learners to participate in a club where they run their own games.

Create an inclusive role-playing experience (**bit.ly/inclusive365-325b**).

Invite learners to create a website to journal about the adventures, reflect on their learning, and to share artwork and other inspirations from the experience of playing.

RELATED RESOURCES

Game to Grow, a Website on Using Role-Playing Games to Help Facilitate Learning (**bit.ly/inclusive365-325c**)

Teaching with D&D, A Website on Using Dungeons and Dragons to Teach Concepts to Learners (**bit.ly/inclusive365-325d**)

Using Dungeons and Dragons to Engage All Students (**bit.ly/inclusive365-325e**)

Figure 325. Learners playing Dungeons and Dragons.

ISTE STANDARDS FOR STUDENTS
1b, 3a, 3c, 4d, 5c, 6b, 6c, 7c

ISTE STANDARDS FOR EDUCATORS
3a, 4a, 4d, 5a, 5c, 6a, 6b, 6d

Fidgeting for Self-Regulation

Fidgeting can serve as a form of self-soothing for many learners. Actually, if you think about it, everyone fidgets—hair twirlers, pencil tappers, and doodlers are all fidgeting! Fidgeting can be supported in many ways, such as giving learners items that spin, that can be squished, and that can be manipulated in hand. Digital fidgeting apps respond to touch with changes in movement, light, color, and sound. Doodling and sketchnoting, both on paper and digitally, are also ways that learners can fidget while still being engaged in academic tasks.

INCLUSIVE USES

Educators often express concern that when learners fidget, they are a distraction to other learners in a shared space, particularly when using the popular fidget spinner or apps that have sounds or are visually of high interest. Fidgeting is possible in multiple ways while learners complete tasks, including as a nondistracting, in-hand tool that learners don't need to see as they use it. Learners can also use tools that support fidgeting when they feel anxious or frustrated and to calm or soothe themselves in a break from a challenging task or situation.

SAMPLE TOOLS

Gravitarium is an iOS app that allows learners to make designs with movements of their fingers (**bit.ly/inclusive365-326a**).

Paint Splash is an Android app for drawing with your finger and then shaking and rotating the device to create splatter art designs (**bit.ly/inclusive365-326b**).

Virtual Fidget Spinner is a web based version of the physical object that provides similiar feedback to the learner. Simply click with the cursor to activate the spinner (**bit.ly/inclusive365-326c**).

EXTENSION OPPORTUNITIES

Invite learners to doodle while listening to audio content, like a podcast. Learners might draw images either on paper or digitally using a drawing application.

Invite learners to build their own virtual fidget spinners using a coding program, like these examples made by using Scratch (**bit.ly/inclusive365-326d**).

Invite learners to build a low-tech fidget, such as adding clay to a balloon to manipulate in their hand, or adding a wing nut and bolt to a pencil top to spin around.

RELATED RESOURCE

The Body-Brain Connection: How Fidgeting Sharpens Focus (**additudemag.com/focus-factors**)

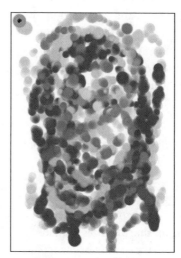

Figure 326. Paint Splash app.

ISTE STANDARDS FOR STUDENTS
1c, 6a

ISTE STANDARDS FOR EDUCATORS
2b, 3b, 4b, 5a, 6a

Interpreting Emotions through Facial Expressions of Digital Avatars

Communication is more than just speaking. Facial expressions convey emotions, too. It takes practice to learn how to interpret facial expressions and how others might interpret your facial expressions. Learning how to read and react to other's facial expressions and to match your own facial expressions to feelings are skills necessary to form healthy, meaningful relationships. Proficiency in understanding nonverbal cues can make the difference between a fruitful and a frustrating experience when collaborating with others. Digital avatar generators allow learners to make digital representations of themselves or others. Creating an avatar provides practice making and interpreting facial expressions by matching the avatar's expression to a corresponding emotion.

INCLUSIVE USES

Learners working on social-pragmatic goals may find creating digital avatars and matching them to different facial expressions a way to work on recognizing emotions.

SAMPLE TOOLS

Bellus3D is a mobile app that allows users to create a three-dimensional version of their face. Users can take multiple images using different expressions matched to emotions (**bellus3d.com**).

Storyboard That is a cartoon generator that provides users with an opportunity to create characters with different expressions (**storyboardthat.com**).

EXTENSION OPPORTUNITIES

Invite learners to create a multimedia slideshow, video, or other form of expression where they create images of themselves making different facial expressions. Pair these pictures with the text labeling the emotion or with an image of something that causes that emotion, such as being sad when ice cream drops off the top of a cone or happy when someone sees a friend.

Invite learners to use a digital avatar to create the facial expression of a character in a video or piece of literature reacting to a particular event in the story.

RELATED RESOURCE

The Powerful Use of Avatars in Social-Emotional Learning (**bit.ly/inclusive365-327a**)

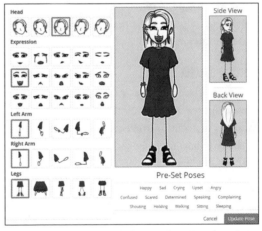

Figure 327. Creating a digital avatar using Storyboard That.

ISTE STANDARDS FOR STUDENTS
2b, 3d, 5c, 6a, 6c, 6d, 7a, 7b, 7c

ISTE STANDARDS FOR EDUCATORS
2b, 3a, 4c, 4d, 5a, 5b, 6d, 7a

Taking Brain Breaks Using Hydration and Movement Timers

It can be easy to get lost in the flow of working on a project. Hours of primarily sedentary tasks can take place in front of a digital screen when one is focused on completing the tasks. People can feel an addicting sense of accomplishment, coming out of the zone after they have worked for a number of hours straight. In the short term, this can look and feel very productive. Over time, however, a lifestyle of minimal movement can have long-term health risks and have an overall negative impact on productivity. Learning to schedule frequent breaks to move and drink water helps both the body and brain stay strong and sharp. Setting and responding to a timer as a reminder to get up, walk around, stretch, and refill their water bottle can help a person maintain both physical and mental health and well-being.

INCLUSIVE USES

Taking a break to move and hydrate is important for any learner to help regulate, manage, and maintain healthy work practices in order to sustain long-term social, emotional, and physical health.

SAMPLE TOOLS

The Google browser provides both timer and stopwatch functions. Just enter the word timer into the search window at Google.com and both will appear at the top of the search results.

OnlineClock offers free, web-based timers in a variety of different styles and visualizations (**bit.ly/inclusive365-328a**).

A search for "timers" in YouTube results in numerous videos featuring countdown timers (**bit.ly/inclusive365-328b**).

EXTENSION OPPORTUNITIES

Invite learners to reflect on the time periods they'd like to set their timer for. Some learners might find it useful to set a timer to go off at variable intervals, such as every 17, 22, or 36 minutes. These irregular times can help make setting the timer more interesting and individualized. Educators can then inquire with learners about how and why they made their choices.

Depending on the sensory needs of the learner, a timer might need to provide a visual, auditory, or tactile indicator when it reaches zero. The timer might flash to the front of the screen, provide a buzzing noise, or vibrate when touching a part of the body, like on a watch or bracelet.

RELATED RESOURCE

StandUpKids provides learners with experiences related to movement and physical exercise, and promotes the idea of standing up while working (**standupkids.org**).

Figure 328. Setting timer in Google browser to five minutes.

ISTE STANDARDS FOR STUDENTS
1a, 1c

ISTE STANDARDS FOR EDUCATORS
3c, 5a, 6a

Building Community for Distance or Hybrid Learning with Games

Games are fun, encourage teamwork, and provide the opportunity to connect secondary and post-secondary learners and even adults through play. Use of games in education has a basis in research as an evidence-based practice for improving outcomes, whether through gamification of the learning process or simply as a means of engaging learners. Use of digital games can provide a means of bringing people who may be separated by distance learning, together as a community.

INCLUSIVE USES

Digital games that provide accessibility through text-to-speech, narration, and accessible dice or spinners remove barriers to learners.

SAMPLE TOOLS

Kahoot allows educators to create games that can be played live or presented as a learner-paced game. In live games, via distance learning platforms, learners connect with each other at home and can play on teams in real time. Learners can play self-paced "kahoots" anytime and anywhere on their own devices. Learners can also play in single-player mode for practice with a topic or skill (**kahoot.com**).

Quizizz offers gamified single-player practice, group games available across screens on different devices, and live polls. Additionally, it integrates with Google Classroom (**quizizz.com**).

LessonPix allows educators to create custom board games and bingo games, and with the PowerPoint add-in, offers built-in custom spinners, dice, and the ability to draw from a hat. With remote cursor access, learners can manipulate their own game pieces, spin, and throw dice (**lessonpix.com**).

EXTENSION OPPORTUNITY

Invite learners to create their own games as a check for understanding or as the conclusion of a project.

RELATED RESOURCES

Creating a School Community (**bit.ly/inclusive365-329a**)

10 Important Research Findings on Games in Education (**bit.ly/inclusive365-329b**)

Teacher Hosts Virtual Kahoot! Family Fridays to Maintain a Feeling of Community (**bit.ly/inclusive365-329c**)

Targeting Social-Emotional Learning with Role-Playing Games (**bit.ly/inclusive365-329d**)

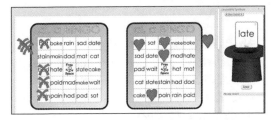

Figure 329a. Digital bingo game in LessonPix.

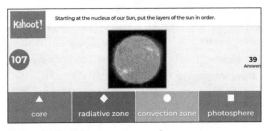

Figure 329b. Kahoot game example.

ISTE STANDARDS FOR STUDENTS
7a, 7b, 7c

ISTE STANDARDS FOR EDUCATORS
3a

STRATEGY 330

Reflecting on Emotions Using Augmented Reality

Providing a visual representation of an emotion can be an effective way for learners to understand their feelings. Visuals in the form of three-dimensional animated characters that move and interact using augmented reality not only provide an engaging experience but also provide learners with multiple modalities to learn about emotions. Learners can use the visuals to reflect on their own emotions, relating their own feelings to those of the characters.

INCLUSIVE USES

Learners who are experiencing a moment of intense emotion may find other skills impacted, like communication or judgement. Individuals learning about emotions and how to communicate their feelings to others may find manipulating animated 3D characters fun and effective during intense moments.

SAMPLE TOOL

Moment AR is an augmented reality application that works with the Merge Cube and represents emotions as 3D characters (**bit.ly/inclusive365-330a**).

EXTENSION OPPORTUNITIES

Invite learners to scan the different sides of a Merge Cube and enlarge them. Once printed, the Moment AR app can be used to create a larger version of the characters in the app. Learners can then interact with these larger characters to learn about emotions.

Invite learners to explore the different characters and talk about which character they related with in the given moment. Learners can then learn to express their emotions without necessarily speaking aloud.

RELATED RESOURCES

Moment AR: Full Demo
(**bit.ly/inclusive365-330b**)

Talking With Tech Episode #13: Kevin Chaja—Using Augmented Reality to Teach Social Skills
(**bit.ly/inclusive365-330c**)

Figure 330a. Moment AR app as displayed on a Merge Cube.

Figure 330b. Animation of a character representing the emotion of happy.

Figure 330c. One of the animations of a character representing the emotion of angry.

ISTE STANDARDS FOR STUDENTS
1c, 6a, 6c, 7a

ISTE STANDARDS FOR EDUCATORS
2b, 3a, 4c, 6b, 6d, 7a

Managing Stress and Anxiety with Exercise Videos

Physical exercise has been shown to reduce anxiety and stress (The Mayo Clinic, 2020). Kinesthetic experiences are proven to help stimulate brain activity and facilitate learning. Using videos to guide whole-group physical exercises enhances learning while reducing stress. Dancing and making silly movements while following the lead of likable characters in a video is fun! Participation in a kinesthetic experience immediately prior to an experience that requires sedentary movements only or one that is considered highly stressful to a learner can be particularly helpful. When movement cannot be designed as part of a learning experience, encourage active, gross motor movements prior to, during (as breaks), and after the completion of the experience.

INCLUSIVE USES

Learners working on regulating their emotions might find participating in gross motor exercises led by humorous or musical characters useful in managing stress and anxiety. Self-reflection on how learners feel before and after physical exercise can help raise awareness of the effect exercise has on one's emotions. Learning this regulation strategy can support following a regular exercise routine, participating in a sport, or taking up a hobby related to physical activity later in life.

SAMPLE TOOLS

GoNoodle provides humorous videos and other experiences to help learners and educators incorporate movement into daily routines. It has a specific set of experiences focused on learning how to manage stress. Log-in to GoNoodle > Categories > SEL and Mindfulness > Manage Stress (**bit.ly/inclusive365-331a**).

Move to Learn is a brain-break video channel geared toward teenage learners (**bit.ly/inclusive365-331b**).

EXTENSION OPPORTUNITY

Encourage learners to record their stress and/or anxiety levels before and after the video exercises and discuss how these impacted their ability to self-regulate. The idea is to build self-awareness and promote metacognitive strategies for life-long implementation.

RELATED RESOURCES

Brain Rules by John Medina. Rule #1: Exercise Boosts Brain Power (**bit.ly/inclusive365-331c**)

Exercise and Stress: Get Moving (**bit.ly/inclusive365-331d**)

Figure 331. Learners doing yoga with GoNoodle.

ISTE STANDARDS FOR STUDENTS
1a, 1b

ISTE STANDARDS FOR EDUCATORS
5a, 5c, 6a, 6b

STRATEGY 331

Making Choices Using Digital Decision Trees

A decision tree created using a flow chart provides a visual way for learners to make choices by asking and answering a series of if-then or true-false questions. A learner can progress through the flowchart by asking themselves a series of questions leading to a decision.

INCLUSIVE USES

Learners who have difficulty making choices might find it useful to identify potential consequences of their choices by seeing potential outcomes of the different options. Depending on the design, decision trees can help the learner visualize the outcome of potentially ineffective choices.

Learners who are stuck when making a difficult or perplexing choice or unsure of how to proceed in a decision-making process may find it useful to use a decision tree to help them move forward.

SAMPLE TOOLS

Lucidchart is a web-based graphic organizing tool that provides various templates that can be customized to make decision charts (**bit.ly/inclusive365-332a**).

Diagrams.net is a free, web-based graphic organizer that could be used to set up a decision tree (**bit.ly/inclusive365-332b**).

Google Forms allows for conditional branching. Questions can be set to go to different next questions based on the responses. This tool provides a text-based option where users do not see all options (**bit.ly/inclusive365-332c**).

EXTENSION OPPORTUNITIES

Learners could be invited to create their own decision trees based on previous decisions made and share those for others to use when they have decisions to make. These decision trees can be published as open-source documents, allowing others to remix the tree to make something that suits their personalized needs.

Invite learners to use a contingency map to help them determine the potential consequences of the choices they might make. Templates, such as those offered by OCALI (**bit.ly/inclusive365-332d**), can be used to help develop the map.

RELATED RESOURCE

Decision Trees: The Simple Tool That'll Make You a Radically Better Decision Maker (**bit.ly/inclusive365-332e**)

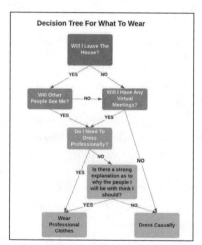

Figure 332. Simple, low-tech decision tree to support a learner's choice in selecting clothing when going to different environments.

ISTE STANDARDS FOR STUDENTS
1a, 1c, 1d, 6a, 6d

ISTE STANDARDS FOR EDUCATORS
1a, 2a, 2c, 3a, 3b, 4a, 4b, 5a, 6a

Managing Anxiety with Self-Regulation Resources

Learners experience varying levels of anxiety when faced with tasks they perceive as difficult. Some degree of anxiety can be helpful for learning; however, increased levels of anxiety can be disabling for some learners. The ability to self-regulate anxiety is a life-long skill and requires cognitive awareness as part of anxiety management. There are a variety of technology tools that support individuals in learning to manage and gauge their anxiety in the moment and implement a cognitive intervention that has been customized for the learner.

INCLUSIVE USES

All learners can benefit from learning and incorporating skills for self-regulation for anxiety management. When learners manage their anxiety, they enhance their learning. This is particularly important for learners whose quality and quantity of work production is impacted by increased levels of anxiety.

SAMPLE TOOLS

MindShift CBT is a free iOS or Android app that uses cognitive approaches to manage anxiety (**bit.ly/inclusive365-333a**).

SAM is a free app for self-regulation and anxiety management and includes tools for developing an anxiety toolkit and tracking anxiety patterns (**bit.ly/inclusive365-333b**).

EXTENSION OPPORTUNITY

Invite learners to track their progress in managing anxiety and identify implementation strategies that are effective in promoting self-regulation and success.

RELATED RESOURCES

Ten Ways to Help Students Who Struggle with Anxiety (**bit.ly/inclusive365-333c**)

Getting Started with MindShift CBT (**bit.ly/inclusive365-333d**)

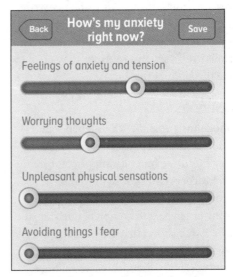

Figure 333. Gauging current level of anxiety with the SAM app.

ISTE STANDARDS FOR STUDENTS
1a, 1c, 4d

ISTE STANDARDS FOR EDUCATORS
2b, 5a, 6a

STRATEGY 333

Modeling Using Video

Imagine being asked to do a task made up of actions you've never heard of, let alone practiced. Some tasks are difficult for learners to complete because they have no experience with, or even a conceptual framework for doing them. Whether the issue is the number of steps necessary to achieve success or difficulty understanding the process in general, video modeling can support learners who need help managing the various processes and routines they need to complete throughout the day.

INCLUSIVE USES

Video modeling can aid with independent completion of multistep tasks and provide necessary executive function support for many learners. Learners can choose to watch the video multiple times until they understand the routine or pause it to complete one step at a time. Research shows that video modeling is an important strategy to use with learners on the autism spectrum as it decreases reliance on adults, promotes independence, and leads to generalization of skills (Bellini & Akullian, 2007).

SAMPLE TOOLS

A camera on a mobile device can be used to take videos of each step of a process and save them in order in the device's library for learners to review when needed. Another option is to embed each video clip on the pages of Book Creator (**bookcreator.com**).

Choiceworks is an iOS app that breaks down each step of a routine using either video or picture support for task completion (**bit.ly/inclusive365-334a**).

EXTENSION OPPORTUNITIES

Discuss with learners the daily tasks that need to be completed. Do they have difficulties

remembering/completing all the steps each day? Create a video model to assist them.

Invite learners to create the videos for peers who may benefit from the use of video modeling.

Create a library of videos that can be used throughout the learner environment, by multiple learners.

RELATED RESOURCES

Choiceworks app user guide (**bit.ly/inclusive365-334b**)

Meta-Analysis of Video Modeling and Video Self-Modeling Interventions for Children and Adolescents with Autism Spectrum Disorders (**bit.ly/inclusive365-334c**)

Evidence-Based Practice Brief: Video Modeling (**bit.ly/inclusive365-334d**)

Figure 334. Video models can be embedded within the steps delineated in the Choiceworks app. *Image ©2011 Bee Visual LLC.*

ISTE STANDARDS FOR STUDENTS
1a, 5c, 5d, 6a

ISTE STANDARDS FOR EDUCATORS
2b, 3a, 4b, 5a, 6a

Visualizing Progress with a Temperature Chart

When learners set goals and track their progress, they foster self-agency and this can positively impact their achievement. Charting progress helps learners realize that they are capable of learning new skills. Learners who digitally chart their progress by creating a data chart in a spreadsheet learn practical math and data collection skills at the same time. Creating a thermometer chart in Excel allows learners to visually see their progress as they reach their learning goals.

INCLUSIVE USES

Setting personal learning goals is critical for all learners. It is especially critical for learners who are working to build confidence in their abilities to develop new skills. Charting one's own progress helps learners develop persistence and visualize how small steps help them move closer to long-term goals.

SAMPLE TOOL

Microsoft Excel allows users to create a visual thermometer by creating a progress chart that calculates the percentage of the task completed, then displaying the percentage as a clustered-column chart (**bit.ly/inclusive365-335a**).

EXTENSION OPPORTUNITIES

Invite a group of learners to create a digital chart to track progress on a community goal, such as the number of words written, or another target that is agreed upon as beneficial to all learners.

Invite learners to periodically share the progress being made on collaborative goals to bolster confidence, motivation, and collaboration.

RELATED RESOURCES

The Effects of Goal Setting (**bit.ly/inclusive365-335b**)

Creating a Simple Thermometer Chart (**bit.ly/inclusive365-335c**)

Creating a Thermometer Chart From a Bar Chart Video (**bit.ly/inclusive365-335d**)

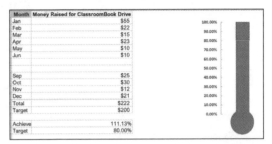

Figure 335. Temperature chart tracking money raised for a community library.

ISTE STANDARDS FOR STUDENTS
1a, 5b

ISTE STANDARDS FOR EDUCATORS
5a, 6a

STRATEGY 336

Building Community with Getting-to-Know-You Presentations

Educators need to find creative ways to build community and help learners get to know each other. The goal of community-building experiences is social-emotional in nature, not academic. By using tools that emphasize photos, video, audio, and graphics over text, learners can share the information they want without the demands of writing. Providing options for which tools to use is essential so that learners can be independent with this beginning of the school year task. These presentations can then be kept and shared throughout the year to new learners coming into the community, to help them get acquainted and build connections with peers.

INCLUSIVE USES

Emphasizing the use of images and other media over text makes this activity accessible to a wide range of learners, including those who have yet to master writing abilities.

SAMPLE TOOLS

Sway is part of the Microsoft 365 suite of online tools. It provides a visually oriented presentation, with the ability to easily add and share text, links, and other media. An easy-to-use accessibility checker also provides tips for making a Sway presention accessible for learners with vision impairments or reading challenges (**sway.office.com**).

Use Google Slides to create a descriptive visual presentation with added text that can be shared with peers (**docs.google.com/presentation**).

Use Flipgrid to create a video introduction, including how learners pronounce their names (**info.flipgrid.com**).

EXTENSION OPPORTUNITIES

Challenge learners to define themselves using only six words, images, or slides to introduce themselves. This forces learners to think critically about what they are including in their presentation, and to be sure that the words and images that they choose are powerful.

Combine the presentation slides into one presentation and share it with new learners who transition into the learning community.

RELATED RESOURCES

Sway for Education (**bit.ly/inclusive365-336a**)

Six-Word Memoirs (**bit.ly/inclusive365-336b**)

Figure 336. Microsoft Sway learner introduction.

ISTE STANDARDS FOR STUDENTS
3a, 6a, 6b, 6c, 6d

ISTE STANDARDS FOR EDUCATORS
2a, 3a, 5a, 5c, 6d, 7a

Learning Social Skills Using Empathy Mapping

An empathy map is a type of graphic organizer that invites learners to think about and understand someone else's point of view. Learners answer questions like:

- Who is the other person?
- What does that other person do?
- What does that other person see?
- What does that other person say?
- How do you think that other person feels?

Learners plot responses to questions on the map, which provides a visual way to organize abstract information. Invite learners to create empathy maps as a way to practice social exchanges.

INCLUSIVE USES

Learners with social-emotional and/or social-pragmatic goals who have strengths or preferences to process information visually might find using empathy maps particularly useful.

SAMPLE TOOLS

Google Forms is a web-based tool that provides a means for users to answer a series of reflective questions, including those asked when developing an empathy map (**bit.ly/inclusive365-337a**).

Visual Paradigm Online is a free website featuring online diagrams, including an empathy map template (**bit.ly/inclusive365-337b**).

EXTENSION OPPORTUNITIES

Invite learners to complete an empathy map after watching a video, hearing a story, or reading text of a social exchange to help illustrate how each party may have felt during the interaction.

Invite learners to complete an empathy map after experiencing media about a current event. Learners can use the empathy map to understand the perspectives of the people involved in the event.

RELATED RESOURCES

Teaching Empathy Mapping To Students with Autism (**bit.ly/inclusive365-337c**)

Empathy Mapping In the Teaching and Training Classroom (**bit.ly/inclusive365-337d**)

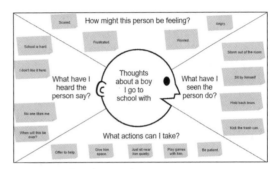

Figure 337. Sample empathy map.

ISTE STANDARDS FOR STUDENTS
1b, 1c, 2a, 2b, 2c, 3a, 3d, 4d, 5c, 6c, 6d, 7a, 7b, 7c

ISTE STANDARDS FOR EDUCATORS
2b, 3a, 4d, 5a, 5b, 5c, 6a

STRATEGY 338

Using Visual Cues to Check for Understanding

Checking for understanding is important in the instruction process. Asking questions like, *Does that make sense?* is often ineffective and results in awkward, uncertain silence. Publicly showing their level of comfort with a learning situation may cause anxiety and fear for some individuals. Low-tech visual cue solutions can utilize items around the learning space (or home in the virtual learning environment) and can be personalized to each learner.

INCLUSIVE USES

Checks for understanding should be developed collaboratively with each learner. Including the learner in the discussion helps develop the metacognitive skills essential for self-reflection and builds agency. Those learning to regulate anxiety, increase attention, and learn appropriate social behaviors may find subtle cues and signals helpful in showing their understanding of a concept, instruction, or direction.

SAMPLE TOOLS

Placing a coin in a specific position on a work surface can help indicate a level of understanding. Heads up could indicate that the learner understands and doesn't need any help, where tails would indicate that assistance is being requested. Another way to use a coin (or any small object) is to move it to different areas of the work surface. For example, a coin on the top left corner might mean, *I'm completely lost!*, A coin in the middle might mean, *Please come over to me when you get a chance* and placing the coin on the right might mean, *I got this!*

Learners can use sticky notes to indicate a need for assistance. No sticky note might mean, *I am understanding everything*, where a blue sticky note might mean, *I need some help when you get a chance*, and red sticky note might mean, *I need urgent assistance!*

Plickers enables learners to indicate their understanding by holding up a piece of paper with a QR code-like visual. The learner orients the paper to indicate the answer to a multiple-choice question choosing either A, B, C, or D (**plickers.com**).

EXTENSION OPPORTUNITIES

Invite learners to be actively involved in identifying a visual cue system that works best for them. Offer several alternative ways, including low-tech and higher-tech, so that learners can discover what works best.

Agreed upon, nonverbal cues can be useful for other purposes beyond checks for understanding, such as representing levels of anxiety, energy, or emotional state.

RELATED RESOURCES

Why Check for Understanding?
(**bit.ly/inclusive365-338a**)

The Teacher Toolkit: Checks for Understanding
(**bit.ly/inclusive365-338b**)

Figure 338. Placing a coin on the left side indicates understanding, placing a coin on the right side indicates that help is needed.

ISTE STANDARDS FOR STUDENTS
1a, 6a

ISTE STANDARDS FOR EDUCATORS
5a, 7b

Developing Interpersonal Skills with Social Narratives

Social narratives are short, first- or third-person stories written to support specific situations, or for an event new to a learner or group of learners. Narratives provide an opportunity to teach actions one might take during these situations, clarify expected or acceptable actions, and examine coping strategies. Role-play can be used as part of the narrative as a means of preparation and practice. Social narratives can be written and illustrated using digital or low-tech resources.

INCLUSIVE USES

Social narratives can be used by all learners who require support navigating social situations. Learners working on developing pragmatic language skills may find using social narratives helpful in practicing those abilities.

SAMPLE TOOLS

Book Creator allows both educators and learners to create custom social narratives with a variety of templates, including comic book or graphic novel styles (**bookcreator.com**).

LessonPix allows educators to generate social narratives using text, clip art, or custom images. Shared narratives can be downloaded to use or modify to meet your needs (**lessonpix.com**).

EXTENSION OPPORTUNITIES

Invite learners to generate their own social narratives. Discuss how they identified the challenge, the text they chose, and why they selected the images.

Invite learners to collaborate on social narratives for a variety of scenarios. Invite groups to exchange narratives and reflect on how they might help them engage in a situation.

Reflect on the cause of the actions before crafting a social narrative. Is something in the learning environment or educators' actions causing the learner to react in a particular way? Consider writing a narrative from an educator's point of view, discussing what changes the educator will make. The educator and learner can review the narrative together and the educator can follow through with the changes to demonstrate adapting to support others.

RELATED RESOURCES

Vanderbilt University fact sheet detailing the elements of social narratives and how to use them (**bit.ly/inclusive365-339a**)

A.T.TIPSCAST Episode #125: "Proto-Chapter for Technology Tools for Students with Autism, Part 1" (**bit.ly/inclusive365-339b**)

Using Social Narratives to Promote Social-Emotional Success (**bit.ly/inclusive365-339c**)

Once Upon a Scial Story: Advantages, Writing and Presenting Social Stories (**bit.ly/inclusive365-339d**)

LessonPix Sharing Center: Search Results for "Social Stories" (**bit.ly/inclusive365-339e**)

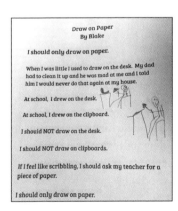

Figure 339. A learner-generated social narrative, dictated to an adult then illustrated by the learner.

ISTE STANDARDS FOR STUDENTS
1a, 1b, 5c, 7b

ISTE STANDARDS FOR EDUCATORS
5a, 5b, 6d

Practicing for New Social Situations and Routines Using Virtual Reality

As a member of a community of learners and in society as a whole, learners need to learn how to prepare and react to new social situations and routines. For example, when the COVID-19 pandemic struck, individuals needed to learn how to maintain new physical distancing norms, prepare for seeing people wearing masks, and practice hand washing protocols. These new situations and routines take time and practice to learn. Learners can participate in virtual reality experiences where they can practice unfamiliar situations and routines in preparation for real-life experiences.

INCLUSIVE USES

Learners working on social-pragmatic goals may find it useful to practice routines using many forms of media, such as slideshows, videos, and virtual reality experiences.

Learners who have demonstrated anxiety due to new social situations or routines may find practicing using virtual reality helpful in preparing for real-life events.

SAMPLE TOOLS

Google Cardboard turns most mobile devices into an inexpensive virtual reality viewer (**arvr.google.com/cardboard**).

CoSpaces Edu is a website with both free and priced plans that allow individuals to create customized virtual reality experiences for learners (**cospaces.io/edu**).

Floreo is a tool that allows learners to practice social experiences in virtual reality (**floreotech.com**).

EXTENSION OPPORTUNITY

Invite learners to draft a script and then create an experience in virtual reality for other learners to practice a social situation or routine. Routines could be things like how to do a particular chore or task, how to perform sequential math, or a demonstration of the meaning of a word.

RELATED RESOURCE

Example of a Practice Routine (COVID-19 Action Plan for Kids) Created in Virtual Reality by CoSpace Edu (**bit.ly/inclusive365-340a**)

Figure 340a. Co-author Chris Bugaj exploring a virtual reality headset and gear.

Figure 340b. CoSpace Edu experience about the coronavirus.

ISTE STANDARDS FOR STUDENTS
1b, 5c, 6c

ISTE STANDARDS FOR EDUCATORS
2b, 2c, 3a, 4d, 5a, 5c, 6b, 7a

Amplifying Diversity through Personal Perspectives

There are three criteria necessary to ensure a strategy is evidence-based. First, the strategy in question needs to be supported by scientific literature. The strategy also needs to be supported by experts working in that specific field of study. Finally, groups of individuals with whom the strategy has been implemented report that it has worked for them. Listening to and learning from those who have experienced improvements to their lives ensures that the strategy actually works. People share what works (and what doesn't work) in various ways including blogs, podcasts, and on social media. Hashtags can be used to organize and amplify diverse voices and perspectives.

INCLUSIVE USE

Listening to diverse voices and to those who have made progress using a particular strategy helps ensure evidence-based methodologies actually work.

SAMPLE TOOLS

The #OwnVoices hashtag is used by individuals who share authentically diverse perspectives.

Individuals using the #ActuallyAutistic hashtag share perspectives from their daily lives.

Individuals who use wheelchairs share stories and insights using the hashtag #WheelChairLife.

The hashtag #AbleismExists is used by individuals to share stories related to discrimination imposed upon people with disabilities.

The #NeuroDiversity and #NeuroDiverseSquad hashtags are two examples used by people sharing how to create a more inclusive future.

EXTENSION OPPORTUNITIES

Invite learners with disabilities to consider sharing what strategies work for them, in the way that works best for them.

Schedule professional learning time to engage in the experience of consuming content shared by people with diverse backgrounds.

Curate a list of contemporary social-media posts, blogs, and/or podcasts that offer perspectives of people from different backgrounds, and share this list with learners.

RELATED RESOURCES

14 Empowering Hashtags For People To Celebrate Their Disabilities Online (**bit.ly/inclusive365-341a**)

Black Disabled Men Talk, a podcast hosted by four Black men with disabilities (**bit.ly/inclusive365-341b**)

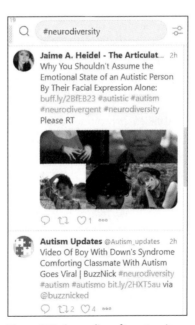

Figure 341. A sampling of tweets using the hashtag #neurodiversity.

ISTE STANDARDS FOR STUDENTS

2a, 2b, 3a, 3b, 3c, 3d, 6a, 6c, 7a, 7b, 7d

ISTE STANDARDS FOR EDUCATORS

2a, 2b, 2c, 3a, 3b, 4a, 4b, 4c, 4d, 5a, 6b, 6d

Self-Paced Learning about Equity and Inclusion

Any educator reading this book is probably also seeking other resources to expand their knowledge about equity and inclusion. Finding resources in varied formats and that educators can explore on their own time is one way to make this ongoing professional learning a part of their busy lives.

INCLUSIVE USES

Self-paced resources that use a variety of media allow educators to find formats and times that best suit their own needs.

SAMPLE TOOLS

The Culture and Diversity in Schools YouTube channel from Education Week is a series of videos that educators can view on their own time. The videos cover a range of topics including Black Student Voices, From the Pueblo to College: The Journey of Two Rural Students, and even Using Hamilton in the Classroom (**bit.ly/inclusive365-342a**).

The Leading Equity Center provides webinars, summits, self-paced courses with online discussions, podcasts, and more on topics such as Teaching Through a Culturally Diverse Lens, Framing Brave Conversations about Race and Ethnicity, and Universal Design for Learning, to help educators explore how to design with equity in mind (**leadingequitycenter.com**).

EXTENSION OPPORTUNITY

Pair-up with a colleague and commit to a regular schedule of exploring equity resources. Sign up for a webinar together, or agree to both listen to the same podcast and then have a discussion about what you have learned. It's valuable to have a peer to reflect with and to have what may be challenging conversations

about the topics. Pairing with a colleague also increases accountability to complete the work.

RELATED RESOURCE

The latest news about diversity in schools, including articles, opinion essays, and special features from Education Week (**bit.ly/inclusive365-342b**).

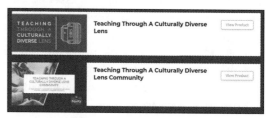

Figure 342. Self-paced course from the Leading Equity Center.

ISTE STANDARDS FOR STUDENTS
7a

ISTE STANDARDS FOR EDUCATORS
1a, 1b, 1c, 2b

Learning to Design Inclusively through Massive Open Online Courses

Massive Open Online Courses (MOOCs) run on platforms that allow individuals to consume content at their own pace. The open nature of the content makes it freely available to anyone with an internet connection. Learners can engage in existing MOOCs, which cover a wide variety of topics, including inclusive design, disability awareness, and equitable practices.

INCLUSIVE USES

MOOCs allow a large number of learners to experience the content asynchronously. Individuals can engage in the content at times that are convenient to their needs and schedules. This flexibility also affords learners the opportunity to re-experience the content multiple times, which may increase comprehension.

SAMPLE TOOL

Coursera is a platform by which people can sign up to participate in MOOCs offered by universities and businesses. The courses cover a variety of topics, including those related to inclusive design and disability awareness (**coursera.org**).

EXTENSION OPPORTUNITY

Invite learners to create their own versions of a MOOC as a possible product of a problem-based learning experience. Learners working to solve a particular problem might recognize that creating a MOOC could be a means of addressing the problem. Learners could create a MOOC by pulling together content and inviting others to participate.

RELATED RESOURCES

Coursera course: Disability Inclusion in Education: Building Systems of Support (**bit.ly/inclusive365-343a**)

Coursera course: Disability Awareness and Support (**bit.ly/inclusive365-343b**)

Coursera course: Basics of Inclusive Design for Online Instruction (**bit.ly/inclusive365-343c**)

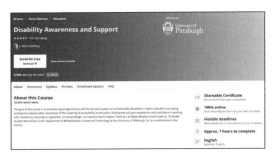

Figure 343. Disability Awareness and Support MOOC taught by Mary Goldberg, University of Pittsburgh.

ISTE STANDARDS FOR STUDENTS

3d, 7a, 7b, 7c, 7d

ISTE STANDARDS FOR EDUCATORS

1a, 1b, 1c

Fostering an Inclusive Mindset with Professional Learning Experiences

Developing an inclusive mindset is essential to truly reach all learners. All learners, adults and children alike, exhibit learner variabilities. An inclusive mindset acknowledges and embraces this reality while understanding that everyone benefits when educational experiences are designed for everyone. There are several online resources to help better understand and develop this mindset and to model a love of lifelong learning through inclusion. Online professional development puts the control in the hands of the viewer for just-in-time viewing and application.

Just by reading this book, you've taken an important step toward fostering your own development of an inclusive mindset. What comes next? What online course will you engage in? Which podcast will you listen to? Which professional learning community will you join? What book will you read next? What will you engage in next to further your own development?

INCLUSIVE USE

Inclusive education, by definition, removes barriers, promotes accessibility, and fosters learner agency by embracing the fact that everyone is unique and by designing awesome educational experiences built with flexibility, empowerment, and joyfulness in mind.

SAMPLE TOOL

Inclusive Classroom Specialization is an online course comprising nine, one-hour learning paths designed by Microsoft and Achievement for All. Topics include Developing a Digitally Literate Learner, Developing a Digitally Literate Pedagogy, The Inclusive Educator, Introduction to Inclusive Digital Literacy, Training Teachers

to Author Accessible Content, and Empower Every Student with an Inclusive Classroom (**bit.ly/inclusive365-344a**).

EXTENSION OPPORTUNITIES

Model an inclusive educator mindset and intentionally collaborate with colleagues to take courses, read books, listen to podcasts, explore tools, and participate in professional learning communities. Similar to a book group, set aside time weekly or bi-weekly to reflect and discuss inclusive practices and brainstorm applications.

School-aged learners and adult learners can participate in experiences centered around inclusive practices together. Sharing stories, reading articles, working on projects, and so much more can be done to work together to build an inclusive future for everyone.

RELATED RESOURCE

What New Teachers Need to Know About Inclusive Classrooms (**bit.ly/inclusive364-344b**)

Figure 344. Inclusive Classroom Specialization homepage.

ISTE STANDARDS FOR STUDENTS

3d, 7a, 7b, 7c, 7d

ISTE STANDARDS FOR EDUCATORS

1a, 1b, 1c, 2a, 2b, 4a, 5a

Learning Asynchronously about Autism and Assistive Technology

There are numerous opportunities to learn, grow, and improve practices to strive for inclusive education. Asynchronous learning experiences invite individuals to learn at their own pace on their own time. These could be 30-minute recorded webinars to full-blown courses comprising multiple learning modules. Save time by learning from pre-made modules, such as strategies from experts in autism or technology for individuals with disabilities.

INCLUSIVE USES

Educators need to continually grow to effectively meet the needs of all learners. Internet-based learning courses can provide that platform for growth. By demonstrating a growth mindset, educators model the practice of lifelong learning we hope to instill in our learners. Intentionally seeking out opportunities to learn effective strategies the learning experience for people with disabilities helps everyone grow.

SAMPLE TOOLS

The OCALI Autism Internet Modules were created with input from practitioners and experts from across the United States. These 40 modules focus on tools and strategies "for anyone who supports, instructs, works with, or lives with someone with autism." Individuals can work through the modules at their own pace and revisit specific portions of the modules when needed (**autisminternetmodules.org**).

The OCALI Assistive Technology Internet Modules, also created with input from practitioners and experts, consist of 50 modules focusing on an assessment process, and implementation, as well as topics, such as seating and positioning, computer access, communication, and more (**atinternetmodules.org**).

EXTENSION OPPORTUNITIES

Since time is a constraint, educators can choose to complete one module that has a direct impact on their teaching. Perhaps there is a learner who has autism and you want to be better equipped to provide schedule support. Review that module, discuss with the educational support team, including the learner and family, and work to implement what was learned.

Invite colleagues to participate in the modules together. Completion dates could be agreed upon with follow-up meetings scheduled to discuss the content in the modules. Focus questions could be generated to guide the discussion and takeaway points could be summarized, followed by the development of an action plan complete with goals to drive sustainable change.

Invite learners to explore the OCALI modules when working to educate themselves about autism, assistive technology, or both.

RELATED RESOURCE

OCALI Inspiring Change Podcast (**bit.ly/inclusive365-345a**)

Figure 345. OCALI Internet Modules webpage.

ISTE STANDARDS FOR STUDENTS
1d, 3d

ISTE STANDARDS FOR EDUCATORS
2c, 3a, 3b, 3c, 3d

Breaking the Ice—Digitally

Icebreakers receive varied reactions; some love them, some hate them! However, when an icebreaker serves as the introduction to the content and helps create a sense of community, it can set a positive tone for the rest of the experience. For virtual professional learning, icebreakers can be even more critical, providing an opportunity to build connections when colleagues cannot be in the same physical space. Consider these virtual icebreakers and adapt based on audience and content:

1. Using only emojis (**emojipedia.org**), share answers to the following questions:

   - What is your content area?
   - What is your ideal learning location?
   - What is your preferred way or mode of learning new information?
   - How do you feel about using the tool/strategy presented in today's learning?

2. Share in the chat a meme, GIF, or song lyric related to the concept being discussed and which shows a bit of your personality.

3. Have participants use the "raise hands" feature in Zoom or another platform to play a version of Never Have I Ever, where you present situations participants might have experienced to get a sense of prior knowledge. Situations might include:

   - Used the tool that you are highlighting or modeling in the session.
   - Had a learner who I couldn't reach at all.
   - Left my mail inbox with unread messages.
   - Served as a peer mentor or coach.

INCLUSIVE USES

Remember that individuals, whether adults or children, have different comfort levels. Provide an opt-out option and keep icebreakers professional by not asking anyone to reveal information that they might not want to share. Well-constructed digital icebreakers give educators and learners an opportunity to interact in a low-stress manner.

SAMPLE TOOLS

Using Emoji Typer, type a word to get/copy the corresponding emoji (**emojityper.com**).

Giphy is a source of free GIFs (**giphy.com**).

Lyrics.com allows users to easily search for lyrics based on the name of the song, the lyrics, the album, or the artist (**lyrics.com**).

EXTENSION OPPORTUNITIES

Have educators reflect on if, why, and how an icebreaker in a digital learning space may serve a different purpose than in a face-to-face learning experience. This could be a follow up to the icebreaker or even one of the cumulative experiences at the end of a learning event.

Engage learners in connecting and interacting with peers using icebreakers that align with learning goals during distance learning.

RELATED RESOURCES

Icebreakers (**bit.ly/inclusive365-346a**)

Why Do Icebreakers with Adult Learners? (**bit.ly/inclusive365-346b**)

Figure 346. Emojis for favorite read-aloud books pasted into a Zoom chat. Can you guess what the books are?

ISTE STANDARDS FOR STUDENTS
7a, 7b

ISTE STANDARDS FOR EDUCATORS
1a, 1b, 2a, 2c

Contacting Your State Assistive Technology Act Program to Borrow Equipment

The purchase of tools is sometimes required to meet the unique needs of a learner. The group could use the Loan Libraries, available through each individual state's Assistive Technology (AT) Act Project, as a resource to help develop ideas of technology to try. Each state (and territory) has an AT Act program and many have a statewide lending program that provides opportunities to "try it before you buy it."

INCLUSIVE USES

At times, learners need specialized technology in order to access their education in the least restrictive manner. These tools, when designed to meet the specific needs of an individual, may have a significant cost. Educators, families, and learners can meet to consider AT needs and develop ideas about how to meet those needs. Once they have agreed on an option, they can contact the AT Act program so that the learner (and team) is given a chance to try out the option without the need to purchase anything first.

SAMPLE TOOL

The National Assistive Technology Act Technical Assistance and Training (AT3) Center provides training and technical assistance for all AT Act Section 4 state and territory AT programs. It supports a website that makes general information about assistive technology available to anyone who needs it. It contains a directory for educators to find the AT Act program for each state (**at3center.net**).

EXTENSION OPPORTUNITY

Provide learners with case studies that reference another group of learners, each of whom is having trouble accessing their education.

These case studies should be anonymous yet authentic, describing individuals at different institutions of learning. Invite the group to research options that might help eliminate the barriers by first listing the needs and then looking for features of technology that might meet those needs. The group could use the Loan Libraries, available through each individual state's AT Act Project, as a resource to help develop ideas of technology to try. The group of learners could then present the ideas they have generated to help those in the case study.

RELATED RESOURCE

AT3 Center's list of state AT Act programs (**bit.ly/inclusive365-347a**)

Figure 347. Find your state's AT Act program at the AT3 Center website.

ISTE STANDARDS FOR STUDENTS

1a, 1b, 1c, 1d, 3a, 3d, 4a, 4b, 4c, 4d, 7b, 7c, 7d

ISTE STANDARDS FOR EDUCATORS

2b, 2c, 6b, 7a, 7c

STRATEGY 347

Learning Together with Professional Study Groups

Reading a book and/or listening to a podcast can be a meaningful way to learn and consider new ideas. After all, you're engaging in one of those activities right now! Individuals exploring the exact same content often have different takeaways depending on prior knowledge and experiences. Sharing those sparks of inspiration about changes to practices and awesome implementation strategies can be meaningfully discussed during collaborative study groups. Participants can develop a schedule where they take turns taking the lead by creating a series of questions to be asked about a chunk of content, such as a chapter of a book or a podcast episode. Participants experience the content asynchronously and then meet synchronously to reflect and discuss collaboratively.

INCLUSIVE USES

Research and innovative practices continuously evolve. Learners with and without disabilities benefit from educators who are informed and challenged to think in new ways.

Learning is a lifelong endeavor and learners benefit when they see educators who model a love for lifelong learning.

SAMPLE TOOLS

Applications in the Google Workspace— Docs, Slides, or Sheets—could be used to organize questions and collect responses (**workspace.google.com**).

Software in the Microsoft Office Suite—Word, PowerPoint, and Excel—could be used to pose questions and responses (**office.com**).

Facebook public or private groups can be used to organize a book study (**facebook.com**).

EXTENSION OPPORTUNITIES

Share some takeaways from participating in group events with learners. Educators who participate in learning groups are also modeling for learners a methodology for how they can work together in their own learning groups.

Advertise the title and topic of the next group event with other educators to invite participation.

Organize a professional study group for this book! Meetings could happen weekly, monthly, or quarterly for educators to discuss the strategies and share how they've implemented them.

RELATED RESOURCES

How to Plan an Awesome Book Study (**bit.ly/inclusive365-348a**)

The New Assistive Tech: Make Learning Awesome for All! Book Study: Part 4 (**bit.ly/inclusive365-348b**)

Talking With Tech Podcast Episode #152: Cuyahoga AAC Podcast Social Group: Benefits of a District-Wide AAC/AT Social Group (**bit.ly/inclusive365-348c**)

Figure 348. Educators reflecting on a chapter of a book they've all read.

ISTE STANDARDS FOR STUDENTS
1a, 1b, 1c, 2b, 3b, 3d, 6c, 7a

ISTE STANDARDS FOR EDUCATORS
1a, 1b, 1c, 2a, 2c, 3b, 4a, 4b, 4d, 5a, 6a

Hosting Video Watch Parties

Watching television shows and movies together provides an opportunity for friends and family to have a shared media experience. Viewing together spurs discussions and allows people to share their thoughts, feelings, and opinions about the media. These same phenomena can occur with educators when they watch a form of media together. Colleagues can participate in webinars or other synchronous and asynchronous events to discuss the meaning, share insights, and generally discuss their impressions and takeaways.

INCLUSIVE USES

Learners can participate in watch parties as well. This can occur in the same room or remotely with learners viewing the same media synchronously. Choose a platform that allows learners to interact using different modalities, including text and/or video. The social experience of watching media together helps learners working on social-emotional skills while providing the opportunity to formulate responses in their own time using text. When participating remotely, a learner could access other supports that are not obvious to other viewers. Learners can use scripts, prompts, or even in-person coaching while participating in the watch party.

SAMPLE TOOLS

Google Meet is a videoconferencing tool that could be used to create a video watch party (**meet.google.com**).

Zoom is a videoconference platform that could be used to host or participate in a video watch party (**zoom.us**).

Netflix Party allows you to watch Netflix shows together as a group. Synchronized viewing allows for pausing and discussion through a group chat (**netflixparty.com**).

EXTENSION OPPORTUNITY

Prior to a watch party, establish a shared document. This document can be a blank canvas on which to share questions, insights, and takeaways, or it could be a more structured template with predetermined questions or fields acting as a guide.

RELATED RESOURCE

Watch parties—The Go-to Group Watch Feature (**bit.ly/inclusive365-349a**)

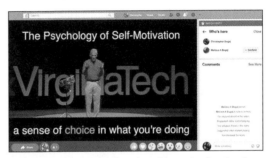

Figure 349. YouTube video played through a Facebook watch party portal.

ISTE STANDARDS FOR STUDENTS

1b, 2b, 3a, 3b, 3c, 3d, 7a, 7b, 7d

ISTE STANDARDS FOR EDUCATORS

2a, 2c, 3a, 3b, 4a

Hashtagging to Enhance Social Media Posts

Hashtags, or a string of text preceded by an octothorpe (the # symbol), are omnipresent in social media; however, many people do not realize that a hashtag actually creates a link that gathers together all posts tagged in the same way. Educators can use hashtags when posting to a learning community or to find information that is specific to a hashtag used by others. For example, if a group of educators are frequently posting about an upcoming event, such as a back-to-school night, they can tag related posts in a consistent manner, such as #Inclusive365. Then, if parents or community members search the hashtag within Twitter, Facebook, or Instagram, all the information about the event will be in one linear feed. This is also frequently done at conferences, like #ISTElive21, so attendees or those who could not attend but want to see information shared can see information posted about the event.

INCLUSIVE USES

Hashtags provide a way for educators or learners to see all posts for a particular topic with one search, rather than looking through individual accounts. Hashtags help keep conversations organized and streamlined, reducing the cognitive load required when searching multiple locations.

SAMPLE TOOLS

Facebook, Twitter, and Instagram all use hashtags.

Hootsuite is a social media management dashboard that allows you to set up a feed dedicated to a specific hashtag, making it easy to quickly scroll through tagged posts (**hootsuite.com**).

TweetDeck sorts the information in a Twitter feed into distinct columns. In order to find and organize relevant information, columns can be sorted by hashtags, Twitter users, or search terms. TweetDeck helps streamline and organize the experience of participating in Twitter chats (see Strategy 356) by sorting pertinent tweets into one column (**tweetdeck.twitter.com**).

EXTENSION OPPORTUNITIES

Invite learners to create or use an existing hashtag for a group or learning community to use when studying a particular topic or issue.

Invite learners to analyze the metrics of a hashtag to discover how much it is being used.

Review social media posts pertaining to this book by using the hashtag #Inclusive365.

RELATED RESOURCE

How to Use Hashtags: A Quick and Simple Guide for Every Network (**bit.ly/inclusive365-350a**)

Figure 350. Results for #ISTE2019 on Instagram.

ISTE STANDARDS FOR STUDENTS
1b, 2b, 3d, 7a

ISTE STANDARDS FOR EDUCATORS
1b, 1c, 2b, 4c, 6d

Sharing Meaningful Ideas TED-Style

"You have something meaningful to say, and your goal is to re-create your core idea inside your audience's minds." The owner and curator of TED, Chris Anderson, makes this statement in his book, *TED Talks, A Guide to Public Speaking*. TED Talks have become known for presenting a personal message by sharing the narrative journey of a lesson learned on a topic of importance to the speaker and the listeners, typically in under twenty minutes. Educators who are providing professional development can take a page from Anderson's book, and deliver their own TED-style talk when sharing best practices with colleagues.

INCLUSIVE USES

TED-style talks are a perfect medium for engaging the disengaged educator who is tired of the standard presentation and professional learning experience. Educators or learners who are not comfortable creating a complex (and maybe boring!) slide presentation may thrive with a more narrative presentation style.

SAMPLE TOOL

TED Masterclass, available on iOS and Android, provides a series of short videos led by Chris Anderson. The program takes you through the process of identifying a great idea, crafting it into a compelling narrative and presenting it so that others listen (**masterclass.ted.com**).

EXTENSION OPPORTUNITY

Invite learners to give a TED Talk on their favorite topic or as a summative assessment choice. The TED-Ed Student Talks program has resources to support educators in facilitating TED Talks with their learners (**ed.ted.com/student_talks**).

RELATED RESOURCES

The Secret Structure of Great Talks (**bit.ly/inclusive365-351a**)

Ten Tips for Speaking Like a TED Talk Pro (**bit.ly/inclusive365-351b**)

Anderson, C. (2018). *TED talks: The official TED guide to public speaking.* London: Nicholas Brealey Publishing

"Disability-Led Innovations for the Masses," Chris Bugaj presenting at TedXAshburn (**bit.ly/inclusive365-351c**)

Figure 351. Chris Bugaj, one of the authors, presenting at TEDxAshburn.

ISTE STANDARDS FOR STUDENTS

6a, 6b, 6c, 6d

ISTE STANDARDS FOR EDUCATORS

1a, 1b, 2c, 3b

STRATEGY 352

Igniting Learning via Fast-Paced Professional Development

Long-winded professional learning can be frustrating and boring for participants. Shorter sessions with poignant topics can help focus attention and spark interest. An Ignite Talk works on the notion that brevity is an enticing elixir. Ignite Talks were conceived in Seattle in 2006 by Brady Forrest and Bre Pett, and live by the motto, "Enlighten us, but make it quick." During an Ignite Talk, presenters get 20 slides, which automatically advance every 15 seconds. This means that the presenter gets a grand total of five minutes to present the topic, make the point, and influence others. It forces a presenter to keep content to the key points and deliver the presentation in a succinct way. Five minutes of lightning learning is all the presenter gets! What would you say? *How* would you say it?

INCLUSIVE USES

With the short presentation time, only key information is shared, which would enable a learner or educator to learn the key aspects of a topic quickly. Learners who are distracted or overwhelmed by numerous facts or ideas during a lengthy presentation may find that information presented in short, meaningful bursts make a greater impact.

SAMPLE TOOLS

Any presentation software that has a timer feature to auto-advance slides, such as Microsoft PowerPoint (**microsoft.com/powerpoint**) or Google Slides (**docs.google.com/presentation**), can be used.

EXTENSION OPPORTUNITIES

Invite learners to create their own Ignite Talk on a topic of interest to them. It could be anything from making a peanut butter and jelly sandwich to how to log in to a Chromebook.

Starting with something familiar empowers them to focus on identifying and conveying the key points.

Embrace the short presentation style of an Ignite Talk at a staff meeting. Since each talk clocks in at five minutes, this could offer a nice respite during long meetings and allow educators to highlight a new strategy/tool they are using.

RELATED RESOURCES

Ignite Talks searchable directory of presentations on an array of topics (**ignitetalks.io**)

Chris Bugaj: Ignite Talks at VSTE 2012 (**bit.ly/inclusive365-352a**)

Figure 352. Mike's Ignite Talk on the Raspberry Pi. Talk fast because the next slide is coming in 3...2...1...

ISTE STANDARDS FOR STUDENTS
1b, 3d, 7a, 7d

ISTE STANDARDS FOR EDUCATORS
1b, 2a, 2b, 2c

Engaging in Participant-Led Learning Experiences

Edcamps were started in 2010 by a group of educators in the Philadelphia area as organic learning experiences organized and led by participants. Arriving at an edcamp is a "leap of faith." There is no posted schedule of events. Instead, participants arrive and brainstorm topic ideas, filling in a grid with topics they'd like to discuss during set times and locations. Once the grid is filled, the edcamp begins.

Edcamps are flexible learning environments that allow people to discuss topics relevant, pertinent, and important to them as individuals. There are four tenets of the edcamp model (outlined by the Edcamp Foundation):

- **Free.** There is never a fee to participate.

- **Participant driven.** Participants choose the topics and collaboratively manage the learning environment.

- **Experience, not experts.** Conversations, not presentations, are at the heart of an edcamp. Open discussions that engage all participants give everyone a voice.

- **Rule of two feet.** As the conversation progresses, if you find it isn't right for you, get up and leave without any hard feelings. You are encouraged to go find another concurrent conversation that is more aligned with your learning goals.

INCLUSIVE USES

An edcamp can be organized around any topic, including those that promote inclusive practices and the development of an inclusive mindset. Some examples are EdcampAccess Boston and EdcampAccess NJ.

SAMPLE TOOL

Although an edcamp can be organized using a shared spreadsheet, when an in-person event is scheduled, all that is needed is a blank wall, some tape to create a grid, and some sticky notes and pens to write topic choices.

EXTENSION OPPORTUNITIES

Traditionally, edcamps are for educators but an edcamp event can be conducted for learners, parents, or the community at large.

Invite learners to provide their perspectives in sessions, which validates their voices and contributions.

RELATED RESOURCE

The Edcamp Organizers Handbook from the Edcamp Foundation (**bit.ly/inclusive365-353a**)

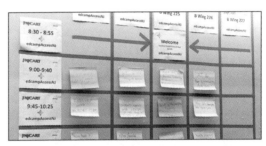

Figure 353a. Every edcamp event starts with building the schedule. Participants suggest conversation topics, which are organized into a grid with room and times.

Figure 353b. Participants gather to discuss topics *they* are interested in. Notice that there are no presentation slides.

ISTE STANDARDS FOR STUDENTS
1b, 3d, 7a, 7d

ISTE STANDARDS FOR EDUCATORS
1b, 2a, 2b, 2c,

Sharing How You Designed Inclusive Educational Literacy Experiences

Other educators need to learn from you! Once you've designed and delivered an awesome literacy experience it is time to share and collaborate with others who are passionate about literacy. The National Council of Teachers of English (NCTE) and the International Literacy Association (ILA) provide an opportunity to submit a description of how you designed the experience as well as to review what others have contributed. Join a global community of literacy experts creating an outstanding free literacy resource for educators who work with learners at all skill levels. We're all in this together!

INCLUSIVE USES

Educators are encouraged to share options they have provided to learners, including possible tools learners were invited to use, to participate in the experience. These options can include any tools, including built-in accessibility features to available technologies, that can be used to help learners have an engaging and empowering experience.

SAMPLE TOOL

ReadWriteThink looks for educators to contribute lesson plans and activities to their site and also to review the submissions of other contributors (**bit.ly/inclusive365-354a**).

EXTENSION OPPORTUNITIES

Explore the resources that are available on the ReadWriteThink website (**readwritethink. org**) to discover what additional resources, lesson plans, or ideas could benefit the design of educational experiences. Evaluate current lessons with an accessibility lens. Would learners of varying abilities be able to interact with the experience you've designed?

Once you've shared the description of the experience you've designed and delivered, consider sharing a link to that description on social media so other educators in your professional learning network can use the idea with the learners they are guiding.

Learners and educators can collaborate on the design of an educational experience related to literacy. As co-designers, educators and learners can submit contributions jointly.

RELATED RESOURCES

NCTE homepage (**ncte.org**)

ILA homepage (**literacyworldwide.org**)

Figure 354. ReadWriteThink contribution page.

ISTE STANDARDS FOR STUDENTS
4b, 6d, 7a, 7c

ISTE STANDARDS FOR EDUCATORS
1b, 2a, 2c, 5c

Learning from Peers with Pineapple Charts

The pineapple is the universal sign of hospitality. The pineapple chart is a system to invite educators into each other's learning spaces to informally observe and learn from one another. The pineapple chart is a physical (or virtual) board that educators use to show when they are implementing a particularly interesting experience, resource, tool, technique, or strategy. When they post to the chart, they welcome their colleagues to observe during the indicated time. This provides just-in-time professional learning in an informal, collegial atmosphere that builds collaboration. Locate the board in a highly visible spot where educators will see it frequently, such as in the staff lounge, by mailboxes, or as a pinned announcement on a website or learning management system.

INCLUSIVE USES

The pineapple chart system promotes inclusivity by providing educators with the opportunity to observe practices that support learners with diverse learning needs in any setting, as well as practices that use Universal Design for Learning to benefit all learners.

SAMPLE TOOL

A shared spreadsheet, such as Google Sheets or Microsoft Excel, could be used as a pineapple chart. Individuals could use notification rules to be alerted that someone has posted to the chart (**bit.ly/inclusive365-355a**).

EXTENSION OPPORTUNITIES

Administrators can provide time and coverage for educators in different locations and learning environments to observe each other. This could be particularly useful for educators in music, art, physical education, or special educators including speech/language pathologists and occupational therapists, who have no match at their own places of learning to observe.

Learners might also use pineapple charts to share what they are currently learning about. Learners could share when they are working on a particular topic of study, when they are using a particular piece of software, or when they are attempting something new, inviting others to join them.

RELATED RESOURCES

How Pineapple Charts Revolutionize Professional Development (**bit.ly/inclusive365-355b**)

Hacking Education: 10 Quick Fixes for Every School by Mark Barnes and Jennifer Gonzalez. The pineapple chart and other professional development ideas are included in this quick read from the *Hacking Education* series (**bit.ly/inclusive365-355c**).

Figure 355. Educator signing up to share his expertise with colleagues on a pineapple chart.

ISTE STANDARDS FOR STUDENTS
1b

ISTE STANDARDS FOR EDUCATORS
1b

Expanding Your Personalized Learning Network (PLN) via Twitter Chats

Building a personalized network empowers one's own learning. It also allows individuals to expand their thinking by challenging presumptions and biases and learning from those from varied backgrounds. Social media can allow us to come together to experience alternative viewpoints, share methodologies, and move the needle toward a more inclusive future.

Twitter chats are a means for professionals to ask and answer questions and share information, resources, and experiences. These chats are primarily synchronous events that follow a consistent format where facilitators ask thought-provoking questions around a topic. Participants then respond by reflecting and commenting. The chats are organized using a common hashtag. If people cannot participate in real-time, the conversation lives on in the platform.

INCLUSIVE USES

There are a number of Twitter chats related to designing inclusive learning experiences. Many organizers of Twitter chats post questions ahead of time. This gives people more time to compose responses. Posting the questions ahead of time in a way that can be read aloud by screen reading technology respects various text input methods and creates a more welcoming atmosphere.

SAMPLE TOOL

TweetDeck sorts a Twitter feed into distinct columns. Columns can be sorted by hashtags, Twitter users, and search terms. TweetDeck helps streamline and organize Twitter chat participation by sorting pertinent tweets into one column (**tweetdeck.com**).

EXTENSION OPPORTUNITIES

A Twitter account is not required to read tweets, however, an account is necessary to post. Create an account and complete a profile sharing professional interests, roles, expertise, and a concise biography. Include a picture to help make a personal connection.

Learners learn by examples set by educators, such as seeking out opportunities to learn and improve. Educators could share when they intend to participate in a Twitter chat, invite questions and conversations from learners about the topic, share Tweets that made an impact and shaped perspectives, and/or reflect transparently about personal takeaways.

RELATED RESOURCES

How to Cultivate your Twitter Profile to Increase Effectiveness (**bit.ly/inclusive365-356a**)

Twitter support: How to use TweetDeck (**bit.ly/inclusive365-356b**)

Education Chat Calendar (**bit.ly/inclusive365-356c**)

Figure 356. Explore a Twitter chat via Tweetdeck.

ISTE STANDARDS FOR STUDENTS
2a, 2b, 3d, 6a, 7a, 7d

ISTE STANDARDS FOR EDUCATORS
1b, 1c, 2a, 2c, 3a, 3b, 4a, 5c, 7b

Backchanneling for Learner Discussions

All learners have something to contribute, but not everyone enjoys participating verbally. A backchannel discussion is a digital space where everyone (educators or learners) can add comments, questions, and other contributions during or after in-person experiences. This can be enticing to those who, for whatever reason, cannot or do not prefer to participate verbally in real-time. Learners can choose which modality works best for them. Backchanneling can be useful during professional events where colleagues share experiences. These discussions promote choice, respect different forms of communication, reduce stress, and can be used as evidence of learning.

INCLUSIVE USES

A backchannel tool can provide a flexible, accessible method for collecting information and including the learner in the discussion. Learners who have oral language challenges or are multilingual learners can take the time needed to compose and post their message. Learners not comfortable turning on their microphone during distance learning can be active participants using a backchannel.

SAMPLE TOOLS

YoTeach! is a chat tool to use as a backchannel discussion board. Educators create a room and share the link. Signing up for an educator account allows for multiroom management options (**yoteachapp.com**).

Padlet provides educators the opportunity to moderate posts. The profanity filter prevents any messages containing expletives, even if the chat isn't moderated (**padlet.com**).

Backchannel Chat was made specifically for educators to use for backchannel discussions. It provides moderation and does not require a learner to have an email address. It also has a private messaging feature that can be used between the learner and the educator (**backchannelchat.com**).

EXTENSION OPPORTUNITIES

Bring backchannel discussions into the "front channel" and review information shared as part of the experience to illustrate how learners are participating even if not responding verbally. This validates the sharing and demonstrates respect for every form of communication.

Backchanneling is usually thought of as a synchronous experience ongoing during a presentation or other real-time event. A backchannel can also occur during a longer event where learners can be invited to participate whenever and wherever to build community.

RELATED RESOURCES

New Features of YoTeach!
(**bit.ly/inclusive365-357a**)

The Backchannel: Giving Every Student a Voice in the Blended Mobile Classroom (**bit.ly/inclusive365-357b**)

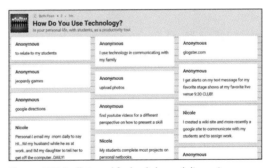

Figure 357. Padlet used for backchannel discussion on how educators are using technology in their lives.

ISTE STANDARDS FOR STUDENTS
1b, 2a, 2b, 3d, 6c

ISTE STANDARDS FOR EDUCATORS
2a, 3a, 3d, 4c, 5b, 6d

Smacking It Down to Learn Something New

Professional learning experiences need not be long events with only one or two presenters. Information, resources, and ideas can be exchanged in brief flashes shared by a multitude of willing individuals. Smackdown events invite educators to share with brevity in mind. Educators line up at the microphone and share something that works for them in three minutes or less. The ideas are meant to be Short, Meaningful, Actionable, Collaborative, and Keepable (SMACK!). Smackdowns can be themed events where educators are invited to share around a central topic, such as technology applications, resources related to a particular content area, or even other professional development strategies. Those organizing or facilitating the smackdown can further expand the experience by offering an online, editable, collaborative document where participants can comment and add additional ideas or resources related to what is being shared. This document can then be referenced as an on-demand resource in the future and shared with those who could not attend the event in real-time. Smackdown events can be created as either an in-person or virtual event.

INCLUSIVE USES

Smackdown events can be focused around shared inclusive strategies, which can help continue to foster the development of an inclusive mindset and promote a culture of inclusive practices. Audio and/or video recordings of a smackdown event can allow people to experience the event repeatedly in a modality that works for their individual needs.

SAMPLE TOOLS

Google Sheets can be used to collect information being shared (**docs.google.com/ spreadsheet**).

YouTube can be used to record and livestream Smackdown events (**youtube.com**).

EXTENSION OPPORTUNITY

Invite learners to organize and participate in a themed smackdown-style event where they each share a tool, resource, or strategy that works to help them learn.

RELATED RESOURCES

Assistive Technology Industry Association App Smackdown Spreadsheets (**bit.ly/inclusive365-358a**)

App Smackdown: Assistive Technology Industry Association professional development resources spreadsheet (**bit.ly/inclusive365-358b**)

Figure 358. Social media post from @wernedat sharing the standing-room only Smackdown event.

ISTE STANDARDS FOR STUDENTS

1d, 2b, 3a, 3b, 3c, 6a, 6c, 6d, 7a, 7b, 7c

ISTE STANDARDS FOR EDUCATORS

1b, 2a, 2b, 2c, 3a, 3b, 4a, 4b, 4c, 4d, 5a, 5b, 5c, 6b, 6d

Automating Electronic Messages to Promote Anytime Learning

Electronic mail continues to be a primary method of communication and collaboration between professionals. This method of asynchronous messaging provides an opportunity for automating the transfer of information to promote the spread of inclusive practices. Professionals can add resources to the signatures of their emails, enticing readers to learn more. Similarly, engaging and empowering away-message responses can be drafted to include resources that help spread knowledge and awareness of resources that promote inclusion, while encouraging a culture of coaching and empowerment.

INCLUSIVE USES

The resources and messages shared with other professionals can help promote awareness of practices that promote an inclusive mindset.

SAMPLE TOOL

Popular email services, such as Outlook and Gmail, invite users to add customized signatures and away messages which are included automatically in outgoing email correspondence.

EXTENSION OPPORTUNITY

Invite learners and other educators to craft their own signatures and away messages with embedded resources which promote inclusion.

RELATED RESOURCES

A.T.TIPSCAST Episode #123: Spreading the Virus—Professional Development So Easy, a Zombie Could Do It (**bit.ly/inclusive365-359a**)

Sample Automatic Email Reply Message (**bit.ly/inclusive365-359b**)

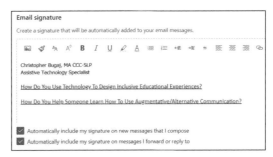

Figure 359. Sample email signature in Outlook.

ISTE STANDARDS FOR STUDENTS

2b, 5b, 6a, 6b, 6c, 7a, 7b, 7c, 7d

ISTE STANDARDS FOR EDUCATORS

2a, 2b, 2c, 3a, 3b, 3c, 3d, 4a, 6d

STRATEGY 360

Listening To Podcasts From Edtech Coaches

Subscribe and listen to podcasts during your commute, while exercising, doing chores, or anytime to further your learning about research, evaluation, and the implementation of tools and strategies related to educational technology.

INCLUSIVE USES

Invite educators to listen and/or subscribe to specific episodes to further their own understanding about specific topics related to using technology to design educational experiences for all. When educators increase their knowledge base about technology they are better able to use that technology to support the diverse learners they work with.

SAMPLE TOOLS

House of Edtech podcast, hosted by Christopher Nesi, highlights technology educators can use to change the learning experience (**bit.ly/inclusive365-360a**).

Easy Edtech Podcast, hosted by Monica Burns, brings you tips, tricks, and strategies to use in your learning spaces (**bit.ly/inclusive365-360b**).

The Edtech Take Out podcast, hosted by Mindy Cairney and Jonathan Wylie, offers up bite-sized technology tips to support educators (**bit.ly/inclusive365-360c**).

EXTENSION OPPORTUNITIES

Educators and learners can explore episodes together and critically review the information. Collaboratively rich discussions can ensue to identify opportunities to infuse that knowledge into the learning environment.

Invite families to subscribe and listen to podcasts together (perhaps while in the car or while using public transportation) to learn about technology that can support learning.

Invite other educators to participate in collaborative learning teams (CLTs) to discuss specific topics shared in podcasts. Like a book study, the team could listen to one episode a month and meet to discuss the topic, sharing takeaways and action steps. Each month one member of the team could pick an episode to share and lead the discussion by generating a list of guiding questions. The CLT could meet in person during the workday, after hours at a local establishment, at someone's personal residence, or virtually on any number of platforms.

RELATED RESOURCE

How to Listen to Podcasts: Everything You Need to Know (**bit.ly/inclusive365-360d**)

Figure 360. Educators can improve their skills anywhere, anytime, through the power of listening to podcasts.

ISTE STANDARDS FOR STUDENTS
1b, 2b, 3d, 7a

ISTE STANDARDS FOR EDUCATORS
1b, 1c, 2b, 4c, 6d

Listening to Podcasts to Learn about Dyslexia

Subscribe and listen to podcasts during your commute, while exercising, doing chores, or anytime to further your learning about research, evaluation, and the implementation of tools and strategies related to dyslexia and other learner variabilities related to reading.

INCLUSIVE USES

Learners can be invited to listen and/or subscribe to specific episodes to further their own understanding.

SAMPLE TOOLS

The Dyslexia Quest podcast, hosted by Elisheva Schwartz, provides interviews and insights related to dyslexia (**bit.ly/dyslexiaquestpodcast**).

The Dyslexia is Our SuperPower podcast by Gibby Booth features both fictional and non-fictional content related to dyslexia (**bit.ly/inclusive365-361a**).

EXTENSION OPPORTUNITIES

Invite families to subscribe and listen to podcasts together, perhaps while in the car or while using public transportation.

Invite learners and families to investigate becoming part of the communities of practice that surround the different podcasts made up of other listeners. Individuals could be encouraged to ask questions, leave comments, and otherwise participate in discussions about topics presented during individual episodes of the show.

RELATED RESOURCE

Top 10 Dyslexia Podcasts You Must Follow (2021) (**bit.ly/inclusive365-361b**)

Figure 361. Cartoon of people listening to podcasts in different environments.

ISTE STANDARDS FOR STUDENTS

1a, 1b, 1c, 1d, 4b, 4c

ISTE STANDARDS FOR EDUCATORS

1a, 1b, 1c, 2a, 2b, 2c, 4c, 4d, 5a, 5b, 6a

Learning from Others Using Hashtags

Social media has been a transformative learning tool for many innovative educators and the primary reason is through the power of the hashtag. Traditionally, educators expanded their knowledge through professional development that was assigned to them within their own district or by attending conferences. With social media, learning is always just-in-time and available. Educators ask for help with challenging situations or share their awesome ideas using a specific hashtag that can be followed and responded to by others. Find your peeps, your subject, or passion using specific hashtags to model a love for life-long learning with learners.

INCLUSIVE USES

Hashtags facilitate the search for topics, strategies, or ideas, which increases efficiency for educators. Hashtags are often hyperlinks that consolidate and organize information, streamlining the experience of learning from the shared content.

SAMPLE TOOLS

Twitter, Instagram, and Facebook all use hashtags as part of their platforms. Search and follow any hashtag listed in the Complete Guide to Twitter Hashtags for Education (**bit.ly/inclusive365-362a**).

To discuss strategies shared in this book, use the hashtag #Inclusive365.

EXTENSION OPPORTUNITY

Invite your colleagues to create and use a professional development hashtag for your district. Colleagues could share new strategies, ideas, and resources for innovative instruction across your entire school district.

RELATED RESOURCES

How to Create and Use Hashtags (**bit.ly/inclusive365-362b**)

The Best 100 Education Hashtags for All Educators on Twitter (**bit.ly/inclusive365-362c**)

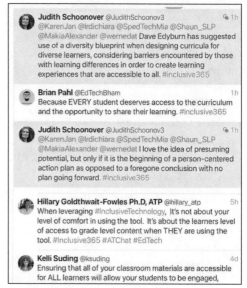

Figure 362. Follow a Twitter hashtag like #Inclusive365 to continue learning and building your professional learning network.

ISTE STANDARDS FOR STUDENTS
1b, 2b, 3d, 7a

ISTE STANDARDS FOR EDUCATORS
1a, 1b, 1c, 2a, 2b, 2c, 4a, 4c, 6d

Exploring Educator-Created Interactive Documents

Hyperdocs are specially designed, interactive documents with embedded hyperlinks to all of the resources for a given educational experience. Digital technologies allow educators to easily collaborate and share hyperdocs with other educators around the world. The willingness to share created resources is a hallmark of a digitally connected educator.

INCLUSIVE USES

Hyperdocs support learners and educators by simplifying the processes of locating the resources needed to participate in a learning experience. Everything is contained in one location, making the experience accessible to every learner.

SAMPLE TOOL

Educators have collaborated to create the HyperDocs Academy website to support other educators in effectively using technology for instruction and to inspire, engage, and transform learning. This website shares information about hyperdocs including pedagogy, video support, and instruction about how to create your own. The site also contains samples, templates, and numerous hyperdocs to use relative to a variety of topics (**hyperdocs.co**).

EXTENSION OPPORTUNITY

Invite learners to adapt and/or create hyperdocs for specific or preferred topics to involve them in their own learning.

RELATED RESOURCES

Getting Started with Hyperdocs (**bit.ly/inclusive365-363a**)

Samples of HyperDocs for Every Subject (**bit.ly/inclusive365-363b**)

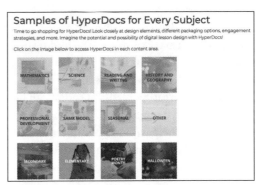

Figure 363. Hyperdoc topics from HyperDoc Academy.

ISTE STANDARDS FOR STUDENTS
1b, 3c, 6b, 6d

ISTE STANDARDS FOR EDUCATORS
1b, 2a, 2c, 3b, 5a, 5b, 5c, 7b

Generating Certificates of Completion Automatically

Documenting professional learning is an important way to demonstrate attendance and commitment to professional and personal growth. Beyond the desire to further their learning, some educators are provided with incentives to complete professional learning experiences, such as pay increases, elevated roles, micro-credentials, or even an allowance to wear more casual clothing in the middle of the week! Organizers, designers, and deliverers of professional learning experiences can help participants by creating certificates that can be distributed upon completion of the experience. Technology can help with the creation and distribution of certificates so more time can be spent on the learning the experience.

INCLUSIVE USES

All learners should be provided with an opportunity to be celebrated for their professional learning accomplishments. Providing a certificate of completion promotes enrollment, engagement, and completion of learning tasks. Digital delivery allows participants to search and locate certificates without needing to be in one physical location.

SAMPLE TOOLS

Google Forms and Google Sheets allow users to collect attendance or participation information through forms and spreadsheets. The form can contain the name of the event, feedback about the delivery of the experiences, and, most importantly, ways they plan to implement what was discussed to improve their practice. The form can then be set to automatically create and populate a spreadsheet.

The Autocrat add-on within Google Sheets enables an automatic merge process to take the raw data from the Google form and convert it into completed fields on a certificate (**bit.ly/inclusive365-364a**).

EXTENSION OPPORTUNITY

Create certificates for school-aged learners as they master concepts. These certificates can be kept in a portfolio, demonstrating evidence of their learning. Learners can insert those certificates into a Google Site to produce and share their digital portfolio of educational accomplishments.

RELATED RESOURCES

How to Use Autocrat to Create Certificates (**bit.ly/inclusive365-364b**)

How Do I Use Google Forms and Sheets to Automatically Generate Custom Certificates? (**bit.ly/inclusive365-364c**)

Figure 364a. Google form used to collect educator data for professional development.

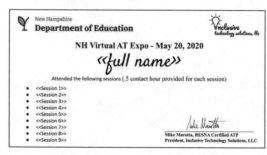

Figure 364b. Certificate template using Google Slides.

ISTE STANDARDS FOR STUDENTS
1a, 1b

ISTE STANDARDS FOR EDUCATORS
1b, 1c, 2a, 2c, 3a, 3b, 4a, 5c, 7b

Promoting a Culture of Inclusivity by Establishing a Learning Brand

You may see it on your Instagram feed or on educational blogs that you visit—posts that have a certain identifiable look to them. And when you are scrolling, you know to stop there because you will find the content valuable. Creating a brand as an educator is a way to signal to followers in a busy digital world that you have something important to share. Using a consistent font, colors, and graphics are a part of branding that makes social media posts easily recognizable and impossible to scroll past. Make sure that your important message about inclusive education is seen!

INCLUSIVE USES

A recognizable learning brand engages the reader or social media consumer, allowing important information about education and learning to be disseminated more effectively.

SAMPLE TOOL

Canva allows educators to quickly and easily create graphics for social media posts and blogs (**canva.com**).

EXTENSION OPPORTUNITY

Invite learners to create their own brand. Have them consider what colors, font, and graphics represent their personality and best communicate their message.

RELATED RESOURCE

Branding your Business (**bit.ly/inclusive365-365a**)

Figure 365. Graphic from the @aaccoach (Kate McLaughlin).

ISTE STANDARDS FOR STUDENTS
6b, 6c, 6d

ISTE STANDARDS FOR EDUCATORS
2a, 5c, 6d

Creating a To-Stop-Doing List

It is obvious that change comes with taking action, however, sometimes those actions can and should be about what individuals and institutions choose *not* to do. To assist in the quest of bringing authentic, inclusive practices to their local education agency, educators can make a table with three columns. The first two columns can be labeled To Do Now and To Do Soon. This book is filled with strategies to help educators populate the first two columns. Putting these strategies in place results in more inclusive practices and positively impacts lives. Educators can then label the final column To Stop Doing and populate those with methods that do not support inclusive practices. To populate that column, educators are invited to reflect on the following questions:

- What methods are we currently implementing that hinder inclusive practices?

- Which tools are we using that present barriers to inclusive instruction?

- What practices might we rethink to help learners become included?

- What policies exist that challenge our goals of providing inclusive experiences?

- Who are the decision makers that I need to reach to facilitate change? How do we collaborate for effective, inclusive change?

- What legacy techniques have been around for so long that we haven't even considered questioning them?

To help educators with this endeavor, consider a list of strategies the authors did not put in this book. The following are methods intentionally omitted:

- Worksheets

- Paper handouts

- Presentation of materials without checking accessibility

- Compulsory homework

- Timed assessments

- Rote exercises

- Round-robin oral reading

- Round-robin quizzing

- Permission to use the bathroom

- Mandatory use of cameras during distance learning

- Assigned seating

- Columns or rows of desks of uniform size and shape

- One-size-fits-all seats

- Fluorescent bulbs as the only source of light

- Carrot-and-stick activities—extrinsic rewards

- Withholding recess

- Banning personal device use

- Using singular points of data to inform instruction

- Comparisons to peer performance

- Grades

- Standardized testing

- Mandatory homework

- "Because I'm the teacher. That's why."

- "Because that's the way we've always done it."

- "A child's job is school."

- "Becoming college ready."

- Anything else that removes agency or choice

- Anything else that forces learners to do the exact same thing in the same way at the same time.

INCLUSIVE USES

All learners benefit when practices that hinder inclusivity are abated and replaced with practices that promote individual growth, personalization, and agency.

SAMPLE TOOL

Use this Google Doc template to create your own To Do Now, To Do Soon, To Stop Doing List (**bit.ly/inclusive365-366a**).

EXTENSION OPPORTUNITIES

Invite learners to create their own To Do Now, To Do Soon, To Stop Doing lists, reflecting on actions that would improve their lives

Invite learners to collaborate with educators on the creation of To Do Now, To Do Soon, To Stop Doing lists. What might learners in your own local educational agency say they'd like to see happen or to stop happening?

RELATED RESOURCES

43 Things We Need to Stop Doing in Schools (**bit.ly/inclusive365-366b**)

I Sued the Education System! (**bit.ly/inclusive365-366c**)

Figure 366. A stop sign inviting educators to reconsider legacy practices that present barriers to inclusion.

ISTE STANDARDS FOR STUDENTS

All of them

ISTE STANDARDS FOR EDUCATORS

All of them

Afterword

You did it! You read a year's worth of strategies. Where do you go from here? Following are some ideas:

- Share your favorite strategies or derivations far and wide. Although the contents of this book are copyrighted, the ideas are not. You are encouraged to share your learning with others. One option is to visit **www.inclusive365.com** and select the link at the top of the page to share your experience.

- Create a personalized action plan for yourself. Write three measurable, achievable goals about what you'd like to implement within the next year. Document the steps you'd need to take to reach the goals.

- Collaborate with colleagues to develop a plan to improve the integration of inclusive practices in your local educational agency. Write one or more measurable, achievable goals that can be accomplished within a year, and then at least one more that can be achieved in three years. Make a list of steps the team will enact to create sustainable change.

- Invite learners to read this book. Empower learners to internalize the strategies in this book and consider which they might choose to adopt.

- Invite parents and families to read this book. Learners are better supported when educators work collaboratively with families. Sharing inclusive strategies can help families support learners as they work to achieve their goals.

The future of education is in our hands. Will we accept the mission of creating a new environment where individuality and diversity are valued, respected, honored, cherished, embraced, and celebrated? Educators will best support each learner by realizing that variability, flexibility, and agency should be at the center of educational design.

A new tomorrow is coming. What part will you play in making it more inclusive?

References

Anderson, C. (2018). *TED talks: The official TED guide to public speaking*. Nicholas Brealey Publishing.

Bureau of Justice Statistics. (2016). Crime Against Persons with Disabilities 2009–2014 Statistical Tables. Retrieved from www.bjs.gov/index.cfm?ty=pbdetail&iid=5844

Bellini, S., Akullian, J. (2007). A meta-analysis of video modeling and video self-modeling interventions for children and adolescents with autism spectrum disorders. *Exceptional Children*, Spring 2007. Retrieved from bit.ly/3fD7Aiu

Bouck, E. C., Satsangi, R., & Park, J. (2017). The concrete-representational-abstract approach for students with learning disabilities: An evidence-based practice synthesis. *Remedial and Special Education, 39*(4), 211–228.

Collaborative for Academic, Social, and Emotional Learning (CASEL). casel.org.

CommonLit |. (n.d.). Retrieved from www.commonlit.org

Cunningham, P. M., & Hall, D. P. (2009). *Making words first grade: 100 hands-on lessons for phonemic awareness, phonics and spelling*. Boston: Pearson Education.

Dawson, P., & Guare, R. (2018). *Executive skills in children and adolescents: A practical guide to assessment and intervention*. New York: Guilford Press.

Deci, E. L., Koestner, R., & Ryan, R. M. (2001). Extrinsic rewards and intrinsic motivation in education: Reconsidered once again. *Review of Educational Research, 71*(1), 1–27. doi:10.3102/00346543071001001

How does dual coding improve learning? (2020). Retrieved from bit.ly/3uceEGY

Erickson, K. A., & Koppenhaver, D. (2020). *Comprehensive literacy for all: Teaching students with significant disabilities to read and write*. Baltimore, MD: Paul H. Brookes Publishing.

Evmenova, A. S. Lights! camera! captions!: The effects of picture and/or … (2008). Retrieved from bit.ly/3wfy8wl

Fisher, A. V., Godwin, K. E., & Seltman, H. (2014). Visual environment, attention allocation, and learning in young children. *Psychological Science, 25*(7), 1362–1370. doi:10.1177/0956797614533801

Flipped Learning Network. (2014). "Definition of Flipped Learning." Retrieved from bit.ly/2QV889k

Hammond, Z., & Jackson, Y. (2015). *Culturally responsive teaching and the brain: Promoting authentic engagement and rigor among culturally and linguistically diverse students*. California: Corwin.

Hammond, Z. (2020, June 13). 3 tips to make any lesson more culturally responsive. Retrieved from bit.ly/31EkvZl

Harrell, E. Crimes against persons with disabilities, 2009–2015 … (2016, November 29). Retrieved from www.bjs.gov/content/pub/pdf/capd0915st.pdf

Hattie, J., & Timperley, H. (2007). The power of feedback. *Review of Educational Research, 77*(1), 81–112. doi.org/10.3102/003465430298487

Hattie, J. (2017). *Visible learning for teachers: Maximizing impact on learning.* London: Routledge.

Huang, H., & Eskey, D. E. (1999). The effects of closed-captioned television on the listening comprehension of intermediate english as a second language (esl) students. *Journal of Educational Technology Systems, 28*(1), 75–96. doi:10.2190/rg06-lywb-216y-r27g

Huyck, D. & Dahlen, S. P. (2019 June 19). Diversity in children's books 2018. Retrieved from bit.ly/3sI0wFa

International Society for Technology in Education (2016), ISTE Standards for Students, Retrieved from www.iste.org/standards/for-students.

International Society for Technology in Education, (2017), ISTE Standards for Educators. Retrieved from www.iste.org/standards/for-educators

James, K. H., & Engelhardt, L. (2012). The effects of handwriting experience on functional brain development in pre-literate children. *Trends in Neuroscience and Education, 1*(1), 32–42. doi:10.1016/j.tine.2012.08.001

Sutton, R. M., Douglas, K., & Hornsey, M. (2012). *Feedback the communication of praise, criticism, and advice.* New York, NY: Lang.

Ma, X., Yue, Z., Gong, Z., Zhang, H., Duan, N., Shi, Y., . . . Li, Y. (2017). The effect of diaphragmatic breathing on attention, negative affect and stress in healthy adults. *Frontiers in Psychology, 8.* doi:10.3389/fpsyg.2017.00874

Maurer, E., & Patrick, J. (2017). Where are the women? A report on the status of women in the United States social studies standards. Retrieved from bit.ly/3wjtLjJ

Mayo Clinic. (2020, August 18). Exercise and stress: Get moving to manage stress. Retrieved from https://mayocl.in/31EK1Oa

Meyer, A., Rose, D. H., & Gordon, D. T. (2014). *Universal design for learning: Theory and practice.* Wakefield, MA: CAST Professional Publishing.

Rello, L., & Baeza-Yates, R. (2013). Good fonts for dyslexia. *Proceedings of the 15th International ACM SIGACCESS Conference on Computers and Accessibility.* doi:10.1145/2513383.2513447

Rodrigues, P. F., & Pandeirada, J. N. (2018). When visual stimulation of the surrounding environment affects children's cognitive performance. *Journal of Experimental Child Psychology, 176*, 140–149. doi:10.1016/j.jecp.2018.07.014

School Library Journal Staff (2019) An updated look at diversity in children's books. *School Library Journal.* Retrieved from bit.ly/3ma1B6a

See, think, wonder. (2019). Retrieved from pz.harvard.edu/resources/see-think-wonder.

Shmoop Editorial Team. (2008, November 11). Homework help & study guides for students. Retrieved from www.shmoop.com

Statista. (2021). The 100 largest companies in the world by market capitalization in 2020. Retreived from www.statista.com/statistics/263264/top-companies-in-the-world-by-market-capitalization.

Student Privacy Resource Center. (2020, November 4). Student privacy compass. Retrieved from studentprivacycompass.org

Tomlinson, C. A. (1999). *The differentiated classroom: Responding to the needs of all learners.* Alexandria, VA: ASCD.

Trafton, A. (2014). In the blink of an eye. *MIT News.* Retrieved from news.mit.edu/2014/in-the-blink-of-an-eye-0116.

US Department of Education. (2020, April 22). Protecting Student Privacy. Retrieved from studentprivacy.ed.gov

Visa. Practical Money Skills. (2020). Retrieved from practicalmoneyskills.com/about/mission

Ward, S. (2016, December). Strategies for improving executive function skills to plan, organize, and problem solve for school success. Retrieved from bit.ly/3dwiaFz

Whittingham, J., Huffman, S., Christensen, R., & McAllister, T. (2013). Use of audiobooks in a school library and positive effects of struggling readers' participation in a library-sponsored audiobook club. *School Library Research, 16.*

Willis, J. (2007) The Neuroscience of Joyful Education. *Educational Leadership.* Retrieved from bit.ly/3mcYpqd

Indexes

INDEX OF STRATEGIES

This index cross-references strategies by category. The bold number ranges indicate a section of the book dedicated to that category.

Cross Content

1–97, 101, 106, 107, 108, 119, 120, 121, 123, 127, 131, 134, 141, 147, 150, 151, 156, 161, 171, 172, 180, 192, 197, 202, 206, 213, 223, 240, 243, 244, 246, 248, 249, 250, 253, 254, 256, 257,258, 259, 260, 261, 262, 263, 267, 270, 272, 273, 277, 282, 286, 287, 289, 294, 295, 307, 317, 319, 322, 323, 334, 335, 336, 343, 345, 347, 350, 357, 363, 366

Reading

17, 32, 62, 77, 80, **98–156**, 157,189, 191, 195, 199, 245, 255, 281,325, 354, 361

Writing

33, 62, 78, 86, 89, 95, 139, 141, 145, 148, 151, **157–201**, 250, 251, 265, 266, 268, 269, 273, 324, 354

STEAM

33, 52, 53, 111, **202–239**, 247, 262, 276, 335

Research & Studying

8, 10, 12, 62, 63, 77, 78, 121, 125, 144, 145, 169, **240–274**, 325, 360

Executive Functioning

14, 20, 27, 48, 49, 50, 51, 54, 66, 90, 216, 242, 250, 252, 263, 264, 266, 267, 268, 271, 273, 274, **275–308**, 309, 313, 315, 321, 326, 331, 334

Social Emotional

13, 14, 19, 20, 27, 29, 82, 83, 90, 188, 216, 303, 304, **309–340**, 349

Professional Learning

7, 16, 23, 41, 42, 44, 45, 46, 51, 58, 61, 80, 81, 87, 94, 96, 97, 102, 117, 188, 240, **341–365**

The Un-Strategy

366

INDEX OF TOOLS

This index lists alphabetically the name of every tool that appears in the book.

#

#AbleismExists, 341
#ActuallyAutistic, 341
#NeuroDiverseSquad, 341
#OwnVoices, 341
#WheelChairLife, 341
3-2-1 Reflection Template, 94
360 Thinking, 300
44 Phonemes Video, 99
60 Second Recap, 154

A

ABCya, 144
ABCya Animate, 52
Acapella Voices, 323
Accessibility review checklist, 46
Actively Learn, 123
Adaptive Controller for xBox, 309, 320
    Adaptive Switch Kit by Logitech, 309, 320
Adobe Acrobat, 17
Adobe Connect, 19
Adobe Spark, 156
AEM Pilot, 3, 46
All Sides, 254
Alt text, 36
Amazon, 148, 199
Amazon Alexa, 248
A Mighty Girl, 64, 101
Anchor, 74
Animaker, 53
Animoto, 95
Anki, 296
AnswerGarden, 169
Apple Pencil, 165
Apple Podcasts, 264
Arcade Game Generator, 87
AR Flashcards, 110
Assembly, 97
ATMakers, 217
Audacity, 75, 116
Autocrat, 364
AudioMaker, 56
AudioNote, 273
Avaz Reader, 114, 138

B

Backchannel chat, 18, 357
Battery Interrupter, 43
Beeline Reader, 136
Bellus 3D, 327

Bensound, 28
Bit.ly, 61
Book Creator, 39, 95, 180, 316, 339
Bouncyballs, 50
Brainscape, 296
Breakout EDU, 16
Breathe app, 321
Breathing Zone, 321
Brix Build, 226
Bubbl.us, 168, 270

C

Canva, 258, 365
Cast of Wonders, 125
Catchy Words, 110
CC Search Browser Extension, 30
Certify'em, 88
Character Trait graphic organizers, 154
Chat Editor, 115
ChatterPix, 191
ChatterPix Kids, 191
Checker Plus for Google Calendar, 305
ChoiceWorks, 302, 303, 334
Chrome Bookmark Bar, 284
Chrome Browser, 151
Chrome Browser Group Tabs, 285
Chrome Extensions Manager, 286
Chrome Music Lab, 233
Chrome Operating System, 34
Chrome Operating System Dictation, 160
Chrome Operating System Magnifier, 65
Chrome Operating System On-Screen Keyboard, 162
Chrome Operating System Text-to-Speech, 106, 192
Chromavid, 78
Citation Machine, 241
Ck12.org, 60
CK–12 Concept Maps, 223
ClaroPDF Pro, 152
Class Dojo, 318
Classroomscreen, 207, 295, 319
Classroom Tools: Random Name Picker, 319
Class YouTube Channel free template, 31
Clicker Writer, 171, 173, 179
Cloud Audio Recorder, 62
Clips, 82, 146
Code and Go Robot Mouse, 237
Common Lit ,126, 142
Copy Machine, 41
CoSpaces, 340
Coursera, 343

Creative Commons, 30
Culture and Diversity in Schools YouTube Channel, 342
Custom-Cursor.com, 66

D

Decoste Writing Protocol, 159
Design Your Classroom, 10
Desmos graphing calculator, 212, 225, 226
Didax, 203
Diigo, 152, 263, 283
Disability Arts Online, 15
Diagrams, 292, 332
Digital Classroom Timers, 300
Distraction-free mode, 287
DIY Stylus, 33
Document Camera, 54
Dualless, 307
Ducksters, 64
Dungeons & Dragons, 325
Dyslexia Is Our SuperPower podcast, 361
Dyslexia Quest podcast, 361
Dyslexia Simulator, 100

E

Earth School, 202
Easy EdTech podcast, 360
Eco Education, 63
Edcamp, 353
Edmodo, 21
EdTech Takeout podcast, 360
Edublogs, 2
Edpuzzle, 244, 316
EmojiCopy, 188
Emojipedia, 188, 281
Emoji Typer, 346
Envision AI, 315
Epic Books, 64, 105, 127
EquatIO, 205, 210, 211
Evernote, 282
Executive Skills questionnaire (Dawson and Guare), 275
Extensis Fonts, 102
Extensity, 286
EZ GIF Makers, 124

F

Facebook, 2, 190, 311, 348, 350
Fact Check, 254
Fit and Fun Playscapes, 14
Flexible seating, 280
Flickr, 6
Flipgrid, 20, 25, 39, 81, 104, 149, 187, 213, 215, 261, 304, 336
Flocabulary, 269
Floorplanner, 8, 9
Floreo, 340

Fluency Tutor for Google, 116
Focus Keeper, 291
Folder Marker for Windows, 10 279
Free Logo Design, 97
Free online file converter, 72
Free online graph paper, 222, 226

G

GBoard, 164
Geoboard, 219
Geogebra, 220
Giphy, 124, 346
Glogster EDU, 317
Glow Word Books, 201
Goodreads, 140, 199
Good Night Stories for Rebel Girls podcast, 257
Google Arts and Culture, 52, 247, 261
Google Autodraw, 70
Google Assistant, 248
Google Calendar, 279
Google Cardboard, 69, 340
Google Classroom, 38, 194
Google Dictionary, 121
Google Docs, 1, 105, 149, 157, 158, 170, 173, 176, 184, 197, 198, 292
Google Drawings, 76, 186, 204, 255
Google Drive, 90, 240, 279
Google Earth, 59, 256
Google Fonts, 132
Google Forms, 4, 13, 16, 22, 58, 81, 84, 85, 88, 91, 92, 105, 272, 277, 314, 332, 337, 364
Google GMail, 359
Google Jamboard ,109, 112, 166, 204, 246, 322
Google Keep, 105, 131, 165, 166, 171, 193, 195, 240, 252, 263, 271, 274, 279, 282, 290, 294, 322
Google Meet, 19, 24, 44, 349
Google Mix Lab, 232
Google My Maps, 243
Google Poly, 83
Google Semi-Conductor, 234
Google Sheets, 105, 140, 172, 197, 267, 355, 358, 364
Google Site, 89, 149
Google Slides, 35, 42, 45, 62, 68, 79, 145, 149, 150, 197, 274, 317, 336, 352
Google Suite for Education, 34, 348
Google Translate, 161
Google Tour Builder, 59, 83
GoNoodle, 231, 331
Granger Academic, 28
Gravitarium, 326
Green Screen, 78
Guess the Feeling game, 312
Gynzy, 10, 12

H

Headliner, 77
Headspace for Educators, 310
Hemmingway Editor, 196
Highlights Tool for Google Docs, 200, 245
High School E-sports League, 309
Hipster Logo Generator, 97
Holt Interactive KWL chart, 272
Hootsuite, 350
House of EdTech podcast, 360
HyperDocs, 363

I

IMGFlip meme generator, 86
Inspiration Maps, 71, 265
Instagram, 2, 190, 350
Instructables, 228
Immersive Reader, 138, 139, 155
Inclusive Classroom Specialization online course, 344
Interactive Phonics song, 99
Interactive Ten Frame, 209
iOS Color Filter, 137
iOS Location Reminders, 290
iOS Magnifier, 65
iOS On-Screen Keyboard, 162
iOS Photos, 150
iOS Picture-in-Picture, 242
iOS Pointing Device Settings, 40
iOS QuickPath, 164
iOS Screen Recording, 53, 67, 253
iOS Screen Time, 288
iOS Shortcuts, 289
iOS Split View, 307
iOS Spoken Content, 106, 107, 192

J

Junior Achievement, USA 216
Just a Line, 227

K

Kahoot, 329
Kaizena, 93, 184
Kami, 152
Keyboard stickers, 163
Keynote, 35
Khan Academy, 202
Kidlit, 105
Kids Wordsmyth, 174

L

Language is a Virus, 182
Leading Equity Center, 342
Lee and Low, 101, 206
LessonPix, 27, 79, 129, 207, 302, 303, 323, 329, 339
Lessonsinherstory, 64

LibriVox, 103, 125
Lifeliqe, 221
Link to text fragments, 37
Loom, 53, 253
LucidChart, 332
Lyrics, 346

M

Mad Takes, 201
Make: Projects, 228
MakeBeliefsComix, 141
Makers Making Change, 230
Mathigon, 218
Mathplanet, 218
Mathway, 214
Math Learning Center, 203
Math Number Rack, 208
Meme Generator, 258
Mercury Reader, 287
Merge Cube, 262
Micnote, 250
Microsoft, 365 34, 348
Microsoft Excel, 172, 197, 335, 355
Microsoft Edge, 135
Microsoft Forms, 13, 91, 92, 314
Microsoft Lens, 131, 240
Microsoft Math Solver, 210
Microsoft OneNote, 16, 93, 165, 167, 185, 205, 250, 271, 274, 279, 282
Microsoft Outlook, 279, 359
Microsoft Planner, 293
Microsoft PowerPoint, 35, 42, 45, 47, 62, 68, 79, 150, 166, 191, 197, 274, 352
Microsoft Stream, 146
Microsoft Sway, 336
Microsoft Teams, 19
Microsoft Whiteboard, 109, 112
Microsoft Word, 151, 157, 158, 161, 170, 194, 196, 197, 241, 260, 289, 292
Mindomo, 299
Minecraft Edu, 63, 224
Mindshift, 333
Moment AR, 330
Mood Meter, 312
Momentum, 297
Move to Learn, 331
Museum Art and Culture Consortium, 247
MyLife, 321
MyPerfectResume, 324
My Script Calculator, 2, 210

N

National Assistive Technology Act Technical Assistance and Training Center, 347
New Oxford American Dictionary, 121

Newsela, 120, 126, 134
Netflix Party, 349
No Fear Shakespeare, 154
Noisli, 49
No Red Ink, 178, 183
Notability, 273
Note Board Chrome Extension, 294
Now Comment, 313
Number Frame app, 209
Nuvoice, 115

O

OER Commons, 60, 259
OCALI Autism internet modules, 345
OCALI Assistive Technology internet modules, 345
Office 365 for Educators, 5
One World Posters, 101
OneTab, 278, 285
Online Assessment of Writing Methods, 159
Open Dyslexicfont, 132
OpenStax, 259
Otter.ai, 268
Overdrive, 103

P

Padlet, 18, 58, 105, 143, 169, 293, 294, 301, 317, 357
Paint Splash, 326
Panoform, 69
PASS software, 129
Periodic Table of iPad apps for primary students, 7
Photomath, 214
Pics4Learning, 6, 28
Piclits, 186
Picture-In-Picture by Google, 242
Pinterest, 317
Pixabay, 6, 28
Piktochart, 76
Pixton EDU, 29, 141, 323
Photo Scissors, 47
PlayPosit, 244
Plickers, 22, 338
Podcastle AI, 56
Poetry Machine, 182
Poetry Templates, 182
Poll Everywhere, 22
Pomodoro Timer Software, 291
Polypad, 203
Popplet, 168, 169, 270
PowerPoint templates from Microsoft, 57
Power Thesaurus, 174
PracticalMoneySkills, 216
Project-Based Learning customized editing checklists, 193
Project Gutenberg, 103
Puppet Master, 147
PublicDomainImages, 28

Q

QR Code Monkey, 96, 149, 304
Quiver Augmented Reality, 262
Quizzizz, 4, 85, 329

R

Raspberry Pi, 236
Read&Write for Google Chrome, 23, 56, 93, 108, 119, 132, 133, 155, 167, 184, 185, 200, 245
Reading Mindset Snapshot, 98
Readtopia, 126
Readworks, 120
ReadWriteThink, 71, 354
ReClipped, 266
Remind, 318
Remove, 47
Rescue Time, 288
Rewordify, 134
Roblox, 63
Rocket Note, 266

S

Safari Reader View, 287
Safeshare.TV, 31
SAM, 333
ScannerBin, 41
Scratch, 111
Scratch Jr, 111
Screencastify, 53, 67, 253
Seeing AI, 130, 315
Seesaw, 38, 39, 90, 213, 318
Session Buddy, 278
Shake Up Learning Chrome Extension Database, 7
Shmoop, 128, 154
Simple English Wikipedia, 134
Sketchbook, 255
Sketch.IO, 255
Skype a Scientist, 206
Siri, 248, 298
Slides Carnival, 57
SlidesMania, 57
Smithsonian American "Because of Her Story" Women's History Initiative, 64
Snapcalc, 214
Snap&Read Universal, 119, 133, 151, 155, 241, 272, 287
Snopes, 254
Social Justice Books, 101
SodaPDF, 17
Speakflow, 80, 117
Special Olympics virtual movement, 27
Sphero, 237, 238, 239
Spritz, 118
Starfall Geometry, 3D 235
Sticky Notes, 301, 338

Storyboard That, 29, 141, 323, 327
StorylineOnline, 105
Sutori.com, 156
Swift Playgrounds, 202
Switch Control for iOS, 32
Synth, 23

T

Tab Resize, 307
Tab Snooze, 285
TableTop Audio, 49
TarHeel Reader, 32, 130, 177, 180
Tate for Kids, 52
Talking Magnetic Alphabet, 112
Tagxedo, 175
Teachers Pay Teachers, 102
TED Talks master class, 351
TEDTalk YouTube channel, 249
Textcompactor, 122
Thingiverse, 113, 228
ThingLink, 308
TimeGraphics, 156
Timer.OnlineClock, 328
Timestorm podcast, 257
Time Timer, 300
Tinkercad, 113
TinyURL, 61
ThingLink, 55, 308
Tomato Timer, 291
Tommy the Turtle Learns to Code, 235
Toontastic 3D, 52, 189
Transo, 265
Trello, 293
TweenTribune, 126
Tweetdeck, 350, 356
Twisted Wave, 75
Twitter, 2, 153, 181, 190, 350, 362

U

Understood, 100
Unite for Literacy, 127
Unsplash, 6, 11, 28
Use Immersive Reader on Websites, 5, 138, 139

V

Very Best Code Switch episodes for kids, 257
Virtual background in Zoom, 11
Virtual fidget spinner, 326
Virtual tours of National Parks, 59
Visor, 135, 137
Visual effects for Google Meet, 11
Visual Paradigms online diagrams, 58, 81, 337
Visuwords, 251
Voice Control, 48
Voice Note, 93

VoiceThread, 20, 191, 215, 246
Voice Typing, 160
Voxer, 21, 23

W

Wakelet, 31, 143, 263, 283
Waypoint, EDU 26
Water Bottle Dice Shaker, 229
WeVideo, 67, 73
Wheel of Names, 319
Whiteboard.Chat, 322
Wikki-Stix, 163
Windows, 34
Windows Magnifier, 65
Windows on-screen keyboard, 162
Wonderopolis, 261
WonderWorkshop, 239
Word banks, 171
Word clouds, 144
Word cloud add on, 175
Word Cloud Generator, 175
Wordpress, 148
Write About This, 178
Writereader, 179
Wriq, 198

Y

YiNote, 266
Your Logical Fallacy, 276
YouTube, 49, 264, 311, 358
YoTeach!, 18, 357

Z

Zoom, 19, 22, 24, 44, 349

BOOK INDEX

A

AAC (augmentative and alternative communication), 115, 129
abstract resources, 205
accessibility
    document templates for, 170
    ebook library, 105
    of learning materials, 3, 46
    scanning text for, 41
    of slide decks, 35
accommodations, xvii
accountability partners, 313
acknowledgments, viii–ix
actions, automating, 289
activities, as term, xxiii
adjustable work surfaces, 9
agency, 2
AI (artificial intelligence), 52, 247
alphabet brainstorming, 173
alt text, 36
ambient noises/music, 49
amorphous visual schedules, 301
animation, 53, 124, 147
annotating text digitally, 152
anxiety, managing, 310, 331, 333
apps, 1
AR. *See* augmented reality (AR)
arcade games, 87
arguments, 276
art, 15, 52, 53, 225, 238
art exhibit field trips, 247
articles, 120
artifacts, 26, 69
artificial intelligence (AI), 52, 247
assessments, 84–85, 87–88, 98, 197
assignments, as term, xxiii
assistive technology, 230, 345, 347
Assistive Technology Act Project, 347
asynchronous discussions, 23
asynchronous learning, 249, 345
audience, authentic, 190
audio
    asynchronous discussions and, 23
    books with embedded, 62
    independence, promoting with, 214
    playback speeds, variable, 264
    recording, 20, 75, 116, 167, 185
    transcribing, 260, 268
    video, pairing with, 77
    web content, turning into, 56
audio feedback, 93
audio stories, 191, 257
audio syncing, 250

audiobooks, 103–105, 125
augmentative and alternative communication (AAC), 115, 129
augmented reality (AR)
art exhibit field trips, 247
artifacts, discovering, 26
collaborating with, 227
emotions, reflecting on, 330
history, reframing, 64
letters and words, learning, 110
STEM and history, visualizing, 262
authentic audience, 190
authentic commentary, 148
authentic inclusion, xv–xvi
authentic problems, 228
authentic resources, 254
authors of this book, about, iv–v
autism, 345
auto captions, 42
automatic scrolling, 117
automatic text substitutions, 167
automating actions, 289
automating email, 359
avatars, 29, 327

B

backchanneling discussions, 18, 357
background knowledge, 120
backgrounds, 11, 47
board games, 229
book, origin of this, vi–viii
book characters, 147, 154
book reviews, 149, 199
bookmarking, 263, 283–284
brainstorming, 169, 173
brands, 97, 365
breakout rooms, 24
breaks, brain, 328
breathing techniques, 321
"Bring Your Own Technology" initiatives, 5
browser extensions, 286
browser tabs, 285
Bugaj, Christopher R., iv, vi, viii
bulletin boards, virtual, 294

C

calculations, 213–214
calculators, 210, 212, 225
calendars, Strategy-A-Day, vi
calling strategies, equitable, 319
camel-casing hashtags, 153
captions, 36, 42, 45, 146
C.A.R. (Comment, Ask, and Respond), 130

caregivers, communicating with, 318
certificates of completion, 88, 364
characters, book, 147, 154
charts, 335, 355
chats, private, 19
checklists, 277
choices, 292, 332
citation generators, 241
citizenship, digital, 30
classes, as term, xxiii
classrooms, as term, xxiii. *See also* learning spaces
closed captioning, 45
coaches, EdTech, 360
coding, 111, 235–236
collaborative augmented reality, 227
collaborative brainstorming, 169
collaborative feedback, 306
collaborative Kanban charts, 293
collaborative online slide decks, 68
collaborative problem solving, 16
collaborative resource lists, 263
collaborative rubrics, 91
collaborative slide decks, 68
collaborative video projects, 73
collectivist learning, 322
color-coding for digital organization, 279
colors
    screen, 137
    text, 136
comics, 141
Comment, Ask, and Respond (C.A.R.), 130
commentary, authentic, 148
communication, 115, 129, 130, 318
community, building, 311, 336
community partnerships, 217
completion certificates, 88, 364
comprehension, 121–125, 144
computational sketching, 225
concept maps, 223, 270
concrete resources, 203
Concrete-Representational-Abstract (CRA) continuum, 203–205
content creation, 30, 60
controllers, universal, 320
copy machines, 41
copyright-free media, 28
Cornell Notes, 267
cost of tools, xviii–xix
counting, 209
CRA (Concrete-Representational-Abstract) continuum, 203–205
creative narratives, 187, 189
creative writing, 186
cues, visual, 139, 338
culture of inclusivity, 365

curation tools, 263
curiosity, 261
cursors, 66
customizing, 66, 157, 163

D
decision trees, digital, 332
decluttering web pages, 287
decorating learning spaces, 51
dice, 229
dictionaries, 121, 145, 155
differentiating materials, 38
digital citizenship, 30
digital sandbox, 63, 224
directions, following, 242
disability art, 15
discussions
    asynchronous, 23
    backchanneling, 18, 357
    Think, Pair, Share and, 21
distance learning
    building community for, 311, 329
    movement, promoting during, 27
    private chats in, 19
    small group opportunities in, 24
    virtual backgrounds in, 11
distractions, limiting, 287
diversity, 6, 101, 127, 257, 323, 341
documents, 17, 170, 240, 363
doodling with graphs, 226
dual coding, 141
dual highlighting, 108, 133
dyslexia, 100, 361

E
Earth, 256
ebooks, 103, 105
edcamps, 353
editing writing, 192–193, 196
EdTech coaches, 360
educational materials. *See* materials
educators, as term, xxii
effectiveness, educational, 1
Eisenhower Matrix, 292
electronic messages (email), 359
emojis, 188
emotions, 312, 321, 327, 330
empathy, 58, 316, 337
engagement, 22, 66, 244
equations, 210
equipment, borrowing, 347
equity, 319, 342
escape rooms, virtual, 16
eSports, 309, 320
ethical content creation, 30

events, sequence of, 150, 156
executive function skills, 275, 280
exercise videos, 331
experiences, as term, xxiii
experts, learning from, 249
expression, 70, 77

F

facial expressions of avatars, 327
fact-checkers, 254
fallacies, logical, 276
families, learning resource access for, 96
feedback, 50, 92, 93, 194–195, 306
fidgeting, 326
field trips, art exhibit, 247
file management, 17, 72
finger tracking, digital, 114
flipped learning, xvi
fluorescent lights, 8
focus bars, 135
folders, digital, 281
fonts, 102, 132, 157
formative assessments, multimedia, 85
forms. *See also* templates
    feedback, 92
    rubric, 91
Frayer Model graphic organizers, 145
future thinking, 308

G

games
    arcade, 87
    board, 229
    community building with, 329
    role-playing, 325
    universal controllers for, 320
    virtual, online, 256
geoboards, 219
geocaching, 26
getting-to-know-you presentations, 336
GIFs, animated, 124
goals, 81, 317
grade levels, as term, xxiii
grammar, 158, 183
graph paper, digital, 222, 226
graphic novels, 141
graphic organizers, 145, 168
graphing calculators, 225
green screens, 78

H

handwriting, 165
handwriting calculators, 210
hashtags, 153, 350, 362
herstory, 64

highlighting text, 108, 133, 200, 245
history, 64, 243, 262
hot spots, image, 55, 308
humorous study guides, 128
hybrid learning, 329
hydration, 328
hyperdocs, 363

I

icebreakers, virtual, 346
images
    backgrounds of, 47
    captions and alt text for, 36
    creative writing with, 186
    digital, 271
    hot spots, 55, 308
    naming digital folders with, 281
inclusion. *See also* specific topics
    authentic, xv–xvi
    culture of, 365
    self-paced learning about, 342
inclusive mindset, xiv–xix, 344
independence, 214, 314
infographics, 76, 81
instruction design, 4
instructional materials. *See* materials
intellectual property, 28
interests, learner, 13, 178, 183
intermittent reminders, 297
interpersonal skills, 339
interviews, 206
introductions, video, 82
invite, as term, xxiii–xxiv

J

Janowski, Karen, v, vi–vii, ix
journeys, historical/literary, 243

K

Kanban charts, 293
keyboarding, 34, 44, 201
keyboards, 162–163
knowledge, 67, 76, 120
KWL charts, digital, 272

L

language, 129, 239
learner-centered philosophy, xvi
learners
    defined, xxii
    engagement of, 22, 66, 244
    interests of, 13, 178, 183
    management of, 295
    needs of, 7, 19, 38
    voices of, 74

learning
    asynchronous, 249, 345
    collectivist, 322
    distance, 11, 19, 24, 27, 311, 329
    flipped, xvi
    hybrid, 329
    reflecting on, 94
    self-paced, 202, 342
    social–emotional, 304, 325
    video, 54
learning brand, 365
learning environments, defined, xxiii
learning goals, 81
learning groups, as term, xxiii
learning intervals, spacing out, 291
learning materials. *See* materials
learning spaces
    decorating, 51
    defined, xxiii
    designing with diversity in mind, 101
    light in, 8
    noise in, 50
    seating options in, 12
    shared, 227
    work locations in, 10
learning tasks, 159
lessons, as term, xxiii
letter tiles, 109
letters, 110, 113
libraries, 104–105
light, natural, 8
linear visual schedules, 302
links, web, 37, 61, 284
listening, 125, 211, 264, 360
literacy, 111, 129, 142, 146. *See also* reading; writing
literary journeys, 243
literature, 125, 128, 143
literature reviews, 149, 199
location, reminders set to, 290
logical fallacies, 276
logos, 97
logs, reading, 140

M

making, 228
"Making Words," 112
maps and mapping
    concept, 223, 270
    creating, 243
    empathy, 58, 337
    mind, 265, 299
    semantic, 251
Marotta, Mike, v, vii, ix
Massive Open Online Courses (MOOCs), 343
materials

accessibility of, 3, 46
    authenticity of, 254
    differentiating, 38
    diversity in, 6
    lists, collaborative, 263
    QR codes for, 96
    reading, 126–127, 259
    supplemental, 142–143
    switch-accessible, 43
    task, organizing by, 278
    web links to, 37, 61
math
    abstract resources, 205
    concrete resources, 203
    digital sandbox and, 224
    geoboards, digital, 219
    graph paper, digital, 222
    music and, 231
    representational resources, 204
    robots, practicing with, 237
    text-to-speech and, 211
    3D models for, 220
    transformations in, 218
    voice assistants and, 248
meditation, 310
memes, 86
mind mapping, 265, 299
mindset
    inclusive, xiv–xix, 344
    platform-agnostic, 5
    reading, 98
mistake-tolerant instructional tools, 39
mobile devices, 40, 48
modalities, multiple, 143, 169, 273
modeling using video, 334
money skills, 216
MOOCs (Massive Open Online Courses), 343
mouse, controlling tablet with, 40
movement, promoting, 27
movement timers, 328
multilingual learners, 151, 161
multimedia formative assessments, 85
multimedia science lab results, 215
multimedia virtual tours, 59
music, 49, 231–234, 269
muted text-to-speech, 119

N

narrative writing, 187, 189
narratives, social, 339
natural light, 8
navigation, 37, 44, 307
needs, learner, 7, 19, 38
noise, 49–50
nonlinear visual schedules, 301

notes
audio, transcribing for, 260
audio syncing and, 250
digital, 267, 274
multiple modalities for, 273
pictures, pairing with, 271
sketchnoting for, 255
tagging, 282
transferring between tools, 252
from web-based video, 266
number racks, 208
number sense, 208–209

O

Open Educational Resources, 60
operational tutorials, 304
optical character recognition, 240
oral storytelling, 191, 257
orchestrating virtual music performances, 234
organization, digital, 279
outlining, 265

P

parents, communicating with, 318
participant-led learning experiences, 353
participation, promoting, 20
partners, accountability, 313
partnerships, community, 217
passion projects, 2
passive voice, 196
peers, learning from, 355
personal finance skills, 216
personalized learning networks (PLNs), 356
perspectives, personal, 316, 341
phonemes, 99
phonics, 112
photo albums, 150
picture dictionaries, 155
picture prediction, 70
picture-in-picture videos, 242
pineapple charts, 355
platform-agnostic mindset, 5
playback speeds, 107, 264
playground equipment, 129
PLNs (personalized learning networks), 356
podcasts, 74, 360, 361
poetry writing, 182
polls, 22
Pomodoro Technique, 291
portfolios, online, 90
Poss, Beth, v, vii–viii, ix
pre-assessment tools, 4
Predictable Chart Writing, 180
preference surveys, 13
pre-writing, 166, 167

prioritizing, 292
privacy, xix, 29
private chats, 19
problem solving, 16, 207, 228, 235, 299
productivity, 49, 285
professional development, fast-paced, 352
professional learning experiences, 344
professional study groups, 348
professionals, interviewing, 206
progress, 140, 197, 335
projects, 72, 75
public domain media, 28
public speaking, 80

Q

QR codes, 25, 96, 149, 304
quality assurance rubrics, 1
quotations, 258

R

radar chart ability infographics, 81
random calling, 319
Raspberry Pi, 236
read alouds, 131
readability, 102, 134, 153, 157
reading
commentary, authentic, 148
font options, 132
highlighting for, 133
love of, 103
progress, tracking, 140
screen masking for, 135
shared, 130
syllable markers for, 138
text color and, 136
3D printed letters/words, 113
visual cues for parts of speech, 139
reading comprehension, 122–123, 125
reading fluency, 116–119
reading logs, 140
reading materials, 126–127, 259
reading mindset, 98
reflecting, 94–95, 207, 330
reminders, 290, 297–298
repetition, spaced, 296
representational resources, 204
researching, 272
resources. *See* materials
resumes, 89, 324
reviews
book, 149, 199
self-based, 54
rituals, 311
robots, 237–239
role-playing games, 325
rubrics, 1, 91

S

sandbox, digital, 63, 224
scaffolds, xxiv, 123
scanning text, 41
scavenger hunts, 25
schedules, 301–303
schools, as term, xxiii
science, 215, 221
screen masking with focus bars, 135
screen recordings, 67, 253
screens, 33, 65, 137, 307
scribbling, digital, 179
scrolling, automatic, 117
seating, 12, 280
security, xix
See, Think, Wonder, 246, 261
self-based review, 54
self-grading assessments, 88
self-monitoring, 198
self-paced learning, 202, 342
self-regulation, 326, 333
semantic mapping, 251
sensory details in writing, 184
sensory paths, 14
sequence of events, 150, 156
sequential single word display, 118
shared reading, 130
shared writing, 177
sight words, 115
silent text-to-speech, 119
silly stories, 201
singing, 269
single word display, sequential, 118
sketching, computational, 225
sketchnoting, 255
slide decks, 35, 57, 62, 68, 79, 150
slide typing, 164
smackdown professional learning events, 358
small group opportunities, 24
social engagement, 309
social media, 190, 350, 362
social narratives, 339
social situations, 340
social skills, 337
social studies concepts, 63
social–emotional learning, 304, 325
sources, citing, 241
spaced repetition, 296
speech parts, 139
speech-to-text, 160. *See also* text-to-speech
spelling, 158, 248
splitting screens, 307
STEAM, 202, 217, 223, 262
stickers for keyboards, 163
sticky notes, 166

stories
    audio, 191, 257
    silly, 201
Strategy-A-Day calendars, vi
stress management, 310, 331
students, as term, xxii. *See also* learners
study buddies, 313
study groups, professional, 348
study guides, humorous, 128
study skills, 296
styluses, 33
summarizing text, 122
surveys, 13
switches, 32, 43
syllable markers, 138
symbols, 129

T

tablets, 40
tabs, open, 45
tagging notes, 282
task completion, 271, 277, 300
tasks, 278, 292–294, 302, 306
teachers, as term, xxii
technology analytic trackers, 288
technology features, 7, 323
TED talks, 249, 351
teleprompters, 80
temperature charts, 335
templates. *See also* forms
    document, 170
    poetry writing, 182
    resume, 324
    slide deck, 35
ten frames, digital, 209
text
    alt, 36
    annotating digitally, 152
    color of, 136
    digital, 165, 245
    handwriting converted to, 165
    highlighting, 108, 133, 200, 245
    readability level, adjusting, 134
    scanning, 41
    slide typing for entering, 164
    substitutions, automatic, 167
    summarizing, 122
    transcribing audio to, 268
    visual presentation of, 157
text-to-speech
editing written work with, 192
highlighting in, 108, 133
math, listening to, 211
playback speed, 107
silent, 119

voice options, 106
thesauruses, 174
Think, Pair, Share, 21
thinking, 167, 213, 308
3D animation, 189
3D artifacts, 69
3D models, virtual interactive, 220–221
3D printing, 113, 230
3-2-1 strategy, 94
time management, 288, 301
timelining, 156
timers, 300, 328
tone in writing, 185
To-Stop-Doing lists, 366–367
tours, virtual, 59
transcribing audio, 260, 268
transformations in math, 218
transitions, 83, 95, 303, 314
translation tools, 151, 161
tutorials, 253, 304
Twenty Percent Time, 2
Twitter chats, 356

U

understanding, 22, 47, 86, 338
universal controllers, 320
Universal Design for Learning, xvii–xviii, 25

V

Venn Diagrams, 71
version history, 197
video
    animated, 53
    audio, pairing with, 77
    captioned, 146
    exercise, 331
    green screens and, 78
    introductions via, 82
    learning via, 54
    modeling using, 334
    narrative writing with, 187
    participation, promoting using, 20
    pausing intermittently, 244
    phoneme instruction with, 99
    picture-in-picture, 242
    playback speeds, variable, 264
    playlists of, 31
    projects using, 73
    scavenger hunts and, 25
    screen recording tutorials, 253
    watch parties for, 349
    web-based, 266
video conference tools, 44
virtual reality, 69, 83, 340
vision boards, 317

vision needs, 65, 137
visual cues, 139, 338
visual feedback, 50
visual schedules, 301–303
visual supports, 295
visualizing, 55, 154–155, 258, 308, 335
vocabulary, 124, 155, 171, 173, 251
voice
    playing musical instruments with, 232
    in writing, 185, 196
voice assistants, 248, 298
voice commands, 48
voice options for text-to-speech, 106

W

watch parties, video, 349
web links, 37, 61, 284
web pages, decluttering, 287
women in history, 64
word banks, 171, 186
word choice, 167, 174, 175
word clouds, 144, 175
word count, 198
word display, sequential single, 118
word walls, digital, 172
words
    augmented reality for learning, 110
    digital, 112
    length boundaries, 181
    sight, 115
    3D printed, 113
work locations, 10
work surfaces, 9
writing
    for authentic audience, 190
    book review analysis and, 199
    creative, 186
    digital graphic organizers and, 168
    editing, 192–193, 196
    emojis in, 188
    feedback on, 194
    learner interests, capitalizing on, 178
    learning task and, 159
    narrative, 187, 189
    sensory details in, 184
    shared, 177
    silly stories, 201
    social media, 190
    tone in, 185
    version history, assessing progress using, 197
    virtual keyboards for, 162
    visual presentation of, 157
    voice in, 185, 196
    word length boundaries in, 181